Ed Glinert was born in Dalston. His fascination with people and place, coupled with his expert knowledge of his city's history and his forensic gift for digging out obscure stories, have made him one of the most acclaimed writers about London. He is the author of *East End Chronicles*, *Literary London*, *The London Compendium* and most recently *The Manchester Compendium* and leads a variety of walking tours around the city of London.

# ED GLINERT

# West End Chronicles

*300 years of glamour and excess in
the heart of London*

PENGUIN BOOKS

PENGUIN BOOKS

Published by the Penguin Group
Penguin Books Ltd, 80 Strand, London WC2R ORL, England
Penguin Group (USA) Inc., 375 Hudson Street, New York, New York 10014, USA
Penguin Group (Canada), 90 Eglinton Avenue East, Suite 700, Toronto, Ontario, Canada M4P 2Y3
(a division of Pearson Penguin Canada Inc.)
Penguin Ireland, 25 St Stephen's Green, Dublin 2, Ireland (a division of Penguin Books Ltd)
Penguin Group (Australia), 250 Camberwell Road, Camberwell, Victoria 3124, Australia
(a division of Pearson Australia Group Pty Ltd)
Penguin Books India Pvt Ltd, 11 Community Centre, Panchsheel Park, New Delhi – 110 017, India
Penguin Group (NZ), 67 Apollo Drive, Rosedale, North Shore 0632, New Zealand
(a division of Pearson New Zealand Ltd)
Penguin Books (South Africa) (Pty) Ltd, 24 Sturdee Avenue, Rosebank, Johannesburg 2196, South Africa

Penguin Books Ltd, Registered Offices: 80 Strand, London WC2R ORL, England

www.penguin.com

First published by Allen Lane 2007
Published in Penguin Books 2008
1

Copyright © Ed Glinert, 2007
All rights reserved

The moral right of the author has been asserted

Typeset by Palimpsest Book Production Limited, Grangemouth, Stirlingshire
Printed in England by Clays Ltd, St Ives plc

978-0-141-02464-6

www.greenpenguin.co.uk

Penguin Books is committed to a sustainable future
for our business, our readers and our planet.
The book in your hands is made from paper
certified by the Forest Stewardship Council.

*To the memory of Betty Glinert*

# Contents

| | *Introduction* | ix |
|---|---|---|
| 1 | Capital of Chic | 1 |
| 2 | Vile Bodies | 4 |
| 3 | The Making of the West End | 31 |
| 4 | Revolution | 60 |
| 5 | Visions | 89 |
| 6 | Temptations | 100 |
| 7 | Art | 123 |
| 8 | Boho | 144 |
| 9 | War | 163 |
| 10 | Foul Play | 189 |
| 11 | Day | 219 |
| 12 | Night | 242 |
| 13 | Style | 283 |
| | *Acknowledgements* | 290 |
| | *Bibliography* | 291 |
| | *Index* | 294 |

# Introduction

The West End is the beating heart of London, the centre of glamour, style and sophistication. It is a land of glitz and gold. Here are the bright lights and red lights of Soho, the romantic mews of Mayfair, the elegant but rigid streets of Marylebone, and the chic enclaves of Fitzrovia. Here is Oxford Street, London's most congested shopping stretch; here are the flashing neon signs of Piccadilly Circus, the most famous landmark in the world. Here is Regent Street, the ultimate in urban grandeur, and Old Compton Street, the epitome of hard-core hedonism. But it is also a place of loose morals, premeditated violence and necessary secrecy; the ulterior motive behind the gleaming smile.

Unlike its dark alter ego – the East End – few books have been written about the West End as a single entity. Many are the volumes on Soho or Mayfair. There are various titles on Marylebone and Fitzrovia. Regent Street has several tomes just to itself. But as far as the West End as a whole is concerned there is a limited collection.

The West End is an easy place to locate. Controversy surrounding its borders is minimal compared to that which accompanies the East End, for instance. The West End consists of four constituent areas, each of which radiates away from Oxford Circus. Running clockwise from the north-west they are Marylebone, Fitzrovia, Soho and Mayfair. Such enduring names, yet their etymology is the usual catalogue of chance and contrivance. Marylebone has been Marybone and the awkward St Marylebone but derives from St Mary-by-the-Bourne (the popular name for the River Tybourn or Tyburn). Some locals still like to pronounce it 'Marlybone', probably to differentiate the still somewhat working-class section north of Marylebone Road, near Marylebone Station, from the up-market doctors' quarter around Harley Street.

Mayfair and Soho are names with less sombre origins. Mayfair was built around the setting of the ancient spring fair. 'Soho!' was a hunting cry and is of uncertain origin. Of the four West End quadrants it is Fitzrovia, by far, that has the most interesting etymology. Until the mid twentieth century it was variously described as North Soho (glib) or Bloomsbury (too far west). Surely it deserved its own title? Thanks to those writers and artists who patronized the Fitzroy Tavern on Charlotte Street in the 1930s it received one: the obvious but ingenious Fitzrovia, with which it could sit confidently alongside Belgravia and Tyburnia.

Even then, it took until the end of the twentieth century for the name to be accepted by Londoners, map-makers and guide-book writers. Detractors pointed out that the name had been made up, as if 'Chalk Farm', 'the Isle of Dogs' and 'Havering-atte-Bower' were handed down to Moses with the commandments on Mount Sinai.

In the 1990s there was even a newspaper campaign to kill off 'Fitzrovia' and replace it with the horrible Americanism 'Noho', sometimes written even more outlandishly as 'NoHo'. This rightly failed to take off, probably when would-be users wondered whether New York's similar sounding SoHo (south of Houston Street) implied that Noho was the land north of (H)oxford Street, as might be pronounced by an aspiring cockney chimney sweep from *My Fair Lady*.

The borders around the West End separating it from ordinary London are mostly well-defined. To the north there is Marylebone Road / Euston Road – formidable, traffic-choked, a road of such strength and speed the casual geographer is immediately awakened to the idea that the areas on either side have little common bond. This road was London's first bypass, built in 1756 to ease the manoeuvring of troops and allow drovers to take their cattle to Smithfield Market without having to use Oxford Street and Holborn.

To the east is Tottenham Court Road, a tedious stretch of hi-fi shops and dreadful pubs beyond which lies the intellectual Georgian vistas of Bloomsbury, and further south Charing Cross Road, with its ever-threatened bookshops. West of the West End is the obvious other world of Hyde Park, a much-needed respite from all the brick, glass and concrete of the West End, although north-west of Marble Arch the green oasis gives way to the slightly shabby spoils of Bayswater.

The West End's southern boundaries are not so clear. Piccadilly is an obvious border, for beyond there is another, smaller, green lung – the pedestrianly named Green Park – before the super-expensive real estate of St James's comes into view. But heading east to meet Charing Cross Road again it is not always easy to make out what belongs to the West End and what does not. Chinatown does; it is the West End in microcosm – cosmopolitan, fiercely independent, shabby but stylish, workaholic but relaxed. Trafalgar Square does not. It is the window on to Whitehall. It belongs to Westminster. As for Leicester Square, to many *the* social centre of London, it sometimes lies within (historically it was never quite accepted by Westminster), sometimes without (when the preponderance of fire-eaters and skittle jugglers send the discerning West End aesthete heading back to the unfussed decadence of Soho).

Then there are those parts of London near the West End that *aren't* in it: Bayswater, Bloomsbury, Charing Cross, Covent Garden, Holborn, Kensington and St James's. For the idle wanderer there is even a handy rule of thumb: 'W1' is found in small letters on the road names throughout the West End, a tactic that fails only in a few streets around Leicester Square.

The West End thus defined geographically, what is its purpose socially? Despite lacking the visual architectural splendour of Amsterdam or Edinburgh, it is the sheer brazen scale of the West End that dwarfs all its rivals. The West End is a place which millions – Londoners and out-of-towners – are instantly familiar with. It is enticing to explore and exciting to read about. Its place in London life is not based around the court (like St James's), religion (Westminster) or Mammon (the City), but it tolerates a little of each. After all, Soho Square was built around the seventeenth-century home of Charles II's illegitimate son, the Duke of Monmouth; the West End has played host to several mystical visionaries, particularly William Blake and Joanna Southcott, and the more bizarre quasi-religious groups, such as the Hermetic Order of the Golden Dawn; and Mammon, too, makes an appearance, for though an area like Mayfair is more of a rich person's playground than a money-making exercise in its own right it is here that both the epic department store and the small specialist shopkeeper are to be found *in excelsis*.

Most of all the West End is a place built around enjoyment and entertainment – clubs, music venues, theatres, dance halls, comedy stores, brothels, cinemas, grand restaurants, cosy cafés, corner pubs, drinking dens. It has been home and host to the greatest of revellers and hedonists: Casanova, George IV, Oscar Wilde, Dylan Thomas, Nina Hamnett, Aleister Crowley,

Henrietta Moraes, Tony Hancock, Syd Barrett, Francis Bacon ... a list that continues to grow. It is one of the few locales not just in London but in Britain where Bohemian behaviour is tolerated, expected even. *West End Chronicles* in some small way tries to explain why.

# I

# Capital of Chic

They come from afar to marvel at the capital of chic, the centre point of style. When they arrive in the West End they find glamour, glitz and glitter. They find chic finery, glorious elegance, dripping opulence. They find wealth; uncountable, unimaginable riches – Baroque mansions, walled gardens, stucco façades, Classical motifs, Georgian terraces, desirable town houses and Adam squares.

This West End is a vast store of treasures, conspicuous in its confidence, found on and around some of the most famous streets in the world – Piccadilly Circus, Regent Street, Oxford Street, Savile Row, Carnaby Street, Fitzroy Square, Park Lane. Here the shops are bigger and the goods fancier, the food in the restaurants tastier, the drinks in the pubs smoother, the streets livelier, the nightclubs louder, the nights out longer, the people happier, even the prostitutes – of either sex, sometimes both – better looking.

What other locale can match an area that contains the excitement of Soho, the refinement of Fitzrovia, the gentility of Marylebone and the class of Mayfair? Even Soho, long the sleaze capital of London, exudes a stylish sort of sleaze, style with rough edges – a potent mix. Shabby yet sophisticated, urban and urbane, Soho has long been *the* target for any self-respecting reveller, superior in every way to Camden Town, Brixton, Brick Lane, Notting Hill, Hampstead, or any other come-lately haven of hedonism. Its streets cater for everyone. While the discerning film goer sits in the Curzon Cinema on Shaftesbury Avenue, watching a rep classic directed by Michelangelo Antonioni, only a few hundred yards away on Winnett Street gullible northern football fans down for the weekend to watch the match are probably holed up in an illegal sex club, about to be stumped £295 each for consorting with a 'hostess' who a week previously was making a precarious journey from deepest Montenegro to London in the back of a lorry full of stolen cigarettes. That's style, even if it comes with a hefty price.

On the other side of Oxford Street from Soho the mood changes as the tasteful, continental-style chic radiated by Fitzrovia fills a perfect arrangement of streets; some long (Whitfield), some small and straight (Tottenham), some atmospheric (Charlotte), some twisty and teasing (Hanway), some shaded by trees (Percy), some framed by towers (Howland), some lined with Georgian vistas (Fitzroy). Even the area's much vaunted recent rebranding as a media village, its advertising agencies, graphic-design studios and satellite-TV companies lumped together around the absurd neologism 'Noho', an incongruous Americanized take on the word 'Boho' and the phrase 'North of Soho', has failed to dissipate Fitzrovia's charm.

To the west, Marylebone has become an elegant, urban twenty-first-century village. Credit for ridding London of the old dull Marylebone of spiritless shops and sober Georgian town houses goes to the Howard de Walden estate, which owns the freehold for much of the area. When company executives looked around in the 1980s they saw a dreary if prosperous backwater of the West End that seemed to have little to offer other than the revered private clinics of Harley Street. Even the main route through the village – Marylebone High Street – had been ruined by too many takeaways and tacky shops. A change came when estate executives bought up the long leases of local properties so that they could choose which retailers they allowed in, thereby setting up a template for how planners across the country could shape a community if they so wished.

They convinced Waitrose to open a branch. Never has the opening of a supermarket had so galvanizing an effect on an area. Soon there was a Conran shop and niche outlets. A fishmonger moved in, as did a French furniture company and Daunt's, the upmarket bookshop. Now Marylebone is one of the most thriving communities in London. Even the austere streets which Benjamin Disraeli compared to a 'large family of plain children' have a new sparkle.

Then there is Mayfair, the south-west section of the West End. Mayfair exudes an air of smug self-satisfaction. Its offices, home of prestige companies dealing in property, advertising, PR, wines, spirits and oil, were once the town houses of the aristocracy and the super wealthy who left for Kensington and Richmond in the 1950s and 1960s. Although there was a brief residential revival after the Arabs quadrupled the price of oil in 1974 and the sheikhs began moving into the area, Mayfair doesn't really need much of a population. Not when it has Savile Row, still the home of bespoke tailoring. Not when it has Cork Street, a few hundred yards to the west, lined with the country's most prestigious art galleries. And not when it has hotels like the Connaught, Claridge's and the Dorchester exuding an air of priceless panache.

Deep into Mayfair there is the elegant simplicity of Shepherd Market, where a villagey atmosphere prevails barely a quarter of a mile north-east of roaring Hyde Park corner. In the centre of the community the letters SHEPHERD MARKET can still be picked out in bold *sans serif* lettering on the parapet of one block. All around are low-rise, flat-faced brick houses, nestling everywhere they can find a space amongst the chaotic, romantic street pattern which appears to rearrange itself every time the visitor returns. It is a mix of country market town and French hamlet, where the cafés have pavement seats and the dark alleys lead nowhere, often ploughing through buildings to get there. To the south, on winding White Horse Street, where the brick has turned a ferociously deep black, there is an old-fashioned cobbler and other relics of pre-chain store neighbourhood shopping which thus far have eluded the clutches of the planners and redevelopers.

If there is one place which effortlessly captures the style of the West End it is a secluded location deeper still into the heart of village Mayfair. It is where Waverton Street doglegs into Charles Street, south of Grosvenor Square. No sound from the interminable traffic at Hyde Park Corner, only a few hundred yards away, can be heard. No screaming ambulances tear round the corner, and no hooded youths hang around. By the bend in the road is a pub, the Red Lion, with a mews alley to the side. Opposite is the aquamarine weatherboarding of Carpenter House, built by John Philips as his workshop in 1754. Around the corner, the start of the lofty, narrow, exquisite Georgian town houses on Charles Street are dwarfed by the immense Baroque stucco folly wall which is all that remains of the mansion of Chesterfield House. Beyond, to the east, there is a delightful kink in the tiny, painfully narrow roadway as it nears Chesterfield Street, where Somerset Maugham wrote *Of Human Bondage* and *The Moon and Sixpence*.

This surely is a style that any corner of any city would love to emulate. But such splendours, such wealth, comes at a price. If only those fortunate enough to be guarding the soul of the West End weren't so easily corrupted by Mammon.

# 2

# Vile Bodies

The West End has long been ruled by dynastic families – the Cavendishes, the Dudleys, the Rothschilds, the Londonderrys, the Cassels, the Grosvenors. These aristocrats and grandees, the super-rich overspill from the Georgian court, formed an empire centred on the grandly ostentatious streets that give the West End its most enviable image.

It is a society empire that began to take shape after London was forced out of the Old City by the Plague and Fire of the 1660s. High society colonized much of the West End, particularly Mayfair, gradually bricking over the sweet gentle lanes of the late medieval village into a plutocrat's playground. Mayfair was a likely setting, for the River Thames was an inconvenient barrier, Westminster was for royalty itself, not for its extended families or the nouveau riche, the land west of Westminster – the Five Fields – swampy and plagued by villains, its mid nineteenth-century transformation into Belgravia unforeseen, the vicinity of the Abbey was dotted with villainous rookeries, and the territory further east the haven of an even more dangerous poor.

Mayfair began to attract an intensity of wealth and power that London had never seen before and has barely seen since. This new West End society empire grew apace through the eighteenth century, reached the peak of its powers in the Victorian period, remained buoyant during the Edwardian early twentieth century and even outfoxed the Great War and the economic crises of the 1920s and 1930s, until it crashed with the Second World War. Its tentacles spread out across the West End, but its power base was south of Oxford Street, close to Piccadilly and west of Regent Street, where the pokey, twisty dark streets of Soho warned of darkness and danger.

Park Lane was its western boundary. It had been an insignificant narrow rutted track leading to the Tyburn gallows in medieval times, but by the mid nineteenth century was a boulevard as glorious and opulent as those of Paris or Florence. Here, overlooking Hyde Park, was the grandest stretch of houses in London, each a millionaire's paradise decked out with marble interiors, sweeping stairwells, velvet seats, gold wallpapers, the most glorious *objets d'art*, chandeliered ballrooms dripping with rococo splendour, décor that switched from Japonnaise to Renaissance, from Gothick to Gothic, from Louis XV to Louis XVI; each a Xanadu missing only an Alph, the sacred river running through caverns measureless to man down to a sunless sea.

From its earliest days those bringing their own mini-empires of conspicuous consumption to the West End have attracted the most wagging tongues, the sharpest brickbats, their every move guaranteed to attract equal measures of notoriety and opprobrium. Take James Scott, the Duke of Monmouth, Charles II's bastard son, for instance. He lived in one of the first buildings ever put up in the West End – Monmouth House – constructed in 1677 on what is now Soho Square.

The duke gained considerable political power in the late seventeenth century. Only the king's brother, James, Duke of York, who went on to become James II, and the king were more prominent. Monmouth embodied the hopes of all those who wanted a Protestant succession at a time when those closest in line to the throne were Catholics. But he was sent into exile after the unmasking of the notorious 'Popish Plot', when Protestant extremists contrived a conspiracy (to frighten people against Rome) that the Catholics were about to seize power. Monmouth later returned to London without permission, and in Soho was greeted by the ringing of church bells and celebratory bonfires. After the death of his father, Charles II, in 1685 he tried to seize the throne with help from West Country supporters. He was vanquished at the Battle of Sedgemoor, arrested and put to death at Tower Hill in a ceremony which ranks as the most botched execution in English history.

The first blow made by Jack Ketch, the notoriously unreliable executioner, made only a slight wound, and after the second the duke's head refused to budge. Eventually Ketch had to call for a knife to complete the decapitation. When the headless duke was taken to the Tower the authorities realized that no official portrait of him existed, so they asked the royal surgeon to stitch the head back on and tie a white cravat around his neck to make him look more appealing. A portrait artist was then given twenty-four hours to complete the job before the decomposition of the body would make his task harder. The picture now hangs in the National Portrait Gallery, only a few hundred yards away from the site of his Soho Square house.

Wherever there was a grand new West End property there was a rogueish, gadabout tenant or an impecunious aristocrat who had fallen foul of the family fortune. So at Leicester House, built in the 1630s on a section of Soho fields known as Swan Close, now the north side of Leicester Square, lived Elizabeth, Queen of Bohemia. She came to England penniless in 1661 but died only a week after moving in. A generation later, in 1717, Prince George (later George II) moved from St James's Palace into Leicester House after a row with his father, the king. He brought with him a large retinue of attendants and servants, who moved into the adjacent Ailesbury House. When George I died in June 1727 the prince was crowned king in the gateway of Leicester House, and he moved back to St James's Palace. Prince Frederick took his place at Leicester House, and the property became a new centre of political activity until Frederick died suddenly from pleurisy in spring 1751. A few days later, the writer Horace Walpole heard some workmen outside the house talking about the late prince: 'He has left a great many small children,' remarked one. 'Aye,' replied the other, 'and what is worse, they belong to our parish.'

Drama surrounded events at Clarendon House on Piccadilly, named after its first owner, Edward Hyde, Earl of Clarendon, Charles II's Lord Chancellor. One of the first West End mansions, its foundations were made with stone originally intended for the new St Paul's Cathedral. It was immense and impressive, and cost the then astronomical sum of £50,000. Clarendon was not popular. As Pepys recorded in his diary for 14 June 1667, 'some rude people have been at my Lord Clarendon's, where they cut down the trees before his house and broke his windows'. The 'rude people' even erected a gibbet, and rumours spread that Clarendon's funds must have been obtained by fraud or treason. That December, the great diarist and designer John Evelyn went to visit and found him in the garden 'sitting in his gowt wheelchair. After some while deploring his condition to me, I took my leave. Next morning I heard he was gone' – he had fled to France to avoid prosecution.

On the adjacent site grew the formidable shape of Berkeley House / Devonshire House, which occupied a large chunk of land between Piccadilly and Berkeley Square. It was built in 1665 for the first Lord Berkeley of Stratton, with a garden designed by John Evelyn. Evelyn praised the house's immensity but was saddened at seeing London extended *this* far into the countryside. It was here that Princess Anne of Denmark (the future Queen Anne) lived from 1692 until 1696 when the Duke of Devonshire bought the property and renamed it Devonshire House. In October 1733 a fire, started when a pot of workmen's glue boiled over and ignited some wood shavings, destroyed Devonshire House while the Prince of Wales was there having breakfast. The house was rebuilt in the 1730s by William Kent, the celebrated Palladian architect, also responsible for Horse Guards off Whitehall. He gave it an exterior so plain that one critic compared it to an East India Company warehouse. Within, though, Kent lavishly poured on the grand décor – gilded ceilings, entablatures, carved marble fireplaces, chandeliers dripping with crystal, and the finest and most fashionable furniture, designed by Thomas Chippendale of Covent Garden and laced with rococo, Gothic and a hint of Chinese, the armchairs given padded seats and mahogany arms.

At the end of the eighteenth century, Devonshire House came to be at the centre of a dazzling social circle that revolved around Lady Georgiana Spencer, wife of the fifth duke, William Cavendish. He was a gambler and ally of the powerful Whig politician Charles James Fox. She canvassed for Fox, dressed in a hat decorated with foxes' tails, and traded kisses for votes with the butchers of Covent Garden, despite not having a vote herself. She was also a fashion leader who convinced West End ladies to wear tall feathers to increase the height of their headdress. One woman was so desperate to follow suit she scoured London in vain for such feathers until she found a compliant undertaker who sold her some from his hearse.

Georgiana lived in a *ménage à trois* for some years with the duke and his mistress, Bess (Lady Elizabeth Foster), her best friend. She also conducted an affair with the Earl of Grey, with whom she had a daughter whose most famous modern-day descendant is Lady Sarah Ferguson, the Duchess of York. Another branch of her family gave the world Lady Diana Spencer, the late Princess of Wales.

## PRINCES OF GREED

When it became clear in the early years of the nineteenth century that George III was too mad to be allowed to continue ruling, his incorrigible son, George

Augustus Frederick of Hanover, Prince of Wales, Earl of Chester, Duke of Cornwall, Duke of Rothesay, Earl of Carrick and Baron of Renfrew – 'Prinny' to everyone not in his earshot – took the throne.

George IV was insufferable, powered by greed and green-eyed gluttony. He surrounded himself with a large retinue of mostly toadying lackeys, and although he spent most of his time in Westminster or his Brighton summer palace he was occasionally forced to slum it in the West End. He married his mistress, Maria Fitzherbert, in secret at her house on Park Street, near Park Lane, on 15 December 1785. It had to be in secret. She was a Catholic and he wouldn't be able to take the throne if the truth emerged. The felony was compounded by the vicar, the Reverend Robert Burt, who was then in debtors' gaol but who agreed to perform the service for the £500 he owed his creditors. Ten years later the prince was pressed into an 'official' marriage with Caroline of Brunswick.

Meanwhile, Prinny's set swarmed into the West End as their mentor's power grew. More popular than the prince was Lord Alvanley, who many regarded as the wittiest man of his day and who threw regular dinner parties at which there were always eight – and only eight – guests present, and where the menu always included apricot tart. More famous than any of this extended crew – more famous even than the Prince himself – was the dandy and well-dressed man, Beau Brummel. He was ostracized by the Prince after an amusing incident at a ball in 1813. Momentarily ignored by the Regent, Brummel turned to Alvanley, remarking loudly: 'Ah, Alvanley, who is your fat friend?' Prinny never spoke to him again.

Not all the West End power-brokers were as grotesque as the Prince Regent. At Apsley House, a Robert Adam mansion built in the 1770s by what is now Hyde Park Corner, the Duke of Wellington exhibited trophies from the 1815 Battle of Waterloo, including Napoleon's coach. And it was here he preferred to stay at the expense of 10 Downing Street when he was prime minister in the 1820s, sitting on the roof inconspicuously watching his troops march by. Apsley House is now a museum, best known for its charming soubriquet – No. 1 London – awarded in honour of being the first house east of the former Hyde Park toll gate.

To the immediate east of Apsley House, where the Park Lane traffic now thunders into Hyde Park Corner, stood 145 Piccadilly, home from 1927–36 of the Duke and Duchess of York, who became George VI and Queen Elizabeth, the eventual Queen Mother. Mayfair society was shocked when they moved in, not only because the Duke and Duchess were downsizing from a palace to a mansion, but because for the first time members of the royal family were living in a house with a number rather than a name; a sure sign that the country was irretrievably moving towards unbridled socialism. On assuming the throne in 1936, following the shock abdication of his brother, Edward VIII, the duke returned home in a daze (he had never expected to become king) and asked his curtsying daughters, the Princesses Elizabeth and Margaret: 'If anyone comes through on the telephone, who should I say I am?' The house was saved from becoming a twenty-first-century museum, like Apsley House, by being destroyed during the Second World War.

## THE WAY WE LIVE NOW

Uproar, war, international crises; they didn't appear to have too much bearing on West End life in the eighteenth century. The aristocracy had won their little local battle in 1697: the assurance that a Protestant would be on the throne; whether it was the throne of England or Britain didn't really bother them, as long as it wasn't a Catholic. And if Popery did look as if it was going to rear its head, the London mob would beat it down, as was seen so emphatically during the 1780 Gordon Riots (p60–62). However, one event had a significant effect on the West End by *not* happening. The failure of the English to execute a French-style revolution made life for the rich in the Regency period more pleasurable. Though radicals, foreign anarchists and other assorted political troublemakers were tearing each other apart in the intellectual battles that raged in Soho pubs, the rich of Mayfair and Marylebone could continue to live a life that was leisurely and gentlemanly, as those battles rarely left the debating rooms.

This state of affairs was sent up exquisitely by William Thackeray and Anthony Trollope. In *Vanity Fair*, published, ironically, in 1848, the year of revolution in Europe, Thackeray noted how the Crawleys have a 'very small comfortable house in Curzon Street and can live on "nothing a year"'. Europe might be ablaze but London was not, and so in the West End, Rawdon's sister lives in an 'exceedingly snug and well-appointed house in Park Lane'. In *The Way We Live Now* (1875), Trollope captured the magnificence of this aristocratic playground perfectly when describing Madame Melmotte's ball: 'It was a ball on a scale so magnificent that it had been talked about ever since

Parliament met, now about a fortnight since ... The house had been so arranged that it was impossible to know where you were, when once in it. The hall was a paradise. The staircase was fairyland. The lobbies were grottoes rich with ferns. Walls had been knocked away and arches had been constructed. The leads behind had been supported and walled in, and covered and carpeted.'

But this was nothing compared with the dinner thrown in honour of the Emperor of China that July. Workmen came 'throwing up a building behind, knocking down walls, and generally transmuting the house in Grosvenor Square in such a fashion that two hundred guests might be able to sit down to dinner in the dining-room of a British merchant'. Trollope's masterpiece may have been a satire, 'instigated by what he conceived to be the "commercial profligacy of the age,"' as he once explained, but it can also be taken as a celebration of the lengths the rich of Mayfair would go to in indulging their passion for lavish occasions.

What else did life offer the new West Enders when they weren't entertaining? Horace Walpole, the Gothic novelist, went to the opera five times a week. Dr Johnson, the Dictionary compiler; Joshua Reynolds, the artist; and the actor, David Garrick, went to The Club. Not just any club, but *The* Club, a literary affair which met first on Greek Street and then moved to 9 Gerrard Street, in what is now Chinatown, in the 1760s. Here Johnson held court, as recounted by James Boswell in his *Life of Johnson* biography.

William Douglas, fourth Duke of Queensberry, better known as 'Old Q', who lived at the turn of the eighteenth century in a large property that stood between Old Burlington Street and Savile Row, probably had more fun. Old Q was one of the last Mayfairians to employ a running footman, and would test the ability of new recruits by watching them speed off from an upper window. In his eighties he would stand in the same window watching the street for teenage girls. When one took his fancy he would order his manservant to approach her. Few resisted when they saw his evident wealth. An acquaintance explained how 'in his dressing room he performed the scene of Paris and the three goddesses with three of the most wonderfully beautiful girls in London, dressed like Homeric goddesses on the Mount of Ida while he in a shepherd's costume rewarded the one he considered the most beautiful with a golden apple.' Douglas had other, more disconcerting, eccentricities, like consuming a supper of roast poulet and lime punch every midnight, and then being woken at three in the morning to take a meal of veal cutlet.

Those with less ravenous appetites went to the Pantheon – Wordsworth's 'stately Pantheon'. This grand entertainment palace was built between 1770 and 1772 by James Wyatt on an Oxford Street site where Marks and Spencer's Pantheon store now stands. It contained galleries framed by Corinthian columns and niches modelled on those of St Sophia, Istanbul. The opening ceremony was attended by more than 1,500 people. The writer Horace Walpole, unsure whether to marvel or mock, exclaimed: 'Imagine Balbec in all its glory! The ceilings, even of the passages, are of the most beautiful stuccos in the best taste of grotesque. The ceilings of the ballrooms and the panels painted like Raphael's loggias in the Vatican.' He later decided the building was 'the most beautiful edifice in England'. Although the Pantheon became the most talked about venue in London, it wasn't as commercially successful as expected and was converted into a theatre in 1791. A year later it perished in a fire, which may have been an arson attack caused by those involved with the rival King's Theatre, Haymarket.

The rich pioneered Oxford Street as one of the most intense stretches of shopping in the world. Sophie von la Roche, a German novelist, wrote of the street with unrestrained euphoria in the 1770s. 'Just imagine, a street taking half an hour to cover from end to end, with double rows of brightly shining lamps . . . to gaze at the splendidly-lit shop fronts in comfort.' The shops were small, and few survived into modern times. It wasn't until the late nineteenth century that the great names of today first appeared. But mostly the new West Enders, when they weren't eating, shopping, sleeping or fornicating, gambled. They bet not just on horses, but cocks, prize-fighting bouts and cricket matches – even on the length of a vicar's sermon. They bet on whose father would croak first, and on who would be the first to seduce a lady in a balloon. Gambling clubs formed for all subdivisions of wealthy West Enders. Young men who had returned from the Grand Tour met in establishments where they bet while eating macaroni, the taste for which they had acquired while in Italy. At Almack's club in 1770 the Earl of Orford staked his house – 11 Berkeley Square – on a game of cards and lost. Wagering took place everywhere. Walking along Bond Street, Charles James Fox and the Prince of Wales bet on how many cats they would see on either side of the street. Fox chose the sunny side and won 13–0. Lord Orford and Lord Rockingham wagered £500 on the outcome of a race between five turkeys and five geese on the road from Norwich to London. When Lord Arlington staked £3,000 on which of two raindrops would fall first the nadir had been reached. Or rather it was when the first drop hit the bottom of the pane.

## ROTHSCHILD ROW

If the most powerful West Enders at the beginning of the nineteenth century were those surrounding the preening Prinny, then as far as the rest of the century was concerned it was an entirely more sober and sombre set – the Rothschilds. So many of the great banking dynasty took up residence in the grand houses along Piccadilly, just off Hyde Park, that the enclave became known as Rothschild's Row – especially after Alfred Rothschild's pet goat began roaming the street at will and its owner was seen racing along Piccadilly in a carriage pulled by a team of zebras.

Nathan Meyer Rothschild was the first scion of the dynasty to settle in London. Born in Germany, he moved to 107 Piccadilly in 1825. His marriage to a sister-in-law of Moses Montefiore, one of the leaders of London's Mediterranean Jewish community, united the two wings of Anglo-Jewry. Rothschild was one of the most powerful figures on the continent, 'a true Lord of Europe', as Lord Byron described him in *Don Juan*. He transferred gold bullion from Britain overseas, so that it could be used by the army, and arranged stock exchange loans when reconstructing the continent after Napoleon's defeat. He was ruthlessly organized, running a pigeon-post service between England and Europe to be first with all the important news. It worked during the Battle of Waterloo, for Rothschild's agent, Rowerth, stood primed for action with his finest bird at Ostend, ready for the latest news from the battlefront.

Rothschild wasn't perfect. He was distinctly uncultured. At one of his concert parties at 107 Piccadilly presented by Louis Spohr, the violin virtuoso, he congratulated the German composer, jingled some coins in his pocket and explained: 'That's my music.'

Nathan's son, Baron Lionel Nathan de Rothschild, lived at 148 Piccadilly, a property six storeys high, its unfinished cornice a memorial to the destruction of Jerusalem. The house was dominated inside by a double marble staircase that took its immaculately gowned and tailed guests to a gilt ballroom and dining room laden with a 650lb silver table service. It was a home more than fit for the first Jew to be elected to the House of Commons, even though Lionel was unable to take his seat until a change in the law in 1858.

Here in November 1875 the prime minister, Benjamin Disraeli, was dining when Rothschild received a telegram from a Paris associate revealing that the Khedive of Egypt had offered his 177,000 shares in the Suez Canal to the French government, but was becoming impatient with their procrastination. Rothschild requested the Khedive's price, and the meal grew cold while they waited for his answer. Eventually it came. The Khedive wanted one hundred million francs (four million pounds). Rothschild and Disraeli agreed that Britain needed to move quickly and discreetly. Unfortunately, with Parliament in recess the sum could not be sanctioned, and the Bank of England was forbidden by law to loan money to the government while the House was in recess.

The only solution was for N. M. Rothschild & Sons, Lionel's family bank, to sanction the loan. Disraeli won approval from the Cabinet, and within two days of the arrival of the telegram it was announced that 'N. M. Rothschild & Sons had credited to the account of the Khedive the sum of four million pounds, and that all the latter's shares in the Suez Canal Company had passed into possession of Her Majesty's Government.' Nevertheless, Queen Victoria refused to grant Lionel Rothschild a peerage on the grounds that 'one who owed his wealth to loans with foreign governments or successful speculation on the stock exchange' didn't deserve the honour. The canal remained in the British Government's possession, yielding enormous profits, until 1956, when it was seized by Egyptian leader Gamal Nasser. A few years later No. 148, by then seen as symbolic of imperial obsolescence, was wiped away for a road scheme.

More and more Rothschilds moved into the Hyde Park Corner end of Piccadilly and the surrounding streets. At 1 Seamore Place, later razed to extend Curzon Street west, lived the colourful Alfred de Rothschild, who liked nothing more than to stage circuses at home with himself as ringmaster, cracking a long whip. He had his servants well trained. When a guest once asked for milk in his tea a powdered flunky responded in a flash: 'Jersey, Hereford or Shorthorn, sir?'

At 143 Piccadilly lived Ferdinand Rothschild, from the Austrian branch of the family, who later became Liberal MP for Aylesbury. Here in 1865 he married his cousin, Evy, daughter of Lionel of No. 148, a union that was tragically curtailed when on the same day their son was stillborn and Evy died from the labour. Ferdinand once threw a ball to honour Crown Prince Rudolph of Austria. During the evening he presented gowns to twelve of the most beautiful guests, including Lillie Langtry, mistress of the Prince of Wales (later Edward VII). Lillie was later shocked to receive a bill from the designer for the petticoat she wore with the gown; Ferdinand Rothschild had sanctioned the gown, but not the petticoat. No. 143 has also been demolished, as have all the Piccadilly area Rothschild mansions, apart from Leopold's at 5 Hamilton Place, now Les Ambassadeurs Club, where the Beatles filmed the casino scene in *A Hard Day's Night*.

# THE RANDLORDS

On Piccadilly the power and glory was in the hands of the Rothschilds. Around the corner into Park Lane it was in the hands of diamond merchants, mostly South Africa-based, such as Barney Barnato and Alfred Beit – the Randlords.

These Mayfair Jews dominated the world diamond market at the end of the nineteenth century. It was a market worth dominating, for what was more alluring, more captivating, more dazzling, more valuable, more ancient than the diamond whose antiquity dated back three billion years, considerably longer than that of man, merely its toy.

Although diamonds mostly came from Africa in Victorian times, little of their liquid wealth remained on the continent or trickled back there. Instead much of it flowed to the West End. When the 83-carat Star of South Africa was discovered by a witch doctor in Zandfontein in 1868 there was a stampede for the jewels. John O'Reilly, the *verneuker* trader who took care of the stone, was laughed at when he carved his initials in a tavern window using the gem to prove its qualities. The stone was wrenched from his grasp and thrown into the street but O'Reilly recovered it after manically scrambling around in the dirt. This time he guarded it more carefully. He sold it for a large sum to the Earl of Dudley, owner of Dudley House at 100 Park Lane, who had it mounted with ninety-five smaller brilliants as a head ornament and presented it to the countess.

But the Star of South Africa is a mere bauble compared to the Cullinan I or Star of Africa. It was discovered in 1905 by the superintendent of the Cullinan mine. At 3,106 carats it was then the largest diamond ever discovered and has only been superseded once to this day. The mine's owner, Thomas Cullinan, sold the stone for £150,000 to the Transvaal government, who in turn presented it to Edward VII for his sixty-sixth birthday on 9 November 1907. But how would the authorities get the jewel to the king?

Edward sat down with his private banker and closest confidante, Ernest Cassel, who lived on Park Lane. Cassel was a German who had arrived in England in 1869 with only a bag of clothes and a violin. On making his first million he converted from Judaism to Catholicism, merely to aid his career, as had Gustav Mahler to gain the directorship of the Viennese Opera House, rather than through any genuine theological calling. Later he was involved in funding a new railway line under the West End: the Central Line.

Once he had accumulated a seven-figure bank balance, Cassel moved into a Park Lane mansion, Brook House. Built by T. H. Wyatt in 1869, it stood where Woods Mews and Upper Brook Street now meet the top end of Park Lane. Brook House was typical of Park Lane's grandeur. There were halls of Tuscan marble, and a dining room, oak panelled, which could hold a hundred guests. Cassel also bought the adjacent 27 Upper Brook Street, which he decorated with 800 tons of imported blue and white marble, lapis lazuli pillars for the hall, and Van Dyck portraits for the walls.

The king and Cassel discussed the implications of owning this gem – so valuable, so exclusive – and the unparalleled security measures needed to protect its journey to Britain. They primed the newspapers to announce the passage of the jewel from South Africa to London by steamer, and the papers responded excitedly, according to plan. The public was impressed. Villains licked their lips. But it was all a diversionary tactic. The Cullinan was posted in a parcel bearing a three-shilling stamp that travelled in an altogether different vessel. The address on the parcel: Brook House, Park Lane.

The arrival of the jewel in the West End set into motion the next exciting chapter in its adventures. Edward VII wanted to keep the jewel uncut, but Cassel and his circle urged him to send it to Amsterdam where it could be treated by the Asscher Brothers firm. Consequently, the Keeper of the Royal Jewels very publicly hired the Royal Navy to transport what was in fact an empty box across the North Sea. Even the captain of the vessel was unaware that the closely guarded box in his cabin contained nothing. Meanwhile, Abraham Asscher came over from Amsterdam and travelled a different route back from the West End, by train and night ferry, with the Cullinan Diamond in his pocket. None of his fellow passengers knew who he was or what he was carrying. Once cut, the many smaller Cullinans were incorporated into the Crown Jewels in the Tower of London.

Yet as far as the Park Lane Randlords were concerned, diamonds were more of a curse than a blessing. Alfred Beit, like Ernest Cassel, was a German-born self-made millionaire. He hurried to Cape Colony in 1875 to take advantage of the diamond rush at Kimberley and later joined the board of De Beers, still the world's best-known diamond company. Beit financed an unsuccessful coup to seize the government of Transvaal in South Africa in 1895, yet somehow found time to acquire one of the world's most coveted art collections with works by Goya, Velázquez, Gainsborough, Vermeer's *The Lady Writing a Letter* (the latter's last work to remain in private hands), and Gainsborough's *Madame Baccelli: Dancer* which is still so popular with thieves it has been stolen four times from its Irish stately home address in recent years.

When Beit announced in 1897 plans to build Aldford House at 26 Park Lane the freeholder, the Duke of Westminster, worried that the proposed new property might not be of a sufficiently high standard, sent Beit a memo stipulating that he must spend at least £10,000. Beit explained by return post that he intended to spend that much on the stables alone. But his creation was a monster. The Portland stone was too roughly cut and jarred with the Alloa granite of the Park Street entrance. The Winter Garden, with its rock garden, oases of ferns and palms, tessellated pavement and electric fountain, was simply outré. And to what avail? Aldford House, with its grand augmentations, lasted barely a generation. It was pulled down in 1929 and rebuilt as a block of flats bearing the same name.

Beit co-ran South Africa's most powerful late nineteenth-century financial house, Wernher, Beit and Co. This was a time of rampant asset-stripping and unbridled colonialism, what Joseph Conrad called 'no end of coin by trade' in *Heart of Darkness*, foisted on South Africa to enrich Britain. In 1895 Beit was behind the so-called Jameson Raid when more than 500 rebels tried to engineer a coup in Transvaal and divest the white Dutch settlers of power, not to hand it to the native black population but to empower Britain. The raid was unsuccessful but did its job in precipitating war – the Boer War – between Britain and the descendants of the Dutch who had colonized South Africa (the Boers).

In London Beit quickly earned the wrath of the socialist press. *Justice*, the journal of the Social Democratic Federation, the leading left-wing organization in those pre-Labour Party days, had no scruples about mixing pacifist, internationalist ideas with anti-Semitism, and warned its readers that Beit and Co. were aiming for 'an Anglo-Hebraic Empire in Africa stretching from Egypt to Cape Colony'. But Beit had more pressing concerns. The announcement of the new Cullinan diamond fields in 1902, findings that threatened his profitability, was too much for his heart, which failed to stand up to the strain. He suffered a cardiac attack from which he never recovered.

The Duke of Westminster was equally unwelcoming to another of Park Lane's grandees, Barney Barnato, a former East End barrow boy and one-time partner of Queen Victoria's chief empire builder, Cecil Rhodes. When Barnato attempted to buy land locally in 1897 the Duke stopped him on the grounds that Barnato did not 'stand in a high position in South Africa and that he is a land speculator'. As far as the duke was concerned Barnato would lower the tone of the place. It wasn't that he was Jewish, as some conspiracy theorists have alleged, for so was Sir Moses Montefiore, stockbroker, philanthropist, tireless campaigner for Jewish welfare, who had recently lived at No. 99. No, it was that Barnato had been born above a shop in Aldgate, that he had been a music hall turn and staged boxing exhibitions, that he had traded in everything from feathers to garden vegetables. The duke didn't want nouveau riche, *arriviste* riff-raff enjoying London's most prestigious address. But even the Duke of Westminster couldn't keep Barnato out for ever, and the rough edge of the East eventually smoothed its way into the smooth side of the West, for Barnato eventually acquired a property at Park Lane's junction with Stanhope Gate at the southern end of the street.

Sadly, no sooner had Barnato gained a Park Lane address than his businesses crashed. Opponents rubbed their hands with glee. This was the man who had salted his unproductive mines with diamonds found at other sites to get prospectors digging away in the hope of finding something lucrative. Now he was ruined. The stone statues on his Park Lane roof, detractors joked, were creditors petrified at the thought of having to wait for their payments. In Johannesburg Barnato's mistress found him trying to scrape diamonds out of the wallpaper to raise a few rand. The only thing left for Barnato to do was to return to London. He called a housewarming party at Park Lane for 22 June 1897, the day of the Queen's diamond jubilee, and took a ship home. In mysterious circumstances he fell overboard near Madeira. Even over a hundred years later at the beginning of the twenty-first century his granddaughter was adamant that he had been pushed – by his own nephew, Solly – who knew he would inherit Barnato's fortune.

More venal than Beit or Barnato was J. B. Robinson, owner of Dudley

House. This Park Lane mansion had fourteen reception rooms, a ballroom and a eighty-foot long picture gallery. It is one of the few surviving nineteenth-century properties on the street, headquarters until recently of the property company Hammerson, who in 2005 put the property on the market for £40 million. Robinson became one of the most despised men in Britain and South Africa in the early twentieth century. He was notorious for his stinginess and lack of public spirit, the living embodiment of the lying, scheming, cheating, frauding Melmotte from Anthony Trollope's Mayfair society chronicle *The Way We Live Now*. 'Sour-visaged and unsympathetic. As yellow as a bad apple,' one colleague described him.

In 1922, after the South African authorities fined Robinson half a million pounds for fraud, he bought a British peerage from Lloyd George for £30,000. Parliament was horrified. How could a man of such disreputable character become a lord? Pressure was exerted, and Robinson, gallantly, it seemed, declined the elevation to the Upper House. Lloyd George himself went to the Savoy Hotel to deliver the letter accepting Robinson's refusal. However, the disgraced merchant had not stood down out of moral concerns. When he saw the note he knew he had understood what was wrong all along, reached for his cheque book and asked: 'How much more?' Robinson's popularity continued to decline, and when he died the *Cape Times*'s obituary broke the usual protocol to damn 'the loathsomeness of the thing that is the memory of Sir Joseph Robinson'.

The Duke of Westminster, who had been so inhospitable to Beit and Barnato, was a Grosvenor, one of the four richest families in Europe, the last family to be awarded a dukedom. Their Park Lane mansion, Grosvenor House, at Nos. 87–89, had a colonnaded screen, huge pedimented stone arch and wrought iron gates. Within, a phalanx of servants was employed in everything from servicing the Duke's phaeton and state coach to tidying up the schoolroom. On the walls there were seven Rembrandt portraits to entertain diners as well as works by Titian, Turner, Stubbs, Gainsborough (*Blue Boy*, no less), Velázquez's portrait of Don Balthazar. There was even a Rubens room crowned with his *Adoration of the Magi*, now at King's College Chapel, Cambridge.

Guests were impressed. Walking through its palatial halls with the poet Richard Le Gallienne, Oscar Wilde drooled: 'Ah, Richard! This is how a gentleman should live.' Revellers were entertained. At a ball hosted by Shelagh, Duchess of Westminster, the Kaiser's son mysteriously disappeared.

He was eventually traced to a bedroom where he was found taking a rest. But he was not alone. The shape of what could only be a comely maiden was noticeable in another part of the bed. The following day the thankful crown prince sent the lady a dazzling diamond, unaware that he had sent her one of the German Crown Jewels, which were not his to dispatch. When the Kaiser found out he was most vexed and demanded the jewel be returned. The lady refused. After much tussling the Kaiser's shame was saved, but not the depth of his wallet. Grosvenor House was demolished after the Great War and replaced by the luxury Grosvenor House Hotel.

## VULGAR FACTIONS

'There are lots of vulgar people live in Grosvenor Square,' claimed the Duchess of Berwick in a magnificent solecism from Oscar Wilde's *Lady Windermere's Fan*. In 1892, the year the play was published, twenty-two of the square's fifty-one addresses contained titled people. A Grosvenor Square address was prestigious and exciting. For instance, it was at No. 4 that news of Wellington's victory over Napoleon at Waterloo officially arrived in London on 21 June 1815, three days after the battle. A chaise and four decorated with French flags pulled up outside the property and out stepped the Honourable Henry Percy, Wellington's *aide-de-camp*, bearing a dispatch confirming the victory for the Earl of Bathurst, the war secretary, who was dining inside with the British cabinet.

So who could have been the Duchess's target? Surely not Lord Randolph Churchill, father of Winston, Chancellor of the Exchequer in Lord Salisbury's 1886 government, who died at No. 50 on 24 January 1895. It must have been another of those repugnantly recidivist Randlords, probably Lionel Phillips, of 32 Grosvenor Square, who like Park Lane's Alfred Beit had helped organize the coup against the Transvaal government in 1895.

Unlike Beit, Phillips was arrested by the Transvaal authorities, who discovered incriminating letters he had sent his co-conspirators and sentenced him to death. Although it seemed that rough justice was about to take place in this semi-lawless territory, the power of Phillips' purse came to bear. First the sentence was commuted to fifteen years imprisonment, and then by a strange quirk to a fine of £25,000 and a promise from Phillips that he would not interfere in Transvaalian affairs again. Yet when Phillips returned to

Britain he was knighted, and during the First World War he was awarded a post in the Ministry of Munitions. Some punishment.

Linking Grosvenor Square and New Bond Street in the heart of the village is Grosvenor Street. In some ways it is just another opulent Mayfair street, in other ways it is a paradigm of West End social history, where practically each house hides some colourful intrigue. At No. 34, from 1903 to 1940, lived Jack Barnato Joel, nephew of diamond magnate Barney Barnato. Next door at No. 33, now the Malawian Embassy, lived a princess, Clara Huntington, who moved there in 1912 after the death of her husband, Prince Franz Edmund Joseph Gabriel Vitus von Hatzfeldt-Wildenburg. On moving in the princess ripped out the Gothic woodwork, which had been installed by the previous occupant, and replaced it with French panelling and Grinling Gibbons-style carvings. No problem. One tasteful opulent design replaced by another.

No. 16, where the Marquess of Hertford kept twenty-two servants in the 1740s, was home from 1909 to the Keppels. They were visited practically every day for a year after moving in by Edward VII, who was having an affair with Alice Keppel, ancestor of Camilla Parker-Bowles, and whom the Keppel daughters called 'Kingy'. After the Great War No. 16 was bought by Laura Corrigan, a dazzling Wisconsin-born beauty, bald under her wig. To the horror of Mayfair society, Corrigan was made of new money and had once worked as a waitress in Ohio. She had only become fabulously wealthy after marrying the owner of the Corrigan-McKinney Steel Company who, tragically, died soon after consummating the marriage from a heart attack, but who fortunately had found time to leave her $60 million in his will. Failing to win acceptance in American high society, Corrigan moved to Mayfair. Here she became famed for her solecisms and malapropisms. She once complained that the Chippendale chairs were spoiled by their 'petit pois' covers, and when listing the merits of Gothic architecture discoursed on a cathedral's 'flying buttocks'. Few could resist her invitations, but one who did so was the playwright George Bernard Shaw who, receiving a card that read: 'Mrs Corrigan At Home 6–8pm', replied 'GBS Ditto'. During the war Corrigan sold her jewellery to leading Nazi Hermann Goering, head of the Luftwaffe, who wore most of them under his uniform. She spent the proceeds feeding French prisoners of war in Paris.

Sir Edgar Speyer, an American merchant banker, spent a quarter of a million pounds decorating Nos. 44 and 46 Grosvenor Street in the early twentieth century, connecting the two houses by a staircase copied from the

Scala dei Giganti in the Doge's Palace, Venice. Speyer rescued London's Bakerloo tube line after its founder, Whitaker Wright, was convicted of fraud, left the court protesting his innocence but swallowed the cyanide capsules he had hidden about his person. Speyer himself later met with ignominy, holding the unfortunate dishonour of being the last individual to be expelled from the Privy Council, a fate which befell him in 1921 for supposed pro-German activities during the Great War. Subsequently, No. 46 was requisitioned by the Government and became the Japanese Embassy.

Lower down the social scale Mayfair sports many secluded streets lined with fine houses, too small to have been considered habitable by the Edwardian magnates of Park Lane or the titled folk of Grosvenor Square, but classy enough to be something most would be proud to own, a pinnacle of social achievement, a fitting realization of a lifetime of hard work or a worthy fulfilling of an inheritance to gain a foothold in West End society.

Take Chesterfield Street, halfway between Berkeley Square and Park Lane. To the upper echelons of traditional Mayfair society Chesterfield Street barely registered. It had been formed from the *gardens* of the long demolished Chesterfield House mansion, and thus was a sad little thing indeed. Yet for those starting from the other end of society to live in Chesterfield Street was something wonderful. Such it was for the resident at No. 6 in the early years of the twentieth century – W. Somerset Maugham.

When Maugham moved to 6 Chesterfield Street in 1911 he was a successful playwright and an aspiring novelist. By the time he left in 1919 he was being fêted for one of the most ambitious and rewarding novels of the era – *Of Human Bondage*, written mostly in Mayfair. A *bildungsroman* – a novel based on the development of a youthful protagonist, like James Joyce's *A Portrait of the Artist as a Young Man* – *Of Human Bondage* showed critics that Maugham could deal with weightier formats than drawing-room dramas, and allowed him to exorcize his childhood demons; his nervousness, inferiority complex, embarrassment at his own social awkwardness, sexual confusion and his stammer, which in the novel manifests itself as hero Philip Carey's club foot.

Living in Mayfair meant he had a place on the invitations list of the great Mayfair hostesses (Lady Ottoline Morrell, 'at home' on Thursdays; the Duchess of Sutherland 'at home' on Fridays), although when he left one soirée early with the excuse 'I have to keep my youth', the duchess replied: 'Why don't you bring him with you?' Living in Mayfair meant the ability to wander from auction room to art gallery, snapping up prized portraits, such as Zoffany's take on Garrick, which once belonged to Henry Irving. Alas, the fine life was brought to a swift end with the outbreak of the Great War. There would be no hiding away in a cocooned world of refined manners for Maugham, even though his war duties could have been as painless, if he had so wished, as those of his fellow writer Lytton Strachey, who stayed at home and knitted mufflers 'for the soldier and sailor lads'.

Without waiting to hear back from Winston Churchill, First Lord of the Admiralty, Maugham left with an ambulance expedition headed for France as an interpreter. He was later caught up in the Battle of Ypres, returning home to learn how to be an ambulance driver after discovering they were more scarce than interpreters. Eventually Maugham wound up in Moscow, where he gained sensitive political information for the prime minister, David Lloyd George, carefully writing down his conclusions so that he might deliver them without stammering. After hostilities ended Maugham returned to Chesterfield Street with a sense of personal achievement that went beyond that usually found in cold-bloodedly money-mad Mayfair to write another masterpiece, *The Moon and Sixpence* (1919), partly based on the life of the primitivist tropical painter Paul Gauguin.

## BRIGHT YOUNG THINGS

The Great War brought privations for West End society. For instance at the Ritz, the grand hotel on Piccadilly, the lavishness of the fare was rationed to little more than creamed soup, lobster, half a chicken, three rashers of bacon, three tomatoes, fruit salad and coffee per person, as Francis Meynell exposed in the *Daily Herald*. At Asprey's, the famous jewellers of New Bond Street, customers who were used to visiting three times a day, each time in different dress – morning suit, afternoon lounge clothes and evening dinner suit – would now only turn up twice a day, without changing.

Many magnificent Mayfair buildings were requisitioned. The Duke of Devonshire gave over his London residence, Devonshire House, which had become an embarrassment, with statues littering the garden (they are now at Chatsworth), the glorious gambolings of Georgiana long forgotten, so that it could be used as the Voluntary Aid Detachment headquarters. Londonderry House became the HQ of the Women's Legion; Grosvenor

House a hospital for invalided soldiers; and Crewe House the Ministry of Propaganda.

At the end of the Great War, however, society returned to the grand houses. Although well-heeled West Enders were alarmed to find that Lady Dorothy Cavendish, the nineteen-year-old daughter of the Duke of Devonshire, had become engaged to a commoner, her father's ADC, no less, a thin-faced, moustachioed chap by the name of Harold Macmillan, it looked superficially as if nothing had changed or would ever change in the dignified mansions by Hyde Park and Green Park. Sure, the Bolshevik revolution in Russia had led to the assassination of the royal family there, but a rabble of syndicalists, socialists and communists was not yet tearing down Park Lane. And if the mob were soon to lay waste Mayfair then the monied classes may as well continue as they had done for centuries, while they still had the chance. The ladies could continue to change costume four times a day – dressing in linen and lamé, satin and starch, georgettes and *crêpes-de-chines*. The season could resume with the opening of the Covent Garden opera, garden parties at Buckingham Palace, the Eton v Harrow football match, the Henley Regatta, Royal Ascot ... The meals could return: breakfasts of devilled kidneys, kedgeree and broiled trout, lunch of cold pigeon and ptarmigan, afternoon refreshments at Gunter's on Berkeley Square of sandwiches, iced cakes, iced coffee and Turk's Blood.

Better still, the gay and carefree parties could be revived. As Evelyn Waugh waxed in *Vile Bodies*, there were 'masked parties, savage parties, Victorian parties, Greek parties, Wild West parties, Russian parties, circus parties ...' There were the parties thrown by Lady Maud Cunard, nicknamed 'Emerald' on account of her dazzling jewellery, at No. 7 on the east side of Grosvenor Square (now demolished), which the leading society diarist Chips Channon explained were 'a rallying point for most of London society'. There was the Mozart Party hosted by David Tennant on Burlington Gardens, behind the Royal Academy of Arts. There was the party thrown by the nymphomanic actress Tallulah Bankhead, who opened the door at her Farm Street, Mayfair, pad naked to lead guests to the bathroom for cocktails. People talked of the circus party thrown by the fashion designer Norman Hartnell at 10 Bruton Street, off Berkeley Square, a few doors along from the house where the future Queen Elizabeth had been born three years previously, the guests including acrobats, Siberian wolf cubs and a white pony led up the staircase by Lady Eleanor Smith, daughter of the redoubtable Tory peer Fred Smith.

Everyone agreed over breakfast of kippers and cocoa at dawn that this was the most magnificent, most exclusive, most splendiferous party the West End had ever seen.

Not all the parties went down well. Cynthia Asquith, daughter-in-law of the Great War-era prime minister H. H. Asquith, was nonplussed by a bash at which society mothers were 'throwing their daughters at the Prince of Wales. I saw the Prince of Wales dancing round with Mrs Dudley-Ward, a pretty little fluff . . . He is a dapper little fellow – too small – but really a pretty face . . . I have never seen a man talk so fluently while dancing. He obviously means to have fun.' The prince may have, but Cynthia didn't, for she moaned about the 'teasing catastrophic music thrummed out by those leering Negroes, and the stuttering, furtive, modern dances which can't be as much fun as our valses.'

The most fêted party hostess of the period was the poisonous Ronnie Greville. A snob with a barbed tongue, she was married to the Hon. Ronald Greville, previously part of Edward VII's circle, and lived at 16 Charles Street, near Berkeley Square. A serial solecist and malapropist, she once called the poet John Drinkwater 'Mr Bayswater', and when corrected apologized to 'Mr Bathwater'. Osbert Sitwell obliquely described her parties, which were attended by many European royals, including the Queen of Spain and the King of Egypt, as 'like jazz night at the London Palladium'.

When the Duchess of York (the future Queen Mother) came to dinner, Greville's two dypso butlers, Boles and Bacon, bobbed up every minute or so offering the duchess whiskey. At another party Bacon, taking a dish of baby tongues into the dinner, was so overcome by gluttony he stuffed them one by one into his face. Although the sauce was now running down his shirt, he disguised this well when he appeared apologetically in front of the guests and explained that the reason why there were no tongues on the plate was that none were to be found in the market that morning. On another occasion Bacon was so drunk Mrs Greville wrote him a note on a place card saying: 'You're drunk. Leave the room at once.' With a stroke of genius he took the card and presented it to the Tory grandee Austen Chamberlain, who was so mortified he said nothing for the rest of the evening.

Mrs Greville was a vociferous supporter of Adolf Hitler. Leading Nazis in London took her seriously. Von Ribbentrop, the German ambassador to Britain, courted her and invited her to a Nuremberg rally. But Harold Nicolson, the society diarist, was furious. 'The harm which these silly selfish hostesses do is really immense. These people have a subversive influence. They wine and dine our younger politicians and they create an atmosphere of authority.'

No one could remember at which of the Duke of Sutherland's fancy dress dos Edward, Prince of Wales, ten years before his shameful abdication and his flirting with Hitler, attended dressed first as Bonnie Prince Charlie and then as a Chinese coolie. Or the one at which he came in a Ku Klux Klan robe, a feat ignored by the press who eighty years later were riled by Prince Harry's wearing of a Swastika at a West End ball.

But reaction even to Harry's *faux pas* was nothing compared with the hysterics that greeted a Bright Young Things bash at St George's Baths in which guests danced in bathing costumes. Barbara Cartland's mother exclaimed to her daughter: 'I've never heard of anything so improper . . . and watched by black men! I'm very glad you weren't there.' Ironically there was no more indefatigable party-goer and socialite, no more glittering debutante and no more star-struck West End chronicler than Cartland. Her memoir, *We Danced All Night*, even managed to open with the most preposterous passage of purple prose in the history of publishing: 'Darling, I love you! Will you marry me? I can't live without you.'

## HEARTBREAK HOTELS

Changes were afoot between the wars. There were major demolitions on Park Lane and Piccadilly. Grand hotels replaced the grandiose mansions. Devonshire House was the first to go. The Duke of Devonshire sold what had been one of London's greatest houses, with its three-acre garden, for one million pounds to a firm of building contractors in 1919. They in turn sold it on to Laurence Harrison, a Liverpool ship owner, and Shurmer Sibthorp, a developer. Harrison and Sibthorp wanted to build an entertainments centre – 'a super cinema restaurant dance hall and tea room' – on the site. Realizing how unpopular this would make him, Sibthorp added apologetically: 'Call me a vandal for pulling down Devonshire House, but personally I think the place is an eyesore.' Not all of Devonshire House was destroyed. Harold Macmillan's mother bought the mahogany doors for her new house in Sussex, and the grand wrought-iron gates tipped in gold were moved across Piccadilly to adorn the entrance to Green Park. But nothing came of the grand entertainments palace, and the replacement that stands above Green Park station on the north side of Piccadilly is more of an eyesore than was Devonshire House.

Dorchester House on Park Lane came down after Robert McAlpine & Sons and Gordon Hotels acquired the site in 1928 for £500,000. When the plans to demolish the mansion were first announced Lady Beecham, wife of the redoubtable conductor Sir Thomas, wailed: 'It is too terrible to contemplate. If the public wish to save the house for London they must make a strong protest before the completion of the sale.' They didn't. The mansion was re-erected in Scotland and later sold to an American, Paul Knight, who transported its 58ft stairway to Texas. Other fittings went to the Walker Art Gallery in Liverpool, the dining room to the V&A, and individual bricks to several London homes, not as trophies but as early examples of sustainable resourcing.

Those responsible for the new building on the site – the Dorchester Hotel – announced it would be the most luxurious in the British Isles. Owen Williams, architect of Wembley Stadium, was chosen as designer, but a disagreement between him and the McAlpines saw the appointment of a different architect, William Curtis Green, only twelve months before it was due to open. The main theme of the new property was the use of concrete. Another was immensity: 2,000 miles of steel rods for the reinforced concrete; 20,000 cork slabs, two inches thick, to line the external walls; 160 miles of pipes to supply water, drainage and radiator systems; the same number of miles of cable for lighting, telephones and bells. The new Dorchester Hotel opened in 1931. It had 600 bedrooms and walls soundproofed with seaweed and cork. The cream of society booked to stay there: Marlene Dietrich, Judy Garland and Laurence Olivier. Indeed it is at the Dorchester in the Soho beat film *Expresso Bongo* that Bongo Herbert takes a suite when he is on his way up, sharing the rooms with fading star Dixie Collins, who is on the way down.

The Dorchester was the first setting for Foyle's literary luncheons. In their early days these featured the novelist D. H. Lawrence, the actor Charlie Chaplin and the Ethiopian ruler, Haile Selassie. When Sir John Gilbey of the gin distillers spoke for one and a half hours, causing a guest to fall asleep, William Foyle, the bookstore's owner, approached the sleeping gentleman and hit him on the head with his gavel, only to be told by the awakened guest: 'hit me harder, I can still hear him.' An unusual guest at the Dorchester in

1932 was Princess Stephanie Julianne von Hohenlohe, a Jewish member of a well-to-do German family and a close friend of Adolf Hitler. She was a valuable source of information, according to Lord Rothermere, owner of the *Daily Mail*, who himself briefly flirted with fascism in the early 1930s, and he paid her an annual retainer of £5,000 (£200,000 in today's prices) to provide him with information. In 1937 she arranged for Lord Halifax (who later lost out to Winston Churchill in becoming PM) to travel to Germany and meet Hermann Goering, the leading Nazi. The same year she began an affair with Fritz Wiedemann, aide to Hitler, and left the Dorchester to join him in San Francisco, where he was Consul-General. Princess Stephanie acted as a go-between for various English aristocrats who were sympathetic to the Nazis, ferrying information between them, and when Rothermere stopped paying her as war neared in 1939 she sued, claiming he had promised to maintain the payments for life. She lost.

Brook House on Park Lane, turn-of-the-century home of Ernest Cassel, Edward VII's confidante, experienced a different fate to the Dorchester's. After Cassel died in the Brook House library in September 1921, his granddaughter, Edwina, inherited the property. She married Lord Mountbatten, Queen Victoria's great-grandson, who became the most conspicuous minor royal of the twentieth century, mentor to Prince Charles and assassination victim of the IRA. The couple fitted out Brook House with London's first penthouse, which could only be reached by an express lift, then a rarity for London, in which Queen Mary became stuck when she visited.

Mountbatten, a naval officer, commissioned a redesign with a marine theme. He turned one room into a replica of the cabin on his navy ship, lined the walls and ceilings with cork, installed a regulation officer-size bunk with a brass handrail, and decorated his personal bathroom with rocks, seaweed, shells and pictures of fish. Yet despite all the hard work the Mountbattens put into reformatting Brook House for modern marine living, they put the property on the market in 1931, claiming that heavy taxation under the new 'socialist' Government meant they could no longer afford to live there. Brook House was demolished soon after, and luxury flats, charming, desirable, costly, but not quite as luxurious as what went before went up in its place.

Londonderry House survived longer than most of its neighbours. The seventh Marquis of Londonderry, Charles Vane-Tempest-Stewart, was a Tory MP who had fought on the Somme in 1916. As Minister of Education in Northern Ireland he 'officially' met the great Irish nationalist leader Michael

Collins, an encounter arranged by Winston Churchill. Collins baulked at being so close to one who bore a surname traditionally aligned with the hated British rule in the North, but warmed to the man. 'Try to imagine what it means to be a man like myself,' he explained, 'entirely self-made, self-educated without background and trying to cope with someone like Lord L, a man who has every advantage I lack.' The marquis in turn pronounced himself impressed with Collins's 'enthusiasm and stirring phraseology'.

Londonderry was one of the great socializing Tory MPs of the day, throwing parties that rank as the 1920s predecessors to Jeffrey Archer's shepherd's pie and Krug affairs of the 1980s. He was catering his way into the Cabinet, Lord Birkenhead claimed, and in due course became Secretary of State for Air, not in a Tory regime but as part of the National Government of 1931, mainly because prime minister Ramsay MacDonald had a crush on Edith, Lady Londonderry. Indeed the PM was desperate to be invited to join Lady Londonderry's elite club, the Ark, which met at Londonderry House and whose members were identified by the name of an animal or mythical creature, with Lady Londonderry as 'Charley the Cheetah' and Churchill 'Winston the Warlock'.

The Londonderrys were soon openly courting Hitler, whom the marquis described as 'very agreeable . . . a kindly man, with a receding chin and an impressive face'. To Edith he was 'a man with wonderful, far-seeing eyes . . . simple, dignified, humble,' and she later wrote to Hitler: 'You and Germany remind me of the Book of Genesis in the Bible.' Signs of the property's imminent demise must have been obvious by the 1940s, when Londonderry began answering the front door himself. It hadn't been so long since the staff included twenty-eight servants in the kitchen alone and sixteen in the stewards' room. Londonderry House was partly destroyed by German bombing during the Second World War. This was a tragic irony given that in the 1930s Joachim von Ribbentrop, the Nazi German ambassador to Britain, had been a regular guest, and it was an irony not lost on General Raymond E. Lee, the US military attaché in London, who in noting the owners' pre-war courting of the Nazi attaché remarked as he passed the bomb site one day: 'I could only wonder what that chump Londonderry thinks now of his friends Hitler, Ribbentrop and Goering'. Londonderry House was demolished in 1962, by which time it had been dwarfed by the monstrous new Hilton Hotel. It was also replaced by a hotel – the Metropolitan – which features the exclusive Japanese restaurant, Nobu. It was at Nobu that a two-minute encounter in a broom cupboard in 1999 between the tennis player Boris Becker and the Russian model Angela Ermakova resulted in a million-dollar paternity suit for the former Wimbledon champion.

As for Grosvenor House, after the Great War the Duke of Westminster, the richest man in Europe (his yacht is always moored beneath the balcony of Elyot's and Amanda's room in Noël Coward's *Private Lives*), didn't have the stomach to return. Before leaving for nearby Bourdon House, a more modest affair, he had a fire sale of his extraordinary art collection. Gainsborough's *Blue Boy* was sold at sea, which caused a public outcry. The property was bought in 1924 by Lord Leverhulme, the soap magnate, who announced he did not want to live there himself but would turn the place into a public art gallery. Unfortunately, he died in 1925 before he was able to oversee the project. Executors decided the site was ideal for a hotel, predictably to be named the Grosvenor House Hotel. It was designed by Edwin Lutyens, no less, had 478 en-suite bedrooms (a radical concept at the time), 160 private apartments, running iced water and an ice rink in the basement. An office even opened in New York to take bookings, until the Wall Street Crash of 1929.

In 1935 the new hotel was the setting for a most unusual event, an aromatic dinner held by a strange new organization – the Smell Society – founded by the eccentric lawyer Ambrose Appelbe, who later represented Mandy Rice-Davies. Appelbe hoped to refresh London nostrils with sheets of paper impregnated with the smells of the seaside and create new words to describe the smell of things such as roast turkey and tar. In this he was unsuccessful, but he did create quite a stink by going about for years in glasses that had belonged to the 10 Rillington Place murderer Christie, one of his less esteemed clients.

As war approached most of the great Mayfair houses were abandoned. No one was sure what the enemy was planning, but they wanted to take few chances. As the fictitious Mrs Jan Buyl explains so succinctly in Norman Collins's exuberant novel of the time, *London Belongs To Me*, 'The Germans are coming over here with ten thousand planes straight away, as soon as war's been declared, if not before, and they're going to destroy London.' Heinrich Brüning, the German chancellor shortly before Hitler, put it a different way. He told Lady Freda Valentine, who lived at 26 Green Street, Mayfair, that the Nazis wouldn't bother with declaring war but simply annihilate London with a sudden deluge of bombs.

Neither happened, but the British government did step in and requisition Lady Freda's Green Street home for foreign diplomats and other military personnel who were to be stationed in central London. Meanwhile, Victor Rothschild cleared 148 Piccadilly, the dynasty's London town house where in 1875 Lionel de Rothschild and Benjamin Disraeli mulled over news of the Khedive of Egypt's negotiations with the French government about shares in the Suez Canal. Hampden House in Green Street, where the Duke and Duchess of Sutherland had thrown their fancy dress parties (Lord Blandford came as a female cross-Channel swimmer in 1926), closed down. Before Lady Cunard's Grosvenor Square place went the same way she threw a dinner party. There, Lady Oxford told guests that gas masks were unnecessary and air raids not dangerous. Laura Corrigan moved her people to the Ritz, Paris, where her suite ran the length of the building.

At 48 Upper Grosvenor Street the family of Margaret Sweeny, who became the sex scandal-mongering Duchess of Argyll in the 1960s, taped up the windows, disconnected the phones, turned off the water and locked up, before abandoning the property. At the end of the war Sweeny returned and found not a thing damaged. Everything worked. Alas, Mayfair Society had upped and left, never to return.

# 3

# The Making of the West End

The West End was a late starter as far as the capital's history is concerned. The two cities – London and Westminster – have hundreds of years on it. Covent Garden and the East End are also older. The West End post-dates them because it wasn't as immediately interesting geographically. It was featureless land at the bottom of the Forest of Middlesex with no Thames to fuel it and feed it. There was just a stream, the Tyburn, the course of which is followed by the modern-day Marylebone Lane. But because the land lay near the great palaces of St James's, Whitehall and Westminster it was ideal for new development when the capital burst its ancient boundaries, particularly after the Fire of London in 1666 destroyed all existing notions of London's size and shape.

## SOHO! TALLY HO!

Monmouth House, on what is now Soho Square, was the first major building to go up on the land between the palaces and the southern edge of the forest. It was built in 1677 by 'Mr Ford, a joynor' for James Scott, Duke of Monmouth, Charles II's bastard son, whose father granted him the freehold of the old hunting fields west of St Giles-in-the-Fields church. The land acquired the name 'So-Ho', an old hunting cry, in 1632, and when the Duke went hunting he would use the cry 'Soho! Tally Ho!' on catching the hare.

Gregory King, a developer, formed a square around the property – King's Square – which later became Soho Square. It has a grassed central area, as with so many late Stuart and Georgian squares in London, such as Hanover Square, but no church, unlike an otherwise similar-looking square built at the same time in the East End – Wellclose Square. Whereas Wellclose Square had a Danish church designed by Caius Gabriel Cibber, Soho Square has Cibber's ungainly statue of Charles II – all that is left of the original structure, which included a stone Baroque fountain resplendent with statues of river gods representing the four great English waterways of the Tyne, Humber, Severn and Thames.

Monmouth House boasted huge wrought-iron gates mounted on stone piers, an ample courtyard for carriages and perfect Renaissance detailing. But despite its grandeur it was demolished as early as 1773. By then it had been joined on King's Square by the first of two separate neighbouring properties called Carlisle House; the one sporting a dramatic history, the other of little consequence. The interesting Carlisle House stood in the south-east corner, where St Patrick's Catholic church can now be found. It was built in the 1680s for the second Earl of Carlisle, was later leased by the King of Naples, and by the 1760s was in the hands of Teresa Cornelys, Venetian soprano, courtesan and occasional lover of Casanova. Here she threw the most fêted balls of the day. Even Lord North, the much derided prime minister responsible for losing the American colonies, capered in harlequin clothes. At another party Joseph Merlin, inventor of roller skates, slalomed through the ballroom at high speed while playing a violin – until he went crashing through a mirror. Long after the parties abated Cornelys met an unfortunate end, dying of cancer and screaming out: 'The devil is dragging me down!' Carlisle House was demolished in 1791.

In the first decades after the Fire of London, when Londoners rich and poor were moving into uncharted territories, developers were keen to build on any available plot of land, and to ignore Elizabeth I's royal proclamation of 1582 against building tenements within three miles of the City. Speculators took leases in the Soho fields, and a lattice of streets appeared: Dean, Frith (occasionally known as Thrift), Greek and Old Compton – all now world-famous names. To the west was Colman Hedge Lane, which later became Old Soho, and is now Wardour Street.

Such development wasn't always popular. In 1592 a mob of around forty Soho residents destroyed the new fences that had been put up on what until recently had been common hunting land. And the problems continued after the houses went up. In many cases they were barely able to stay upright. William Hogarth mocked the jerry-building of the day in his infamous 1752 engraving *Gin Lane*, which shows the houses around St Giles crumbling away around their owners.

The new streets attracted not just Londoners moving from the old centres, but a large number of immigrants and refugees who couldn't afford better. There were Huguenots, French Protestants fleeing hostile Catholics; Greeks fleeing the Ottomans in the 1670s; and later Jews, Germans and Italians. The Huguenots, mostly artisans – milliners, jewellers, tapestry makers – made the most impression. They introduced new foods to the English diet, such as oxtail soup and saveloys, and brought a level of intricate workmanship never before seen in the capital. By the early eighteenth century Soho was full of silversmiths, clock-makers, engravers and gun-makers. Although their skills and mores remained for generations, their community was short-lived, quickly subsumed into the greater demography.

In west Soho was Knave's Acre, small narrow streets – Beak, Brewer, Broad(wick) – which refused to run straight, crammed with flat-faced brick houses that sported few adornments. It was on Beak Street that the Italian artist Giovanni Antonio Canal, better known as Canaletto, had his studio (at No. 41, from 1746–56). Canaletto came to England from Venice when he was forty-nine, having made much money selling views of Venice to Englishmen passing through on the Grand Tour. His first London pieces were almost square and included views of the Thames, especially in Richmond. But not everyone was impressed, and the poor quality of some pictures led critics to suggest that the Canaletto who settled in Soho was an impostor.

Here in west Soho the centrepiece to rival Soho Square in east Soho was Golden Square. 'A very handsome open place', as John Strype described it in his 1720 Survey of London. Golden Square was created in 1674 as a luxurious address for the gentry, the design overseen by Christopher Wren. Taking advantage of this prestigious location was Henry St John, the first Viscount Bolingbroke, who lived at No. 21 on the south side from 1701–1704. Although Bolingbroke publicly supported the Hanoverian accession of George I, he was secretly plotting for the return of the Stuarts, and when his scheme was uncovered he fled to France. There the Catholic James Edward Stuart (the Old Pretender), son of the exiled king, James II, appointed him his Secretary of State. Back home Bolingbroke's name was mud, and was swiftly removed from the House of Lords. After eight years in exile, during which time the Jacobites failed to achieve their aims, Bolingbroke returned to England. He was only able to do so because his mistress, Marie Claire Deschamps, bribed George I's mistress, the Duchess of Kendall, at a cost of £11,000, to ease through his repatriation.

Because gunpowder stores and breweries (commemorated by modern-day Brewer Street) were so close to Golden Square the aristocracy and super-wealthy soon vacated the locale for Mayfair. Middle-class foreigners took over the houses. One such was the twenty-five-year-old painter Angelica Kauffmann (at No. 16 from 1767–81), a founder member of the Royal Academy who was the first woman involved in the organization. Kauffmann captivated the Danish prime minister, Count Bernsdorff, who described her as having 'a most peculiar and womanly dignity'. She also quickly captivated much of the West End. Even Sir Joshua Reynolds, then Britain's most influential artist, came to pay homage, as did Dr Johnson who had his portrait done. But Golden Square was soon filled with cheap hotels, their rooms taken, as Charles Dickens noted in *Nicholas Nickleby* (1838), by 'dark complexioned men who wear large rings', and foreign legations from Bavaria and Portugal. Mostly Catholics, these newcomers, such as the Portuguese ambassador Don Sebastian Joseph de Carvalho, could enjoy the rare privilege of being able to worship legally – at the time Catholicism was barred in England – in the chapel at the back of Golden Square's Bavarian Embassy. But this had a downside. In 1780 the mob began outside the building the week-long violence – the Gordon Riots – that partly destroyed London.

# STUCCONIA

Running across the West End from Marble Arch to St Giles's Circus is Oxford Street, effectively London's high street. Originally part of a Roman road running from Hampshire to the Suffolk coast, bypassing the forts at Londinium, it has enjoyed a succession of names including The Waye from Uxbridge, The King's Highway, The Road to Oxford and The Tyburn Way. The name Tyburn honoured the Tyburn or Tybourne brook which ran underneath and is culverted at the spot now marked by Stratford Place.

At the street's western end stood the Tyburn Tree, for centuries London's main hanging site. At the eastern end the road's rigid forward lunge broke into a curve which took it towards St Giles's church. That change in direction has historically marked the eastern edge of the West End.

In the late eighteenth century piecemeal development of the area north of Oxford Street began. This had been the manor of Tottenhall, land stretching north to Highgate which belonged to the canons of St Paul's at the time of the Domesday Book (1086). By the eighteenth century it was covered with fields, ponds, and few buildings other than a windmill and William Rathbone's timber yard. Its eastern boundary was a lane that became Tottenham Court Road. The northern boundary was unclear until the Duke of Grafton financed a major new route that allowed cattle being taken to Smithfield meat market to miss out Oxford Street. This was given the ungainly title 'The New Road from Paddington to Islington' and opened in 1756. It is now Marylebone Road to the west and Euston Road further east, insufferably and unrelentingly choked with traffic, a formidable barrier between the elegant West End and decrepit Somers Town to the north.

Development of the land to the west of Tottenham Court Road was mostly the work of another of Charles II's sons: Henry Fitzroy and his (legitimate) issue, the Duke of Grafton and Earl of Euston. After the Peace of Paris signalled the end of the Seven Years War in 1763 the rich, their coffers boosted, were keen to create new estates further away from Westminster and the City. Charles Fitzroy, second Duke of Grafton, commissioned the Adam Brothers, masters of the use of ornament, to design a new London square: Fitzroy Square.

When Robert Adam died in 1794 only the east and south sides had been completed to his grand designs. The other two sides were finished skilfully according to the same pattern in the 1830s. Until the south side was damaged in the Second World War the square showcased the best of Adam's work, described by John Summerson, the great chronicler of Georgian London, as 'glamorous, gay, original, full of affectations'. It became the home of the wealthy, of patrons of the arts who supported local concert halls and pleasure gardens. Ford Madox Brown, the artist, mentor to the Pre-Raphaelites, lived at No. 37. George Bernard Shaw and Virginia Woolf occupied No. 29, at different times, and the Georgian Group is now at No. 6, a house typical of Adam architecture, with iron lanterns set in the original railings, a wide, proud front door with fanlight, and rooms that feature plaster cornices and marble fireplaces.

Further west in Marylebone in 1719 John Prince laid out a rigid grid pattern of streets. Here the symmetrical houses feature wrough-iron balconies, tall sash windows, often with a balcony running the entire length, and a solid double front door with decorated fanlight. As houses began to cover the fields the indefatigable pamphleteer and writer Daniel Defoe noticed 'a world full of bricklayers and labourers who like gardeners dig a hole, put in a few bricks and presently there goes up a house', a description turned into a complaint by the Duke of Chandos who noted how the air was 'poisoned with the brick kilns and the other abominate smells which infect these parts'.

Work soon began on new houses to the north-west of where Oxford Circus now stands, what became Cavendish Square. The Duke of Chandos was central to the new developments. This was the man who bought his second wife, Anne Jefferies, at a Newbury market despite, or perhaps because of, the rope around her neck. He owned much land between here and Canons, his mansion in Edgware, which Defoe described as 'the finest in England', and announced that he would build himself a mansion to take up the north side of the new square, lining the twelve-mile route to Canons with luxurious properties that would form a grand processional way. But his plans were spoiled by the South Sea Bubble financial crash of 1720 in which he lost a fortune, and he settled for just two mansions at the northern corners of the square.

On the west side of Cavendish Square Thomas Archer designed Harcourt House for Lord Bingley, Chancellor of the Exchequer. It became Portland House when the Duke of Portland moved there in 1825. Later in the century it was at the centre of one of the strangest legal tussles London has ever witnessed. A Mrs Druce, the daughter-in-law of a local shopkeeper, the late Thomas Druce, petitioned the Home Secretary for permission to open her father-in-law's coffin on the grounds that Druce and the Duke of Portland, who had also passed away, were one and the same; that the duke had created the shopkeeper persona as an elaborate hoax. The coffin would be empty, she explained, and she would be entitled to a share of the millions that the childless Duke of Portland had left in his will.

A legal battle of Jarndycean proportions ensued, but Mrs Druce remained unsuccessful in her attempts to prove that her father-in-law's coffin was empty. The coffin remained unopened, and after seven years Mrs Druce was consigned to a mental hospital. Meanwhile, the Druce family formed a public company to continue the case, and speculators, sensing a killing, took up their cause. At last, in 1907, the coffin was opened. Inside, to no one's surprise, was the body of Druce. The case collapsed.

Another new estate, developed as part of the prosperity that London enjoyed after the ending of the Seven Years War in 1763, was the Portman

Estate. It was begun by Henry William Portman to capitalize on the Building Act of 1774, and centred on Portman Square. It had no great architectural aspirations – 'Stucconia', Charles Dickens called it after the stucco plaster-work liberally stuck onto the bases – but it became the most fashionable square in London outside Mayfair in the early nineteenth century.

Portman Square's social nuances captivated the novelists William Thackeray, who set many scenes from his novels locally, and Anthony Trollope, who featured the square in *Phineas Finn* and *The Small House at Allington*. The two main Portman Square properties were Home House and Montagu House. Home House, which still stands, was designed by Robert Adam in 1772–6 for Lady Home, heir to a fortune made in Jamaica, who was notorious for her foul language. The inside has some of the most exquisite designs in London, including paintings by Angelica Kauffmann.

Montagu House was the work of James 'Athenian' Stuart, built for Elizabeth Montagu who ran a literary salon that became known as the Blue Stocking Society after she told one of the guests, Benjamin Stillingfleet, who complained of having no formal wear, to come in his 'bluestockings' – ordinary clothes. Every May Day Montagu, described by the novelist Fanny Burney as 'brilliant in diamonds, solid in judgment', hosted a dinner for London's chimney sweeps, serving roast beef and pudding on the lawn. When one chimney sweep, David Porter, became a builder he created a square, Montagu Square, in her honour a few hundred yards to the north-west. It was here, at No. 39, that the early Victorian West End's greatest chronicler, Anthony Trollope, lived. He was an insufferable workaholic, and his amanuensis, Florence Bland, who was also his niece, was not allowed to so much as speak while he was dictating to her. When she did once he tore up the whole chapter. Montagu House was destroyed in the Blitz but parts of the gate are now in the grounds of Kenwood House, Highgate.

The northern reaches of Marylebone, near the park, were built over in 1753. Here the most important street was named after Edward Harley, second Earl of Oxford, the ground landlord. In its early days Harley Street attracted army officers such as Wellington, who was plain Sir Arthur Wellesley when he left No. 11 in 1808 to wage the Peninsular War. Then came politicians. William Gladstone moved into No. 73 in 1878, and had his windows smashed by the mob protesting against his opposition to Disraeli's pro-Turkish policies. But Harley Street is best known for its connections with medicine. In 1828 John St John Long, the so-called 'King of the Quacks', opened a practice for wealthy women clients at No. 84. He would ask his clients to inhale from a long length of pink tubing filled with a potent gas, noting how their resistance to his massage sessions would usually then decrease at a similar rate to how much the gas increased. Long's star waned after the death of two of his patients, and he was convicted of manslaughter, for which he received the paltry punishment of a £250 fine.

In 1853 Florence Nightingale became Superintendent of the 'Establishment for Gentlewomen During Illness' at what was then 1 Upper Harley Street. Here, her improvements to nursing including piping hot water to every floor and arranging for the installation of a lift to bring patients their meals. A year later Nightingale left for the Crimean War, where her nursing work reduced the death rate among soldiers from 42 to 2 per cent. Other eminent early Harley Street specialists include Morell Mackenzie, the first doctor to suggest a link between smoking and lung cancer, who had his consulting rooms at 19 Harley Street. There he treated Frederick, Emperor of Germany, Queen Victoria's son-in-law, but was unable to save him dying from cancer of the larynx.

By the end of the nineteenth century there were 157 private doctors operating here. More than a hundred years later Harley Street is still the home of London's leading private clinics, patronized by the well-heeled of not just London but of the international jet set. For instance, it was at the grandly named London Clinic in October 1998 that General Pinochet, the one-time Chilean dictator, was treated for back pain, that was until he was arrested in the middle of the night for alleged crimes against humanity.

Eventually the entire territory between Oxford Street and Marylebone Road was filled with what Benjamin Disraeli called 'our Gloucester Places and Baker Streets and Harley Streets and Wimpole Streets, and all those flat dull spiritless streets resembling each other like a large family of plain children, with Portland Place and Portman Square for their respectable parents.' Edward Gibbon, author of *The Decline and Fall of the Roman Empire*, who lived locally, was also among Marylebone's detractors. He noticed how members of the aristocracy were not particularly interested in spending so lavishly on their town houses as they would on their country seats. 'We should be astonished at our own riches, if the labours of architecture, the spoils of Italy and Greece, which are now scattered from Inverary to Wilton, were accumulated in a few streets between Marylebone and Westminster.' These streets may have not been to Disraeli's or Gibbon's taste but they remain the bedrock of the West End – elegant if a little austere, carefully maintained, harbouring a balance of residential use and commerce.

## THE MAKING OF MAYFAIR

Whenever the poor indulged themselves in merriment the authorities were quick to stamp it out. Consequently the May Fair didn't last long. It began in 1660, took place every spring for a fortnight near Haymarket, moved to what is now Shepherd Market in 1686, and was banished to Bow, east London, in 1764 after the Grand Jury of Westminster complained that it was a 'publick nuisance and Inconvenience' patronized by 'loose, idle and disorderly persons'.

In its prime the fair had been riotous. For the first three days it was a cattle market. Then out came the stalls where political satire was conducted using puppets. There was also donkey racing, bull baiting, diving for eels, and duck hunting, the odds being heavily and obviously stacked against the ducks, which had to fend off the huntsman's dogs in the pond where Hertford Street now runs.

Once the fair had gone the open country by the banks of the Tyburn stream on which it had taken place were ripe for the surveyor and bricklayer. In 1715 Sir Nathaniel Curzon bought a three-acre field there and built a chapel on what is now Curzon Street. Edward Shepherd, whose name lives on in Shepherd Market, erected himself a glorious mansion nearby. Best known as Crewe House, it served as Ministry of Propaganda during the Great War, and is now the Saudi Arabian Embassy.

Mayfair's prospects as a desirable address were vastly improved in 1783 when the hangings ended at Tyburn (now Marble Arch). Tyburn Road then became Oxford Street, and Park Lane was no longer the haunt of the rabble flocking to the public executions. The area grew around three great squares (Grosvenor, Berkeley and Hanover) and two grand routes (Bond Street and Piccadilly). In 1720 local landowner Sir Richard Grosvenor, whose name comes from the French *gros veneur* – fat hunter – designed a grid pattern of streets for the new Grosvenor Estate. The land was bounded by Oxford Street, Park Lane and the Tyburn brook, with what would be one of London's largest squares as its centrepiece. When Daniel Defoe visited the development in September 1725 he noted 'an amazing Scene of new Foundations, not of Houses only, but as I might say of new Cities, New Towns, New Squares and fine Buildings, the like of which no City, no Town, nay no Place in the World can shew'. Grosvenor Square was complete by 1770, one of the first examples in the capital of terraced houses grouped together behind one monumental façade, as if it were a single building. A hundred years later it was the last part of the capital to be lit by gas rather than electricity.

Grosvenor Square was immediately popular with the aristocracy and politicians. Lords Rockingham, Grafton and North, all British prime ministers at various times, lived here in the late eighteenth century. The Grosvenors were granted the Duchy of Westminster in 1874, at which point they were Europe's wealthiest family after the Rothschilds. Descendants are still the area's major landowners, the estate office being situated on Grosvenor Street. Yet some kind of curse must have been placed on the square, for few London locations have endured such a history of concentrated, premeditated violence.

In 1780 Grosvenor Square was caught up in the anti-Catholic Gordon Riots, when Lord Rockingham's house at No. 4 was blockaded to fend off an expected siege, guns pointing from the windows. A little while later, after the riots were over, Dr Johnson, the Dictionary compiler, was walking along the square when he felt a pickpocket's hands about his person. He accosted the fellow, seized his collar and slapped his face so hard the assailant fell back on to the pavement. Around the same time a couple of footpads attacked the Neapolitan ambassador's carriage in the square. In 1820 anarchist conspirators schemed a plot to kill the entire Cabinet while they were dining at No. 44, but were foiled. Fast-forward to the mid 1960s when the square, by now home to the American Embassy, was besieged by tens of thousands of demonstrators opposing the Vietnam War. And, no surprise, it was Grosvenor Square which featured at the top of the list of targets for the revolutionary anarchist terrorist Angry Brigade at the end of the decade. Even as recently as 2006 Grosvenor Square was still featuring in the darker side of London life when it was revealed that an ex-Russian spy who was assassinated by ex-KGB officers using a radiation overdose may have been poisoned in Grosvenor Square's Millennium Hotel, a building standing on the very site where the Cato Street Conspirators had plotted their mass assassinations.

Berkeley Square, made famous by Eric Maschwitz's 1940 song 'A Nightingale Sang in Berkeley Square', was named after the first Lord Berkeley of

Stratton, Royalist commander during the Civil War. It was not planned architecturally but came together haphazardly to the north of the peer's 1660s mansion, Berkeley House, outside which the carriages of the Whig grandees would roll along the gravel forecourt amongst the lilacs and crocuses.

Pride of place went to Lansdowne House, a Robert Adam creation of 1768, built for Lord Bute, who sold it before it was finished. Adam considered the Eating Room his greatest creation, even if he did admit he copied the design from the palace of the Emperor Diocletian in Spalato, Dalmatia. Alongside was a narrow alley, privately owned and open all but one day of the year when Lord Lansdowne's men would lock the gates. An obvious target for imaginative writers, it formed the setting for Michael Arlen's 1920s ghost story 'The Loquacious Lady of Lansdowne Passage'. Lansdowne House now survives in severely corrupted form as the Lansdowne Club, and the rest of Berkeley Square, like Grosvenor Square, has been spoiled by unimaginative rebuilding.

There are other ghosts on Berkeley Square 'in which gloomy locality death seems to reign perpetual', as Thackeray put it in *Vanity Fair*. Two generals supposedly haunt No. 7, having died precipitately when they fell through a trap door arguing about how the Duke of Marlborough should have waged the Battle of Blenheim. Then there was Admiral Byng who lived at No. 40 in the 1750s. Inconsequential in life, he has endured an infamous afterlife, for it was he who was executed in 1757 *pour l'encourager les autres*, according to Voltaire.

Clive of India died a more agonizing death – of excessive laudanum – at No. 45 in 1774 as the West End's first celebrity drug casualty. The great soldier and statesman took vast quantities of laudanum for stomach pains, which gave him more pains, and led him to take more laudanum. His biographer, Sir John Malcolm, explained that 'the remedy, while alleviating the pain, produced a mental stupor which caused the loss of all self-control.'

Moving round the square in a clockwise direction, Nos. 7–8 were Negri's tea rooms in the eighteenth century. It was founded by an Italian pastry cook, Domenico Negri, 'making and selling all sorts of English, French, and Italian wet and dry sweetments'. It became Gunter's in 1799, popular for its ices and sorbets, which gentlemen would eat while leaning against the railings watching the ladies in their carriages eating theirs. No. 11 on the east side was home from 1747 to Horace Walpole, the eighteenth-century novelist and Gothic revivalist. He was so taken with the view that he compared the statue of George III in the middle to the work of the Athenian Phidias, something of which he would have been barely aware, having failed to reach Greece on his Grand Tour.

At the north-east, less fashionable, corner of Mayfair is Hanover Square, which was begun on farmland in 1714 soon after George, Elector of Hanover, took the British throne as George I. Despite a slow start to house building following the South Sea Bubble financial collapse of 1720, it was an immediate success, attracting Whig soldiers who had fought for Marlborough. Few of the original brick houses survive, despite the square's 'traditional' look. Long demolished are the Hanover Square Concert Rooms, which opened on the east side on 1 February 1775, where Johann Christian Bach gave the first of many concerts the following year. In 1791 the prolific symphonist Joseph Haydn made the first of several visits to the Rooms, and later wrote Symphonies Nos. 93–104, popularly known as the London Symphonies, many of which were introduced here, in honour of his visits. Hanover Square gradually lost its residents but has remained an elegant address thanks to the number of prestigious offices, fashion houses and clubs that can be found here.

The locale's focal point – St George's church – is not on the square itself but a hundred yards south. The parish church of Mayfair, built in 1721–4, it was financed through money raised by a tax on coal, and designed by John James, who had been apprenticed to Christopher Wren. St George's was meant to be one of fifty new churches for Londoners, built to meet the needs of the population that had moved away from the City following the Fire, but in the end was one of barely a dozen that were finished.

At a nearby rival, Mayfair Chapel, on Curzon Street, Alexander Keith soon began to host cheap marriages at a guinea a time, without banns or licences. Dr Trebeck, rector of St George's, was furious, and launched a lawsuit against Keith, who was duly excommunicated by the Bishop of London. Keith in turn held a service at the chapel in which he hopefully excommunicated the rector, the bishop and the judge of the court that had ruled against him. Meanwhile St George's became *the* place for weddings. Those who married here include the poet Shelley in 1814 to the nineteen-year-old Harriet Westbrook, with whom he had eloped three years earlier and who later drowned in the Serpentine; the author George Eliot to John Cross in 1880 when she was sixty and he forty (she died a few months later);

and the American politician Teddy Roosevelt, who described himself as a ranchman when he married Edith Carow here on 2 December 1886. St George's best known marriage is fictitious – that of Alfred Doolittle in George Bernard Shaw's *Pygmalion*, as embodied in the song 'Get Me to the Church on Time' in the play's musical incarnation, *My Fair Lady*.

Bond Street is the only street to run the full north-south course through Mayfair, linking Oxford Street and Piccadilly. Its name is misleading for there is no Bond Street as such; the northern section is New Bond Street, the southern Old Bond Street. Thomas Bond developed the street and locale after his group of financiers bought the Duke of Clarendon's gardens from the Duke of Albermarle in 1686. A close friend of King Charles II, his family motto was fittingly 'Non sufficit orbis' – Not even the world is enough. But for a while only a short section of the street was. The money ran out when Bond Street had made it only as far as from Piccadilly to Burlington Gardens. It is this section that is Old Bond Street. The longer stretch to Oxford Street – New Bond Street – had to wait a few decades.

Bond Street – Old and New – was never one of impressive architecture, but it soon became London's most luxurious shopping street, home in the eighteenth century of the Bond Street lounger whose walk, the Bond Street Stroll, was imitated by Regency dandies. Some of the more unusual shops that gave the street its character until recently have now gone. Truefitt's, wig-makers to George IV, is no more; nor is the chemist's Savory and Moore, located at 143 New Bond Street until the 1970s. Savory and Moore was famous for its laxative, Seidlitz Powders, and in 1853 it won the contract to make medical supplies for troops fighting in the Crimean War. But (New) Bond Street is still one of London's most exclusive streets. At 165–9 is Asprey's, official jeweller to the royal family, where a box of Christmas crackers containing earrings and a crocodile-skin lighter cover can be bought for more than a thousand pounds. All around are fine-art galleries (such as Richard Green), auction houses (Sotheby's) and exclusive fashion stores, purveyors of Versace, Farhi, Armani, Halston, Gucci, Fiorucci ...

Mayfair has an obvious southern boundary: Piccadilly. Originally it was Hide Park Road west of Berkeley Street, where a stone bridge took it over Tybourne stream, and Portugal Street to the east, in honour of Queen Catherine of Braganza, wife of Charles II. Its name change was a nod to the pickadell, frilled collars sold by Robert Baker who lived in a hall off Great Windmill Street he named Pickadell Hall.

Piccadilly was the terminus of long-distance mail coaches until the advent of the railways in the nineteenth century. It was best known for its unparalleled succession of grand properties on the northern side, the Georgian answer to medieval Strand, which itself was lined with a succession of mansions when the royal court was based nearby at Whitehall Palace.

Only two original Piccadilly mansions survive. One is Burlington House, which Sir John Denham designed for himself in 1664, and is now home to the Royal Academy. Denham sold it unfinished to the first Duke of Burlington shortly after the Fire of London, but it was the third Earl who gave the house its identity. A great patron of the arts, the earl carried a copy of Andrea Palladio's *I Quattro Libri dell'Architectura* with him while on his Grand Tour, making copious notes in the margins, and when he returned he hired the fashionable architects of the day – Colen Campbell and William Kent – to rework the property, which they carried out in the Palladian style from 1718–39, with a nod to the Palazzo Porto at Vicenza.

Not everyone was impressed with the grandiosity and grandiloquence of Palladianism, which was fashioned from a set of rules. Critics pulled up Burlington for having only limited first-hand knowledge of the style, as he spent only one night in Vicenza, the Palladian capital, and they berated Campbell for never having set foot in Italy. William Hogarth, in his first print, *Masquerades and Operas: The Taste of the Town* (1724), satirized aristocrats with a taste for Palladian architecture. Another who mocked was the irascible poet Alexander Pope who on seeing the building quipped: "'Thanks, Sir," cried I, "'tis very fine / But where d'ye sleep, and where d'ye dine?'" Nevertheless many of the leading writers and artists of the mid eighteenth century, including Jonathan Swift and the ailing composer Handel, gathered at Burlington House. During the early years of the nineteenth century the property was the unofficial headquarters of the Whig Party, and it was here that the Elgin Marbles, after being filched from Greece, were stored until they were moved to the British Museum.

The other Piccadilly survivor, Albany, lies to the immediate east of Burlington House. It was built by William Chambers for Lord Melbourne in the 1770s, and designed in a style that contrasted with the Adam brothers' geometric Classical forms. Chambers set the house well back from Piccadilly behind a high wall, and added coach houses and stables. Melbourne's wife, Elizabeth, was a great society hostess, a rival to Georgiana – 'No man is safe with another's secrets, no woman with her own,' she explained – whose lovers included George IV.

In 1791 the Melbournes decided to swap houses with Frederick, Duke of York and Albany, George III's eldest son, who would have reigned had he lived. A plan to demolish the property and build a terrace of elegant houses to line up with Savile Row came to nothing. Instead it was converted in 1802 into chambers for gentlemen and renamed Albany, never *The* Albany. A rare survivor on Piccadilly, the house rules, in place until the 1920s, stated that no one could keep a musical instrument or a wife. It has been home to Lord Byron, who moved into No. 2 in 1814, disguising Lady Caroline Lamb as a page boy to get her into the building; the writers Arnold Bennett, Aldous Huxley and Graham Greene; and wealthy socialites such as Anthony Armstrong-Jones (Lord Snowdon) and the diarist Alan Clark.

## THE GOLDEN VISION

George IV may well have been the most reviled monarch to have ever sat on the British throne – in 1812 the publisher Leigh Hunt described him as 'a man who has just closed half a century without one single claim on the gratitude of his country or the respect of posterity' – but he was a discerning patron of the arts and presided over a golden age of architecture in the West End.

What is now known as Regency architecture dominated good taste in the second decade of the nineteenth century. It was based mostly on Classical Greek ideas touched up with Egyptian and even Chinese flourishes, and became the vogue after Lord Elgin returned from Athens with pieces of the Parthenon in his possession. The driving force for the new but Classic look was an architect in the government's Woods and Forests department. Just as Christopher Wren gave the City of London its shape, so John Nash made his mark in the West End. At the end of the eighteenth century he won a competition to build a grand processional way linking the Houses of Parliament with the royal estate of Marybone Park (now Regent's Park), a road through the heart of the West End that would bulldoze its way through the shabby streets at the west of Soho.

Nash foresaw a London as spectacular and sumptuous as the great

European capitals. His new grand artery – Regent Street – would be a Royal Mile that would dwarf the Champs Élysées in magnificence. As the diarist Crabb Robinson put it, Regent Street would provide 'a sort of glory to the [Prince] Regent's government which will be more felt by remote posterity than the victories of Trafalgar and Waterloo'.

In 1813 the New Street Act was passed to build Nash's route. Finance came from an insurance company, and later from the Bank of England. Demolition began, a sewer was built and sites were let. For a while nothing else happened, and it looked as if everything would all grind to a halt, except for the lust for work of the builder James Burton. Then Nash found investors willing to take an option on the land who were fired by the prospect of building hotels, large private houses, banks and churches. The road began to take shape. It ran north from the Prince Regent's Carlton House stately pleasure dome, cut a swathe through the small slummy twisting streets that bridged Soho and Mayfair, ploughed on across Oxford Street through the more restrained elegance of Marylebone, and arrived triumphantly in parkland, soon to be renamed Regent's Park. Alongside, new stucco buildings were designed by the greatest names of the day: John Soane, Decimus Burton, Charles Cockerell.

Alas Nash's Golden Vision of a grand processional route never materialized as planned. Obstacles stood imperviously in the way. Carlton House lay too far east to allow Nash to delve north in a straight line with ease. He could begin Regent Street slightly to the west of the Hay Market but could not continue north of Piccadilly without landing in Golden Square. To avoid crashing headlong into the square Nash took the route through 'a small Circus where the oblique lines meet in Piccadilly'. Such modesty. Such understatement. What was originally Regent Circus (South), was later renamed Piccadilly Circus and is now the most famous landmark in the world.

Heading north Nash took the road along a graceful curve, a quarter circle known as the Quadrant, full of shops 'appropriated to articles of fashion and taste'. The Quadrant sported a covered walkway built to protect the clothes of the nobility who would saunter there while taking refuge from the climate. To the north the grand boulevard ploughed on further. How would it meet Oxford Street? A simple crossroads would be too mundane, so Nash created another circus. For a while it bore the name Regent Circus (North). Later it became Oxford Circus, inferior in scope and size to Piccadilly Circus, a landmark bereft of memorable features, the briefest of respite for shoppers.

On the new route went north of Oxford Circus where there was one huge obstacle preventing it taking a straight course: Foley House. No problem. It was demolished. A kink in the road was needed further north so that Regent Street would merge into the Adam brothers' sumptuous Portland Place, then the widest street in London, 125 ft from pavement to pavement. Beyond the West End, in Regent's Park, Nash's route met a different kind of disappointment. His idea for a garden city in the middle of the park with twenty-six villas was severely curtailed. With twenty-first-century eyes this was a blessing in disguise, preserving the park's green lusciousness and open vistas. The astonishing Palladian-style panoramas at the edges are a delightful complement, ensuring Regent's Park status as one of the most exclusive addresses in London.

Despite the disruption to London, the old houses in Soho abandoned and left to rot, and the clouds of dust that appeared from the builder's works to part suffocate tens of thousands, Nash's work had no shortage of admirers. To James Elmes, writing in 1827, Regent Street was as sublime an achievement for the Prince Regent as was Rome for Augustus, who 'made it one of his proudest boasts that he found it of brick and left it of marble'. Nevertheless, a few detractors carped and cavilled. Parliament ridiculed the spire of Nash's new church of 1824, All Souls, cleverly situated by the twist in the road north of Oxford Circus. A cartoon published that year puts Nash uncomfortably perched on top of the church spire, his bottom making contact with the spikiest point. He took it good-humouredly: 'See, gentlemen, how criticism has exalted me!'

There has been gradual change to Nash's Regency road since. The worst decision was the destruction of the Quadrant arcades just north of Piccadilly Circus in 1848, removed because they had become the haunt of prostitutes. Many were shocked. To visitors this *was* London, a recognized symbol worldwide in the days before Tower Bridge was built. Foreign prints which captured the colonnade were captioned 'Ville de Londres'. Did the prostitutes leave the area? On the contrary, they proliferated (see Chapter 6).

Elsewhere along the route the stylish houses north of Oxford Circus have survived while the great shopping stretch south of Oxford Circus on Regent Street remains a testimony to late nineteenth-century Beaux Arts redesign, Portland Stone monsters created to impress shoppers and visitors. It is one of the world's busiest and most visited streets.

## MAYFAIR I

The West End was central to the growth of one of the most exciting developments in twentieth-century living – the notion of shopping for shopping's sake. Nearly all the best and most expensive stores arrived in the West End; only Kensington was a rival.

The entrepreneurs whose names live on as symbols of retailing at its best – William Debenham, D. H. Evans and John Lewis – arrived locally in the nineteenth century. Debenham went into partnership with a Thomas Clark in a shop that overlooked Cavendish Square in 1813. Gradually, the premises were expanded until by the end of the century the firm was supplying furs to royalty across Europe. In 1903 the store acquired the iconic phone number Mayfair 1, but it had many nearby competitors. D. H. Evans was named after Dan Harries Evans, a Welsh lace-maker, who bought a property at 318 Oxford Street in 1879 and opened a draper's store. Evans stayed with the firm until 1915 when he lost his money in an unsuccessful property deal that saw him die penniless in 1928. In 2000 the store was renamed by its new owners, the House of Fraser.

Neither Debenham's nor D. H. Evans have ever been able to match the pull of John Lewis. Lewis himself was a silk buyer who opened a shop at the corner of Oxford Street and Holles Street in 1864. When he tried to expand into nearby Cavendish Square at the end of the century he found the conditions of his lease forbade commercial activity there. Unimpressed, Lewis entered into litigation with the landlord, Lord Howard de Walden, and erected a sign outside the shop pointing to the latter's house in Cavendish Square, what he called de Walden's 'Monument of Iniquity'. The peer suggested a compromise: Lewis should change the shop façade to resemble a private house. But the store owner rejected the offer. Sent to prison for disobeying a court order to reinstate the property, he drove off to Brixton Gaol in his own carriage, and later won the case.

In 1906 Lewis bought Peter Jones's store in Sloane Square, making it over to his eldest son, John Spedan Lewis, on the condition that the latter worked a full day at the Oxford Street store before attending to the new shop. John and Spedan later clashed over the development of the company, but it was Spedan's policies of equitable sharing that were implemented. In 1929 Spedan transferred his shares to a trust 'for the happiness of all its members', which is set to expire twenty-one years after the death of the last descendant of King Edward VII alive at the time of its creation. At the beginning of the twenty-first century only two descendants remained alive: Queen Elizabeth II and Lord Harewood.

Lording it over all other Oxford Street department stores – even John Lewis – since 1909 has been Selfridge's, London's best known store other than Harrods and Harvey Nichols, located at 400 Oxford Street. Its creator, Gordon H. Selfridge, was a self-made Chicago millionaire who arrived in London determined to build the capital's first American-style superstore. Selfridge planned everything on a gigantic scale and failed to be dissuaded by the authorities' petty refusal to let him incorporate a St Paul's-style dome within or the Central Line's rejection of his proposal to call a new nearby underground station 'Selfridge's' rather than the disingenuous 'Bond Street'.

The store featured 130 departments, a post office, roof garden and soda fountain. It was shopping on a scale never previously witnessed in London. The store opened with the slogan: 'Why not spend the day at Selfridge's?', thereby introducing the idea of shopping as leisure pursuit in its own right. Believing that the British knew how to make goods, but not how to sell them, Gordon Selfridge concentrated on developing a new retailing philosophy using credit schemes, sales, innovative window displays, a bargain basement, publicity and advertising. He was rewarded by the arrival of a million shoppers in the first week.

## TREASURES UPON EARTH

The West End may be a land without industry and factories, but it is not without invention. In 1801, Humphry Davy, a twenty-three-year-old medical student, began lecturing on the nature of gases at the Royal Institution, a gentlemen's and intellectuals' club based on Albemarle Street in Mayfair, founded for 'diffusing the knowledge of useful mechanical inventions'.

He was soon appointed professor – Britain's only professional scientist other than the Astronomer Royal – and his lectures drew huge crowds. By this time thinkers had moved on from a religious view of nature to a secular one. They had abandoned alchemy, which had united religion and science, for chemistry, a secular subject free of religious ephemera.

In 1807 in his Mayfair laboratory Davy isolated two new elements, potassium and sodium, after holding the alkalis potash and soda in a platinum spoon over a flame and passing an electrical current through them. He gave a lecture about his findings to an audience that was amazed and impressed at the new discoveries taking place in the West End. Davy explained how he and his assistant, his cousin Edmund, arranged twenty-four batteries of zinc and copper plates to obtain a powerful electric current, how the charge passed through the wire to a solution of caustic potash, and how that reacted violently with water and harmed the skin when touched. He described how as the water separated into hydrogen and oxygen, bubbles of gas began to appear on the wires. But how as the potash remained unaffected the experiment was largely unsuccessful.

Instead of being discouraged, Davy suggested repeating the experiment without water. This time he held a platinum spoon containing dry potash over a flame until the substance melted. He then connected the batteries to the spoon containing the melted potash. Davy surmised that if the mixture contained an undiscovered element it would burn with a new colour as soon as the element was isolated. Sure enough sparks exploded from the flame and after a few fiery minutes the mixture began burning with an unusual lilac hue which disappeared as soon as the current was removed.

Davy knew he had been successful, but as he explained, he still had no means of isolating this new element. Next he tried sending a current through cold potash, with no success. Refusing to give up, he decided a new approach – allowing the dry potash to react with the air for only a few seconds, enough to allow the electricity to pass through. Now Davy was successful. Tiny silver globules began appearing on the molten potash and after reacting with the air were soon covered by a white film. Davy had discovered that potash contained a metal, something no one had previously suspected. The metal turned out to be the eighth most abundant element on earth, which he called potassium.

One of Davy's assistants was the Prussian scientist Friedrich Accum, who lived at 33 Old Compton Street in the heart of Soho. Accum pioneered gas lighting in London but achieved his main success with his ground-breaking findings on how shopkeepers doctored food. In 1820 his paper 'A treatise on adulterations of food, and culinary poisons' caused bakers, brewers and millers considerable embarrassment. It highlighted how bakers filled their bread with alum and used flour containing chalk; how brewers added iron sulphate to beer to help froth the liquid, and how grocers diluted milk with water and added sand to sugar. Eventually, thanks to Accum's findings, the government passed the Adulteration of Food Acts (1860).

In 1812 Davy resigned from the Institution to go on a continental tour. His place was taken by his assistant, Michael Faraday. In the Royal Institution's basement laboratory in September 1821 Faraday discovered electro-magnetic rotation, the principle that led to the invention of the first telegraph, introduced in 1838 along the Paddington–West Drayton railway line. The telegraph meant that for the first time it was possible to communicate with people beyond one's own vicinity and that humanity now needed new rules about the nature of time.

In August 1831, ten years after his discovery of electro-magnetic rotation, Faraday discovered electro-magnetic induction. This enabled electricity to be adapted for everyday purposes. He spent the remainder of the decade engaged in further experiments in electricity, proposing the notion that it was a force which passed from particle to particle, and coining a number of new scientific terms, now part of everyday speech, including electrode, anode and cathode. Faraday's crowning achievement came at one of his Friday evening lectures in 1846 when he suggested that matter was not made of billiard ball-like indestructible atoms but of wave-like particles.

The era of gentlemanly science conducted in smart West End addresses was soon due to end. In the new century science would be colder and more clinical. It would be in university laboratories that scientists like Rutherford would split the atom and James Watson's team discover the double helix structure of DNA.

Yet the West End hadn't seen its last maverick creators. In 1925 John Logie Baird, a self-taught Scottish inventor, rented out an attic workshop at 22 Frith Street, above what is now Bar Italia, to work on improving his crude 'televisor' machine. At the time scientists accepted the notion that television might be possible, even if they hadn't yet seen the results. Having borrowed £200 to indulge in experiments, Baird developed a sophisticated model using a large rotating disc studded with a spiral of holes to achieve a scanning effect. That March there was a knock at the Frith Street door. It was Gordon Selfridge, owner of London's leading store. Baird gave Selfridge a demonstration of 'televising', transmitting from one room to another a crude outline of a paper mask. The store owner was impressed enough to hire Baird to give personal demonstrations of the new device at the Selfridge's store for three weeks at a payment of £25 a week. Indeed Selfridge was beside himself with excitement over the promotion and drew up adverts which proclaimed:

*Selfridge's*
*Present the First Public*
*Demonstration of Television*
*In the Electrical Section (First Floor)*
*Television is to light what telephony is to sound –*
*it means the INSTANTANEOUS transmission of*
*a picture, so the observer at the 'receiving'*
*end can see, to all intents and purposes, what is a*
*cinematograph view of what is happening at the*
*'sending' end.*

*The demonstrations are taking place*
*here only because we know that our friends will*
*be interested in something that should rank with*
*the greatest inventions of the century.*

Now that Baird had succeeded in displaying stationary objects on screen, he began work on more ambitious plans – televising people. On 2 October 1925 he placed 'Bill', a ventriloquist's dummy, in front of a transmitter. Thus far the dummy's head had appeared on the receiving screen in a fuzz with a group of blobs where there should be a nose and eyes. But this time Bill appeared as a recognizable image. As Baird proudly described it in his autobiography 'the image of the dummy's head formed itself on the screen with what appeared to be almost unbelievable clarity.'

Now Baird needed a real-life version. He rushed downstairs to the Cross Pictures company and borrowed the office boy, William Taynton. Baird tried to screen Taynton without success. The boy, scared by the intense light, had moved too far away from the equipment. To win Taynton's co-operation Baird handed him a half a crown. This time Taynton kept his head in the right position. The inventor, watching in the next room, saw the boy's head on screen in what was the first recognizable television picture of an individual.

Moments later a group of Soho prostitutes knocked on the door. They thought the tenant was spying on them with a large telescope. That was not the only drama to greet this prototype television screening. Some years later

John Hart, a fellow Scot, who had been one of Baird's helpers, claimed he, not Taynton, was the first man to be televised. Later a doorman at a London club claimed that on the contrary *he* was the first. In 1951, at the unveiling of a plaque to Baird at 22 Frith Street, a third man, a J. E. Hamelford, showed the assembled throng a letter written and signed by Baird saying that he, Hamelford, was the first person to be televised. Regardless of which of the three was the genuine first, Baird's *second* subject, Peter Dawson, the Australian baritone, failed to pass his screen test. He had to stop singing as only the middle of his body was showing on screen.

In January 1926 Baird invited forty members of the Royal Institution of Great Britain, clothed in full evening dress, to Frith Street to see his work. Two years later Selfridge's on Oxford Street made the world's first sale of a television set.

# THE WRECKERS

The Second World War made little dent on the West End compared with the devastation that hit the East End. Yet around the same time the area was a prime target for the new breed of property developer who sensed there was a killing to be made out of reshaping one of the richest areas in London.

Mayfair in particular lost much of its resident population at the start of the war as the titled families fled a location so close to the centre of London in the wake of Hitler's bombs and government requisitioning orders. While the Luftwaffe planes were banked up in the sky, poised to bomb London, property magnates were sat in their West End offices poised, pen and cheque book in hand, for a different kind of battle. They were taking no chances. If the Germans won the old order would crumble and everyone's plans would be laid to waste. If the Allies won the capital, pock-marked with bomb sites, would need rebuilding, so they might as well be prepared anyway. And as Mayfair was unlikely to be one of the bombers' favourite targets it would become a most popular and attractive location after the war, they surmised.

Typical of the new breed were Dudley Samuel, the Harris Brothers, Joe Littman and Sir Henry Price. In 1918 at the end of the previous war Samuel had been sent by his father to work for a West End estate agent at wages of

£1 a week. After a year he won promotion. He was now head of department, earning £4 a week. Samuel rushed home euphoric to tell his father, but Mr Samuel Senior was nonplussed. 'Oh dear,' he replied, 'I had to give your boss £1 a week to take you on. Now I will have to give him £4.'

The Harris Brothers, Bob and Harry, based in Mill Street, Mayfair, bought up a number of West End sites. They sat on their new plots, literally, living frugally and lunching on sandwiches while perched uncomfortably on office benches. Meanwhile the value of the land rose spectacularly. Joe Littman was a refugee from rural Russia who targeted Oxford Street as his plaything and became skilled in sale-and-leaseback – buying property, selling it for a small profit, taking a lease on it from the buyer, and making a bigger profit by sub-leasing it to a retailer. The practice became known in the trade as the 'Littman Cocktail'.

Repeating this over and over again, Littman went from owning one property on Kilburn High Road to owning most of the street in the 1930s. He then turned to Oxford Street, continuing the practice oblivious, it seemed, to the wartime bombs. Colleagues remembered his huge hands and his eccentricities. When the phone rang he would clutch it bear-like, completely enveloping the receiver while mumbling something barely intelligible into the mouthpiece. At one meeting with bankers he stumped those present by remarking: 'I once went to my physician and he said to me "I don't deal in consoles I deal in tonsils."'

Sir Henry Price was even more manic. The day after a bombing raid he would phone a nearby estate agent and ask: 'Did you hear the bombs last night? There must be some bargains around this morning.' At the other end of the line the contacts could almost see Sir Henry rubbing his palms with excitement. Sometimes those with an eye for a killing didn't even bother to wait for the bombs to fall. They would go along to a likely building, usually one in a street already hit, armed with a pickaxe and set to work so that the structure would be declared dangerous the next morning.

After the war gross redevelopment began in earnest. It was not the noise of carriages, dinner-suited parties, men in spats and wing collars, and ladies in diamante-sprinkled gowns that resounded across Mayfair but the thud of the wrecking ball and the click of the surveyor's theodolite. Grosvenor Square, where news of Wellington's victory over Napoleon officially arrived in London three days after the 1815 battle, where the Cato Street Conspirators planned to assassinate the entire British cabinet in 1820, was soon decimated. The houses on the west side were replaced by the relentless concrete massing of the American Embassy. After the building was completed in the early 1960s one of the first visitors was President John F. Kennedy. Noting how the United States owned the land on which all their embassies were built, apart from the one in London, he asked the Duke of Westminster if he could buy the freehold. The duke replied that Kennedy could have the land in exchange for the American territory the US government had seized from his ancestors in the 1770s, which included the Cape Canaveral rocket launch site.

Elsewhere on Grosvenor Square developers gathered vulture-like. When conservationists objected to the demolition of the south side, including the house where the Cato Street Conspirators hoped to enact their murderous putsch, they were overruled on the grounds that to keep these houses would spoil the overall redevelopment. But that was the whole point; to stop the complete eradication of the place. A preservation order was slapped on one Grosvenor Square property, No. 44, but in 1961 the trustees appealed and won. The Britannia Hotel was built there.

In Mayfair the most coveted prize was Park Lane. There amongst the grandiose luxury hotels were smaller, quainter, older properties, dating back a few generations to Park Lane's days as London's nouveau riche playground. But in the 1950s Park Lane became a different kind of playground, one where wheeling and dealing took place, as developers fought over this prime real estate.

It was the age of the planner, the sinister town hall figure salivating at the prospect of wiping out vast chunks of London for a high rise city of glass and granite towers set in 'landscaped' grounds connected by podiums. There were even plans to glass over much of Soho at roof level and build six twenty-four-storey towers, each equipped with heligarages for helicopter parking and canals to transport people around the area on hi-tech boats. To introduce the scheme seventeen-storey Kemp House was built at the bottom end of Berwick Street market. The scheme eventually sank, and Kemp House remains as a folly, barely noticeable among the Victorian shops, fruit and veg stalls and sex shops.

It was the age of the financier. Money was cheap and borrowing easy. Charles Clore, the retail magnate who owned the British Shoe Corporation and later Selfridge's, acquired a slither of land bounded by Park Lane, Hertford Street and Shepherd Street. He bought it from Tim Abel-Smith who despite inheriting the land was so short of money he sold it to Clore for a bargain half a million pounds, without ever meeting him.

Clore demolished the properties, which included several charming Gothic houses that had been partly bombed during the war. After all, why bother rebuilding London with charm and grace, patching up a fine house, when you can demolish the lot and plonk a monstrous money-making machine on the site? Consequently he gave Park Lane the hideous, elongated, unlovable Hilton Hotel, one of the greatest abominations on the face of London, a viable contender for the role of Prince Charles's 'monstrous carbuncle'.

When the Hilton opened in 1963 it was London's tallest building, a title previously held by the Tower of London, Canonbury Tower, St Paul's and Senate House. Now the view east towards London from the park was ruined. Worryingly, guests staying on the upper floors could see the Buckingham Palace gardens. Clore was triumphant. He had no concerns about aesthetics. As he wrote to the property journalist Oliver Marriott: 'I do not believe in great architecture that ends in bankruptcy.'

This was the way of the new West End plutocrats. Their avaricious consumption was not part of a grand plan to win acceptance within West End Society, as had been the *métier* of their late Victorian predecessors. It was profit for profit's sake. They were international jet-setters, their boundaries far beyond the West End, their stamping ground stretching from Monaco to Miami via Meribel and Marrakesh.

Clore had plenty of rivals for the title of king of the London Property Boomers, among them Edward Erdman and Jack Cotton. Erdman developed Euston station, which meant that it was he, more than any other, who was responsible for the wanton destruction of the magnificent Euston arch. Like so many property developers Erdman was a dab hand at sale-and-leaseback, and in this way he acquired some of the first retail units in the West End for W. H. Smith, Burton's, and Marks & Spencer.

Erdman began as an office boy with the estate agent Gordon Thomas on Oxford Circus in 1923, earning five shillings a week. Soon he was making the tea and doing some typing. Eventually he was taking part in the important arts of negotiating and bargaining. In 1934 Erdman set up his first property firm on Maddox Street, then one of the West End's main red-light districts. Disconcerted with the number of prostitutes around the block, he moved the firm to nearby Hanover Street, the first floor of No. 10. Alas the flats upstairs were also occupied by street ladies. Unwilling to share his door-plate with their name cards, Erdman set himself up as a human contraceptive. Every time a punter rang the bell he would emerge on the landing and demand: 'What do you want?' The ladies soon left for somewhere more amenable.

In 1946 Erdman braved out an embarrassing incident which surprisingly left him only £25 out of pocket. At a trade dinner he knocked back too much red juice and found himself asking the editor of the *Hackney Gazette* whether he would like a photo of the Conservatives' parliamentary candidate for Hackney North dressed in a tight bathing costume bending down to pick up a sixpence. Leaving in some confusion, he drove back to Mayfair, but only made it as far as Canonbury where he pulled over and fell asleep at the wheel. He awoke in Islington police station, and when asked if he would object to examination by a police doctor responded: 'I don't care a hoot if William the Conqueror examines me.' Later he told police that he had finished the meal 'with 10 brandies'.

More circumspect was Jack Cotton, boss of City Centre Properties, never seen in public without a bow tie and carnation. One journalist described him as a 'rags-to-riches' figure, which he didn't mind, even though it wasn't true. Another called his father a 'small businessman'. Now he was mortified. 'There is nothing, I repeat nothing, small about my father,' he thundered. Cotton achieved something many schoolchildren dream of but never carry out: he pulled down his own school. He was educated at King Edward's, Birmingham, and years later bought the site, demolishing the old block and replacing it with shops and offices.

After financing the building of the Pan-Am skyscraper in New York, Cotton targeted one of the few West End locations even more desirable than Park Lane – Piccadilly Circus. By chance in 1954 his company bought the world-famous neon-lit block on the circus between Shaftesbury Avenue and Glasshouse Street. It was known disingenuously as the Monico site after the unassuming café located there. Cotton's men came up with various plans for rebuilding the plot, as did the London County Council. Eventually the authorities agreed to approve Cotton's scheme for a bland, flat-faced, glass-plated, twelve-storey, L-shaped office block – the kind of tedious tower that nowadays dominates nothing suburbs like Enfield and Harrow, but which would have been disastrous for Piccadilly Circus.

Euphoric, Cotton called a press conference and unveiled the monster to the world. One picture showed a side of the new building adorned in large zany letters: 'Snap, Plom, Vigour . . . Wat Ze Time [*sic*].' There was an outcry from MPs, journalists and the Royal Fine Art Commission. Henry Brooke, the Minister of Housing, capitalized on a loophole in the council's decision and called an enquiry. Opposition to the scheme intensified. Cotton lost, defeated by hubris. Even the Ministry of Housing inspector said as much in his report: 'The applicants must now greatly regret that they put out the perspective sketch which they did at Mr Cotton's press conference in October 1959.'

The project was abandoned. Piccadilly Circus was saved from tasteless-ness. Not so part of Park Lane, where there has always been more opportunity for wielding a pickaxe. Cotton pulled down No. 45, which had briefly been the home of the incorrigible 'Randlord' Barney Barnato, he who fell to his death from the ship that was bringing him back for his housewarming party, and replaced it with a property made of brutalist concrete, its design over-seen by the once inspired Walter Gropius, founder of the Bauhaus, that immediately qualified as London's ugliest building. Remarkably, given the building's unsightliness, it became home of the Playboy Club, epitome of louche Swinging London hedonism.

Meanwhile, the most vociferous opposition to the developers came not from the general public but from a small, politically attuned section: squat-ters. They decided to occupy various West End buildings as a protest against the new schemes. Especially targeted was 144 Piccadilly, an abandoned hotel opposite Green Park in what had been Rothschild Row during the nineteenth century. In 1969 a group calling themselves the London Street Commune squatted the building as part of a double-edged protest against the emptying of this and similar large properties and the wanton destruction of vast swathes of London to build council homes, often at no discernible benefit to the population.

The new residents daubed the slogan 'Property is Theft', coined by the French anarchist Pierre-Joseph Proudhon, in tall letters on the wall, as the world's media gathered outside. But on 21 September 1969 the police raided No. 144 under the pretext of a drugs bust, swarming over the ad hoc drawbridge the squatters had erected as they were pelted with water-filled balls, roof slates, pieces of wood and iron bars thrown from the roof. Once inside the police evicted hundreds, the original number boosted by French students who had been involved in the recent *événément* political riots in Paris. The *Daily Mirror* headlined their report the following day 'Fall of the Hippy Castle'. Three years later the building was demolished.

Remarkably, given the needless destruction of so much of London since, the West End has escaped almost intact. Preservation orders and listing means that in an area where so much thought and attention went into its creation there can now be no major changes to the fabric, thereby preserving the Classic elegant face of the West End for years to come. As for what goes on inside those buildings, no laws imposed from above can prevent the most extreme machinations.

# 4

# Revolution

The streets of the West End have long played host to the brightest stars in the revolutionary firmament, the greatest figures, the incontestable leaders. Here Lenin, Trotsky, Stalin and Mussolini have raged and raved, preached, practised and propagandized alongside a host of lesser known figures. Yet since Oliver Cromwell's anti-royal coup of 1649 no political revolution has ever been successful in London. No charismatic political leader has emerged since to seize power, confidently expecting to tell the masses, like Napoleon did to the French in 1799, 'The Revolution is over. I am the Revolution.'

Before upheaval gripped Paris, London had its own political turmoil, short-lived rather than epoch-making. The Gordon Riots were a week of mayhem and madness in June 1780 which featured the worst political violence London has ever seen.

The riots were that rarest of political animals: a reactionary rather than a revolutionary campaign, for the perpetrators wanted to *preserve* rather than upset the status quo. Trouble broke out after the Protestant Association learned that the government wanted to change the law to allow Catholics to join the army to make up for a shortage of new soldiers. The new legislation would be introduced as part of a package allowing Catholics new rights, for at that time, nearly a hundred years after the Glorious Revolution had seen the Protestant William III replace the Catholic-leaning James II on the throne, Catholics were not allowed to be members of Parliament, buy land, keep arms, practise medicine or teach.

The authorities believed antipathy to Rome had softened, but they horribly misjudged the public mood. Lord George Gordon, secretary of the Protestant Association, spread rumours that 20,000 Jesuits were hiding in a network of secret tunnels under the Thames, ready on the orders of Rome to overrun the capital. On Friday 2 June 1780 Gordon delivered an anti-

Catholic petition to Parliament as MPs debated the new legislation. Thousands of supporters joined him, many wearing blue cockades and carrying blue flags bearing the legend: 'NO POPERY'. Outside the Palace of Westminister they booed, hissed and jostled MPs. They pulled Lord Bathurst, Lord President of the Council, from his carriage to cries of 'silly old woman' and 'Pope!', and tried to storm the doors of Parliament as the peers within picked up their swords, pledging to use them if attacked.

When Gordon failed to win Parliamentary approval for his anti-Catholic petition (by 192 votes to 6), the mob left Westminster and headed to the two places in the capital where Catholics could openly worship: the Sardinian Chapel by Lincoln's Inn Fields and the Bavarian Chapel on Warwick Street, Soho. On Warwick Street rioters broke windows, forced the doors, ransacked the house and threw out all the furniture, which they burned in the street. Luckily they never found the large horde of contraband tea which the minister had smuggled into Britain and buried in the Warwick Street cellars to supplement his meagre income, and which a German blacksmith had hidden along with the chapel valuables in a house on Swallow Street. The chapel was only saved from destruction when the army appeared.

The rioters soon went in search of prominent Catholics. Their main target was Bishop Richard Challoner, the ninety-year-old Vicar Apostolic of London. He had fled to Finchley, and his Bloomsbury property survived destruction only because when the rioters arrived on (Old) Gloucester Street they could not agree which house was his. By noon of the Saturday it appeared as if the violence was over. But in the afternoon soldiers escorting a group of prisoners to Bow Street Magistrates' Court were jeered and pelted with mud. Around the same time riots broke out in the slums of Soho where Irish immigrants, in a desperate bid to protect themselves, chalked: 'No Popery' on their doors, or displayed strips of blue silk to show their support for the Protestant Association. In the Jewish parts of Soho householders chalked the words: 'This is the home of a true Protestant' on the door.

Confronted by the rioters, the Justices of the Peace, magistrates, aldermen and even the Lord Mayor shrank from their duties. Violence continued sporadically throughout the week, as did unusual behaviour. For instance, on the Monday a procession marched to Lord Gordon's house in Welbeck Street, Marylebone, to bring the nonplussed peer trophies of relics ransacked from the looted chapels. It was left to the army – some 10,000 troops – to bring the riots to an end. Those arrested were tried at the Turk's Head tavern on Gerrard Street, at the southern tip of Soho, and twenty-five of them were hanged, with one rioter, a hangman, pardoned so that he could hang his fellow rioters. By the end of the week 173 people had been severely wounded and 200 people had died.

The Gordon Riots had given the poor the chance they and various political agitators had been waiting for to air their grievances with as much violence as they could muster. Yet neither the rioters nor their leaders had much in the way of a political agenda. They were mostly either drunk on a sense of their own temporary, anarchic power, or just plain drunk. Their number included no demagogues waiting to seize the moment and turn anarchy into revolution. The best they could offer were James Johnson, 'a giant of a man', according to reports, whose voice 'boomed like the crack of doom', and Thomas Taplin, who on horseback led a gang of fifty juveniles into battle, and was subsequently executed.

Five years after the riots the Vatican sent two Jesuits to Lord George Gordon's Welbeck Street home to poison him. The Jesuits brought with them a vial of liquid and a note supposedly written by the local chemist urging the peer to drink the mixture. Suspicious of the strangers with the unusual request and package, Gordon had the contents examined and discovered their toxic nature.

Bizarrely, given the trouble he caused, Gordon later forsook the Anglican church for Judaism, changing his name to Israel Abraham George Gordon. He died at the age of forty-two in Newgate prison, where he had been incarcerated for libelling Marie Antoinette.

## RIGHTS OF MAN

The French Revolution of 1789 sorely tested the authorities' nerve in London. It was only a matter of time, politicians mused, before the mob took to the streets again, causing turmoil, as they had during the Gordon Riots. The very fabric of English society was at risk, and the only solution, as far as the government was concerned, was to adopt authoritarian measures: strict censorship, political repression, even the suspension of *Habeas Corpus*.

Nevertheless it was in the West End, in the smart but featureless residential streets of the leisured classes, away from the new factories and furnaces of the North and the Midlands, away from the revolutionary fervour of

France, that fervent political debate raged. It was in one such property at 7 Upper Marylebone St (now 154 New Cavendish Street) that Thomas Paine, author of *The Rights of Man*, went into hiding in 1792.

*The Rights of Man* was a polemic so powerful that the government wanted Paine prosecuted for seditious libel. In the work Paine attacked hereditary government and argued for equal political rights. He suggested that all men over twenty-one in Britain be given the vote, called for family allowances, the instigating of old-age pensions and maternity grants, and the abolition of the House of Lords. He was forthright on the so-called divine right of kings to rule: 'A French bastard [William I] landing with armed banditti and establishing himself as King of England, against the consent of the natives, is in plain terms a very paltry rascally original. It certainly hath no divinity in it.'

A year previously in France the revolutionary court had sentenced Paine to death for opposing the beheading of the king. He escaped with his life, but only because his gaoler failed to see the chalk mark on the cell door identifying him for the guillotine. Holed up in Marylebone, Paine was visited by William Blake, Mary Wollstonecraft (author of *A Vindication of the Rights of Woman*), and the French and American ambassadors, who persuaded him to flee, but not the British authorities, who couldn't find him. Nevertheless they prosecuted Paine in his absence. After two years he left for the New World, where his anti-religious work – *The Age of Reason* – upset many people, and he lost the popularity he had enjoyed during the War of Independence. Unable to return to Britain, Paine remained in America until his death in New York on 8 June 1809. His one great achievement over the water was to coin the term 'the United States of America'.

While Paine was in hiding in the West End, Thomas Spence, a Newcastle schoolteacher, arrived in the capital to distribute subversive literature. Spence founded a radical debating club which met at the Cock Tavern in Grafton Way, near where Warren Street station now stands, and published political texts from 9 Oxford Street. His group, the Spenceans, believed land in Britain should be shared out equally, as there was enough to give every man, woman and child seven acres each. (They never explained how they would ensure that every individual kept to their exact seven acres.) Spence did not advocate a centralized political party. Instead he encouraged his followers to form small groups that could organize direct action. This involved the Spenceans walking the streets of London at night chalking on the walls slogans such as: 'Spence's Plan and Full Bellies' and 'The Land is the People's Farm'.

This MO was ultimately their undoing. How could the masses build the revolution if they were divided into hundreds of groups, rather than one body? Nevertheless the authorities were worried enough about Spence's activities to send him to jail a number of times.

When Spence died in September 1814 he was buried by forty disciples who promised to keep his ideas alive. They formed the Society of Spencean Philanthropists, and were duly watched over by a government spy who reported to the Home Office that the Spenceans were planning to encourage rioting at a mass meeting, overthrow the British government, and storm the Tower of London and Bank of England. The spy wasn't over-reacting; the Spenceans *were* planning exactly that. And they had a new, more powerful figurehead: Arthur Thistlewood. His declared aim was nothing less than a plot to murder the entire British cabinet before seizing control of the main buildings of state.

Thistlewood assembled a gang of revolutionaries which included George Edwards, who supplied them with blunderbusses and cutlasses; Richard Tidd, a shoemaker; James Ings, a butcher; and William Davidson, son of the Attorney General of Kingston, Jamaica, a known sufferer of what he himself called 'psychotic tendencies'. Its headquarters was a barn on Cato Street in Marylebone. From there it was only a mile or so to Grosvenor Square where, they discovered, the entire Cabinet would be dining at the home of Lord Harrowby on 23 February, 1820. Thistlewood and Co. planned to rush the door, overcome the servants, storm the dining room and attack the party. 'We are going to kill His Majesty's ministers and will have blood and wine for supper,' they boasted. 'We will cut off every head in the room and bring away those of Lord Castlereagh and Lord Sidmouth in a bag'.

Castlereagh, leader of the House of Commons, was their main target. He was especially hated for having suspended *Habeas Corpus* during the unemployment demonstrations of 1817 and had been vilified by the poet Shelley, an occasional West End resident, in the latter's 'Mask of Anarchy' poem, a diatribe against the 1819 Manchester Peterloo Massacre, brought about, it was said, by Castelreagh's repressive policies.

> I met Murder on the way
> He had a mask like Castlereagh
> Very smooth he looked, yet grim
> Seven bloodhounds followed him
>
> All were fat; and well they might
> Be in admirable plight,
> For one by one, and two by two,
> He tossed them human hearts to chew
> Which from his wide cloak he drew.

But things didn't go according to plan for the Cato Street Conspirators. Gang member George Edwards was an *agent provocateur*, a government stooge. The dinner was a ploy; the participants were ready and waiting for their adversaries ... who never came. The police had caught up with the rebels at Cato Street. There they found some twenty men armed with guns, swords and other weapons standing next to two sacks, sacks in which they intended to carry off the heads of the ministers. When one constable, George Ruthven, shouted: 'We are officers! Seize their arms!', Thistlewood picked up his sword and thrust it into the body of another officer, Richard Smythers, who cried out: 'Oh my God, I am done.' As the *Morning Chronicle* described it the following day, 'Smythers received a stab in his right side and was carried away quite dead.'

There was further fighting, shooting and stabbing. Four of the conspirators, including Thistlewood and his Number Two, John Brunt, escaped out of a window. They were soon arrested but Thistlewood escaped, only to be recaptured the following night near Moorgate. After being imprisoned in the Tower he was hanged outside Newgate prison on, ironically, 1 May, and for being a traitor as well as a murderer he was decapitated after being hanged. Brunt's demise was equally dramatic. He refused a blindfold, calmly took a pinch of snuff, and announced to the crowd, 'It is better to die free than to live like slaves.'

While Thistlewood's gang was foiled by a fifth columnist, the Chartists never got that far. Their brand of radicalism, which occupied much discussion in West End taverns, particularly the King and Queen at 1 Foley Street, Fitzrovia, in the early decades of the nineteenth century, was limited to 'The People's Charter'. This document, drafted by William Lovett in 1838, set out six demands: annual parliaments, universal male suffrage, equal electoral districts, voting by ballot, an end to property qualification for MPs and payment of MPs.

But the Chartists lacked organization and funds. Their core belief – that parliament could right economic exploitation – was too insipid to capture people's imaginations. Factory workers dismissed them as 'middle-class agitators'. The Chartists never appreciated that with employment levels in London not subject to the same violent fluctuations as they were in the North there was never one mass of people suffering at the same time in the capital. In July 1839 the Chartists presented a petition of 1,200,000 signatures to Parliament, but MPs refused to consider it. The Chartists, by now increasingly disunited, discussed staging a general strike, but then abandoned the idea. Such compromise was typical.

## 'ARE YOU A COMMUNIST?'

Not all political movements conceived in the dusty streets near Oxford Circus in the mid nineteenth century were run by devotees as patient and moderate as the Chartists. In June 1847 a German workers' organization, the League of the Just, held a conference in London. It was attended by Friedrich Engels, a German-born textile industrialist who ran a cotton factory in Manchester. Shocked by the widespread poverty he found in the city's Little Ireland district, Engels had gathered his ideas together in a tough piece of reportage entitled *Condition of the Working Class in England in 1844*. He refused to join the League unless it dropped the slogan: 'All Men are Brothers' in favour of 'Working Men of All Countries, Unite', a phrase coined by his animated German ally, Karl Marx.

Thanks to Engels and Marx the League of the Just became the Communist League. The two Germans were asked to draw up a new manifesto. The result was more like a code of conduct drawn up by a Rosicrucian society with a penchant for call-and-response techniques than a political tract. A typical section ran:

*Are you a Communist?*
Yes.

*What is the aim of the Communists?*
To organize society in such a way that every member of it can develop and use all his capabilities and powers in complete freedom and without thereby infringing the basic conditions of this society.

*How do you wish to achieve this aim?*
By the elimination of private property and its replacement by a community of property.

In November 1847 Marx and Engels brought the outline of their work to the Communist League congress, which was being held at the Red Lion on Great Windmill Street, Soho, a pub which still stands, now in the centre of London's red-light district.

The congress lasted ten days, and Marx made a big impact on the rank-and-file delegates. According to Friedrich Lessner, a Hamburg tailor, 'He was a born leader of the people. His speech was convincing and compelling in its logic.' Marx won all the arguments and at the end of the congress was asked, along with Engels, to tidy up the draft for publication. The two men laboured slowly. By January 1848 they still had not finished the great work. Leaders of the Communist League sent them an ultimatum: 'If the [text] does not reach London by 1 February further measures will have to be taken ...' This did the trick and the work was soon complete.

*The Manifesto of the Communist Party* must have seemed strange at the time. No such body as the Communist Party then existed nor, as Francis Wheen explained in his 1999 biography of Marx, was the work really a manifesto. As a piece of literature *The Manifesto of the Communist Party* is clumsy and pedestrian. Its famous early line –'The history of all hitherto existing society is the history of class struggles' – pales alongside its precursor, Rousseau's great epithet from the *Social Contract*: 'Man is born free; and everywhere he is in chains.'

But as a piece of political propaganda its resonance has been phenomenal. Only one other book – the Bible – and that is of unsure translation – has had such an impact on humanity. *The Manifesto of the Communist Party* is the most influential book that ever arose from a pub meeting in Soho, the cornerstone of a philosophy that powered the Soviet Union, China, Mongolia, North Korea and much of eastern Europe for the latter half of the twentieth century, and still propels political thought worldwide.

Its 17,000-odd words can be categorized into a few main themes. There is the notion of history as class struggle rather than as a collection of swash-buckling tales of kings and conquerors. There is the classifying of society into strata: 'freeman and slave, patrician and plebian, lord and serf . . . in a word, oppressor and oppressed.' There is the explanation of how the working class is exploited by the bourgeoisie. There are the economic theories about the value of goods and services based around the notion of labour. Finally there is the call for revolution to bring about socialism and the rallying cry at the end: 'Working men of all countries, unite!' And nearly all this thrashed out in endless semi-drunken meetings above the Red Lion, Soho.

Not all the *Manifesto*'s predictions were accurate. The most famous alleged that capitalism is a temporary phenomenon which would bring about true revolution. It isn't. Ironically, one tiny, but significant, prop supporting the menace of international capitalism to this day is the phenomenal sales of *The Communist Manifesto*, still a bestseller at the beginning of the twenty-first century.

Not all the *Manifesto*'s discourses were morally honest. All rights to inheritance should be abolished, thundered Marx and Engels, but the former was quick to accept £6,000 from the family estate. But some of the crystal-ball gazing within the *Manifesto* was eerily prescient: 'In place of the old wants, satisfied by the productions of the country, we find new wants, requiring for their satisfaction the products of distant lands and climes.' The modern-day reader will immediately think of their local supermarket stacked high with tasteless tropical fruit and veg out of season at the expense of honest-to-goodness English greens, peas and runner beans to realize the quality of Marx's vision.

The *Manifesto* was typeset by the Workers' Educational Association in London, printed in the City, and published in German on 24 February 1848. That day in Paris, with consummate coincidence, a feverish mood that had been growing around economic grievances saw an outbreak of street fighting and the flight of the king, Louis Philippe. A provisional government was formed and universal male suffrage announced. It soon looked as if a revolution or two was going to break out across Europe. In March 1848 Prince Metternich, the Austrian chancellor, was toppled. Similar political turmoil broke out in the Rhineland, Vienna, Berlin, Milan and Venice. Refugees poured into London.

In the British capital attention focused once again on the Chartists. At least they were a movement, as opposed to Marx's drinking and debating club. A massive rally was planned for 10 April at Kennington Common and a crowd of around 150,000 attended. The authorities, fearing insurrection, hired extra special constables and stationed 5,000 troops at strategic points across the capital, including Hyde Park, the Tower and the Bank of England, to ward off the mob. The royal family and a number of landowners fled London. But after the Chartist leader, Feargus O'Connor, agreed to the authorities' demand – that the crowd could not accompany the main Chartists to Whitehall to deliver their petition – events passed off relatively peacefully.

Chartism never really recovered from this anti-climax. Nevertheless some of its tenets became common currency among all parties the following century. Britain may not entertain annual parliaments, but it does have universal male suffrage, equal electoral districts, voting by ballot, the absence of a property qualification for members of parliament and payment of MPs, having adopted these measures *without* revolution.

During that tumultuous year Marx was on the continent. Ordered out of Belgium on 3 March when the French Republic was declared, he arrived in a Paris strewn with barricades and bloody turmoil, and two days later telegraphed Soho that he had moved the executive headquarters of the Communist League to the French capital and that all members should wear a 'blood-red' ribbon on their coats. When the Paris uprising also failed Marx and other Communist League members returned to their German towns to educate the masses. It looked as if the revolutionary fervour which had gripped Europe – in France, Italy, Austria and Germany – was running out of steam.

Exiled from Germany, thrown out of Belgium and expelled from France, Marx moved back to London, permanently. Britain, with its liberal government – liberal compared with those on the Continent – where many harboured revolutionary ideas but couldn't quite get a revolution organized, presented the biggest challenge. With his wife, Jenny, their maid and various children he rented a house in Chelsea, although they couldn't really afford the rent. There were more meetings. Again these were held at the Red Lion on Soho's Great Windmill Street.

Few such gatherings, not even those of the Huguenots of Spitalfields some 150 years earlier, can ever have rivalled these sessions in their catholic versatility. Subjects debated included astronomy, history, geography and . . .

communism. There were drawing lessons and dance classes. There were debates with titles such as 'What is the present postion of the workers and their attitude towards the bourgeoisie?'

It wasn't long before Marx and family were evicted from their Chelsea lodgings – for not paying the rent. Scores of people watched in Anderson Street, just off King's Road, as bailiffs removed the furniture. Briefly the Marxes stayed in the German Hotel, off Leicester Square, but soon found a place at 64 Dean Street in the heart of Soho, a house now demolished, which stood on a site opposite the modern-day Groucho Club. No. 64 was the ramshackle home of a Jewish lace dealer. The Marxes were wracked with poverty and Jenny, Mrs Marx, who was pregnant (again) went to Holland to beg money from her uncle, Lion Philips, one of the founders of the Philips electric company that now dominates the city of Eindhoven. Philips, worried about the effect socialist activity of the kind that Marx advocated was having on his business, refused her. When Jenny threatened that she and Karl would therefore have to emigrate to America, he explained that such a move would be an excellent idea.

Marx's financial problems were eased by his long-term collaborator, Friedrich Engels, who took a lucrative job in his father's Manchester textile firm and sent bank notes to Marx, cutting them in half and putting them in separate envelopes so that no would-be thief would prosper from opening the envelope. That June of 1850 the *Spectator* printed a letter from a 'Charles Marx and Fredc. Engels' of 64 Dean Street complaining about police spies, whom they had spotted watching their every move around Soho. They some-what ruined their case by admitting they were revolutionaries on the run from Germany, their country of birth.

The Marx family soon moved to rooms further along Dean Street, at the top of No. 28. There in the 1851 Census Marx registered himself as 'Charles Mark, Doctor (Philosophical Author)', signing letters 'A. Williams' just in case the authorities were opening his mail. No. 28 had no toilet or running water, and conditions were so heinous three of the Marxes' children died at this new Dean Street address. A Prussian secret agent who visited the family there reported that they lived in 'one of the worst and hence the cheapest quarters of London. There is not one piece of good, solid furniture in the entire flat. Everything is broken, tattered and torn, finger-thick dust every-where, and everything in the greatest disorder.'

The entire household had to sleep in one room, which meant that the only time Marx and Jenny had for procreation was when the maid was out with the children, an inconvenience which makes it all the more remarkable that Marx also found time to impregnate the maid. Jenny Marx was kind enough to hush up what would have been a choice scandal for the greater good of the movement. By then the Communist League had moved from London to Cologne, as the London branch was deemed to be too obstreperous. This was not a clever move, for by the summer of 1851 all eleven members of the central committee were in jail in Germany on accusations of conspiracy.

Marx was now getting tired of being a member of feuding, bickering committees and outfits, and retreated into his writings. He spent many days researching *Das Kapital* in the British Museum. He would stay up all night working, sleeping on the Dean Street couch oblivious to all the commotion around him for much of the next day. On one occasion he even sought everyday white-collar employment, applying to be a railway clerk, but was turned down on account of his illegible handwriting. When in 1856 Jenny received an inheritance the Marxes left the West End for suburban Kentish Town, four miles north.

Marx returned to the West End on one occasion – purely for hedonistic reasons – a pub crawl. He, Wilhelm Liebknecht and Edgar Bauer started at the Blue Posts, at the corner of Tottenham Court Road and Hanway Street, a pub which survived in altered form until the 1990s when it was demolished for a new Sainsbury's, before moving on to the Black Horse at No. 19; the Rising Sun, still at No. 46; the Rose and Crown, No. 62; the Talbot at 64; the Northumberland Arms, which also survives, at 119; the Southampton Arms, No. 141; the Plasterers' Arms at 157; the Mortimer at 174; the New Inn, 183; the Apollo, 191; the White Hart, 199; the Italian, 236; Fox and Hounds, 264; and the recently demolished Horseshoe, 267. At the last pub they met what they later described as a group of 'odd fellows' who were also out celebrating. A discussion began, which turned into a row when Marx and Bauer began promoting the worth of German culture over English values, and then into a fight. As there were only three Germans and several more English the Germans ran. Wilhelm Liebknecht later recalled how 'Marx showed a turn of speed that I should not have attributed to him. After the chase had lasted some minutes we turned into a side street and there running through an alley we came behind the policeman who had lost the trail.'

Marx also returned to the West End for more typical political fare. The

International Workingmen's Association, better known as the First International, met in the late 1860s in Rathbone Place, a small street north of Soho Square, near Emanuel Barthelemy's salon where Marx practised his fencing. It is strange, given how during the following century Marx's name came to be synonymous with radical politics, that he wasn't a particularly important member of the group. Many experts even wonder how he managed to secure an invitation to its first meeting, one of the defining events in communist history, which was held at St Martin's Hall, Long Acre, Covent Garden in September 1864.

## THE ANARCHISTS

Karl Marx, despite his revolutionary fervour, never took part in outright terrorist activities. He was a fierce debater and indefatigable researcher, but not a bomber, dynamiter or murderer. Not like his old fencing partner, Emanuel Barthelemy. One day Barthelemy left his Rathbone Place salon equipped with weapons and deer shot tipped with sulphur. He intended using these to assassinate Napoleon III, but never made it. On the way Barthelemy called on a contact in Warren Street who owed him money. An argument raged, things turned nasty and Barthelemy shot the man dead. As he fled he was confronted by a former policeman who lived next door. Barthelemy killed him too. But by this time a crowd had gathered. They overpowered the renegade fencer and secured his arrest. He was hanged at Newgate.

Marx vociferously disapproved of the bomb left by the Fenians, the Irish nationalists, at the Clerkenwell House of Detention, on Friday 13 December 1867. It was the first terrorist bomb planted on mainland Britain and part of a campaign to release two of its leaders from prison. 'A colossal blunder,' he called it.

The botched bombing led the British state to hire an Irish barrister, Robert Anderson, to co-ordinate spying and counter-terrorism. At first Anderson was based at Dublin Castle, where he organized a network of informers – mostly butchers, bakers and assorted shopkeepers – across Ireland, primed to watch for anti-British opinion. Before long the British government realized it would make more sense to base Anderson in London. Not in the East End, where an HQ would be too conspicuous, but in the West End, a far better foil. After all, who would suspect the state of monitoring such nefarious activities in the smart stucco streets around Oxford Circus? Anderson set up shop at 50 Harley Street, in what is now London's private clinic land, and called for his best agent, Thomas Miller Beach, alias Henri Le Caron, who conveniently held the position of Inspector-General of the Irish Republican Army.

Throughout the 1870s the state enjoyed some success from its anti-terrorist activities. Citizens went about their business relatively unafraid of being blown up at random. All this changed after the Liberals won the 1880 general election. Anderson was forced to take a six-month sabbatical, and during his absence the United Irishmen of America blew up the Salford Infantry Barracks near Manchester. More bombs left by Irishmen were soon exploding across London, particularly at railway stations.

Yet it was not the Irish who now most worried the defenders of the state. A new menace had gripped London, particularly in the West End – anarchism. The anarchists were soon considered to be more dangerous than the Irish. At least the authorities knew what the Irish wanted, and knew how they were likely to strike, but they could never get to grips with anarchism. The Irish spoke English, so their meetings allowed easy eavesdropping, but the anarchists spoke strange east European languages, some of which didn't even use Roman letters. The Irish were Christians, even if they espoused the 'wrong' brand of Christianity. The anarchists, however, were atheists and Jews, sometimes both. All the British government knew was that the anarchists wanted direct action, not, as with Marx's communists, discussion. They wanted maverick rebellion, not planned revolution, and in all likelihood it would involve terrorism. Henry James caught the mood of the times in *The Princess Casamassima*, his 1886 novel, in which one character explains how 'there's an immense underworld peopled with a thousand forms of revolutionary passion and devotion . . . In silence, in darkness, but under the feet of each one of us, the revolution lives and works.'

The anarchists swarmed to London after every major political drama on the Continent such as the collapse of the Paris Commune in 1871 or the attempts to assassinate the Kaiser in 1878. They spread their propaganda using wandering agitators armed with smuggled newspapers. They met in scores of shabby meeting places in the cramped streets of Soho and Fitzrovia, streets which would be gentrified and prettified decades later, cleared of the filth, rats and urchins. One of their most popular venues was the Social Democratic Club on Rose Street (now Manette Street), by modern-day

Foyle's. The club was popular with members of the English Revolutionary Society, in reality Germans fleeing persecution of socialists. Indeed, there were so many Germans pouring into Soho the Rose Street venue looked more like a railway station than a socialist club, even if the luggage was mostly cases of *samizdat* literature. Another favoured West End location was the basement of 49 Tottenham Street, where visitors at the end of the century included George Bernard Shaw and Keir Hardie. Then there was the International Club in Stephen Mews off Gresse Street. And just in case anyone wasn't sure where to find these places the *Evening News* of 17 December 1894 carried a helpful piece headlined: '8,000 anarchists in London: Where These Enemies of Society Live in This Great Metropolis'.

The authorities spent considerable time debating what they should do with this influx of insurgents, and eventually decided to adopt a *laissez-faire* approach. Leave them in place; just watch over them. It was a policy that often resulted in absurd conclusions. For instance, at the Red Lion on Soho's Great Windmill Street, where Marx ran his Communist debating club, those attending included one Wilhelm Stieber, an agent of the Prussian government. He was watching Marx under instructions from the Prussian Minister of the Interior, Ferdinand von Westphalen, who just happened to be Marx's brother-in-law. Stieber reported back to von Westphalen that the Communists were plotting in code to kill Queen Victoria. Von Westphalen in turn told Lord Palmerston, the foreign secretary, but Palmerston chose to sit on the information. When the Prussians complained that the British authorities were not showing sufficient concern the home secretary explained that 'under our laws mere discussion of regicide . . . does not constitute sufficient grounds for the arrest of the conspirators'.

At the Prussian Embassy on The Mall one agent took his enthusiasm for watching anarchist and socialist refugees too far. He began manufacturing weekly reports of a fictitious communist group, complete with fake minutes of a non-existent Supreme Committee, which resulted in arrests and a court case. There it was proved that the embassy was collaborating in this absurd canard, which set back their subsequent campaigns for some time. The Metropolitan Police made up for the Prussians' incompetence with their own useless raids. In 1885 they descended on the International Club with a posse that included various well known faces whom everybody at the club assumed were ordinary locals but who turned out to have been police agents. Their sole achievement from the raid was to take away all the beer.

By the end of the nineteenth century there were about a thousand German anarchists and some four hundred French anarchists in the West End, mostly based around Charlotte Street. They had no official leaders, for they were anarchists, but a powerful figure amongst them was Johann Most. A dissident German Social Democrat with a rare talent for biting sarcasm, Most had been a member of the Reichstag until a speech sympathetic to those who had been trying to assassinate the Kaiser led him to be sent to jail for six months, much of it spent in solitary confinement. Most was released in December 1878 and given twenty-four hours to leave Berlin. He went to Hamburg. There, local anarchists took fright and advised him to emigrate to America. Instead Most went to London, to Soho no less, where he began publishing the revolutionary journal *Freiheit*.

Editions of the magazine contained instructions on how to make bombs, useful information to a number of readers such as Joe Deakin, a rare English anarchist. Deakin was stopped on Tottenham Court Road by police, searched, and found to have explosives on him. 'It's okay,' he explained to the officers, 'they're not for use in London – they're bound for Russia.' This unusual and original excuse curried little favour with the policemen who took him in for questioning. There Deakin fingered a collaborator: Auguste Coulon of 19 Fitzroy Square. He didn't realize Coulon was a police spy, already suspected by the anarchists for various suspicious activities, including celebrating the blowing up of a cow in Belgium as a 'great and revolutionary act'. Also hauled in during the same sting was Coulon's neighbour, Jean Battola. He was a proper anarchist, and used his trial as the platform he craved. 'Society is based on sham, hypocrisy and theft,' he announced from the witness stand. 'This court is guilty of all the crimes of the age, of all the murders prompted by want, and all the suicides. Long live anarchy!' 'Eight years,' said the judge.

Most even got *Freiheit* into Germany. He arranged for large numbers of one edition to be sewn into mattresses being made in a factory in Hull that were due for export. His confidence boosted by that scam, he made *Freiheit* even more supportive of the anarchists. Every time a figure of political authority was 'eliminated', Most and his magazine were quick off the press with a vitriolic article in favour. When Russian nihilists assassinated the Russian Tsar, Alexander II, in 1881 *Freiheit* published an enthusiastic endorsement entitled: 'At Last'. The British authorities, under pressure from the Russians and Germans, arrested Most. They found him guilty of incitement to murder heads of state. Eighteen months was the sentence. *Freiheit* was closed down soon after, following an article applauding the Fenians' assassination of Lord Frederick Cavendish in Dublin in May 1882. The editorial team left England and reconvened in Switzerland.

In 1886 simmering resentment by the oppressed for the oppressors boiled over into what some historians have excitedly described as the 'West End Riots'. Trouble began that February when the non-radical Fair Trade League met in Trafalgar Square to push for higher customs tariffs to cure unemployment. The Marxist Social Democratic Foundation called a counter-demonstration of the unemployed. There the Foundation's John Burns told the crowd that the House of Commons was 'composed of capitalists who had fattened on the labour of the working man ... to hang these ... would be a waste of good rope ... there must be a revolution to alter the state of things. The next time they met it would be to go and sack the bakers' shops in the west of London. They had better die fighting than die starving'. Evidently at that moment he could not foresee the time when he would be a *Liberal* MP and cabinet minister. Nor could the crowd which, fired up, tore along Pall Mall and looted shops in Piccadilly.

Occasionally a West End anarchist was successful. Martial Bourdin, a tailor who worked on Great Titchfield Street a few yards east of Oxford Circus, took a train from Charing Cross to Greenwich on Thursday 15 February 1894, carrying a bomb. He was planning to destroy the Royal Observatory, 'capitalist' home of time. By accident the bomb went off in Greenwich Park before Bourdin had reached his appointed target, much like the bomb Hasib Hussain carried onto the number 30 bus near the West End on 7 July 2005. But Bourdin, unlike Hussain, was still alive after the explosion even if severely injured. His guts were hanging from his stomach, and a finger had zoomed off to a nearby tree where it was found a few days later.

Bourdin pleaded to be allowed to go home (as if) but instead was taken to the nearby Naval Hospital, where he died. There he was identified through his membership card for the Autonomie anarchist club at 6 Windmill Street, Fitzrovia. Police raided the club using a secret knock learned from infiltrators. A week later, as Bourdin's funeral cortège passed through Fitzrovia, some 15,000 anti-anarchist protesters gathered and a mob smashed the windows of the club. But some good came out of the drama. It inspired Joseph Conrad to write *The Secret Agent*, published in 1907 and set in Soho, an exquisitely drawn, ironic romance of scrupulous prose, the most convincing study of the terrorist mind ever committed to print, in which a mad anarchist known only as The Professor wanders London with a bomb and detonator strapped to his waist. Conrad knew exactly what he was talking about and how the modern terrorist wanted to play. When Chechen rebels took over a Moscow theatre in 2002 they espoused a manifesto which was practically a word for word rewrite of The Professor's speech.

## MAN OF THE STEPPES

Bourdin was small fry, insignificant. More powerful was the pseudonymous Stepniak – 'Man of the Steppes' – real name Sergius Michaelovitch Kravchinski. Stepniak was a Russian of noble stock who had proved his credentials when he killed the chief of the secret police in St Petersburg in 1878. After a spell in Switzerland he arrived in London and headed for the anarchist cells around Charlotte Street. There he helped set up the Society of Friends of Russian Freedom.

Supporters followed Stepniak to the promised land from afar. One was Wilfred Michael Voynich. He was not put off at being sent into exile in Siberia, near the Mongolian border, where his gaolers thoughtfully arranged his cell so that the window faced the gallows, allowing him a good view to watch his friends die. Somehow, Voynich escaped and made his way to Mongolia. There he joined a caravan heading the wrong way, to Peking. Eventually he made it to Hamburg, where he sold his coat and glasses to buy some bread and herring, and a ticket on a boat bound for England. He was penniless, hungry and spoke no English, but what the hell. He was now in the same city as his mentor and comrades!

Voynich had one major problem – finding Stepniak in a city of seven million. His solution was inspired. After getting off the boat near the Tower of London he walked along Commercial Road in the heart of the East End, stopping passers-by at random and thrusting into their face a piece of paper on which was scrawled Stepniak's name . . . in Russian. It didn't take long before a Jewish student knew exactly what this dishevelled creature wanted and took him to meet the great man.

Voynich and Stepniak now hit the West End together, frequenting Charlotte Street's anarchist cafés. Their favourite meeting place was the Épicerie Française at 78 Charlotte Street where the French regulars had helpfully drawn up a list of 'Cockney' phrases written in Franglais which they felt fellow anarchists would need to ingratiate themselves with locals. Simple things like 'Aille ouil poule your nose' and 'if you deun't g'hive mi a sixepen'ce, aille breke your nose'.

Voynich eventually became a great success, but not at anarchism. He acquired a proper job, working as an antiquarian bookseller on Shaftesbury Avenue near Piccadilly Circus, where with his stooped back, caused by the cramped conditions of his Siberian cell, and engaging line in seductive talk he became a West End institution. In 1912, the year when Stepniak, whom he had followed to London, literally from the ends of the Earth, was killed by a train at a level crossing in Chiswick, Voynich's life took a surprising turn. In a secluded Jesuit monastery in Italy he found a remarkable medieval document illustrated with fantastic decorations, strange plants and astronomical drawings written in a hitherto unknown language. No scholar could explain its contents. The finest cryptographic minds have still failed to solve what is now known as the Voynich Manuscript. The British government once even put its entire MI8 department on to the task of unravelling the esoteric incunabula, to no avail, an ironic twist given that the secret services had been engaged in watching Voynich's political activities only a few decades previously.

Besides Stepniak and Voynich there was the Italian, Errico Malatesta. No boundaries or borders could hold him. Egypt, Syria, Romania and Spain were his domain, and eventually so was London where he fled to in 1881 to organize the first International Anarchist Congress. After a ten-year sojourn in Argentina (gold prospecting in Patagonia) and Italy (a three-year jail sentence for criminal conspiracy) Malatesta returned to the West End where he worked as an electrician, bicycle-repair man and ice-cream seller. In 1910 police in the East End searching the Houndsditch crime scene where anarchists had shot officers during a botched jewellery heist found a card bearing Malatesta's name. A police investigation failed to implicate him in the events, and in 1919 he returned to Italy permanently. There he soon met an ambitious, up-and-coming activist – the director of the Socialist daily *L'Avanti!* – Benito Mussolini. Malatesta was shown no favouritism though when the fascists put him under house arrest during the later years of his life.

Not all visiting revolutionaries on the run from their own governments were Europeans. In 1895 Sun Yat Sen, often now described as the founder of modern China, fled to London after staging an unsuccessful attempt to take power in Canton. His coup probably failed because it depended on groups of youthes marching across the country into Peking and seizing the state without bloodshed. When Sun knew it wasn't going to work he went into hiding, leaving on a steam launch, first for Macau and then for Japan where he disguised himself as a native by growing hair on his upper lip.

By then the Chinese government had discovered that Sun was the ringleader. As soon as he arrived in London agents from the Chinese Legation at 49 Portland Place, half a mile north of Oxford Circus, began to tag him. They had been ordered to kidnap Sun before he could raise money for his Young China movement in London, and have him shipped back to China alive, so that he could be tortured. Sun, naively, never thought he would be shadowed or that he was in danger. He joked to his main protector, James Cantlie, later to become a renowned expert on tropical diseases, about going near the Legation, to which Cantlie's wife remarked: 'You'd better not go near it. They'll catch you and ship you off to China.'

On 11 October 1896 Sun was near the building, walking along Devonshire Street in Marylebone, when a Chinaman approached him and asked in English if he were Chinese or Japanese. Sun said he was from Canton. The man said he was too. As they talked they were joined by another who urged Sun Yat Sen to come back with them to their lodgings for a smoke. Naive? Maybe, but Sun was looking for supporters, and so couldn't turn down the chance of making new friends. The men exchanged some good-natured banter on the street as they walked along. When they passed 49 Portland Place one of the men stopped, opened the door of the house and pushed Sun in.

Once Sun realized he had been tricked into the Chinese Legation he took stock of the situation. Maybe there was a way out of his predicament. He met the English official at the Legation – Sir Halliday Macartney – but Sir Halliday was a stooge of the ruling Manchu dynasty and told Sun: 'Here is China for you. You are now in China [i.e. Chinese territory]. Your name is Sun Wen [*sic*] and we have a telegram from the Chinese minister in America to arrest you. You are detained here until we learn what the Emperor wishes to do with you.'

Sun Yat Sen was allowed to contact friends and tell them where he was, but not that he had been kidnapped. On the fourth day of his confinement one of his kidnappers told him that if his life were to be spared he must write to Sir Halliday, in English, admitting that he had been involved in wrongdoing in China, denying he had been wrongly accused by the Chinese authorities, and affirming that he had come to the Legation for help.

It was obviously a trap, a way of extracting a confession. Instead Sun wrote messages and weighing them down with coins threw them from the window. They were all found by the guards. However, an English servant at the Legation contacted Cantlie who went to *The Times*. The fearless Thunderer baulked at upsetting the Chinese but the *Globe* ran an item headlined: 'Startling Story! Conspirator Kidnapped in London! Imprisonment at the Chinese Legation.' Sun was freed thanks to the personal intervention of Lord Salisbury, soon to become prime minister. Cantlie went on to provide the Chinaman with the most fulsome of eulogies. 'I have never known anyone like Sun Yat Sen. If I were asked to name the most perfect character I ever knew, I would unhesitatingly name Sun Yat Sen.'

There was to be another unusual Chinese-revolutionaries-in-London tale. In 1967 Harold Holt, the Australian prime minister, vanished into the sea around his homeland after going for a swim, and was never seen again. Some said it was suicide, others that he was murdered by the CIA after intimating that he was going to withdraw Australian troops from Indo-China. Sixteen years later, in November 1983, allegations surfaced that Holt had not died in a tragic marine accident after all but had been whisked away by frogmen and transferred to a Chinese submarine. He had long been a spy for the Chinese, recruited when he was twenty, in 1929, and even when he was a new minister in the 1950s he had passed information to his Chinese communist masters using an address in the West End on Gerrard Street, so it was alleged. Holt has not resurfaced since; not even in London's Chinatown.

## UNDER THE SPREADING
## CHESTNUT TREE

Lenin, Trotsky, Stalin, Mussolini. Still the aspiring revolutionary leaders poured into the West End. Lenin used to organize debates in the West End of the early 1900s under the guise of the Foreign Barbers of London Association, which met in the Anglers' Club on Charlotte Street under the noses of the piscine trophies on the walls. In 1903 Lenin's party, the Russian Social Democrats, briefly held a congress in a Brussels flour store. When they were ordered out of the country they chose to reconvene the congress in the

West End, on Charlotte Street. Such mystery surrounds the events that to this day no one knows where on Charlotte Street it was held. Bickering amongst delegates resulted in what came to be called the Bolshevik–Menshevik split – the former being the 'majoritarians' (*bol'sheviki* in Russian), the defeated latter, the 'minoritarians' or *men'sheviki*.

Visitors at various times to the Communist Club at 107 Charlotte Street in 1910 included Joseph Stalin and Leon Trotsky. Stalin, who in the 1920s succeeded Lenin as leader of the Soviet Union, ate at the Continental Café on Little Newport Street where a fellow patron remembered he who became one of the twentieth century's most feared dictators as 'a bombastic little man, not very big, but always with an air of mystery about him.' In his wanderings around Fitzrovia Stalin probably ambled along Percy Street, the delightful street of terraced houses lined with lime trees that links Charlotte Street and Tottenham Court Road. If so he wouldn't then have appreciated the significance of the tenant at No. 4, an Austrian waiter called Alois Hitler, half-brother of Adolf, who may have paid a brief visit in 1912 when he was a struggling Austrian artist.

When Benito Mussolini arrived in the West End in December 1922 he was lucky enough to be able to stay at the luxurious Claridge's Hotel. There was no need for the Italian fascist to pay his dues amongst the broken tea cups of Fitzrovia's cheap *pensions* as by this time he was prime minister of Italy, staying in London during a conference on German reparations following the Great War. Journeying to London, Mussolini took the boat train, arriving at Victoria station, where he was greeted by fascists wearing black shirts singing the Italian song 'Giovinezza'. After laying a wreath at the Cenotaph Mussolini paid a visit to the Italian Fascist Soho HQ at 25 Noel Street, where his arrival was met with yet another chorus of 'Giovinezza.' Indeed, wherever he went in London over the next few days Mussolini was surrounded by Italians singing 'Giovinezza', except when he bedded prostitutes in his hotel, which once caused him to miss a press conference. He impressed *The Times*, who wrote how 'Signor Mussolini has an air of authority and a dominating personality.' Part of this 'dominating personality' was his penchant for complaining incessantly about the fog which, he claimed, penetrated his clothes, his bedroom, even his suitcases. Back in Italy he swore he would never go to England again, and never did.

Three years later Mussolini assumed the title *Il Duce* – leader. Now there was to be no opposition in Italy. But in Soho his enemies were free to conspire. At the King Bomba delicatessen, 37 Old Compton Street, in the heart of London's Italian community, behind the awning 'The sole macaroni factory in England', anarchists plotted in 1931 to assassinate the Italian dictator.

In charge of the operation was the deli owner, Emidio Recchioni. In 1899 he had escaped from an island prison where he had been interned for his involvement in an assassination attempt on the Italian prime minister, Francesco Crispi. Now Recchioni was plotting to eliminate another Italian leader. In 1931 he travelled to Brussels, shadowed all the way (not that he knew it), by a Special Branch agent. There he met Angelo Sbardellotto, an Italian anarchist who offered to go to Rome and personally kill Mussolini if Recchioni could provide money and weapons.

Several failed attempts later, Sbardellotto was arrested in Rome, and found with two bombs and a loaded revolver. He made a full confession, listing the dates when he had met Recchioni in Paris. The Italian authorities wanted Recchioni extradited from London, but not only did Recchioni brave out the request, when the *Daily Telegraph* named him as being involved in the failed assassination plot on Mussolini he sued for damages to his reputation as a 'virtuous man' and won.

Lenin, Trotsky, Stalin, Mussolini. All West End visitors, mostly in their powerless days, all mercilessly mocked in the area's most potent polemic, George Orwell's *1984*. An infamous and widely influential novel, mostly conceived in the West End, *1984* is amongst other things a political satire so bleak, so black, that most readers have taken it at face value as political propaganda warning against totalitarianism. But is more likely that Orwell was sending up European political extremism and how it translated into the Britain of 1948, the year in which he was writing, exactly a century after various revolutions had swept across Europe, if not Britain, reversing the last two digits for literary effect.

This was a time when Britain was awash with so many rules and regulations it was hard sometimes not to feel like a criminal, vilified for falling foul of some form of petty bureaucracy. It was a time of rampant state socialism, peddled by Britain's first ever majority Labour government, whose tax-and-spend, nationalization-obsessed regime, intent on running people's lives 'from cradle to grave', features in extreme form in the novel as INGSOC – English Socialism.

Orwell drew on many local experiences in writing *1984*. The interminable, red-tape strewn, war-time BBC meetings, dominated by endless memos about the mirrors in the ladies' loos and the quality of the carpets in the recording booths, had been held in Room 101 at 55 Portland Place. This gave him the idea of using the phrase 'Room 101' in sending-up the idea of the 'worst thing in the world'. During the War a BBC censor vetted all scripts, and when announcers went on air, a 'switch censor' sat alongside, cutting off the speaker if he deviated from the approved text. In *1984* this is taken to its logical, paranoid conclusion, manifested in the form of the telescreen controller able to watch everyone's movements and upbraid every wrongdoer in every home and on every street with an immediate admonition.

The BBC canteen, situated in the windowless basement of the Peter Robinson store near Oxford Circus, where Orwell ate while working for the Corporation on wartime propaganda, was the model for the Ministry of Truth canteen in *1984*. Here basic foods had been replaced with processed alternatives (margarine for butter, saccharine for sugar), the dinner ladies would wheel round mugs of Victory Coffee as part of the BBC's 'V For Victory' campaign, and serve what Orwell called in the novel 'metallic stews . . . which, in among its general sloppiness, had cubes of spongy pinkish stuff which was probably a preparation of meat.' He didn't even need to change much in using this material in the novel.

Inspiration for many of the locations used in *1984* came to Orwell from his daily jaunts around the streets and pubs of Fitzrovia. Newman Passage, the blind alley that links Newman Street and Rathbone Street, is a recurring haunt. It is where Winston Smith, the novel's hero, remembers the junk shop 'where he had bought the blank book which was now his diary', a subversive act that eventually becomes his downfall. At the eastern end of the passage stands the Newman Arms, a pub which before the Second World War sold only beer – it had no spirits licence – and was therefore heaven to Orwell, the fundamentalist beer drinker. It was in the Newman Arms that Orwell set the scene in which Winston, having followed an elderly 'prole' into the pub to learn about life before the Revolution, before it became illegal even to think of doing such a thing, succeeds only in starting a futile, frustrating conversation devoid of meaningful content. Orwell used the scene to strike a body blow against one of his main targets – bumptious bumped-up bureaucrats.

'Lackeys!' he said. 'Now there's a word I ain't 'eard since ever so long. Lackeys! That reg'lar takes me back, that does. I recollect oh, donkey's years ago – I used to sometimes go to 'Yde Park of a Sunday afternoon to 'ear the blokes making speeches. And there was one bloke – 'e didn't 'alf give it 'em! 'Lackeys!' 'e says, 'lackeys of the bourgeoisie! Flunkies of the ruling class!' Parasites – that was another of them. And 'yenas – 'e definitely called 'em 'yenas. Of course 'e was referring to the Labour Party, you understand.

Another one in the eye for the rulers of 1948.

Further east, at 18 Percy Street, was the home of Sonia Brownell, who worked at the Euston Road offices of the literary magazine *Horizon* and became Orwell's second wife. Some years before he wrote *1984* Orwell spent a number of fruitless evenings here, attempting to woo the woman known as the 'Venus of Euston Road'. In *1984* Sonia, who disliked sex but chose to go to bed with writers and intellectuals for the experience, appears as Julia, stalwart of the novel's Anti-Sex League who nevertheless falls in love with Winston. No. 18 becomes the model for the junk shop where Winston and Julia conduct their affair, evidently wishful thinking on Orwell's part as he only succeeded in ensnaring Sonia on his death bed.

Just outside the West End on Bloomsbury Way was a branch of the Express Dairy Company chain which served as the haunt of artists, bohemians and intellectuals – the model for the Chestnut Tree Café in the novel. Nearby, towering over the streets of Fitzrovia, especially in those pre-high rise days, is Senate House, built by Charles Holden in 1927–36 as the University of London headquarters and then the tallest building in London. During the Second World War Senate House was home to the government's Ministry of Information, run by Brendan Bracken, a Tory MP who went by the nickname 'BB' – as does *1984*'s unseen overlord, Big Brother. Orwell used the building's vast bulk as the model for the architecture of *1984*'s four all-powerful ministries, particularly the Ministry of Truth.

One writer engaged by the wartime ministry was Graham Greene, who wrote a short story, 'Men At Work', based on a day in the life of a ministry clerk whose day is taken up entirely with drafting useless memoranda and attending pointless meetings. This gave Orwell the idea for the job performed in *1984* by Winston Smith, who rewrites back copies of *The Times* at the Ministry of Truth.

Orwell himself was a target for the real-life Ministry of Information's wartime censoring. The Ministry cut large extracts from his 'London Letters', which he wrote for the American magazine *Partisan Review*. He later discovered that American readers were unaware that there had been any cuts in the articles. Orwell also fell foul of a ministry civil servant, Peter Smollett, head of the Russian section, whom he believed was a Soviet agent. According to Peter Davison, who edited the complete set of Orwell novels and writings at the end of the twentieth century, Orwell wrote a preface for *Animal Farm* under the title 'The Freedom of the Press', space for which was left at the beginning of the work, as the pagination of the proofs shows, but which was not included. It was not until many years later, after Orwell had died, that the typescript was found. Men from the ministry, led by Smollett, mentioned to at least one publisher that they disapproved of the release of *Animal Farm* because of its untimely political message at a time of pro-Soviet feeling. When Davison's *Complete Works of Orwell* appeared in 1998 Smollett's descendants were furious at how their relative had been cast and demanded an apology. But research soon proved that Smollett had been working for Soviet state security since 1933.

There were targets in *1984* other than the little moustachioed men of the Labour government and their supporters whose equivalents in the novel are forever denouncing citizens that have erred as traitors of the state. The novel was a tirade against all fellow-travellers: all the gullible, guilt-ridden Soviet sympathizers and Stalin supporters who journeyed to Moscow and came back gushing with enthusiasm for the post-revolution regime, ignorant of the slave camps, the famine, the terror, the eliminations . . . and continued to remain pro-Soviet in the face of all evidence that didn't fit their preconceived prejudices. Such dupes were mostly writers, for example George Bernard Shaw, and particularly Sidney and Beatrice Webb. In 1935 the Webbs published an account of their trip: *Soviet Russia: A New Civilization?* Two years later came a revised edition, the title augmented by an obsequious screamer – *Soviet Russia: A New Civilization!* Not that they had much input into the great work, as it was written mostly by the KGB.

In the 1940s Orwell kept a small, pale blue notebook in which he listed what he called 'crypto-communists and fellow-travellers'. At the time no one knew that he was monitoring Stalinists within London Bohemia for a secret wing of the Foreign Office, the Information Research Department, not for any hidden nefarious purpose, but with the notions of free speech and democracy in mind. When the Left discovered this remarkable news in the 1990s it was aghast and Orwell ironically and instantly became an 'unperson' – straight out of the pages of *1984*.

## STREET FIGHTING MEN

Post-war Soho drew a fashionably left-wing crowd to its jazz clubs, pubs and bookshops such as David Archer's on Greek Street. The most popular hangout was the Partisan café at 7 Carlisle Street, next door to the modern-day home of *Private Eye* magazine. Here in the evenings in the early 1960s, amidst much chess playing and flyers advertising CND, the new school of underground poets such as Pete Brown, who later collaborated with Cream, gave readings, and folk singer clones of Woody Guthrie sang about mining disasters and the consequences of the levee breaking – in Memphis, not Charing Cross.

No. 7 also housed a number of 1960s left-wing groups and publications including *Black Dwarf*, set up by leading members of the London left-wing intelligentsia such as the activist Tariq Ali, the writer Sheila Rowbotham and the poet Christopher Logue. The first issue of *Black Dwarf* was emblazoned with the slogan: 'We shall fight, we will win, Paris, London, Rome, Berlin', but the text was impenetrable and there were no pictures. Future issues improved. The magazine threw itself behind the important issues of the day, such as the campaign against the Vietnam War, although attempts to tackle more abstract notions such as feminism were dogged by classified advertisements placed from within like 'Dwarf designer seeks Head girl type to make tea, organize paper, me. Suit American negress.'

At the beginning of 1969 Rowbotham suggested that as 1968 had been 'The Year of the Heroic Guerrilla', 1969 should be 'The Year of the Militant Woman'. Everyone agreed that the notion would be heralded by a series of articles, including a centrespread manifesto entitled 'Women: The Struggle for Freedom' that she would write herself. Prior to publication Rowbotham insisted on proof-reading the article herself so that she could remove any embarrassing errors. When she arrived in the office she soon realized that typographical accuracy was the least of her concerns: the designer had underlain the article with a picture of a naked woman with unimaginably huge breasts.

The 1960s was a time when commentators were claiming that class barriers were breaking down; the dream that Marx had outlined in tortuous rhetoric in 1850s Soho. Old money estates were leaving the West End. Working-class icons such as Twiggy, Jean Shrimpton and the Beatles were the new heroes. The West End was leading the fight against deference at the anti-establishment Establishment satire club and in the pages of *Private Eye*.

Yet Mayfair was soon filled with the sound of anarchy . . . 'marching, charging feet'. The perpetrators were demonstrators protesting about the Vietnam War in which the US was propping up one corrupt (anti-communist) regime against one corrupt (communist) regime. Their target was the US Embassy on the west side of the square.

At the first of these Vietnam Solidarity Campaign marches, held on 22 October 1967, nearly 10,000 demonstrators, irked by the tacit support the British prime minister, Harold Wilson, was lending the US, gathered in Grosvenor Square under banners proclaiming: 'Where has Harold Wilson gone? Crawling to the Pentagon'. They called for victory for Communist Vietnam, and attacked with missiles the 350 or so police officers that had formed a cordon around the square to protect the embassy. It is just as well that few of the demonstrators were simultaneously thinking of Oscar Wilde's learned quote about the locality, put into the mouth of Lady Bracknell in *The Importance of Being Earnest* (1895). 'Fortunately in England at any rate, education produces no effect whatsoever. If it did, it would prove a serious danger to the upper classes, and probably lead to acts of violence in Grosvenor Square.'

Nevertheless, some protesters forced their way into the embassy garden, but were dissuaded from entering by the thought of meeting sterner opposition inside. Yet not all the protesters had serious political intentions. As the main body chanted: 'Ho, Ho, Ho Chi Minh' (the name of the anti-colonialist leader), the Situationist King Mob group, equally sceptical of the establishment and left-wing opponents, sang 'Hot chocolate, drinking chocolate', as in the popular advertising song of the day.

The following March another Vietnam Solidarity Campaign Demonstration centred on the square. Some 20,000 demonstrators had earlier gathered at Trafalgar Square, making their way to Mayfair amid the usual chanting of 'Ho, Ho, Ho Chi Minh'. By the time they got to South Audley Street they were twelve deep, and when police spotted Mick Farren, the flamboyantly Afro'd front man for the counterculture group the Social Deviants among them, they waded through the crowd to aim a truncheon blow at his head.

Once in Grosvenor Square, the crowd stormed towards the embassy, hurling smoke bombs and throwing marbles beneath the hooves of the police horses. One girl who tried to offer a mounted policeman a flower was truncheoned to the ground. The fighting lasted two hours and 117 officers and forty-five demonstrators were injured. Although posters advertising the event had urged the crowd to 'come armed', the Vietnam Solidarity Campaign denied this to be its work. The events inspired Mick Jagger, an onlooker, to write 'Street Fighting Man' for the Rolling Stones, a visceral, uplifting track which took a sardonic swipe at his own inability to do anything more worthwhile than 'play for a rock and roll band' and perfectly summed up the confused political mood in London at that time.

In the run up to the third, the last and biggest anti-Vietnam War demo, on 27 October 1968, the authorities, with the May student riots and strikes in Paris fresh in the mind, tapped phones, opened the mail of leading campaigners and infiltrated socialist groups, often as *agents provocateurs*. On the day itself the Vietnam Solidarity Campaign redirected the march from Grosvenor Square to Hyde Park at the last minute but a splinter group from the Britain–Vietnam Solidarity Front ignored the call and clashed with police outside the US Embassy, leading to forty-two arrests, and injuries to four policemen and fifty demonstrators. The bulk of the 100,000 marchers, however, congregated peacefully at Hyde Park where at the end of the demonstration the marchers and police together sang 'Auld Lang Syne'. The newspapers congratulated themselves at the failure of the campaigners to bring down the government, the Royal Family and world capitalism. Once again Grosvenor Square and the West End had let the revolution down.

# 5

## Visions

If God is everywhere, then He has been particularly so in the West End. Mystics, millennialists, prophets, seers and sages began bearing true witness locally no sooner than the fields north of Westminster were built over in the eighteenth century.

William Blake, who was raised in Soho, is the first to have documented a vision. At the age of nine Blake claimed he saw a tree filled with angels on Peckham Rye, four miles south-east in the countryside. He went home and told his father, who thrashed him, until his mother intervened. Blake also claimed he once saw the face of God pressed against a Broad Street window. Later he discovered, with no surprise, that his birth year – 1757 – had already been marked down by his mentor, the Swedish visionary Emmanuel Swedenborg, as a special year, the year when the last judgement would be accomplished in the Spiritual World.

Although Blake was an intensely religious artist and poet, confusion has long surrounded the identity of which nonconformist sect he was born into. That his parents were nonconformists we know for sure, for they were buried in Bunhill Fields, Moorgate, like Blake himself. Peter Ackroyd, Blake's most extensive biographer, has debated whether William's father, James, was a Baptist on Grafton Street, a Moravian on Fetter Lane, a Muggletonian, Sandemanian, Hutchinsonian, Thraskite or Salmonist, such were the bewildering number of non-establishment Protestant groups present in the West End in those days. Blake's own views were idiosyncratic: he designed his own mythology based upon the Bible and Greek mythology, and rejected what he called 'arid atheism and tepid deism'.

Blake was wary of conventional religion. In *The Marriage of Heaven and Hell* (1790) he wrote: 'Prisons are built with stones of Law, Brothels with bricks of Religion' and 'as the caterpillar chooses the fairest leaves to lay her eggs on, so the priest lays his curse on the fairest joys', a line borrowed from the Biblical book of Proverbs. In his epic poem 'Jerusalem' (1804–20) he posed the ancient queries of the Christian Kabbalists that James I revived when he moved to London from Scotland in 1603 to take the throne: Was Britain the primitive seat of the patriarchal religion? Was Britain home of a purer Christianity than Rome? Was London *the* Holy City, the New Jerusalem, the centre of a world of one God, one religion, one nation?

If it is true: my title-page is also True, that Jerusalem was & is the Emanation of the Giant Albion. It is True, and cannot be controverted. Ye are united O ye Inhabitants of Earth in One Religion. The Religion of Jesus: the most Ancient, the Eternal: & the Everlasting Gospel – The Wicked will turn it to Wickedness, the Righteous to Righteousness. Amen! Huzza! Selah! All things Begin & End in Albions Ancient Druid Rocky Shore.

## PRINCE OF THE HEBREWS

Whereas William Blake channelled his mysticism into art and poetry, his two main maverick contemporaries – Richard Brothers and Joanna Southcott – chose the other well-trodden path, that of prophet. Brothers, a resident of Marylebone, was born in Newfoundland, Canada, in 1757, the same year as Blake, on 25 December, no less. He came to London to work in the Woolwich shipyards but in 1790, after studying various ancient tracts, announced that 'the Spirit of God began to enlighten my understanding'. He then announced he was the Prince of the Hebrews, descended from King David through James, one of the *brothers* of Jesus, hence his fraternal surname.

Alas at the same time Brothers fell into debt. He entered the workhouse and was sent to Newgate Prison to share a cell of fifteen. On being released in 1792 Brothers decided to return to America, but while walking to Bristol to catch a ship found that 'God by his power stopped the action of every joint and limb, commanding me at the same instant to return and wait.' He walked back to London and took lodgings at 57 Paddington Street, Marylebone, where he wrote a book, *A Revealed Knowledge of the Prophecies and Times*. It was a mixture of extracts from the Bible interspersed with his own commentary, which adopted some of the more outré Protestant teachings of the day: Rome as the great whore of Revelations 17, the Pope as the scarlet-coloured beast, the cardinals as the ten horns, and so on.

Soon Brothers was issuing a precise date for the Second Coming: 19 November 1795. *The Times* nicknamed him 'The Great Prophet of Paddington Street'. His book became a bestseller, and he was visited by large numbers of people, followers and detractors alike. The authorities took fright. In March 1795, worried about the scope of Brothers's influence, they arrested him. He was interviewed by the Privy Council and declared insane. Prison was a grim and ghastly cell for eleven years, amidst the austere brick walls of Canonbury Tower. It was an appropriate asylum, for in the same building Francis Bacon, the philosopher, politician and pioneering scientist, had practised Rosicrucian magic two hundred years previously.

As for the date of the Second Coming, 19/11 passed with no obvious Messianic manifestation. Brothers's influence subsequently waned, except among his staunchest supporters, who saw his plight as proof of his status as a true prophet persecuted by his own people. After his release he had a new plan: to return the Jews to the Holy Land. He hoped help would come from the kings of England, Denmark, Sweden and Prussia, with each state providing a quantity of building material to create the city of sacred geometry outlined in Ezekiel, chapters 40–48. It didn't.


## THE WOMAN CLOTHED WITH THE SUN

Joanna Southcott was a Devonian upholsterer who led a breakaway movement from the Methodists in 1777. She moved to 38 Manchester Street, only a few hundred yards from Brothers's now vacated Paddington Street address, in 1801. That year she announced herself as a millennial prophet: 'the woman clothed with the sun' of Revelations 12 and the 'bride of the lamb' of Revelations 19.

With pamphlets and through speaking tours Southcott amassed some 20,000 followers who cited her as a true visionary and claimed she had accurately predicted the war with France, and the failed harvests of 1794, 1795 and 1797. Thousands signed a petition in support of her desire to overthrow Satan and establish Christ's kingdom on earth. In turn they each received a piece of paper inscribed: 'The Sealed of the Lord, the Elect precious. Man's Redemption to inherit the Tree of Life. To be made Heirs of God and Joint-Heirs with Jesus Christ', their name written above the inscription with Southcott's signature below.

In 1814 at the age of sixty-four Southcott announced she was pregnant. It would be a virgin birth, the child 'Shiloh', as prophesied by Jacob in Genesis 49:10: 'The sceptre shall not depart from Judah, nor a law-giver from between his feet, until Shiloh come,' who as outlined in Revelations 12:5, 'is to rule all the nations with a rod of iron'.

Some twenty doctors asserted that Southcott was pregnant. Supporters sent gifts and a cradle decorated with a gold crown, and the name 'Shiloh' embroidered in Hebrew letters at the head. Southcott assumed many of the usual signs of pregnancy. She developed a fad for asparagus, eating fifty-two heads in one sitting. Supporters suggested it might be best if she acquired a husband prior to the birth, so that the child would not be declared illegitimate. On 12 November 1814 she married John Smith, a steward to the Earl of Darnley. Her followers sold their businesses and travelled to the capital, camping on the outskirts and waiting for the great event.

The newspapers of the day were not enthusiastic. Many journalists alleged that the birth would be of the 'baby-smuggled-in-warming-pan' variety. And as the birth day approached it looked as if they might be right, for by November signs of pregnancy had disappeared. Southcott herself declared it to have been an 'illusion'. The pregnancy over, she grew increasingly weak and died, of dropsy, it is believed, on 27 December 1814. Lord Byron weaved the story into 'Don Juan', noting 'So few are the elect / And the new births of both their stale virginities / Have proved but dropsies taken for divinities.' William Blake was equivocal and commented: 'Whate'er is done to her she cannot know/And if you'll ask her she will swear it so / Whether 'tis good or evil none's to blame / No one can take the pride, no one the shame.'

To Southcott's supporters her death was only a temporary setback. Some explained that Shiloh had indeed been born – on Christmas Day – and had immediately soared to Heaven to save Himself from the dragon. They placed hot water bottles around the late prophetess's body, to keep it warm in expectation of either a resurrection or the appearance of Shiloh. But when neither happened after four days her remains were taken to St John's Wood Cemetery, where she was buried.

Supporters vowed to refrain from shaving their beards until she was reborn, but their wait is still not over. Southcott also left a box which she insisted should only be opened in the presence of twenty-four bishops. It became difficult to find that many bishops willing to take part in the ceremony, and it wasn't until the 1920s, when a group of supporters paraded through the streets of London bearing sandwichboards proclaiming 'The Bishops must open Joanna's Box to save England from ruin', that the box was opened, in the presence of just one bishop at Church House, Westminster. It was found to contain some coins, a pistol, a nightcap, a lottery ticket and a cheap novel.

## THE GOLDEN DAWN

Brothers and Southcott were maverick visionaries without the benefits of an organized body behind them. Such developments came later in the century. One of the best known religious movements of that time was the Hermetic Order of the Golden Dawn. Its creator was Dr William Wynn Westcott, a coroner with an interest in the occult and a master Freemason.

Westcott claimed that he had deciphered an encrypted sixteenth-century document discovered in a bookstall on Farringdon Road and found that the document's arcane alphabet contained details of the alchemical and mystical rituals of a secret Germanic occult order: *Die Goldene Dammerung*. The Germanic group were Rosicrucians, members of a still-active secret society so secret even its main perpetrators have no evidence it officially exists. The Rosicrucians' patriarch, Christian Rosenkruez, was an enigmatic fourteenth-century mystic who travelled to the Orient, and in the caves of Syria was initiated into the teachings of a mystical cult, returning to Europe to found his movement and dying at the advanced age of 106.

As with Freemasonry and other similar movements the main Rosicrucian inspiration is the Kabbalah, the body of Hebrew mysticism which hints at a vast body of knowledge only alluded to in the Bible. Indeed, the story of Christian Rosenkruez is itself based on the tale of Rabbi Shimon, a teacher who lived in the Holy Land during Roman rule and who after being sentenced to death hid in a cave for thirteen years, gaining spiritual awareness by drawing on deep levels of memory and vision stored in his unconsciousness to create the Kabbalah's revered book of Zohar (Splendour).

After its unknown founders issued the Rosicrucian Manifesto in Germany in 1614, Rosicrucian mania swept through Europe's intellectual world. Rosicrucian societies were set up everywhere by those attracted to the lack of any visible bureaucracy or busy clergy, and to a philosophy that could therefore take any form its adherents wished. In England Francis Bacon, philosopher, essayist, Lord Chancellor to James I, operating out of Canonbury Tower, was a particular devotee.

Now Rosicrucianism had a new outlet. Westcott set up the Hermetic Order of the Golden Dawn at the intriguingly named Isis-Urania Temple, 17 Fitzroy Street. The colourful and curious, looking for a God substitute, were attracted by what at once seemed exclusive, esoteric and extraordinary, by the promise of obtaining a glimpse of eternity, of the world's entire knowledge – the knowledge that has been, the knowledge that is, the knowledge that will be.

The poet W. B. Yeats couldn't resist and at Fitzroy Street assumed the mantle *Demon est Deus Inversus* (D. E. D. I., 'The Devil is God Inverted)'. Inside the Temple he underwent a 'spiritual' marriage with Maud Gonne, or as he called her briefly *Per Ignum Ad Lucem* ('Through the Fire, to the Light'). It was remarkable that women were allowed inside the Temple at all. But the Hermetic Order were evidently more progressive than the Masons. Another initiated at No. 17 was Annie Horniman, of the tea family, who later pioneered theatre in Manchester. She was sworn to secrecy lest she be 'slain by the lightning flash'.

The Hermetic Order of the Golden Dawn thrived during 1888. It was London's strangest year since 1666, a year when five East End prostitutes were killed according to Masonic ritual by 'Jack the Ripper' – a killer or killers unknown. By the end of the year the Temple had thirty-two members, who were being schooled in astrology, alchemy, Enochian magic and the Egyptian Book of the Dead. Rituals would begin with a recitation of the eleven Magick Commandments:

> Thee I invoke, O Bornless One.
>
> Thee, that didst create the Earth and the Heavens.
>
> Thee, that didst create the Night and the Day.
>
> Thee, that didst create the darkness and the Light.
>
> Thou art ASAR UN-NEFER ('Myself made Perfect'): Whom no man hath seen at any time.
>
> Thou art IA-BESZ ('the Truth in Matter').

Thou art IA-APOPHRASZ ('the Truth in Motion').

Thou hast distinguished between the Just and the Unjust.

Thou didst make the Female and the Male.

Thou didst produce the Seeds and the Fruit.

Thou didst form Men to love one another, and to hate one another.

Soon the Hermetic Order of the Golden Dawn had a schism. No religious or quasi-religious group would be credible without one. MacGregor L. Mathers, a pioneer of the Tarot, adept at Hebrew, Latin, French, Celtic, Coptic and Greek, wrested control from Westcott. He wanted a Magical Order in which initiates would study his interests in esoteric knowledge centred around the Kabbalist notion of how all things in the universe connect via the Tree of Life.

In 1892 the Order's leaders moved to new premises in the West End: 24–25 Clipstone Street, a few yards north of Oxford Circus. The building was far from heavenly. 'It was 'dirty, noisy, smelly and immoral,' noted one member. The neighbours, prosaically, were a hairdresser, a dairyman, a confectioner, two sculptors, cabinet-makers, French polishers, a piano tuner, and the officials of the German Waiters' Society. In 1900 Mathers was exposed as a fraud and expelled from the Order. But by this time members had come under a more potent influence, that of Aleister Crowley.

The self-proclaimed 'Great Beast', Crowley, born into the Plymouth Brethren fundamentalist Christian sect, exhibited a taste for what he called 'sex-magick', as well as drug-taking, assorted hedonism and antisocial behaviour. He claimed to be the reincarnation of various colourful historical characters, including the incorrigible Pope Alexander VI (a Borgia), the eighteenth-century Sicilian mystic Count Cagliostro and the Kabbalist writer Eliphas Levi. He adopted as his personal motto 'Do What Thou Wilt Shall Be The Whole Of The Law,' and his party piece was the Serpent's Kiss – biting the wrist of women with teeth specially filed for that purpose. Once the newspapers discovered Crowley, they dubbed him 'the Wickedest Man in the World'.

Crowley's declared aim was to produce a 'monster baby' after the 'ultimate orgasm', to which end he produced pills made from his own semen. At a chemist's shop on Stafford Street, off Old Bond Street, he collected the ingredients needed to aid his sex drive: kyfi, an Egyptian incense;

the perfume and oil of Abra-Melin; and onycha, the powder from the horned shell of a mollusc found in the Red Sea. Crowley also clashed regularly with other members of the Order. W. B. Yeats objected to his pornographic writings, blasphemy and alleged immorality, and ensured that when Crowley tried to win promotion to a higher level within the Order he was turned down. Crowley sued the Order, which in turn sued him. The prolix, labyrinthine machinations were enlivened by Crowley's habit of assuming full Highland dress, his face covered in a black mask, an enormous gold cross around his neck and a dagger by his side in court while the case dragged on without solution or satisfaction to either party.

## DEATH ON SWIFT WINGS

Half way between the sites of the Golden Dawn's temples, barely noticeable in a Fitzrovian backstreet despite its blood-red 227ft brick spire, stands the church of All Saints. The architect William Butterfield ingeniously fitted the building into a claustrophobic space on Margaret Street, a few hundred yards north-east of Oxford Circus, in the 1850s. He provided a choir school and clergy house on the site, and cleverly designed a small court in the front around which he set the smaller service buildings. All Saints is an extraordinarily powerful Gothic structure, built for the Oxford Movement or Tractarians, Anglo-Catholics who believed Gothic was the only true Christian style of architecture.

Despite the church's austere style, which fits in with the Tractarians' views on minimal external show, the internal décor is rich in detail. There is excellent use of granite, alabaster and marble, its chequered patterns, polished piers and stained glass are exquisitely detailed and coloured, and the interior is replete with the finest furnishings. All Saints became a major influence on the Gothic revival, being one of the first nineteenth-century churches to use brick decoratively, and was described by John Ruskin, the leading mid nineteenth-century art critic, as 'the first piece of architecture I have seen built in modern days which is free from all signs of timidity and incapacity'.

One West Ender who used All Saints regularly during the 1940s, when respite from the war was needed, was George Orwell, who passed the church daily journeying from the BBC to the pubs of Fitzrovia. He came to

All Saints infatuated, but not to worship. For Orwell was obsessed with the Anglo-Catholic church, which he mercilessly mocked in his novels. *A Clergyman's Daughter* (1935), one of Orwell's earliest, features a rector who has 'the deepest contempt for the Anglo-Catholic movement. It had passed over his head, leaving him absolutely untouched; "Roman Fever" was his name for it'. Another character in *A Clergyman's Daughter*, Victor Stone, is an 'Anglo-Catholic of the most truculent *Church Times* breed – more clerical than the clerics, knowledgeable about Church history, expert on vestments, and ready at any moment with a furious tirade against Modernists, Protestants, scientists, Bolshevists, and atheists.'

With the decline of belief in London during the twentieth century, West Enders, sceptical of God, became more prone to the claims of charlatans and idolaters. The capital was gripped throughout the 1920s by the supposed curse of Tutankhamun, the Egyptian boy king of antiquity. Tutankhamun's tomb remained undisturbed until November 1922 when the British excavator Howard Carter found the burial chamber in the sands of the Valley of the Kings in Egypt. Once the tomb was turned over, more than twenty of those involved in the exhumation perished over the next few years. Indeed, only one lived into old age. The credulous pointed to the legend written in hieroglyphics near the entrance of the tomb: 'Death will slay with his wings whoever disturbs the peace of the pharaoh.' Proof, surely, of the curse of Tutankhamun!

Nowhere in the world seemed to be safe for those who had invoked the ire of the Egyptian death gods, even the West End. Discovery of the tomb had immediate repercussions in Soho. At Kate Meyrick's exclusive 43 Club near Leicester Square the brother of King Fuad of Egypt told the hostess herself: 'It is ill work. The dead must not be disturbed. Only evil can come of it.' He was right. A few weeks later Lord Carnarvon, who had sponsored the expedition, was fatally bitten on the cheek by a mosquito. At the exact moment of his death there was a power failure in Cairo. Seven years after the filching of the tomb Howard Carter's personal secretary, Richard Bethell, was found slumped over in a chair at the Bath Club, 43 Brook Street, Mayfair. The cause of death was never scientifically determined. A few months later, Bethell's father, Lord Westbury, leapt from his seventh storey apartment near Piccadilly. Although Westbury had never even seen the tomb, he possessed a small collection of Egyptian antiquities, and had frequently been heard to mutter 'the curse of the pharaohs'. When the hearse made its way down the street a week later an eight-year-old girl was accidentally killed.

A generation later another group of charlatans and idolaters appeared. They were followers of a little-known science fiction writer, L. Ron Hubbard, who arrived in Fitzrovia after the Second World War and took lodgings at 102–104 Whitfield Street. In the early 1950s Hubbard established the London Church of Scientology at 37 Fitzroy Street, only a few doors from the site of the temple run by the Hermetic Order of the Golden Dawn. Church or cult, the Scientologists believe in the power of a person's spirit to clear itself of painful past experiences through self-knowledge and spiritual fulfilment. Nowadays Scientology is dismissed by many as dangerous, a prop for enticing gullible American celebrities to part with their savings, but these were early, non-controversial years for the organization.

As is usually the way with such groups the Scientologists soon suffered a schism. When two members, DeGrimston Moore and Mary Ann McClean, discovered in 1963 that their Fitzroy Street meetings were being bugged they formed an offshoot, the Process Church of the Final Judgement. Its HQ was on Wigmore Street, Marylebone. When a devotee came into an inheritance they switched to more sumptuous offices in Mayfair, which led to a memorable *Sunday Telegraph* piece in which they were damned as the 'Mind Benders of Mayfair'.

The Process Church adopted many of the eccentricities of the 1960s with aplomb, in particular the teachings of Aleister Crowley, the Great Beast of 1920s Fitzrovia. Devotees wore badges featuring the Goat of Mendes, the devil-headed demon of the witches' sabbath. They gave classes in telepathy and preached at Speakers' Corner in Hyde Park. They touted for custom on Oxford Street. In America they established branches in New York, Los Angeles and San Francisco. Members of the Beach Boys and Rolling Stones attended their sessions, as did the mass-murdering hippie renegade Charles Manson.

But what did the Process Church of the Final Judgement believe in? They touted the work of Alfred Adler, a psychologist who cultivated the idea of the inferiority complex and believed that people were driven by what he called 'hidden agendas' that led to compulsions and neuroses. They cited Matthew 28: 'Heal the sick, cleanse the lepers, raise the dead, cast out devils . . . Provide neither gold, nor silver, nor brass in your purses . . . Behold, I send you forth as sheep in the midst of wolves: be ye therefore wise as serpents, and harmless as doves.'

Alas it was all to no avail. Like West End predecessors such as the Hutchinsonians, the Thraskites, devotees of Richard Brothers and Joanna Southcott, Westcott's original Hermetic Order of the Golden Dawn and MacGregor L. Mathers's offshoot, the Process Church disbanded, in 1993, before the arrival of the Messiah, and its archives were destroyed. Perhaps it was divine wrath.

# 6

# Temptations

Sex in the West End has long covered all manner of permutations, persuasions, proclivities and predilections: from the prospect of a knee-trembler with an underage Albanian asylum seeker in a grotty alleyway off Berwick Street Market to the possibility of upmarket fellatio with a duchess clad in pearls and soaked in expensive mid-European scent in an Upper Grosvenor Street town house. Colin MacInnes summed it up in his late 1950s novel of Soho sleaze, *Absolute Beginners*: 'In Soho, all the things they say happen, do: I mean the vice of every kink.'

As far back as 1764, when Giovanni Giacomo Casanova, still the world's best known lothario, briefly lived in Soho, he visited bagnios held at Carlisle House on Soho Square organized by Terese Cornelys. Entrance to these events cost two guineas a head, which led Casanova to note: 'Here a rich man can sup, bathe and sleep with a fashionable courtesan, of which species there are many in London. It makes a magnificent debauch, and only costs 6 guineas.'

While Casanova was indulging, his continental contemporary, Charles D'Eon, was cross-dressing. D'Eon, a French army officer and spy, had been brought up to wear female clothing, but joined an aristocratic convent as a boy. When presented to the court of Louis XV he was female once more and was sent to Russia where he became a maid of honour at the court of the Tsarina, Elizabeth. D'Eon was transferred to London in 1762 as a diplomat-spy, but after arguing with the king and French Embassy officials he was removed from his position as *chargé d'affaires* and ordered back to France. Because D'Eon refused to obey the instruction the French authorities launched an attempt to kidnap him from the ambassador's Soho Square residence. It failed, but he fled his lodgings in Dover Street, Mayfair, nonetheless, and aided by friends and French deserters took refuge at 71 (then

38) Brewer Street, which he turned into a fortress. Eventually D'Eon left for France where he was accepted as a woman.

His peregrinations in England weren't quite over. He later returned to London as his own sister, keeping the secret until his death when a surgeon performing a post-mortem discovered 'male organs in every respect perfectly formed'. A famous print of the time shows D'Eon's body split vertically into two halves: the left side as a glamorous woman, the right half a gentleman.

Not so exotic, but more influential, were the highbrow sexual explorations conducted by William Blake, the West End's most remarkable polymath, in the early nineteenth century. While living on Soho's Broad Street Blake worshipped at the Moravian Chapel on Fetter Lane where the sect's leader, Count Zinzendorf, would hand newly married couples, such as William and his wife, Catherine, texts which they could recite during climaxes. Consequently, at an orgasmic moment, Mrs Blake might have been heard breathlessly intoning: 'When my dear husband lets his oil sizzle in me, this grace is a sacrament.' At the Moravian Chapel Blake also learned such useful techniques as how to withhold orgasm so that seminal fluid could nourish the brain, the study of which was revived by New Age scholars at the end of the twentieth century. Sex in Soho has rarely been quite so cerebral. Mostly it has been closer in spirit to the seedy backstreet shop in Joseph Conrad's 1907 novel *The Secret Agent* where Adolf Verloc sells smutty magazines and naughty photos.

When Theresa Berkeley took over the White House, a Soho Square mansion with a painted chamber, grotto and skeleton room, in 1787, she installed a vast store of instruments of torture. These included a dozen tapering whip-thongs, cats-o'-nine-tails studded with needle points, supple switches, thin leather straps, curry combs, oxhide straps studded with nails and green nettles. She opened a brothel in 1828 at 28 Charlotte Street, Fitzrovia, which contained a machine for flogging gentlemen and where George IV was a regular visitor. Berkeley took her instruments of torture with her, and according to one Charlotte Street customer, 'they were more numerous than those of any other governess. Her supply of birch was extensive, and kept in water, so that it was always green and pliant. There were holly brushes, furze brushes and a prickly evergreen called butcher's bush.' Clients could be 'birched, whipped, fustigated, scourged, needle-pricked, half-hung, holly-brushed, furze-brushed, butcher-brushed, stinging-nettled, curry-combed, phlebotomized and tortured'. And if the urge for a more active role was irresistible there was a ready supply of willing girls who would be flogged in turn, namely Miss Ring, Hannah Jones, Sally Taylor, One-eyed Peg and the starkly monikered 'Bauld-cunted Poll'.

One reason why the king had to go to such lengths to have seedy sex was his antipathy to his royal bride, Princess Caroline of Brunswick. When George was first introduced to her he was so mortified by her appearance he wiped his brow and stumbled, whispered 'I am not well', and downed a brandy to quell a fit of faintness. George later wrote to a friend: 'She showed such marks of filth both in the fore and *hind* part of her . . . that she turned my stomach and from that moment I made a vow never to touch her again.' Nor was the bride particularly pleased with her groom. After George had departed she asked her lady-in-waiting, 'Is the Prince always like that? I find him very fat and not nearly so handsome as his portrait.' Somehow he managed to make her pregnant.

# THE MODERN BABYLON

Sex in the West End often leads to scandal. When Lord Palmerston, the revered mid nineteenth-century statesman, dallied with a Margaret O'Kane in Mayfair wags mused: 'While the lady was certainly Kane, was Palmerston Abel [*sic*]?' A longer-lasting scandal of sorts was the obsession William Gladstone had for prostitutes. On the night of 10 May 1853 Gladstone, who was then Chancellor of the Exchequer, was walking along Long Acre in Covent Garden when a woman stopped him to engage in conversation. When she invited the Chancellor back to her lodgings in Soho he complied. Yet it was not sex that was on the great man's mind but the chance to explain to the girl the error of her ways. Alas as Gladstone and the woman reached her street a man approached and revealed he'd been following the couple. He then tried to blackmail the Chancellor, threatening that he would inform the newspapers that the politician had picked up a prostitute unless he gave him some money or, more shockingly, found him a job with the Inland Revenue.

Soon the Chancellor's Private Secretary found out where Gladstone had spent the night and he warned him of the dangers. 'What will your wife say if she finds out you have been consorting with prostitutes?', to which Gladstone replied: 'I am bringing them home to see my wife.' The Long Acre incident tested Gladstone's charity to the full. He decided he had nothing to

TEMPTATIONS

fear, and took the case to court where the blackmailer was found guilty and sentenced to a year's hard labour, which some argued was preferable to a job with the Revenue.

As the nineteenth century wore on child prostitution became a more common problem in the West End, its perpetrators spurred on by the canard that intercourse with a virgin cured syphilis. In 1885 W. T. Stead, editor of the society newspaper the *Pall Mall Gazette*, decided to launch a crusade against this vice through the pages of his paper. Stead seemed to be the perfect sort of character to run such a campaign. A solid and seemingly unmovable pillar of Victorian society, he limited the number of times a week he had sex with his wife to two, for 'thrice or four times in the week I got deaf with apparent wax formation in the right ear.'

Aided by volunteers from the Salvation Army, Stead began to uncover a huge network of procurers, midwives, doctors, brothel-keepers and financiers who were profiting from child prostitution. He decided he would shock polite society by showing how easy it was to obtain a child for sex. With the help of a Madam, Rebecca Jarrett, who supplied so-called virgins for West End brothels, Stead learned that a local thirteen-year-old girl, Eliza Armstrong, could be obtained from her mother for the cost of five pounds at a brothel in Poland Street, Soho. After a midwife had certified that the girl was a virgin Stead went to the brothel with his assistant, a reformed prostitute. She undressed the girl and gave her chloroform, a common practice. Soon she was asleep.

Would Stead succumb to temptation? No. His assistant took the girl back to the midwife to prove her maidenhood was still intact and they then whisked her away to a Salvation Army hostel in Paris. Now came the tabloid exposé. In the *Pall Mall Gazette* of 4 July 1885 Stead warned squeamish readers to take extra care with subsequent editions of the paper. Readers were duly treated to four articles under the title 'The Maiden Tribute of Modern Babylon' which detailed the horrific story of 'Lily' (Eliza) sold by her dissolute parents into slavery. 'The brothel-keeper sent for the mother and offered her a sovereign for her daughter,' the piece ran. 'The woman was poor, dissolute and indifferent to everything but drink. The father who was as a drunken man . . . received the news with indifference.'

The campaign backfired. Eliza's mother claimed that Stead had misled her, that he had told her he was taking her daughter into service, not prostitution. She was outraged that the *Gazette* had portrayed her as a drunken mother who had sold her child. Worse still, consent from the father hadn't been obtained. She called the police, and Stead, who *had* fraudulently taken Eliza, was found guilty of an offence, despite the moral virtuousness of his intentions. In court he claimed that he had been guided by his 'senior partner' – God – but he was convicted regardless and sent to Holloway prison.

A new law was passed, the Criminal Law Amendment Act, which raised the age of consent to sixteen. The Act set the penalty for assault on a girl under thirteen as whipping or penal servitude. Stead, meanwhile, concurred that he had done nothing wrong and that it was the system that was flawed. He claimed he had enjoyed his time in jail, where his special privileges included an armchair and comfortable bed. 'Never had I a happier lot than the months I spent in happy Holloway,' Stead boasted, and for years afterwards he walked about London proudly wearing his prison uniform on 10 November, the anniversary of his incarceration.

Stead's demise was equally dramatic. Despite claiming he had ESP, he bought himself a ticket on the *Titanic*. As the ship went down, he sat quietly reading a book in the First Class Smoking Room, probably contemplating the time in 1886 that he had written an article entitled 'How the Mail Steamer Went Down in Mid-Atlantic, by a Survivor', in which an unnamed steamer collides with another ship but due to a shortage of lifeboats leads to much loss of life. 'This is exactly what might take place and will take place,' Stead wrote, 'if liners are sent to sea short of boats – Ed.'

# THE URANIANS

In 1862 Karl Heinrich Ulrichs, a German lawyer, made a brave declaration: he announced his preference for sex with the same sex. One of the first prominent people to do so in modern times, Ulrichs, in his many books, argued that same-sex love was hereditary, and that those who practised such sex, whom he called Uranians (the word 'homosexual' had not then been created), should not be considered as criminals.

In Britain laws against homosexuality traditionally covered only sodomy, or as it was legally known, buggery, and though the penalty since the time of Henry VIII for such behaviour had been execution, no one had ever received so punitive a punishment, legally. Nevertheless, those caught were often dealt with severely. After a raid in 1811 on a gay pub, the White Swan tavern in Vere Street, near Oxford Circus, six men charged with 'assault with the intention to commit sodomy' were put in the pillory in Haymarket. There a crowd of about 30,000 pelted them with mud, offal, dead animals, bricks and excrement.

But none of this seemed to dissuade those who wished to indulge. By 1855 they even had a guide book – *Yokel's Preceptor* – to help them. *Yokel's Preceptor* not only explained where the best gin palaces and gaming houses were in London, but detailed the activities of what it called 'marjeries and pooffs who could be recognized by their effeminate air and fashionable dress', presumably not put off by signs in the windows of Charing Cross pubs warning: 'Beware of sods'.

In 1885 the British government tinkered with the law in a way that would make Uranian practices more problematic. An amendment to that year's Criminal Law Act included the notion of 'gross indecency' for any sexual act between two male persons, whether in public or private. The Act probably didn't have that much bearing on men's behaviour. If anything, it made some more daring. That certainly seems to have been the case for the well-heeled figures who used a male brothel at 19 Cleveland Street, Fitzrovia.

In July 1889 19 Cleveland Street was the setting for one of the major sex scandals of the era. It began when police, investigating the theft of some cash from the London Central Telegraph Office on St Martin's Le Grand, questioned a telegraph boy, Thomas Swinscow, and found him to be carrying the handsome sum of eighteen shillings – several weeks' wages. When Swinscow revealed that he had obtained the money not through theft but by 'going to bed with gentlemen' at 19 Cleveland Street, for four shillings a time, police began watching the house. They spotted 'a number of men of superior bearing and apparently good position' paying visits. On 6 July officers led by Inspectors Frederick Abberline, who had investigated the Jack the Ripper murders a year previously, raided No. 19. Their targets were the brothel-keeper, thirty-five-year-old Charles Hammond, and his eighteen-year-old accomplice, Henry Newlove, whom they wanted to charge with 'unlawfully, wickedly, and corruptly conspiring, combining and agreeing to procure teenage prostitutes to commit the abominable crime of buggery.' They found both men had gone, but they caught up with Newlove at his mother's house and when he told them all he knew he was rewarded with a shorter sentence.

At first the papers barely covered the story, but the *North London Press* was suspicious about why Newlove had received a light sentence and how the brothel owner had found time to make his escape. The *North London Press* editor, Ernest Parke, began digging and discovered that the telegraph boys had fingered prominent aristocrats. On 16 November the paper named the Earl of Euston and Lord Somerset, head of the Prince of Wales's stables, as participants. It noted how the peers had been allowed to leave the country to save the skin of one 'more distinguished and more highly placed', a subtle reference, some informed readers concurred, to none other than Prince Eddy, the incorrigible son of the Prince of Wales.

Parke was eventually jailed for libel. But at another trial, which began on 12 December, the presiding judge told the court that Newlove's defence lawyer had helped the brothel owner to escape to prevent him from testifying against his aristocratic clientele. By this time Prince Eddy, who was only to live a few more years, was nowhere to be found; not in the West End, at least. He had conveniently left for a royal wedding in Greece and a tour of India that would last seven months.

This was not the only scandal with which Prince Eddy has since been connected. One of the more interesting Jack the Ripper conspiracies links him with the murders. The story goes that the Prince's mother, Princess (later Queen) Alexandra, sent him to an art studio opposite No. 19 run by the painter Walter Sickert so that he could gain experience of everyday life, but that the royal heir fulfilled her hopes in a manner unintended by impregnating one of the artist's models, Annie Elizabeth Crook, a Catholic. Eddy supposedly married the model in the East End in front of a few witnesses – mostly prostitutes – who later decided to take the tale to the newspapers unless he paid them sufficient hush money. As a result they were all killed, possibly by the royal surgeon, William Gull, abetted by Sickert, in what came to be known as the Jack the Ripper murders.

In July 1890, exactly a year after the Cleveland Street scandal first surfaced, Oscar Wilde, who was captivated by the events, published *The Picture of Dorian Gray*, a novel laden with homoeroticism, in which Wilde admits: 'To realize one's nature perfectly – that is what each of us is here for . . . The only way to get rid of a temptation is to yield to it.' A review of the book in the Scottish edition of the *Observer* was critical of Wilde's tone. 'Mr Wilde has brains, and art, and style, but if he can write for none but outlawed noblemen and perverted telegraph boys, the sooner he takes to tailoring (or some other decent trade) the better for his own reputation and the public morals.'

For Wilde, who had married in 1884 to affect a 'normal' public persona and to mask his proclivities, temptation was all around. At Albany, the sumptuous gentlemen's residential quarters on Piccadilly where he was a frequent visitor, a secret homosexual club, the Order of Chaeronea, was in full swing. The Order was named after a Greek battle in which Alexander supposedly defeated 300 pairs of gay lovers, and was organized by a George Ives who created a set of rituals, symbols and codes. When Wilde met Ives at a lunch at the Authors' Club in 1892 he asked him: 'Why are you here among the bald and bearded?' and suggested that a pagan monastery be set up on a Mediterranean island, where 'all loves might be free'.

In 1892 Wilde began an affair with Lord Alfred Douglas – 'Bosie' – son of the Marquess of Queensberry. He might have escaped prosecution and public humiliation but for the two men's penchant for flaunting their men friends – uncouth, working-class boys, no less – throughout the West End at venues such as Kettner's, the exquisite restaurant on Romilly Street which is now part of the Pizza Express chain, and the area's most glamorous location, the Café Royal. Such brazenness was too much for West End society. Uranian activities – homosexuality – was one thing, but with rough trade . . .

The Marquess was still seething over rumours about another son, Viscount Drumlanrig, who had been cavorting with the Foreign Secretary, Lord Rosebery, so when he learned what was happening with Bosie he stormed into Mayfair's Albemarle Club in a rage and left Wilde a scrawled note which read: 'To Oscar Wilde Posing Somdomite [sic]'. Wilde issued libel proceedings, and the peer was arrested for 'unlawfully and maliciously publishing a certain defamatory libel'. The Marquess of Queensberry failed to play in accordance with the gentlemanly boxing rules he gave his name to. He employed a former police inspector to force his way into the premises of one of Wilde's rent boys, Alfred Taylor. There he found a list of boys with whom Wilde had supposedly consorted, who were then pressed into testifying against him. Wilde was unable to disprove his opponent's allegations. He lost the case and was now open to prosecution for gross indecency – in effect sodomy, as opposed to somdomy – under the 1885 Criminal Law Amendment Act.

The trial began in the West End at Great Marlborough Street Magistrates Court. Wilde, wearing a white flower in his lapel, arrived in a carriage and pair with a coachman and a cockaded footman. Proceedings then moved to the Old Bailey where the court heard how Wilde had consorted with an Alfred Wood in Langham Street, near Oxford Circus, and a Fred Atkins at 35 Osnaburgh Street, further north, where, according to the landlady, 'the sheets were stained in a peculiar way'. The Marquess triumphed and Wilde was convicted of gross indecency. Although the authorities helpfully gave Wilde ample time to flee the country he lingered instead at the Cadogan Hotel, Belgravia, until the police arrived. He never recovered psychologically from the prison sentence.

## SPORTING LADIES

No sooner were the first West End communities formed than the first prostitutes began plying their trade. As far back as the Restoration period the local sex industry was fuelled by assiduously published guidebooks such as John Garfield's *The Wand'ring Whore*, a racy 1660 work which listed London's most popular prostitutes, each of whom sported their own idiosyncratic name such as 'the Queen of Morocco', 'Peg the Seaman's Wife' and the particularly and peculiarly popular 'Mrs Osbridge's Scolding Daughter'.

More popular was *Harris's List of Covent-Garden Ladies*. This guide, which first appeared in 1757, was published annually and reached a circulation of around 8,000 copies. It listed the name, address, physical charms, specialities and charges of about eighty London prostitutes working the West End and Covent Garden, and was useful for anyone wishing to take advantage of Soho's delights.

For instance, a 1788 edition contained an advert about 'Sporting Ladies' including a Miss B— who resided at 18 Old Compton Street:

Close in the arms she languishingly lies with dying looks, short breath, and wishing eyes. This accomplished nymph has just attained her eighteenth year, and fraught with every perfection, enters a volunteer in the field of Venus. She plays on the pianoforte, sings, dances, and is mistress of every Maneuver in the amorous contest that can enhance the coming pleasure; is of the middle stature, fine auburn hair, dark eyes and very inviting countenance, which ever seems to beam delight and love. In bed she is all the heart can wish, or eyes admires every limb is symmetry, every action under cover truly amorous; her price two pounds.

Jack Harris, who gave his name to the publication, was head waiter at the Shakespeare's Head pub. But he was a mere prop, paid commission by the brains behind the venture, a drunken Irish poet called Samuel Derrick who charged his whores a fifth of their income. Derrick, once described by James Boswell, Dr Johnson's biographer, as 'a little blackguard pimping dog', had reps all over London, greeting girls arriving from the countryside to seek their fortune in the capital.

Being a prostitute in the West End has always been particularly precarious. Clients, even those from the most responsible professions, are not always responsible. Occasionally they are as psychopathic as Dr Neill Cream, a Canadian medic who poisoned a number of London prostitutes with strychnine. Cream was nearly caught before he had really started. His first victim, an Ellen Donworth, had time to blurt out to friends while writhing in agony: 'That gentleman with whiskers and a top hat gave me a drink twice out of a bottle with white stuff in it!'

Cream left the capital but in 1892 returned to London, this time taking lodgings in the West End at Edward's Hotel, near Euston. He met a Louisa Harris by Trafalgar Square, spent the night with her in a hotel on Soho's Berwick Street, and generously gave her two pills to 'improve' her complexion and five shillings to go to the Oxford Music Hall, arranging to meet her there later. Harris cleverly refused to take the pills and threw them away. Cream failed to show, for he assumed she was dead.

Deluded by his own powers, he went to the police to complain they were harassing him over what he called 'the strychnine murders', including that of Louisa Harris. This the officers thought odd, given that he was not a suspect and she was not one of the victims. The police realized they were onto something and printed her name in newspaper stories about the murders. When Harris saw it she realized she was his next intended target and went to the police who arrested Cream. After the victims were exhumed he was found guilty and hanged at Newgate as a screaming mob 5,000 strong waited outside, upset that public hangings had been abolished.

Nevertheless, London's reddest lights continued to shine in Soho throughout the nineteenth and twentieth centuries. The French writer Hyppolite Taine, walking through the area in the 1860s, wrote how he was continually stopped by 'harlots' asking for a glass of gin. Around the same time the great Russian author Fyodor Dostoevsky was shocked walking down Haymarket to see mothers with their daughters looking for clients. Then there was James

Greenwood, author of the *Seven Curses of London*, who in 1869 found Soho filled with street-walkers and counted 152 brothels.

The arrival of the next century didn't seem to make much difference. In 1913 police raided the premises of Queenie Gerald, a Haymarket brothel-keeper, and found her in the bathroom with two girls aged seventeen and eighteen. She was giving them a bath, so she claimed, but when the police searched the flat they found a revolver, whip, cane and a large chunk of money, which led them to believe Queenie was living off immoral earnings. A jail sentence followed.

Once the Great War began in 1914 prostitution increased to meet the demands of soldiers on leave. The *Weekly Despatch* was horrified, and told the story of a young officer staying at a hotel in Regent Street who while walking to Piccadilly Circus station was accosted sixteen times – mostly by children, *pace* Stead. To combat this, the moral guardians of the Women Police Volunteers and the Women's Patrols roamed the West End breaking up copulators, warning them about their actions.

These organizations had wartime powers to curfew working girls and even to search their houses for soldiers, but cynics pointed out that their ranks were augmented by no shortage of voyeurs. The army was equally naive, handing soldiers leaflets which warned that 'your duty cannot be done unless your health is sound. Keep constantly on your guard against any excesses'. Despite such measures, VD among troops in Britain exceeded 100,000, leading many to remark that the authorities should have handed out condoms rather than lectures.

Between the two world wars levels of prostitution soared in the West End. The main red light areas were Shepherd Market, the secluded enclave with an oddly village-like atmosphere near Hyde Park Corner, and Piccadilly, habited, according to one officer, by 'lower type of prostitutes, quite indiscriminate in their choice of client, and persistent thieves'. There was also Maddox Street, off Regent Street, dominated by French prostitutes who, according to Scotland Yard's Superintendent Cole, were 'a colony among themselves, clean and businesslike, who although persistent in their soliciting rarely cause trouble by committing larcenies or getting involved in disputes among themselves.' And where the prostitutes weren't French, they often claimed to be, obliged to assume continental mores as the British weren't turned on by sex in English, although their Gallicity often went no further than slinging back half a bottle of Pernod at the French House on Dean Street.

After American GIs arrived in the West End during the Second World War the number of local prostitutes doubled. The *New York Times* told its readers how the area around Leicester Square was an 'open market', and even though the number of convictions for soliciting fell, because it was easier to hide in the blackout, women came from all over Britain to walk the streets, hustle in hotel lobbies or hang loose in West End clubs and bars. As Billy Hill, the Soho gangland boss, explained in his memoirs: 'Good time girls became brazen tarts, ordinary wives became good time girls. A pair of nylons could buy a woman's body, a diamond ring could buy her for life – or as long as you wanted.'

Just as the Women Police Volunteers and the Women's Patrols had patrolled the streets, their moral truncheons poised, during the Great War, so the Public Morality Council took the moral high ground this time. Two of their officers went walkabout around Piccadilly Circus one day and were accosted thirty-five times over one stretch of 100 yards. It was not just the notion of sex for sale to which they objected, it was the way the cattle market was conducted. Prostitutes would sidle up to prospective clients, mostly those from the uniformed masses, and grab their insignia to see how much they were likely able to afford. The jokes didn't help. 'Heard the one about the new utility knickers? One Yank and they're off,' was a favourite. Nor did the shortage of rubber from war-torn Malaya allow for an ample supply of condoms.

When the Messina brothers ran Soho vice in the 1940s and 1950s the street girls worked particularly hard. Each street shift began at four o'clock in the afternoon and finished at six the following morning. Often their proceedings, which took place in seedy West End flats, were interrupted by men with cameras who would burst in and take shots that could be used for black-mailing punters. But most of the time the girls were clock-watching, for they were bound by the ten-minute rule which stipulated that each client had ten minutes to do his business, after which he would have to go. It meant that no punter was able to demonstrate the kind of sexual prowess, eleven minutes, say, that would have floored any of the Messina brothers. It also meant the Messinas made stashes of money by having their girls cavorting with as many clients as possible. The record was held by Marthe Watts, who managed forty-nine men on VE Day, or rather VD Day.

The war over, the girls could still be found on practically every street around Piccadilly Circus: Air, Archer, Beak, Brewer, Glasshouse, Sackville,

Swallow ... what the *News of the World* called London's 'naughty square mile' or 'the square mile of vice'. Many were the men who now flocked to these lively parts of the West End to research the phenomenon. Alfred Kinsey, the American biologist who had founded the Institute for Sex Research at Indiana University – the popular press predictably dubbed him a 'sexpert' – toured the West End one night in 1955 and was shocked to count as many as a thousand prostitutes plying their trade. In a book on the phenomenon entitled *The Shame of A City*, John Gosling and Douglas Warner noted how 'in doorways and alleys from the edge of Notting Hill in the west down Bayswater Road, through the park to Piccadilly, and eastwards to Stepney, the curious investigator could expect to be accosted every few yards. Everywhere lines of willing prostitutes, often accompanied by scented poodles, tootling their distinctive mating call: "Short time, dearie?"'

*The Shame of A City* appeared in 1960, a year after the Street Offences Act cleared away the prostitutes. Girls convicted of soliciting would now have to pay hefty fines. They responded by fleeing indoors, literally overnight. Shabby properties on Old Compton Street and Frith Street suddenly became home to scores of 'models', the nameplates exuding a European flavour, for sex in those days was still perceived by the British to be a continental affair.

A new take on Harris's *List of Ladies* even appeared, produced by Frederick Charles Shaw from premises in Greek Street. He called it *The Ladies Directory* and it contained names, addresses, telephone numbers of prostitutes and their particular peccadilloes. Shaw went to the police for clarification. Were his activities within the law? The police wouldn't commit themselves. But as soon as he published they prosecuted him – for 'conspiring to effect a public mischief', the theoretical maximum penalty: life. Shaw was convicted, but given only two years. He appealed on the grounds that there had been no such law when he committed the offence but the House of Lords upheld the ruling.

Around Soho's Great Windmill Street, where the lights continued to shine red, there was a new phenomenon for the 1960s: the clip joint. In the doorway an attractive girl would pout and preen, hoping to entice inside gullible men who could be relieved of large sums of money for the chance of talking to a member of the opposite sex. The girl would arrange for the man to follow her to a particular address. She would leave and then he would go, but when he arrived no one knew anything about a girl. Or, once in the club, a girl would invite the dupe to buy her a drink, often water with a hint – a tiny hint – of champagne, marked up to an extortionate price that in a nearby pub would buy twenty of the same. If the client refused to pay when the hefty bill arrived the atmosphere would turn nasty. If he tried to leave he would find his way blocked by a large man or two. The threats of violence were not exaggerated and were often followed by a trip to the nearest bank or, after 1981, the nearest cash machine.

Then there was the blue film racket. Customers would pay good money to watch what they thought were going to be hot, red-blooded, blue romps, only to be shown non-naughty, nudist camps where as *The Illustrated Book of Sexual Records* explained, 'the hero and heroine end up holding hands as the sun sets on yet another game of volleyball'.

Some film clubs were more authentic, more artistic, than others. At the Compton Cinema Club, 60–62 Old Compton Street, Michael Klinger and Tony Tenser used only the finest talents. So George Harrison Marks, the celebrated photographer, directed *Naked As Nature Intended*, starring his wife, Pamela Green, one of the leading pin-ups of the period. The Compton gradually began screening more salacious material. In 1977 they staged a rare showing of Pasolini's controversial *Salò, 120 Days of Sodom*, derided by some critics as the most disgusting film ever made.

Set in a Fascist town in 1944, *Salò* tells the story of four men who collect a group of teenage virgins of both sexes from the local town in order to rape and abuse them. Much pressure was put on the British Board of Film Classification to sanitise the film, but once the censor had declined to do so (on aesthetic grounds) the film could not be shown at mainstream cinemas and was available only to private cinema clubs, such as the Compton. The rulings on the film regarding the obscenity laws remained unclear, and shortly after it opened police raided the Compton, charging the owner with keeping a disorderly house. Every scene that could be construed as obscene was then removed before the film was shown again.

The 1959 Street Offences Act led to the opening of a number of strip clubs. The best known of these was Paul Raymond's Raymond's Revue Bar, where topless and eventually naked dancers paraded under the banner of 'glamour review', rather than striptease. Raymond was soon targeted by the authorities who wanted to clamp down on Soho sleaze. Their main objections were Revue Bar acts such as Bonnie Bell the Ding Dong Girl who danced clad in little bells which punters were encouraged to ring as she called out 'Dinner time . . . supper time'. Yet Raymond's Revue Bar survived to become the socially acceptable face of Soho sleaze, a popular nightspot for clubbers, especially out-of-town football fans.

Another of the new risqué 1960s clubs was Murray's on Beak Street where the guests occasionally included Princess Margaret, and the acts Christine Keeler and Mandy Rice-Davies. Keeler later recalled how her main task was to 'walk around naked in a low-lit room with deep-red carpets and gilt furniture.' Then there was the Windmill Theatre. It was neither a clip joint nor a strip club. A former cinema, it could boast a long and colourful, even somewhat racy, history. It was here in the 1920s that Laura Henderson displayed near-naked girls, mostly in statue-like poses, clutching a feather to hide any glimpse of pubic hair that may have induced apoplexy in the spectator. The girls dared not move, for as far as the omnipotent Lord Chamberlain, the theatre censor, was concerned: 'If it moves, it's rude,' and he had the power to close the place down. When London's theatres were forced to shut briefly at the start of the Second World War the Windmill was one of the first to reopen, and it stayed open throughout the war, consequently boasting proudly: 'We never closed,' which was reworked by detractors, mindful of their reputation, as 'We never clothed.'

Despite the whiff of glamour, the local sex industry was more seedy than sophisticated, laced with the fear of casual violence, an atmosphere expertly evoked by Michael Powell in the 1960 film *Peeping Tom*. One location was the newsagent's on the corner of Rathbone Street and Percy Street in Fitzrovia where suited gents bought 'glamour shots' of partly clothed women. Above the newsagent's the film's protagonist took photographs of models – that was when he was not carrying out murders which, chillingly, he commits while filming the death throes of his victims. The murders take place on Newman Passage, the spooky dog-leg alleyway between Newman Street and Rathbone Street which George Orwell had featured in *1984* and which the West End Chronicler Julian Maclaren-Ross nicknamed Jekyll and Hyde Alley, 'where one sometimes guided girls in order to become better acquainted'.

## PICCADILLY POLARI

Meanwhile the Uranians continued to walk on the wild side, particularly around Piccadilly Circus, before the laws on homosexuality were eased in the 1960s. A favourite spot was the Alhambra Music Hall in Leicester Square, long a haunt of prostitutes of both sexes, or the bars of nearby theatres such as Daly's, also on Leicester Square. One regular customer was Roger Casement, the notorious early twentieth-century spy (or freedom fighter, depending on one's political persuasion), who after a night's cruising would note in his diary the age, nationality and penis size of his contacts, and how much he had paid.

The sumptuous Café Royal on Regent Street was particularly popular. Here men would make eye contact with other men, and the two interested parties would then wander off to a shadowed area where more intimate contact could follow. As Thomas Burke put it in 1922, the Café Royal was the home of 'queer creatures ... hermaphrodites with side-whiskers and painted eye-lashes ... things in women's clothes that slide cunning eyes upon other women. Male dancers who walk like fugitives from the City of the Plain. Hard featured ambassadors from Lesbos and Sodom.'

For those on tighter budgets there was the first floor of the Lyons' Corner House on Coventry Street (what is now Planet Hollywood), renowned for its magnificent frieze, marble décor and bar – the Long Bar – that ran the entire length of the room. The Long Bar was male-only and the clientele an engaging mix of prim civil servants in starched collars, pin-striped suits and bowler hats, exotically dressed queens, and some who fell into both camps. Fittingly it was here in 1932 that a new song was premiered: 'Make Way, Boys – Here Comes a Sailor.'

Deeper into Soho was the Au Chat Noir, 72 Old Compton Street, where in the 1930s the outrageously camp Quentin Crisp and friends spent 'night after loveless night buying each other cups of tea, combing each other's hair and trying on each other's lipsticks'. Crisp, who displayed a haughtiness worthy of the actress Margaret Rutherford in her prime, tried to find a lover, unsuccessfully, and later explained how he 'disliked the coarseness of situations in which I found myself. Courtship consisted of walking along the street with a man who had my elbow in a merciless grip until we came to a dark doorway. Then he said "This'll do." These were the only words of tenderness that were uttered to me.'

A secret code enabled those who wanted to indulge in homosex to communicate in public, to flirt in a made-up tongue. The code went by the name of 'Polari', a take on the nineteenth-century fairground slang, Parlyaree, a word itself etymologically similar to the French *parler* – to speak. Polari, which was also used by prostitutes and beggars, was not a language but a long list of regularly used words based on cod French, Yiddish and Romani. 'Bona', unsurprisingly, meant good or nice; 'riah', palindromically, hair. 'Eek' was face, and 'chicken' young boy. 'Basket' was used in the way that 'lunchbox' would be in the 1990s. Remarkably, Polari was heard regularly on the radio in the 1950s on the comedy show *Round the Horne* during which Kenneth Williams and Co. would suddenly burst into a monologue along the lines of 'Ooh vada well the omee-palone ajax who just trolled in. She's got nanti taste, dear, cod lally-drags and the naff riah but what a bona eek. Fantabulosa!', roughly translatable as 'Have a good look at that homosexual nearby who just came in. He's got no taste, awful trousers and tasteless hair, but what a lovely face. Absolutely fabulous!'

Polari wasn't enough to ward off the police in 1955 when they raided the Fitzroy Tavern, then the West End's most exciting pub, and found it filled with some fifty male prostitutes. As officers noted in their report, 'for the most part its occupants were quite obvious male homosexuals who dyed their hair and rouged their cheeks and behaved in an effeminate manner. The other occupants were sailors, soldiers and marines. There can be very little doubt that this house was conducted in a most disorderly and disgusting fashion.' Polari would have probably remained an obscure slang but for Morrissey's rousing 1990 single 'Piccadilly Palare' with its esoteric chorus: 'So bona to vada, oh you, your lovely eek and your lovely riah' [so good to look at, you, your lovely face and lovely hair], which must have confounded a million fans.

The mid 1960s decriminalization of homosexuality didn't make life safer for its practitioners. They were still prone to the kind of risks that mostly eluded straights. For instance, in August 1980 Billy Sutherland, a twenty-seven-year-old, hard-drinking, male prostitute from Edinburgh met a man in a West End pub. After parting at Leicester Square tube Sutherland approached the man again at the ticket booth, explaining he had nowhere to go. The man invited Sutherland back to his house in Cricklewood but when they arrived he strangled him.

Later that autumn the murderer picked up a tramp near Tottenham Court Road station, took him back to Cricklewood, strangled him, cut up the body and buried it under the floorboards. That wasn't the end of the slayings. On 10 November that year the killer met a Douglas Stewart in Dean Street's Golden Lion. The pub was notorious in the 1950s for attracting men arriving on a Friday night looking for a bit of weekend fun, maybe to pick up a serviceman on weekend leave. Bizarrely, when some of the regulars got married they would invite to the wedding their 'special' friend. But no such social niceties for this man. He took Stewart back to Cricklewood, and probably intended to do away with him as well, except he was stymied when Stewart escaped his clutches and contacted the police. Officers wrote off the incident as a homosexual tiff, and the murderer was free to strike again.

This was no ordinary murderer, but Dennis Nilsen, soon to become one of Britain's most lethal serial killers. At the time Nilsen, a former policeman, was a respectable civil servant by day, working in the Job Centre off Charing Cross Road. That December of 1980, in between murders, he considerately brought into work for the staff Christmas Party a huge iron cooking pot to hold the punch. Not that he told fellow workers it was the pot in which he had cooked the heads of his victims.

Several more times Nilsen picked up men in West End bars or streets, convinced them to return with him, strangled them, and buried the corpse under the floorboards. It was to stop them leaving him, he later explained. Sometimes he dismembered the body, and one victim was helpfully adorned with a tattoo around his neck that read: 'cut here'.

After moving across north London to Cranley Gardens late in 1981 Nilsen murdered three more men. He met his fifteenth and last victim, Stephen Sinclair, on 26 January 1983 at the Royal George pub in Goslett Yard, off Charing Cross Road. The two men went for a burger at McDonald's by Tottenham Court Road station and back to Cranley Gardens where Nilsen strangled him with a tie. The murders ended in February 1983 after tenants complained about Nilsen's drains. Workmen uncovered the manhole and let loose a terrible stench. When police found what looked like human remains one officer asked Dennis Nilsen, jokingly, 'Where's the rest of the body?', to which Nilsen replied: 'in two plastic bags in the wardrobe next door. I'll show you.' He was found guilty at the Old Bailey of six counts of murder and two of attempted murder.

## SCHOOLS FOR SCANDAL

In the swish parts of the West End sex has often taken place behind stucco sophistication unlit in red. A paramour popular with deep-walleted men in the early post-war years was Ethel Margaret Whigham, the Duchess of Argyll, Debutante of the Year in 1930 and the subject of Cole Porter's song 'You're the Top'. In 1963 the duke found photographs of the duchess wearing a three-stringed pearl necklace and a wide smile fellating a man in the bathroom of her Mayfair town house at 48 Upper Grosvenor Street. The photo had been taken so that the man's head was not visible. Nevertheless, the duke sued for divorce, and the public was gripped by the debate over the identity of the 'headless man'.

Expert opinion narrowed it down to two possibilities: the Tory Cabinet Minister Lord Duncan Sandys and the actor Douglas Fairbanks Jnr. Sandys, alarmed by the thought of a sex scandal, said he would resign if it were proved to be him. Prime minister Harold Macmillan hired the legal expert Lord Denning to solve the mystery, and Denning came up with an ingenious solution. He invited Sandys, Fairbanks and an outsider, Sigismund von Braun, the brother of the Nazi rocket scientist Werner von Braun, to the Treasury to discuss the matter. Perhaps he should have added a few more names given that the duke had told the divorce court how the duchess had been enjoying favours with eighty-eight men in all.

Nevertheless Denning solved the problem. Noting that the words 'before', 'during' and 'finished' were written on the incriminating polaroids, he ensured that each suspect signed the Treasury visitors' register. A graphologist matched the handwriting and identified Fairbanks as the culprit. Not that the public knew this at the time. Some years later it was revealed that there were two 'headless men' in the various photographs. Not only Fairbanks, but Sandys as well.

Soon there was a meatier scandal. That same year Christine Keeler, a stripper at Murray's Club, was found to be sleeping with both John Profumo, secretary of state for war, and Yevgeny Ivanov, the Soviet naval attaché. And this at the height of the Cold War, no less. Keeler was living with Stephen Ward, a West End osteopath who met her when she was parading behind a huge ostrich feather at Murray's club. He moved in lofty social circles, tending the sore backs of Elizabeth Taylor and Ike Eisenhower, and he also threw swinging parties at his Marylebone apartment, 17 Wimpole Mews. One day Ward was approached by MI5 who hoped one of his girls could act as bait to lure a Soviet officer into becoming a double agent, perhaps by taking a compromising photograph or arranging some other means of blackmail. His first opportunity to help MI5 came at a party held on 10 July that year at Lord Astor's Cliveden mansion in Buckinghamshire. The guests included the showgirl Keeler; Profumo, the War Secretary; and Ivanov, the Russian diplomat. Keeler met Profumo as she climbed naked from the swimming pool. They were soon having an affair.

When Keeler moved out of Ward's Wimpole Mews pad in 1962 another teenage girl, Mandy Rice-Davies, moved in. Events might have tailed off without further interest but for an incident on 14 December 1962 when Johnny Edgecombe, a West Indian friend of Keeler, followed her to Ward's mews apartment, where she was visiting Rice-Davies, and fired a gun at the building. Fleet Street journalists picked up on the incident and agreed to print Keeler's 'life story'. Prior to publication Ward tipped off Ivanov that he was about to make the Sundays, and he immediately made arrangements to leave London.

Profumo, concerned that news of his dalliances was to be made public, sought help from MI5. He swore that he had had no physical connection with Christine Keeler, making a statement to the House of Commons on Friday 22 March 1963 that turned out to be unfortunate: 'Miss Keeler and I were on friendly terms. There was no impropriety whatsoever in my acquaintanceship with Miss Keeler.' In private Profumo was more forthright and told one colleague: 'Who's going to believe a word of this tart?' Profumo and Harold Macmillan, the Tory prime minister, also tried to blacken the name of Andrew Roth, the journalist who had been leading the investigation into the scandal, threatening to call in the libel lawyers.

Ward was horrified about how events were panning out. Fearing prosecution for pimping, he informed Macmillan about a series of love letters Profumo had sent Keeler. The PM preferred to believe Profumo's word 'as a gentleman', but within a few months Profumo's word had changed. In June 1963 he at last admitted that he had lied to the House – that there *had* been 'impropriety' between him and Christine Keeler – and resigned from the Cabinet. Ward was charged with living off immoral earnings, and after being sent for trial at the Old Bailey took a fatal overdose. This was hardly surprising given that in the days leading up to the trial some of his well-heeled clients, worried that their names might be linked with the scandal, had phoned Ward, urging him to leave the country or cut his throat.

Ward was found guilty in his absence, and Christine Keeler was found guilty of perjury, for which she received nine months in jail. Profumo was so mortified by his behaviour he sought and gained permission from the Queen to resign from the Privy Council. He also quit West End society to perform charitable works, mostly at the Toynbee Hall mission house in Whitechapel, a rare instance of an individual leaving the bright lights of the West to taste the darkness of the East.

Christine Keeler gradually sank into oblivion. In her autobiography, *The Truth at Last*, she claimed Ward was spying for the Soviet Union and wanted her to wheedle out of Profumo information about the placing of nuclear warheads in West Germany. She also claimed that Ward tried to kill her while she was water-skiing to silence her. Mandy Rice-Davies married an Israeli businessman and opened nightclubs in Tel Aviv. She also secured her name in the *Oxford Book of Quotations* after a question from the prosecuting counsel, pointing out that Lord Astor denied having an affair with her or having even met her, elicited the response 'Well, he would, wouldn't he?' Ivanov returned to obscurity and too much drink in Moscow, dying in 1994. Many commentators have since cited this scandal as *the* scandal, crucial in bringing down the Tory government of the early 1960s and ushering in the permissive society more typically associated with that decade.

# A TWIST IN THE TALE

While Soho has long been home of the cheaper brand of prostitute, Shepherd Market, the quaint, antiquated corner hidden away in deepest Mayfair, has usually offered up a more expensive escort; a higher class of hooker.

A regular on the patch in the mid 1980s was Monica Coughlan, an Irish prostitute. At 1 a.m. on 8 September 1986 Coughlan left the Albion Hotel on Gillingham Street, Victoria, with her third client of the evening. They had just had sex in room 6a, and were about to drive back to Shepherd Market in his blue Mercedes when across the street the headlights flashed from an expensive parked car, what looked like a Daimler or Jaguar. Coughlan approached the driver's window, and after a moment's conversation she and the driver entered the hotel. The man with the Mercedes was a businessman, Aziz Kurtha. He claimed he recognized the driver of the other car as being none other than Jeffrey Archer, then deputy chairman of the Tory Party. Coughlan later explained that he had first approached her earlier that evening in Shepherd Market before going to fetch his car.

Despite countless investigations it is still hard to prove that it was Archer who met Monica Coughlan that night to have sex. Coughlan, who died in a hit-and-run accident in 2001, always maintained that Archer was the other man. 'It was over very quickly – with getting undressed and the actual sex ten minutes,' she said in court. 'Because it was over so quickly I suggested that he relax for a while and we try again. He told me he sold cars. He got dressed. He left.'

Aziz Kurtha contacted the *News of the World*, and two months later, on October 26 1986, the paper splashed the story. It included details of how Michael Stacpoole, an Archer associate, offered Coughlan an envelope stuffed with £50 notes to leave the country on Platform three of Victoria Station. On November 2 the *Daily Star* took things further, claiming that Archer had picked up Coughlan at the hotel and paid her £70 for 'perverted sex'.

Archer vigorously denied he had slept with Coughlan. He sued the *Daily Star* newspaper for libel and won £500,000 in damages. Archer's alibis for his movements that night were complex and copious. He told the libel jury that he had dined with his agent at the fashionable Le Caprice restaurant near Shepherd Market but that dinner broke up by 11 p.m. That left him with two hours to account for. Terence Baker, a theatrical agent, explained how he had arrived at Le Caprice around 10.45 p.m. and sat there for about two hours before Archer drove him home to Camberwell. But before he died in 1991 Baker told friends that he had perjured himself.

It was not until 1999 that it all started to go wrong for Archer. When he tried to stand for London mayor Ted Francis, another Archer associate, told the *News of the World* that Archer had asked him to provide a false alibi ahead of his *Daily Star* libel hearing in July 1987. Francis said he had gone along with the false alibi because he thought he was doing it to save Archer's marriage.

Archer stood down as candidate for London mayor and released a statement in which he admitted that he had asked Mr Francis to cover for him. The Conservative Party, keen to eradicate any hint of sleaze from its ranks, removed the whip from the politician. There were various accounts to call in. Tory Party leader William Hague announced: 'This is the end of politics for Jeffrey Archer. I will not tolerate behaviour like this in my party.' The *Daily Star* unsurprisingly demanded the return of £500,000 in damages – plus interest. The police then began an investigation, which resulted in Archer being jailed for perverting the course of justice and perjury.

If not the most salacious of West End sex scandals it was certainly the most costly. But then West End sex always comes at a price.

# 7

# Art

Art in Britain has long been a battle between craft and culture; between those who wish to represent things in naturalistic likeness and those who wish to represent them through their own unique vision. It is a battle that has long been inflicted on the West End: Joshua Reynolds or William Blake? Omega Workshop or the Vorticists? The elegant galleries of Mayfair or the St Martin's School of Art?

As London grew in pre-industrial times, its artistic community moved west; from the City to Covent Garden during the Stuart years and to the streets north of Charing Cross in the Georgian era. This migration meant that during the eighteenth century Leicester Square was home to both Joshua Reynolds and William Hogarth; the former establishment, the latter maverick, a division that would continually return to polarize the art world.

Reynolds, who became the first president of the Royal Academy in 1768, lived on the west side of Leicester Square at No. 47. There he built himself a 'detached gallery and painting rooms' where he entertained writers such as James Boswell, Oliver Goldsmith and Fanny Burney. Reynolds's name endures, but more for his technical skill as a portraitist than for his contribution to the capital's culture and history. With Hogarth it is the other way round.

Hogarth was a supreme caricaturist who captured London scenes, its politics and characters like no one before or since. Born in Bartholomew Close near Smithfield Market on 10 November 1697, six days after the celebration of King William III's birthday (hence his name), Hogarth first took lodgings in the West End at the sign of the Golden Ball, just north of Leicester Square in 1724. This was a West End of closely packed labyrinthine alleyways, courtyards and tenements set in a landscape that predated the wide boundary-creating roads such as Shaftesbury Avenue, Charing Cross Road, Trafalgar Square and Regent Street.

That year of 1724 Hogarth issued his first independent print, *Masquerades and Operas: The Taste of the Town*. It was a satire of the new vogue for Italian culture such as opera which Hogarth thought was un-English and was undermining intelligent discourse as well as threatening the success of theatre. The work shows a fool and a devil herding a masqued throng into Haymarket Opera House while the works of Shakespeare, Dryden and Congreve are carted away to be pulped. British artists displaced by decadent foreigners. Overhead a huge banner promotes Italian castrati, monstrosities that noble English women seemed to find irresistible.

In *Masquerades* Hogarth also attacks aristocrats with a taste for Palladian (i.e. foreign) architecture, in particular Lord Burlington, redesigner of Burlington House, the property on Piccadilly (now the Royal Academy) whose Palladian gateway fills the centre of the painting. With its gates tightly shut to passers-by, the figures of Burlington and his associates are pointing up at the preposterous statue of William Kent kitted out as a Roman Emperor, at whose feet in a deft comic touch lie the enslaved figures of Michelangelo and Raphael.

Hogarth published *Masquerades and Operas* himself, a revolutionary step. The print was a modest success and brought his name to the general public. But pirated copies abounded. This led Hogarth to begin a campaign that eventually resulted in new legislation to protect artists' work. A decade later Hogarth moved into a shop at the sign of the Golden Head at the south-eastern corner of Leicester Square. He made himself a new shop sign, a bust of Van Dyck, the Dutch artist who had settled in England, out of 'several thicknesses of cork compacted together', and on the ground floor built a studio to capture the light from the north.

Here Hogarth began to work on his many 'modern moral subjects': witty, caustic paintings and engravings conveying a moral message. The most famous of these is *The Rake's Progress*, which details in eight parts the tragic life of the irresponsible Tom Rakewell, from birth to fortune to penury, and features a number of London settings. It now resides in the John Soane Museum in Holborn.

In June 1748 Hogarth, the arch Anglophile, visited France to draw. He spent much of his time moaning about the awful food, the pathetic natives and about the buildings, which he saw fit to describe as 'all gilt and beshit'. In Calais, on his way home, Hogarth paused to sketch the ancient gateway built by the English (the town was in English hands from 1347–1558). As he began to draw he was arrested and marched off to the Governor's office, where he was accused of being a spy. Following exchanges that verged on the farcial Hogarth was deported to England.

Incensed, Hogarth returned to Leicester Square to paint the mocking O *The Roast Beef of Old England (The Gate of Calais)*, which savages French claims of superiority and promotes supposedly English virtues such as reliability. Hogarth believed that roast beef was the food of real men, and was a founding member of the Sublime Society of Beefsteaks. The Frenchmen in his picture, effeminate, impoverished, servile, are stock comic French characters: servants in clogs; starving soldiers spilling their soup, all transfixed by the sight of the succulent English beef on its way to the local hotel to feed British visitors. But Hogarth didn't always need to go to France to find inspiration. While having his hair cut one day in Joseph Watkins, barbershop at 121 Tottenham Court Road he saw a boy drop his pie and gravy on the ground. With the shaving soap dripping from his face, Hogarth rushed out to sketch the boy's dismay fresh.

In 1749 Hogarth bought a country retreat in Chiswick, but continued to work occasionally in Leicester Square, which was where he died of an aneurysm on 25 October 1764. He is buried in St Nicholas's church, Chiswick, ironically the same church as William Kent.

## VISIONS OF ANGELS

A few years before the death of Hogarth the West End saw the birth of its first genius. William Blake was born in his father's hosiery shop at 28 Broad Street (now Broadwick Street), Soho, on 28 November 1757. Soho then lay on the extreme northern edge of London, with nothing but fields and market gardens beyond, so the young Blake was able to roam freely in the countryside. Unfortunately, the house was built near an old burial ground, Pesthouse Close, which though filled in by 1733 still exuded a stench that drew regular complaints from residents.

Considered too sensitive to attend school, the young Blake was taught at home by his mother, who introduced him in a rather chaotic way to Latin, Greek, Hebrew, Shakespeare, Milton and the Bible. Blake took up an apprenticeship as an engraver in Holborn, but he continued to live in Soho until his wedding, at which point his father, enraged at his marrying an uneducated woman, drove him out of the house.

The Blakes moved half a mile to Green Street (now Orange Street) by Leicester Square. And it was while living there in the summer of 1783 that Blake witnessed a rare phenomenon – a fiery blue meteorite with an orange tail that shot over the London skies. It lit up much of London and inspired a number of his paintings as well as the line in the poem 'Tyger': 'When the stars threw down their spears/And water'd heaven with their tears.'

Blake later lived on Soho's Poland Street, in a narrow house of four storeys and a basement with a single front and back room on each floor. There he achieved his aim of uniting painting and poetry into a new kind of art form by engraving his own book of verse. The process was painstaking and immaculately technical, and the secrets of it came to him, he once explained, in a dream featuring his late brother, Robert.

Blake's first step, as Peter Ackroyd explained in his biography, was to cut out plates from a large sheet of copper using a hammer and chisel. He then would make a rough design in chalk, and using a camel-hair brush paint the words and images on the plate with a mixture of salad oil and candle-grease. This combination was then strong enough to resist the next mixture needed to complete the work: aqua fortis of vinegar, salt armoniack, baysalt and vert de griz, which bit into the surrounding plate for three or four hours. The most remarkable part was that Blake had to write the words backwards with a quill pen so that when the image was printed they would be the correct way round.

Blake mentions the process in his epic poem 'Jerusalem': 'I must Create a System, or be enslav'd by another Man's. I will not Reason & Compare: my business is to Create.' The main work he created in this new form was 'Songs of Innocence' (1789), which was regularly reproduced on the printing press right up to his death, no two copies ever containing the poems in the same order.

Around the corner to Poland Street, at 9 Marlborough Street, a site now covered by Marks and Spencer, lived Thomas Butts. He was a civil servant who became Blake's most important patron, the only thing that stood between 'the greatest designer in England and the workhouse', according to the artist Samuel Palmer. Butts, like Blake, was a Swedenborgian, and was evidently a keen supporter of the Swedenborgians' belief that men should share a number of wives, given that the 1801 census shows that he lived here with nineteen females. It was Butts who famously went to visit Blake when he was living in Hercules Buildings, Lambeth, and found him and his wife, Catherine, in the garden naked, reading verses from *Paradise Lost* to each other. 'Come in,' cried Blake, 'It's only Adam and Eve, you know.'

When Blake was living in Felpham, Sussex, he would send Butts letter-poems such as the one Peter Ackroyd used as the title of his first chapter of his biography of Blake:

> 'O! why was I born with a different face?
> Why was I not born like the rest of my race?
> When I look, each one starts; when I speak, I offend;
> Then I'm silent and passive, and lose every friend.'

Blake and Butts argued in 1810 and after that no more payments were made, a contributory factor to the poverty in which the sixty-nine-year-old Blake died in Fountain Court by the Strand in August 1827.

Blake spent most of his life in the West End, living at various different local addresses on Orange Street and South Molton Street as well as Poland Street and Broad(wick) Street. He often socialized at the home of the Reverend Henry Matthews at 27 Rathbone Place, Fitzrovia, where he would sing his poems, such as the preface to 'Milton', since renamed 'Jerusalem' (it has no connection to the epic poem of the same name), now the unofficial English national anthem, in a melody unknown, the famous version not written until eighty years after Blake died.

Blake was not fêted during his lifetime. As he was considered by many to be merely a tradesman, few people bothered to keep his letters, and most dismissed him as a crank. *Songs of Innocence and Experience* sold fewer than twenty copies, and only one poem made the anthologies – 'Tyger'. There were few exhibitions of his work, and one that was held at his former Broad Street home received few visitors. By the time Blake died he was already forgotten, but his memory was kept alive by a group of anachronistic early nineteenth-century poets and artists called the Antients: Samuel Palmer, George Richmond, John Giles.

He might have remained an obscure figure but for the efforts of Alexander Gilchrist, an art critic and neighbour of Thomas Carlyle, who in the 1860s began to write a biography of Blake, and found that some of the Antients were still alive and willing to pass on their memories. Gilchrist died before he could complete his work but the biography was finished by his wife, Anne Burrows, and promoted by the Pre-Raphaelites.

As establishment as Blake was maverick was the artist Joshua Reynolds. Blake met Reynolds in 1779 at the Royal Academy schools where he was a student. They soon clashed. Reynolds told Blake that he should tone down his extravagance and correct his drawing. Blake believed that Reynolds's insistence on 'copying nature' was to become a slave to memory, whereas he preferred the vigour of his own imagination. Rather than gazing at an object and painting 'backward' from memory, Blake relied upon looking. He believed that if he stared at an object he could enter it, that it would begin to converse with him. He railed against art blighted by the marketplace. Of all its branches he despised most of all portraiture. 'Only Portrait Painting [was] applauded & rewarded by the Rich and Great. Reynolds and Gainsborough Blotted and Blurred one against the other & Divided all the English World between them.'

In 1808 Blake wrote a damning response to Reynolds's *Discourses on Art*: 'Having spent the Vigour of my Youth and Genius under the Oppression of Sir Joshua and his Gang of Cunning Hired Knaves, Without Employment, and as much as could possibly be Without Bread, the Reader must expect to Read in all my Remarks on these Books Nothing but Indignation and Resentment.'

Whereas William Blake is readily identifiable with Soho, J. M. W. Turner is harder to pin down as a West End figure. Nevertheless, Turner made his home in Marylebone in 1799, taking lodgings on Harley Street, and opening his own gallery in 1804 at what is now 23 Queen Anne Street. It was there that he unveiled works which have since sealed his reputation as Britain's greatest painter: *Thomson's Æolian Harp* (1809); *Snow Storm: Hannibal and his Army Crossing the Alps* (1812); and *Dido and Æneas* (1814). In 1802 Turner was elected to the Royal Academy, the youngest person ever to receive such an honour. Five years later he was made the Academy's Professor of Perspective.

Turner was meticulous and studious. In 1807 he began to produce copious worksheets he called *Liber Studiorum*, in which he recorded his major important compositions. He also began to promote a group of steel-plate engravers who in turn supported his work in their publications. Turner developed a network of discerning patrons drawn mostly from the new mercantile and industrial classes. Concerned about his posthumous reputation, he bequeathed the contents of his Queen Anne Street gallery to the nation.

# THE BROTHERHOOD

The land north of Oxford Street continued to attract inspired painters throughout the nineteenth century. On Charlotte Street digs were shared by W. P. Frith (best known for *Derby Day*, 1858); the wonderfully named Augustus Egg, an associate of Dickens, and Richard Dadd, responsible for the intricately fantastic *Fairy-Feller's Master Stroke* (1855–64). Dadd was an unexceptional figure until he caught sunstroke in Egypt. It must have caused an imbalance in his mind, for one day while walking with his father in the Surrey woods Dadd Jnr. stabbed Dadd Snr. to death. He was arrested a few days later in France (after a fellow coach passenger awoke to find Dadd's hands round his throat), tried and found to be insane, which saw him incarcerated, first in Bedlam, then in Broadmoor. When the police searched his Charlotte Street studio they found painted on the wall behind a screen portraits of Egg and Frith – both with their throats cut.

As the Victorian era proceeded intellectuals and artists began to react vehemently against industrialization, mass production and the way the machine continued to impinge on everyday life. For every tub-thumping capitalist reliant on rapid technological advances, there was a nostalgic romantic advocating handicrafts over mass production, traditional decoration over metallic brutality. Within the arts this was manifested in the revival of English vernacular architecture, embodied by William Morris's Red House in Bexleyheath and the Pre-Raphaelite school of artists.

The Pre-Raphaelites grew around a loose collection of London-based artists, particularly William Holman Hunt and Dante Gabriel Rossetti. In August 1848 Hunt moved into a studio at 46 (then 7) Cleveland Street, and began work on the painting *Christ and the Two Marys*, although he had to stop temporarily when out of a twelve-foot palm leaf he had brought back from Kew Gardens popped a bat that had been nestling therein and dropped down his friend's back.

Sharing the Cleveland Street studio with Hunt was the multi-talented Dante Gabriel Rossetti, born locally, despite his Italianate name, and equally adept at poetry and painting. Rossetti began work on *The Girlhood of Mary Virgin* at Cleveland Street in 1848, painting in oils with watercolour brushes onto a canvas so laden with white the surface became like cardboard, a technique that assured a deep luminosity.

*The Girlhood of Mary Virgin* is steeped in religious imagery. It features a seven-thorned briar (the seven-branched candelabrum of Biblical lore), a cross in the lattice work, a dove (the Holy Spirit) and a red cloak (Christ's robe). These surround a scene in which the Virgin embroiders a lily under the watchful eye of St Anne while her father, St Joachim, prunes a vine. Christina, Rossetti's sister, sat as Mary; his mother as Anne; and Old Williams, the family handyman, uncomfortably as Joachim.

Rossetti wanted to create more paintings in that style, and discussed the idea not just with Holman Hunt but with John Millais, a Bloomsbury-born artist who shared his views. The three objected to the triviality and vulgarity of the Royal Academy. They wanted to set up a group of artists that would create a body of work similar in brightness of colour, attention to detail and honest simplicity to the period of Italian painting prior to Raphael Sanzio (1483–1520). They wanted to follow in the footsteps of the Nazarenes, a group of German artists based in Rome dedicated to religious art. All were influenced by John Ruskin's influential 1843 work, *Modern Painters*, which advocated painting figures using models and landscapes on location rather than in the studio (which wasn't always the best policy, given the English weather).

Rossetti, Hunt and Millais drew up a list of heroes, of which Jesus Christ was top, and a list of aims which ran:

1. To have genuine ideas to express.
2. To study nature attentively, so as to know how to express it.
3. To sympathize with what is direct and serious and heartfelt in previous art, to the exclusion of what is conventional and self-parading and learned by rote.
4. To produce thoroughly good pictures and statues.

The next task was to name their new group. Rossetti wanted to include the then fashionable term 'Early Christian', but Hunt objected and proposed 'Pre-Raphaelite'. Rossetti added the word 'Brotherhood' as he wanted the society to be secret, in line with the Italian political group the Carbonari.

In March 1849 the Pre-Raphaelites staged their first exhibition at the Free Exhibition of Modern Art, near Hyde Park Corner. On display was *The Girlhood of Mary Virgin* which Rossetti had signed 'PRB' to maintain the society's air of mystery. The critics were not particularly impressed, but the Dowager Marchioness of Bath bought the work for £80. Other early paintings were also derided. Holman Hunt's medieval costume drama of death,

*Rienzi*, failed to excite many people initially, and Charles Dickens dismissed Millais's *Christ in the House of His Parents (The Carpenter's Shop)* as 'mean, odious, revolting and repulsive'. But Millais's *Lorenzo and Isabella* (1848), loosely based on the Keats poem 'Isabella', soon came to be appreciated as a fascinating study of tension and simmering violence.

The Pre-Raphaelite Brotherhood fell apart when Millais, whom Ruskin had taken under his wing, was elected to be an Associate of the previously despised Royal Academy, and Holman Hunt left for Palestine. But no group of British artists has bequeathed so detailed, elaborate and sparkling a body of work.

# GREENERY-YALLERY GROSVENOR GALLERY

By the 1870s the Pre-Raphaelites had been supplanted by the Aesthetic Movement. Its leaders extended their predecessors' romanticism into a manifesto that triumphed *l'art pour l'art* – art for art's sake – and in the West End this was reflected in a number of unusual new stores. In 1875 Arthur Lazenby Liberty opened the Liberty's store at 218a Regent Street, selling Japanese prints, Chinese porcelain, silks and other goods from the Orient. Outside shop hours Liberty created the Japanese-style sets for the first run of Gilbert and Sullivan's *The Mikado*. He also engaged William Morris to design prints, and enlisted the painter James McNeill Whistler to help him create what became known as *le style Liberty*. This was a blend of Art Nouveau, Arts and Crafts, and Art Deco created by English craftsmen which included printed cotton cloths and much of the so-called 'Tudorbethan' furniture filling the new villas springing up in the London suburbs.

Success enabled Liberty to expand, and soon the store was the most fashionable place to shop in London. But Liberty's was also constantly prone to ridicule from detractors. Oscar Wilde described a dress designed by E. W. Godwin as 'looking like a badly made salad', while others poked fun at the shop being staffed not by assistants but by 'cicerones', who only spoke when approached and were expected to know the names of all the shop's customers, especially Nicholas II, the last Tsar of Russia, who ordered new furnishings for the imperial Russian palace from Liberty's in 1914 only a few years before his assassination.

Further west from Liberty's was William Morris's shop-cum-showroom at 449 Oxford Street. Morris, a polymath able to veer from epic poetry to fiery socialist rhetoric to concepts of medieval history, often in the same sentence, opened the premises in 1877 for The Firm, his design company. The Firm specialized in painted glass, embroidery, tapestry, carpets and wall-hangings, decorations that were unknown in London at the time. Again, as at Liberty's, many customers came from the new Bohemian-friendly estates such as Bedford Park in Acton, London's first garden village. Another customer was Oscar Wilde, who bought William Morris wallpaper for his Tite Street home in Chelsea, wallpaper which popped and split when poked.

In 1877 London got its first independent art gallery – the Grosvenor Gallery at 135–137 New Bond Street. This was a major breakthrough for London artists, especially for those aligned with the Aesthetic Movement. For whereas securing a place in an exhibition at the prestigious Royal Academy was based on approval by a committee, inclusion at the Grosvenor was based solely upon the invitation of the proprietor, Sir Coutts Lindsay, and he was more favourable to experimental artists than the staid Academy.

The new gallery was painted green and yellow, colours the Victorians thought not only unmanly but a sure sign of sexual depravity, especially once Aesthetic Movement members began appearing in public carrying colour-co-ordinated flowers. Its opening ceremony was attended by major figures from the worlds of art and literature, including Oscar Wilde and John Ruskin. The latter, mentor to many in the world of British art, summed up his thoughts about the new gallery in his monthly letter published under the banner *Fors Clavigera* (Latin – roughly translatable as 'fortune bearing a key'), which he addressed optimistically to 'the workmen and labourers of Great Britain'. Ruskin praised the work of Edward Burne-Jones as 'simply the only art-work at the present produced in England which will be received by the future as "classic" in its kind' and then turned derogatorily to Whistler:

For Mr. Whistler's own sake, no less than for the protection of the purchaser, Sir Coutts Lindsay ought not to have admitted works into the gallery in which the ill-educated conceit of the artist so nearly approached the aspect of wilful imposture. I have seen, and heard, much of Cockney impudence before now; but never expected to hear a coxcomb ask two hundred guineas for flinging a pot of paint in the public's face.

Whistler was mortified. He sued for libel. But though he won damages – of a farthing – the trial ruined him financially. Four years later Gilbert and Sullivan sent up the scene and the type of people who fuelled it in their comic opera *Patience*, a memorable quote from which runs: 'A pallid and thin young man / A haggard and lank young man / A greenery-yallery, Grosvenor Gallery / Foot-in-the-grave young man!' The Grosvenor Gallery closed in 1890, by which time West End art had turned to new horizons.

## 'COME ON! SET FIRE TO THE LIBRARY SHELVES!'

New departures in art often take shape when those of like mind club together to form a group. Some – the Pre-Raphaelites, Cubists, Futurists – win international acclaim; others remain inexorably local. Such was the case in the West End of the early twentieth century with the Fitzroy Street Group, the Vorticists, Unit One, and the Euston Road School.

The Fitzroy Street Group was the brainchild of Walter Sickert, who had worked as Whistler's assistant. In 1883 Sickert was entrusted with taking Whistler's *Portrait of the Artist's Mother* to Paris. There he met Degas, whose work had a profound influence on him. Sickert lived intermittently in Dieppe, northern France, and Venice, but he also spent time in London, in Fitzrovia, where at 8 Fitzroy Street in 1907 he began hosting 'At Homes' – Saturday afternoon tea parties that the critics were soon deriding as a very 'English' set-up. He also hired rooms at nearby No. 19 where he, Harold Gilman, Spencer Gore and other graduates, mostly from the Slade, set up the Fitzroy Street Group of artists.

The Fitzroy Street Group celebrated the minutiae of everyday domestic life in order, as Sickert explained, 'to keep up an incessant proselytising agency to accustom people to mine and other painters' work of a modern character.' Their studios were open to anyone who wanted to peruse their creations and they attracted a loyal clientele who bought works dominated by low women lounging in shabby north London bedsits next to cluttered mantelpieces. Less typical of their work, but one of their most inspired, is Malcolm Drummond's *19 Fitzrovia Street 1913–14*, now in the Laing Art Gallery, Newcastle, in which three men, their backs turned to the viewer, but evidently the local painters James Manson, Spencer Gore and Charles

Ginner, are surrounded by their own paintings, too engrossed in their own art to notice anything else.

In 1911 the Fitzroy Street Group became the Camden Town Group in honour of the then seedy, solidly working-class, inner suburb two miles to the north where some of their members lived. There they continued to observe the shabby, unloved London of canal banks, railway lines and cab stands. Sickert had a particular passion for the seamy underbelly of London life. Indeed, so great was his enthusiasm for consorting with and painting prostitutes, particularly after the murder of Emily Dimmock in the so-called 'Camden Town Murder' of 1907, that many commentators have connected him with the Jack the Ripper murders of prostitutes, and he is now better known as a favourite contender for Jack than for being an artist.

The Fitzroy Group and its Camden Town offshoot belonged to main-stream art. Modern avant-garde art arrived in Britain around that time courtesy of Roger Fry. A scion of the Bloomsbury Group, Fry organized an exhibition entitled 'Manet and the Post-Impressionists' at the Grafton Galleries in Mayfair's Grafton Street in November 1910. He coined the term 'Post-Impressionist' for the show so that he could unite under one banner the works of Cézanne, Gauguin and Van Gogh – names that the public now takes for granted but which at the time were unknown to London eyes.

Not for the first or last time in the West End artefacts not created locally but merely being displayed caused deep ructions. Visitors were shocked by the distorted shapes and brash colours of the Post-Impressionist artists. They denounced the pictures as childish and degenerate, and declared Fry insane. The critic Robert Ross even claimed the show was part of a 'wide-spread plot to destroy the whole fabric of European painting', while the writer and Arabist Wilfred Blunt moaned that the exhibition was 'either an extremely bad joke or a swindle. I am inclined to think the latter, for there is no trace of humour in it. Still less is there a trace of sense of skill or taste, good or bad, or art or cleverness. Nothing but the gross puerility which scrawls indecencies on the walls of a privy.'

Blunt was even more damning of the drawing, which he said was on the level 'of that of an untaught child of seven or eight years old', the sense of colour ('that of a tea-tray painter'), the method 'that of a schoolboy who wipes his fingers on a slate after spitting on them'. Eric Gill, the sculptor and graphic artist (creator of Gill Sans and Perpetua), was more restrained, noting how 'all the critics are tearing one another's eyes out over [the exhibition]. If you are inseparably connected with the generation from which it is a transition, then you don't like it'. There evidently was much to fear in the emotional honesty and brushstrokes full of passion of the Van Goghs, for instance. In 1890, a few months after finishing *The Church at Auvers-sur-Oise*, the artist committed suicide.

Fry was unperturbed by the uproar over the Post-Impressionists. In 1912 he organized a second Post-Impressionist Exhibition of British, French and Russian artists at the Grafton, dominated by the work of Picasso and Matisse. It was all too much for London sensitivities. After all, this was thirty years of artistic development in Paris, itself several light years ahead of London, distilled into two exhibitions two years apart.

Fry's Post-Impressionist show was not the only outré arts event in the West End around that time. A lecture held at the Lyceum Club on Piccadilly in 1910 was given in French by Filippo Marinetti, leader of the Italian Futurists, then the most vociferous new art movement in Europe. Marinetti harangued the audience, slaying the biggest beast in British art criticism. 'Your deplorable Ruskin, whom I intend to make utterly ridiculous in your eyes, with his sick dream of a primitive pastoral life . . . this maniac for antique simplicity resembling a man who, in full maturity, wants to sleep in his cot again and drink at the breasts of a nurse now grown old.'

Marinetti explained that Ruskin's biggest crime was his 'hatred of the machine' – *the* symbol of progress, *the* symbol of the future.' His polemic was art as manifesto, with no compromise. 'Come on! Set fire to the library shelves! Turn aside the canals to flood the museums! Oh the joy of seeing the glorious old canvases bobbing adrift on those waters, discoloured and shredded! Take up your pickaxes, your axes and hammers and wreck the venerable cities.'

Those taking up a less extreme anarchic position shared a sober determination to rid English art of its lethargy and retrospection. In London a new group of artists met for dinner at the Florence Restaurant on Soho's Rupert Street in November 1913. They included Frederick Etchells, William Roberts and Wyndham Lewis. A flamboyant figure, Lewis in those days always dressed in a long dark overcoat and large black sombrero, and described himself as 'novelist, painter, sculptor, philosopher, draughtsman, critic, politician, journalist, essayist, pamphleteer all rolled into one'.

Lewis, the Renaissance man, remains an iconoclastic and controversial figure. It's not difficult to see why he was disliked, scorned even. He was deeply paranoid, and believed that those who complimented his work were obviously only trying to ingratiate themselves before turning him over to his enemies. Few have succeeded in defining and placing him. He liked to be thought of as a mystery man without a past, and indeed his background made him hard to categorize, for though he was educated at Rugby and the Slade School of Art, he was born on a yacht off the Canadian coast, and would become conveniently British or American at will.

Lewis travelled to Paris at the beginning of the century to paint alongside Augustus John, and in the French capital saw Picasso's early works, responding with the colossal *Kermesse*, which he painted for the staircase of the outré Mayfair nightclub, the Cave of the Golden Calf. His Cubist paintings, with their angular scaffolding, were the highlight of a 1913 show: 'The Post-Impressionist and Futurist Exhibition', a brave attempt to link cubism, post-impressionism and futurism, which was held at the Doré Galleries on New Bond Street.

That year Lewis joined Roger Fry's Omega Workshops, based at 33 Fitzroy Square, in the heart of the Adam Brothers' glorious creation, where Fry had padded the walls with seaweed to keep out the noise. Omega had progressive aims. It encouraged men and women to work in equal partnership. It was a world of bright colours and ornamental patterns, and its team used Post-Impressionist ideas to produce hand-painted furniture, ceramics, drapery, textiles and clothing – all signed with the trademark Omega symbol.

Evidently it was all too staid for Lewis. He wanted more of the fast future, less of the pious past. Only that April Marinetti himself had spoken at a Doré Galleries exhibition in the West End, striking wood with a hammer as two big drums in a distant room produced a boom of cannon fire on Marinetti's telephone commands. 'A day of attack on the Western Front, with all the heavies hammering . . . was nothing to it,' Lewis later recalled.

That year Lewis set up his Rebel Arts Centre in Bloomsbury's Great Ormond Street. A few months later he loudly separated from his Omega colleagues by forming a new group: the Vorticists, a name coined by the uncompromising American poet Ezra Pound. Vorticism was launched with the publication of the magazine *Blast*: 'the journal of the Great English Vortex'. This was an aggressive manifesto which 'blasted' the effeteness of British art and culture.

There was no limit to Lewis's targets. Omega was 'Mr Fry's curtain and pin-cushion factory'. The writers Ford Madox Ford and Joseph Conrad – 'Foûtou! Finished! Exploded!' The Vorticists wanted to create a specifically English form of the European avant-garde, one that would be more suitable to the UK's northern weather than to the Latin climate of the Mediterranean countries. Britain, the first industrialized country, should face up to the modern mechanized world in its art with a new aesthetic wrapped up in the latest methods and technology, the Vorticists felt. Artists should love the machine and attempt to capture movement in images with bold lines and harsh colours. Typographics should be revolutionary in their dynamic audaciousness.

The Vorticists soon produced an admirable body of work. What words can fully capture or describe the excitement, the movement, the dynamism of David Bomberg's *Ju-Jitsu* with its angular geometric figures in red, grey, blue and ochre refracted through countless prisms? They were also very visible around town. Their favourite restaurant was La Tour Eiffel at 1 Percy Street, Fitzrovia, where Ezra Pound and Co. had hosted the Poets' Club in 1909. William Roberts's 1962 painting, simply named *The Vorticists at the Restaurant de la Tour Eiffel, Spring 1915*, and now at the Tate Britain, shows a number of key figures from the movement including Lewis, Pound, the painter himself, and the restaurant owner, Rudolph Stulik, who had once been chef to Austrian Emperor Franz Josef. As Roberts once told the *Listener* magazine: 'In my memory la cuisine française and Vorticism are indissolubly linked.' Continental food amid the British weather.

Not all the West End Vorticists were painters. T. E. Hulme was a philosopher and poet who liked to think of himself as a tough, no-nonsense Yorkshireman on a mission to terrorize anaemic, bourgeois, Southern softies. He once left a dinner at the Café Royal, claiming he had a most pressing engagement, and returned twenty minutes later, sweaty and exhausted, to announce that the steel staircase by the emergency exit at Piccadilly Circus station was 'the most uncomfortable place' in which he had ever copulated. Hulme was even more troublesome than Lewis. When the latter dallied with Hulme's girlfriend he found himself tied upside down to the railings on Soho Square, the culprit his jealous rival.

Apart from Lewis the Vorticists championed the arrival of the Great War. Where Lewis thundered: 'I don't want to get killed for Mr Lloyd George or Mr Asquith or for any community except that elusive but excellent one to which I belong,' C. R. Nevinson thought the war would be a 'violent incentive to Futurism, for we believe there is no beauty except in strife, and no masterpiece without aggressiveness.'

The reality was different. The war demoralized the Vorticists, especially when the new exciting machinery helped kill some of its members, like T. E. Hulme, who was blown up in a large explosion at the western front. Lewis, noting the public's suspicion of art movements in the melancholic aftermath of the war, then gave up on Vorticism to concentrate on literature, his only brush work being portraits to pay the rent. In the 1930s his flirtation with fascism made him a pariah in some circles, particularly in Fitzrovia where, ironically, his one-time lodgings, 4 Percy Street, had previously been occupied by Alois Hitler, half-brother of Adolf, who is believed to have paid a brief visit to his relative there in 1912.

By the beginning of the 1930s British artists had fallen into a depression; a feeling that they could never match the unbounded innovation of their contemporaries overseas, that they had talent but not genius. It was an unfortunate state of affairs that was replicated in British music until the mid 1960s. The problem was that British artists, located in a country in which art was not one of the regularly spoken languages, tended to work in isolation. 'They do not make a programme, do not present a united front or generate a common intensity of any kind,' the formidable critic Herbert Read explained, noting how Vorticism was dead and that the Bloomsbury Group had fled Bloomsbury to Sussex and Paris.

Read's polemic worked. British artists came out of their shell. Amongst them were those in the Unit One group: Paul Nash, Henry Moore, Ben Nicholson and Wells Coates. They were based at the West End's Mayor Gallery, located not in Soho, the usual home of the bizarre and unusual, but in Mayfair (on Cork Street), an area dripping with gilt-edged riches. Unit One announced its formation through a letter in *The Times* on 2 June 1933 which explained how it would 'stand for the expression of a truly contemporary spirit'.

As with so many such groups, it was short-lived, splitting after two years, its members unable to agree on its aims. For instance, while Ben Nicholson was comparing painting to a 'religious experience', Wells Coates, architect of the Bauhaus-inspired Isokon building in Belsize Park, was devising the revolutionary idea of assembling prefabricated houses that could be clipped onto the back of a lorry on a Friday evening, taken to the countryside for the weekend, and brought back to town for Monday.

The West End was soon at the centre of more art notoriety. This time the location was the New Burlington Galleries at 5 Burlington Gardens, just behind the Royal Academy, and the cause the gallery's International Surrealist Exhibition of 1936. Keen on gaining publicity, the organizers discussed various strategies. Should they bombard *The Times*'s letter pages with informed comment, as Unit One had done? One suggestion, not carried out, was that they all phone Selfridge's at different times and ask them what surrealism was.

There was no need to worry about publicity. More than 1,500 people crammed into the galleries for the opening of the exhibition on 11 June. The artist Sheila Legge arrived from Trafalgar Square, where she had been photographed as Salvador Dalí's 'la Femme au Tête des Roses', her head obscured by roses, and made her way through the crowd holding an artificial leg in one hand and a pork chop in the other, although she had to abandon the pork chop when it began to wilt in the heat. Dylan Thomas waded through the throng carrying tea cups filled with boiled string, asking those whose glance he caught: 'Do you like it weak or strong?' Dalí himself, the genre's major artist, appeared for a lecture at the gallery accompanied by two borzoi hounds and dressed in a diving suit, the helmet of which made his words inaudible and came close to suffocating him, before he was rescued by a man with a pair of pliers.

The exhibition was a big success. Some 40,000 attended. But as far as the *Observer* was concerned London was not quite ready to have its sensibilities distorted through a clear but wicked lens. The paper dismissed the show as 'practical jokes, abortive from the aesthetic point of view'. A more sober alternative to the excesses of surrealism came from the other end of the West End. The Euston Road School, formed in 1937, was made up of four painters: Claude Rogers, Victor Pasmore, William Coldstream and Graham Bell. Their headquarters was on Fitzroy Street, where Walter Sickert and co. had been based a couple of decades earlier, this time at No. 12, until success saw a move to larger premises at 314–16 Euston Road, after which they assumed their name.

The Euston Road School painters were concerned with the gritty realism of everyday life. Watch the subject, forget Paris. They were united by their normalcy, rather than an interest in the avant-garde, a reaction to the extremist positions of the Vorticists, and a return to Sickert's concern with reality over abstract themes. (Pasmore eventually returned to abstract art, but not till after the war had shattered his sensibilities.) Group members even had day jobs. Pasmore was a clerk for the London County Council. It was very subdued, very understated and very English.

# 'LIFE IS HELL'

What once seemed wild and revolutionary now looks tame and quaint. What was once shocking is now commonplace. Up to a point. Students of West End history will always consider the actions of the avant-garde at the Institute of Contemporary Arts unusual.

The ICA was founded in 1948 in a cinema basement at 165 Oxford Street (the Marquee club began there a few years later). It soon moved to Dover Street, Mayfair, setting up home in a dressmaker's studio that took up part of a Georgian terraced house. From here in 1952 sprang the experimental Independent Group. The group took an iconoclastic line. It argued that no everlasting notion of 'good design' existed, no form of painting was purer than any other, and that timelessness was spurious.

Members included the photographer Nigel Henderson, who would send his students from the nearby Central School of Art around the tobacconists and bookshops of Charing Cross Road for inspiration, and the Scottish-Italian sculptor Eduardo Paolozzi, whose father and grandfather perished in the *Arandora Star* tragedy that sunk many Soho Italians (see p. 175). Paolozzi's huge public works, such as the statue of Newton outside the British Library and the mosaics on the walls of Tottenham Court Road tube station, have made him one of the leading figures in the field. But his first West End project was a collage of photographic images culled from trashy American magazines for the Independent Group – *Evadne in Green Dimension* (1952). It was one of the first examples of what came to be known as pop art.

The ICA continued to purvey the unusual and provocative. In 1953 it held the first exhibition of Jackson Pollock's Action Paintings. It organized strange events. There was the time that the police approached a young Austrian artist in Mayfair's Dover Street while he was thrashing an animal corpse around, splattering the pavement with the blood. This was in 1966, not 2006; all part of Herman Nitsch's symposium, 'Destruction in Art', and it was watched by a group of admirers that included Yoko Ono. Gustav Metzger, who had organized the event, was fined £100 as punishment for Nitsch's dismembering animal parts in the road.

But the institute was more than simply a haven for experimentation. It peddled artistic integrity. With Roland Penrose, indefatigable promoter of surrealism in 1930s London in charge, organizers strove for elitism with impunity. Large numbers attended its lectures. Even the café exuded warmth and cosiness, selling normal food at cheap prices. In 1968 the ICA moved to a more upmarket address on The Mall in Westminster where it has continued to present the most outré of exhibitions and events.

By then the centre of gravity of the London art world had returned to the West End after sojourns in Hampstead and Chelsea. Having Francis Bacon as peripatetic painter-in-residence helped. If the manoeuvrings of the ICA were unusual, what of Francis Bacon's activities? Bacon was more than an artist, even though no artist better represented the agony of modern man. He was the embodiment of degeneracy in a life which encompassed practically every vice man has invented: drink, greed, gambling, lust, promiscuity and wastefulness, along with a delicious disregard for petty authority.

Born in Dublin in 1909, Bacon moved to London when he was sixteen after his father threw him out of the family home for wearing his mother's clothes. At first he was a furniture designer and interior decorator, but in 1933 the Mayor Gallery on Cork Street, Mayfair, included his work in a group exhibition. Bacon painted relatively little in those days, and destroyed much of his early work in the 1940s. He spent the war years running an illegal casino opposite the Natural History Museum, in the same rooms where the great Pre-Raphaelite John Millais had once lived. The casino must have been inspirational, for at the same time he was gaining the aesthetic maturity that made him the most remarkable painter to emerge from the British Isles in the twentieth century. This was signalled in 1945 with his *Three Studies for Figures at the Base of a Crucifixion*, a three-part work consisting of animalian figures with human orifices and long eel-like necks writhing in bloody anguish.

When it was shown at the Lefevre Gallery on Mayfair's Bruton Street that April the critics were torn. They are still torn. Was his warped outlook shaped by the horrors of the war or the horrors of his own mad psyche? Was the work a bold and uncomfortable attempt to link wartime carnage with the suffering of Christ on the Cross? Did his paintings describe the human condition or merely the sado-masochistic gay condition? Was Bacon being truthful when he responded by stating that he had nothing to express about the human condition; that 'life was the horror and his paintings were no match for it?'

Treatise after treatise, critique after critique was produced to argue this way or that. But perhaps the best attempt was one which succinctly summed up the man and his work with the kind of directness Bacon himself always admired. It was the view offered by Margaret Thatcher who, when asked her views on the painter, described him simply as 'that dreadful man who paints those horrible pictures'. Indeed such primitive analysis was once neatly echoed by Bacon himself. When asked by one critic if he had ever experienced an epiphany to rank alongside William Blake's vision of angels in Peckham he recalled the sight of a dog turd on the pavement which made him realize that 'there it is. This is what life is like.' Asked to elaborate he explained his life as 'going from bar to bar and drinking and that sort of thing'.

Indeed the artist's personal life was a riot of wantonness, mostly taking place in Soho, its decadent, cosmopolitan, licentious hedonism making it the perfect backdrop for someone who wanted to remain on the edge of society. Bacon became the living embodiment of the distorted psychic creations found in his tortured paintings, stalking the Colony Club drinking den on Dean Street, where he was paid a retainer by the landlady for bringing in wealthy customers, and Wheeler's fish restaurant on nearby Old Compton Street where he would torment naive Americans with his foul mouth and fouler temper.

Meanwhile, on the other side of Regent Street, in the refined galleries of Mayfair, Bacon was a sensation. In November 1949 the Hanover Gallery at 47 New Bond Street staged the first solo exhibition of his work. It was one of the events of the year. London marvelled at the paintings of tormented heads which induced in the spectator feelings of despair and frustration, summed up by one French visitor in the existentialist 'life is hell and we had better get used to the idea'. Bacon long continued producing heads, including that of a boxed, screaming Pope, based on Velázquez's *Portrait of Pope Innocent X*, that established his international reputation.

Bacon could do no wrong in the art world. There was an ICA retrospective in 1955, another Hanover gallery exhibition in 1957, this one dominated by a series of paintings based on a photographic reproduction of Van Gogh's *Painter on the Road to Tarascon*, which he later denounced as unrepresentative, and the climax, a 1962 Tate Gallery show in which the highlight was the outrageous triptych *Three Studies for a Crucifixion*. In

1989 he became the world's most expensive living artist when another of his triptychs – *May–June 1973* – sold at Sotheby's in New York for £3.53 million.

Bacon's death (in 1992) has failed to stem the controversy surrounding his life, caused as much by his outré paintings as by his turbulent behaviour. To those who knew him well he was generous and amiable. In formal circles he was the epitome of charm and good manners, but when he smelt hypocrisy he assumed a cloak of spontaneous irritation from which emerged a lashing tongue and a barbed wit.

In the late 1980s Bacon received letter from the Tate Gallery asking him to collate all his archive material for the museum's collection. Disgusted at the letter's officious tone, he took everything he could find of interest into the garden and burned the lot. Two years later the same man from the Tate again wrote to Bacon, reminding him that he had still not responded to the original letter. Bacon immediately gathered together another stack of archive material and destroyed it. In 2000 his estate sued his dealer, Marlborough International Fine Art, for allegedly undervaluing his paintings. It then came to light that Bacon had avoided paying tax in Britain by failing to declare payments made by Marlborough to a Swiss bank account. The row was settled in 2002 with Marlborough agreeing to pass to the estate all the documents it owned that had previously belonged to Bacon.

In his will Bacon left most of his estate, worth £10.9m, including his South Kensington studio, to his closest confidante, John Edwards, an ex-publican, subject of some thirty Bacon paintings. Edwards retired, first to the Florida Keys then to Thailand. He died in Thailand in 2003, having squandered Bacon's fortune. The late painter would doubtless have been chuffed to know of the fate of his riches. If only Hogarth had been around to capture the moment in caricature.

# 8

## Boho

Boho. Bohemian Soho. Bohemian from the French *bohémien*, itself from *Bohême* or in English Bohemia, the central European state home to gypsies living the unconventional life. Bohemian as in Henry Murger's sketches of feckless artistes and café philosophers in Paris's Latin Quarter of the 1840s. Bohemian as taken up by W. M. Thackeray in 1848 in *Vanity Fair*, his epic novel laden with West End settings: 'She was of a wild, roving nature, inherited from father and mother, who were both Bohemians, by taste and circumstances.' Bohemian as in 'peregrinator, wanderer, rover, straggler, rambler, bird of passage, gadabout, vagrant, scatterling and landloper,' according to Arthur Ransome's *Bohemia in London* of 1907.

The bohemian was an artist, actor or musician; an intellectual, a dilettante, a sensualist, an absinthe drinker, an opium dabbler, a hopeless romantic leading a life of determined irregularity, drawn towards neighbourhoods like Soho with its louche loose cosmopolitan population, drawn to West End streets such as Berwick, Beak and Brewer; Dean, Frith and Greek; Old Compton and Gerrard; Charlotte, Rathbone, Whitfield and Percy. But the West End bohemian was in particular a writer – Thomas de Quincey, Percy Bysshe Shelley, Samuel Taylor Coleridge, Verlaine and Rimbaud, Oscar Wilde, Joseph Conrad, Ezra Pound, Augustus John, Dylan Thomas, George Orwell – and from its earliest days the West End has played host to such figures.

Thomas de Quincey was the West End's first full-time bohemian. Not only was he a washed-up, penniless writer, enwrapped in the most devoutly romantic web of imagery, able to compose Greek verse in lyric metres and speak the Classical tongue fluently, he was also drug-addled beyond repair. Fleeing his background and school in decidedly non-bohemian Manchester, he wandered through England and Wales in the early years of the nineteenth century before gravitating to Soho.

After frittering his money away De Quincey spent his days mooching through the streets and parks, and his nights sleeping rough in a house on the corner of Greek Street and Soho Square, where 'the noise of the rats made a prodigious echoing on the spacious staircase and hall'. He shared the accommodation with a ten-year-old waif, and they survived by waiting for the owner to finish breakfast so that they could gobble up the leftovers. To keep warm he paced the streets of Soho with Ann, a fifteen-year-old prostitute. When one day he collapsed in Soho Square Ann ran off for help, and returned with port and spices, which revived De Quincey and kept him alive.

Ann was now his saviour. He left for Bristol to borrow some money from a friend, telling Ann he would return to share the bounty with her. They parted at Golden Square where Ann, overcome with grief, threw her arms around his neck and wept into his collar. De Quincey reassured her that he would be gone only a week, after which she should go to the corner of Oxford Street and Great Titchfield Street at 6 p.m. every night until he returned.

De Quincey left, secured the money, came back to London and headed for Great Titchfield Street at the appointed time. No Ann. He returned and returned, but Ann never showed up again. He sought her everywhere. He found the street where she had been staying but knew not the number. He sought her in thousands of female faces passing him in the West End . . . to no avail. Now suffering from the 'real fleshly ills of cold and hunger', De Quincey sought solace in opium – 'dread agent of unimaginable pleasure and pain' – which he bought on a Sunday afternoon, 'wet and cheerless', from a chemist's at 173 Oxford Street, by its junction with Poland Street.

Now a location as urban and prosaic as it is possible to imagine, occupied by Marks and Spencer, it was then on the edge of built-up London, and from there De Quincey could 'gaze from Oxford Street up every avenue in succession which pierces through the heart of Marylebone to the fields and woods'.

Remarkably, his opium eating didn't dent his talent for producing rhapsodical imagery practically without parallel in English literature, as captured in his 1821 testament, *Confessions of An English Opium-Eater*, first published in the *London Magazine*:

I was necessarily ignorant of the whole art and mystery of opium-taking: and, what I took, I took under every disadvantage. But I took it: – and in an hour, oh! Heavens!

what a revulsion! what an upheaving, from its lowest depths, of the inner spirit! what an apocalypse of the world within me! That my pains had vanished, was now a trifle in my eyes . . .

Society's reaction to De Quincey's indulgences was not in accord with the modern-day reaction to literary drug takers such as William Burroughs or Will Self. The editors of the *London Magazine* proudly by-lined him the 'Opium Eater' and no controversy greeted his descriptions; there were few moral judgements from 'shocked' readers or reporters. De Quincey was also adept at cutting satire. When commenting on the 1811 Ratcliff Highway Murders he memorably quipped: 'For if once a man indulges himself in murder, very soon he comes to think little of robbing; and from robbing he comes next to drinking and Sabbath-breaking, and from that to incivility and procrastination.'

It was in 1811 that the poet Shelley took lodgings on Poland Street simply because he liked the name Poland. 'It reminds me of Thaddeus of Warsaw and freedom,' he told his room mate, Thomas Hogg. Shelley was nineteen, and had just been sent down from Oxford for writing the supposedly seditious pamphlet *The Necessity of Atheism*. The pamphlet embarrassed his father who suggested he be put into 'the care and society' of a gentleman tutor whom he would select. Shelley was horrified, and after refusing to comply was ostracized by his family. He and Hogg covered the walls with trellised paper that was decorated with vine leaves and huge clusters of grapes, but despite telling Hogg 'we must stay in Poland Street for ever', Shelley left Soho soon after for Edinburgh, only returning to the West End occasionally to lodge on Great Portland Street.

A year after Shelley arrived in the West End the forty-year-old Samuel Taylor Coleridge, living at 71 Berners Street, off Oxford Street, was finding it next to impossible to produce any work from his lodgings. He rented the property for £60 a year ('very cheap, as houses go'), and while living there Coleridge worked on his masterpiece, 'Kubla Khan', one of the best-known poems in the English language, whose genesis took several years owing to the author's penchant for opium. In October 1813 Coleridge's landlord, Morgan, who was about to be made bankrupt, fled to Ireland to escape his creditors and Coleridge moved away from the West End.

As the nineteenth century proceeded so the unconventionally aesthetic, the London bohemian, increasingly felt the need to adopt French attitudes and affectations, Frenchified clothes, Francophone homilies, Francophile mannerisms. This did not include the French ways of the devout Huguenots, with their staid debating societies and industrious silk-weaving, who had migrated to St Giles on the outskirts of the West End, but the France of debauchery and decadence, the France of the astronomer Alexis Morin who denied the existence of the sun but placated the public by allowing the existence of the moon, the France of the red cap of liberty, the France of *Vive La Revolution!*

It helped if the London bohemian were genuinely French. In 1872 the French poets Paul Verlaine and Arthur Rimbaud fled to London to escape the repercussions their affair had caused to Verlaine's wife and family. They took rooms at 34 Howland Street, close to where the BT Tower now looms over central London. There they found a city of mud and constant fog 'as black as a crow and noisy as a duck', as Verlaine put it.

Rimbaud was equally scathing, moaning, while sitting in the carriage of a Metropolitan Railway train, about the 'sheets of fog spread out in ghastly layers in the sky . . . formed of the most sinister black smoke that the Ocean in mourning can produce'. Rimbaud was perturbed that the gin tasted like 'concentrated sewage water' and that the food was inedible, especially 'the abominable oxtail soup', which led him to thunder memorably: 'Fie on such a horror! A man's sock with a rotten clitoris floating in it.' The only place where they supped satisfactorily was the Hibernia Stores at 23–25 Old Compton Street, a tavern popular with foreign exiles, which hosted radical lectures in an upstairs room. Rimbaud didn't manage to do much work in London. At the British Library the assistants refused to allow him to read the Marquis de Sade's outré sexual ramblings as he was under twenty-one. And although he did try, as he claimed in *A Season in Hell*, to 'derange all his senses' to write a new kind of verse, he had completed all his useful poetry by this time.

Nevertheless both poets continue to inspire near-religious devotion in the bohemian world. A new generation was introduced to Rimbaud and Verlaine in the 1970s when Patti Smith launched into her rock war cry: 'Go Rimbaud and go Johnny, go!' and when they learnt the reasons for Tom Miller's name change to Tom Verlaine in fronting the New York art punk band Television.

The West End's greatest bohemian of the late Victorian period, one who needed no Frenchifying, existed alas only in the pages of Arthur Conan

Doyle's detective stories. Sherlock Holmes loathed 'every form of society with his whole Bohemian soul,' Doyle revealed in 'A Scandal in Bohemia', the first Holmes short story, published in 1891. Holmes would speak to no one for days on end, scrape away endlessly on his violin, was hampered by a cocaine habit and indulged in chemical experiments in his living room. He may have been only fictional but he remains an archetype for the genre.

## THE AESTHETES

At a dinner in the Langham Hotel near Oxford Circus in 1889 Arthur Conan Doyle was commissioned to write the Sherlock Holmes novella *The Sign of Four*. Also at the meal was the figure who went on to epitomize the flamboyant, dandified, debauched real-life late-Victorian bohemian: Oscar Wilde.

No sooner had Wilde arrived in the capital in 1878 after leaving Oxford he was styling himself as a 'Professor of Aesthetics', peddling Aestheticism, the latest in a long line of Victorian bohemian movements. Aestheticism, which promoted romanticism into a manifesto that triumphed *l'art pour l'art* (art for art's sake), was a reaction against the gross industrialization of society. At that time Wilde exhibited little hint of the talent for drama and fiction that now propels his reputation. He was a celebrity who featured in the papers by indulging in flamboyant stunts, such as attending the opening ceremony of Mayfair's Grosvenor Gallery wearing a frock coat designed at the back in the shape of a cello.

Yet within a few years, before he had written anything substantial, Wilde had earned an enviable accolade – being satirized in the Gilbert and Sullivan opera *Patience*. In the opera Gilbert adroitly sent up the Aesthetes. Its two main protagonists, Reginald Bunthorne and Archibald Grosvenor, are composites of several dandified Bohemian West End figures, not just Wilde but the artist James Whistler, with his celebrated white lock of hair, the poet Algernon Swinburne, his lesser known contemporary Coventry Patmore, and the design guru, proto-socialist and epic poet William Morris. The West End setting for their rococo ruminations is memorably identified by Gilbert in Bunthorne's often quoted line: 'Though the Philistines may jostle, you will rank as an apostle in the high aesthetic band, if you walk down Piccadilly with a poppy or a lily in your medieval hand.' This was exactly what Wilde did, and he later explained: 'To have done it was nothing, but to make people think one had done it was a triumph.'

In the 1890s bohemianism in the West End acquired a new prop: *The Yellow Book*. A flamboyant decorative publication, *The Yellow Book* promoted new developments in art and literature with short stories, articles, poetry, and drawings. It was yellow because yellow was the colour of the allegedly wicked and decadent French novel. Holbrook Jackson, in his book *The Eighteen Nineties* (1913), explained how 'nothing like *The Yellow Book* had been seen before. It was newness *in excelsis*: novelty naked and unashamed. People were puzzled, shocked and delighted, and yellow became the colour of the hour, the symbol of the time-spirit.'

*The Yellow Book* was not just bohemian but *bohémien*, for it had been conceived in Dieppe, northern France. Behind it was a group that included the painter Walter Sickert and the illustrator Aubrey Beardsley, still admired for his daring drawings of esoteric erotica, who explained how 'many brilliant story painters and picture writers could not get their best stuff accepted in the conventional magazines, either because they are not topical, or perhaps a little risqué.'

When Oscar Wilde was arrested on charges of gross indecency he was seen to be carrying a yellow book. Mistaking this for THE *Yellow Book*, a mob swarmed to the publication's Vigo Street office, near Piccadilly Circus, and smashed the windows. Some contributors also demanded that Beardsley be fired as art editor because he was associated with Wilde, having illustrated the latter's *Salomé* the year before. *The Yellow Book* never recovered from this unfortunate juxtaposition, and it closed soon after. But then such projects tend to be short lived anyway.

London bohemia was shattered by Wilde's downfall. There had long been a struggle to maintain an air of authentic decadence, and his incarceration for gross indecency suggested that if London tried to become too Bohemian it would quickly be put in its place. Meanwhile, those acquainted with Parisian life mocked London's attempts at decadence. When French friends of the poet Arthur Symons visited him in the early years of the twentieth century they jeeringly asked: 'Where is your Montmartre, where is your *Quartier Latin*?' 'We have none,' he replied. The same inferiority complex haunted London music for much of the next century.

There was one specifically created bohemian establishment in London, however, the Café Royal on Regent Street. Set up by a Frenchman – Daniel Thévenon – in 1865, its décor was lavish, ornate, with velvet seats and elaborate mirrors. The Café Royal attracted Beardsley, Wilde, Whistler, a motley collection of artists, villains, bohemians, pimps, prostitutes and aristocrats, and what the modern-day West End chronicler Phillip Hoare described as 'young men wearing tight suits and nail varnish sipping creme de menthe.' When the writer Max Beerbohm entered the premises for the first time he announced: 'This indeed is life.' It was at the Café Royal that Whistler sallied forth brilliantly one day to be interrupted by Wilde, who drooled 'I wish that I had said that, Whistler,' receiving the perfect response: 'You will, Oscar, you will.'

The menu was super-expensive: *poulet en casserole* with *Coute Mallard*, a popular and purse-ripping choice. For those who wanted to live such a life but weren't blessed with the necessary private income it was possible to drink until 1 a.m. provided one also bought a meal. Fortunately a ham sandwich was legally classed as a meal, but ordering one would inevitably bring the sardonic query from the waiter: 'Do you want that for eating, sir?'

## THE DOORS OF PERCEPTION

For much of the nineteenth century London's drug world centred on Limehouse, where the imperialist policies of the East India Company caused a mass outbreak of opium indulgence amongst the local Chinese population. Pillars of the establishment would head to Limehouse to indulge without guilt. Others would participate from the centre of the capital. The Liberal prime minister, William Gladstone, would take a nip of laudanum before speaking to the Commons, and Queen Victoria was treated with tincture of cannabis for her period pains.

However, at the outset of the Great War the state clamped down. Soldiers on leave were heading down to Leicester Square to score at places like the Leicester Lounge, the Hotel Provence or Wooldridge's, a chemist at 26 Lisle Street. There they would obtain morphine, heroin or cocaine, a drug which, as *Empire* magazine explained, had 'demoralised the Negroes of Alabama and caused outrages of the most terrible description'.

Obviously these people had to be stopped. New drug laws were brought in as part of the 1916 Defence of the Realm Act, but the laws succeeded only in driving the problem underground, criminalizing many for the first time and captivating a new generation with the allure of low-level wrongdoing. It wasn't long before the West End bohemian world was ensnared in the twin naughty pleasures of cerebral recreation and minor misdemeanoury. Cocaine use increased in Soho and Mayfair. Panic spread in non-boho circles. *Empire* magazine wrote of soldiers 'crawling into chemists' shops on their knees, desperate for "snow"'.

It all went wrong at the end of 1918 when a twenty-two-year-old actress, Billie Carleton, was found dead the morning after she had attended a Victory Ball at the Albert Hall. In a gold box on the dressing-room table was cocaine (obtained from a restaurant on Lisle Street). The inquest found that Carleton had not just died of drug abuse. She was an incontestable victim of bohemianism as well. Her lifestyle was not the sort of thing a young woman should be indulging in. Since leaving home in her teens she had come 'under the protection' of a middle-aged man who lavished money on her. She had taken drugs with her transvestite dress designer who had been involved in a homosexual blackmail case. As *The Times* reported she was a regular at Mayfair parties 'where revellers smoked opium at all-night orgies'. Eventually the fuss died down. Carleton's death would be a lesson to all young women thinking of leaving suburbia for Bohemia.

Yet there was soon a new victim: Freda Kempton. She was about the same age as Billie Carleton, and had ingested such quantities of cocaine it made her grind her teeth. One night Kempton returned home after carousing around a number of West End venues with a headache so violent she began to smash her head against the wall, which didn't help, for she went into convulsions and died. She had swallowed too much coke this time.

The police visited her last haunts. One was a Chinese restaurant at 107 Regent Street owned by a pseudonymous Chinaman, Brilliant Chang (Chang being slang for cocaine). Chang had told Kempton that cocaine was only harmful if it was put into water. The press castigated Chang as a purveyor of evil, but found that he had a magnetic effect on white women. To the journalists' revulsion a number of women rushed up to him at the inquest. As the *Empire News* disgustedly reported they 'patted his back, and one, more daring than the rest, fondled the Chinaman's black, smooth hair and passed her fingers slowly through it'. The *World's Pictorial News* was even more aghast, disclaiming the 'half-a-dozen drug-frenzied women' who had joined him in 'wild orgies'.

But Chang wasn't the drugs tsar, or in his case the *huangdi*, running the West End scene. His overlord was a Jamaican, Eddie Manning, who had come to London to read for the Bar but had had his mind subverted after being seduced by a woman he had met in a nightclub. Manning forsook law to be a jazz drummer, dealing on the side until that became more lucrative. He charmed his landlady on Margaret Street, Fitzrovia, despite leaving his revolver on the washstand, and he won over his caretaker Mrs Fox. She let him use her restaurant at 9 Little Newport Street, a few doors down from the Continental Café where the young Joseph Stalin had recently plotted a different kind of world domination.

It was Manning who introduced Brilliant Chang to drugs, and he went down in 1923 for shooting and wounding three rival dealers. The *News of the World*, typically, derived the most cutting headline: 'Evil Negro caught'. Its piece explained how Manning was 'money mad, and how he made it at the sacrifice of the souls of white women and white girls.'

Manning wasn't confined for long. He was released in November 1925, and a few months later gave his own account in *World's Pictorial News*: 'My Life as The Dope King of London' – eight instalments that excitedly told of the corruption of young, upper-class women at Mayfair orgies. 'The women seemed to go utterly mad with excitement,' he explained. 'Dope sapped away all their feelings of modesty and restraint.'

That year cannabis was banned in Britain after the government accepted the findings of the 1925 Geneva International Convention on Narcotics Control, during which an Egyptian delegate claimed 'chronic hashishism had caused most of the insanity in his country'. It wasn't until the early 1950s though that the first arrests for possessing the drug took place in London, in the West End, Soho, in fact, which led the press to rail against black men 'armed with drugs and white women'.

In 1953 Aldous Huxley, the revered novelist, who by then was sixty, decided to test William Blake's assertion that 'if the doors of perception were cleansed, everything will appear to man as it is, infinite.' Huxley searched for the infinite by taking the drug mescalin, a Mexican favourite. He now saw the world as Adam had witnessed it on the first morning, so he claimed, and wrote up his experiences in *The Doors of Perception*.

The effect hit the West End a decade later, not through mescalin but through a new laboratory-contrived, mind-bending drug – Lysergic Acid Diethylamide, better known as LSD or simply 'acid'. Considerably stronger than mescalin, with unpredictable side effects, LSD quickly became the drug of the intellectual elite, the drug of the new West End rock stars such as the Beatles, Jimi Hendrix, Syd Barrett, and members of Cream, the Who and the Rolling Stones.

After a New Jersey bride was stabbed with a pair of scissors and strangled by a dabbler, LSD was banned in America. A few months later a man who had regularly attended the Blues Club on Soho's Greek Street tried to fly from the roof of a chapel in Kentish Town, presumably after taking acid. LSD was duly banned in the UK, joining cannabis, heroin, cocaine *et al.* in the twilight-lit underground of drugs endowed by proscribing governments with a spurious fascination that transcended the boho world.

## THE FITZROVIANS

For those who wanted to indulge in cultured conversation laced with cutting wit without having to compete with a dance band or dancing girls, and who couldn't afford the Café Royal, there was always the Fitzroy Tavern at the corner of Charlotte Street and Percy Street.

What became London's most celebrated pub in the middle years of the twentieth century opened as the Fitzroy Coffee House in 1883 and four years later was renamed the Hundred Marks pub. It was redecorated with *fin de siècle* touches in wood and frosted glass, and the lettering had the finest art-nouveau curves. The Hundred Marks became the Fitzroy Tavern early in the twentieth century with the arrival of Judah Kleinfeld, who, un-usually for the London licensing trade, was not only Polish but Jewish and teetotal.

At that time the Fitzroy was located in an area of the West End that resisted easy definition. It was the German anarchist café area. Some hope-fully called it Bloomsbury (surely not that far west), some North Soho. Others plotted a name change based around the word 'Fitzroy', itself a cor-ruption of Fils Roy, (bastard) son of the king. Indeed a pub on Clipstone Street bore the racy name 'The Bastard Arms' until the mid nineteenth century.

A new name for the area was eventually unveiled, coined by the Labour politician Tom Driberg: Fitzrovia. Such is the power of the well-crafted neol-ogism, the name had by the beginning of the twenty-first century won almost universal acceptance, with mentions in guidebooks, street atlases and news-paper articles.

If Fitzrovia was boho country in the London of the early twentieth century, then its seat of government was a bar stool in the Fitzroy Tavern and its president was Augustus John. A painter known more for his socializing and womanizing than his aesthetic legacy, potent though that was, John lived with his sister, Gwen, at 95 Fitzroy Street, conveniently near the Tavern, where he existed on a diet of nuts and fruit. He then moved out to live in sleaze with fellow art student Ida Nettleship, whose physical beauty out-weighed the ugliness of her name. He grew his hair, left his beard unkempt – reputedly he was the only person in the British army to be allowed to wear one – and donned a wide-brimmed hat, black silk scarf and earrings, a culti-vated wild Dionysian look that made him the epitome of the flamboyant bohemian artist.

Not content with just Ida, he maintained a ménage with other women whom he obliged Ida to accept. One was Dorelia McNeill, 'whose smile opened infinite vistas'. Another was Ottoline Morrell, the literary hostess caricatured in various twentieth-century novels including D. H. Lawrence's *Women in Love* and Aldous Huxley's *Crome Yellow*. Somehow, in between his concupiscence, and draughts of double rum-and-brandy at the Fitzroy, Augustus John found time to produce portraits including those of George Bernard Shaw, James Joyce, W. B. Yeats, Thomas Hardy, and on 30 May 1921 the young Crown Prince Hirohito of Japan. 'I was very much impressed by his tranquil personality and natural dignity,' the painter later recalled of the royal. 'He sat through the hour with complete ease.' Lord Leverhulme, the soap magnate, wasn't so easily placated. He sent back John's portrait of him mutilated, having snipped out the head, explaining that he wished to fit the portrait into a small safe. 'The artistic ethics of the operation performed by Lord Leverhulme is a question I must leave people to decide for them-selves,' was his only comment.

Augustus John was challenged as the chief Fitzroy Taverner in the late 1930s by Dylan Thomas. The Welsh wizard of the wafted word was initially fazed by the place, and would rush back to Wales after what he described as 'too much talk, too much drink, too many girls'. Then he met his amour, Caitlin Macnamara. They took a room above the nearby Tour Eiffel restau-rant, stayed in bed there for several days, and charged the bill to Augustus John's account. Thomas was later bankrolled by Margaret Taylor, wife of the renowned historian, A. J. P. Not that he appreciated the handouts, and he spent many hours running away from her. When Margaret Taylor finally managed to track down Thomas at the Stag public house on New Cavendish Street she didn't even realize, for he hid behind the bar, his hand, according to one onlooker, 'sneaking round the flap, groping for another pint'.

In the Fitzroy Thomas would write poems on beer mats for the tavern's female customers, which was just as well as his poetry, with its idiosyncratic, highly personalized, florid poetic style – 'with the first pint a tall / Story froths over', as Louis Macniece's perfect parody put it – is best read with an ale accompaniment. Thomas left the Fitzroy one day in the 1940s to make a broadcast for the BBC on John Dryden's poetry. Two minutes before he was due on air he was snoring in front of the mike. The producer gave him a shake, prodding him into consciousness just in time for Thomas to announce that he would be reading from 'Shaint Sheshelia's Day'. On another occasion Thomas paused during a live broadcast and announced: 'Someone's boring me. I think it's me.'

The Fitzroy women were no less unusual. Nina Hamnett, who lived above the L'Etoile restaurant, a few doors down at 30 Charlotte Street, was a writer, artist and model. Her modelling career peaked when the French cubist sculptor Henri Gaudier-Brzeska created 'Torso of Nina' in her pose out of a piece of stone stolen from a scrapyard in Putney. Hamnett was euphoric and told everyone she met: 'You know me, m'dear. I'm in the V&A with me left tit knocked off.'

Hamnett went to Paris's Montparnasse *Quartier* where she studied at Marie Vassilieff's Academy. In a local café she sat down next to a man who introduced himself as 'Modigliani, painter and Jew'. She made friends with Picasso, Diaghilev and Jean Cocteau. In London she worked briefly at the Omega Workshops, and in 1932 published her bohemian escapades in *The Laughing Torso*. One unimpressed with her life story was Aleister Crowley, the Great Beast, Satanist and occasional poet. She claimed in turn that he had practised black magic in Sicily, and was connected with the disappearance of a baby. Crowley sued for libel. The court heard how he had performed animal sacrifices, baptised a toad 'Jesus', and forced one man to drink a slaughtered cat's blood (the man joining the cat in the afterlife soon after). The judge then announced that he had 'never heard such dreadful, horrible, blasphemous and abominable stuff as that which has been produced by the man who describes himself to you as the greatest living poet'.

Although Hamnett won the case, she descended into despair and dypso-mania. 'To enter the Fitzroy and not buy Nina Hamnett a drink was in those days and in that world a solecism that amounted to a social stigma,' claimed Thomas's biographer, Constantine Fitzgibbon. But then it *was* hard to ignore Hamnett given that she would rattle a money box in people's faces with the entreaty 'Got any mun, dear?', touting for drinks that ironically included the lethal cocktail Crowley contrived for the Fitzroy: Kubla Khan No. 2, made of gin, vermouth and laudanum.

Hamnett once left the Fitzroy and ventured out into the rest of the world, making a trip to the cinema with Fitzrovia's other great lost literary talent, Julian Maclaren-Ross. They saw *The Lost Weekend*, in which Ray Milland drinks himself into psychotic senselessness. Afterwards Nina had to be administered a stiff rum before she was strong enough to wait for a taxi that would take her back to the Fitzroy. She continued to crumble socially and physically after the Second World War, becoming toothless and drink-sodden, her wit and charm dissipated, a fate that has befallen so many West End bohos over the years. In December 1956 Hamnett heard herself featured in a radio play, Robert Popock's 'Long Past the Time', and took the reference not as it was intended – as an affectionate memory – but as a barbed insult. She jumped from her Westbourne Terrace balcony, impaling herself fatally on the railings below. The late Aleister Crowley was blamed for placing a curse on her.

The spurious and superficial attractiveness of this decadent, boho, Fitzro-vian lifestyle meant that its most talented practitioners rarely found the time to do any real work. Indeed, for some their artistic reputation was forged from the art of doing as little possible for as long as possible. Such was the story of Julian Maclaren-Ross, a 'mediocre caretaker of his own immense talent' according to his biographer, Paul Willetts.

Before taking to writing Maclaren-Ross peddled vacuum cleaners door to door on the south coast, a role which encouraged Graham Greene in creat-ing the character of Wormold in *Our Man in Havana*. Maclaren-Ross began his literary career promisingly with a piece for *Horizon* magazine entitled 'A Bit of A Smash in Madras'. But *Horizon*'s editor, Cyril Connolly, was horrified to discover that the author had never been to India, and told him to change the setting to the imaginary province of Chandrapore, as in E. M. Forster's *A Passage to India*. He also insisted that Maclaren-Ross change the opening line: 'Absolute fact, I knew fuck-all about it.'

Maclaren-Ross set to work on BBC radio plays in which he acted as well, writing them in the early hours of the morning after a hard day's night drinking in the Fitzroy or the Wheatsheaf on Rathbone Place, staying up till dawn reading review copies of newly published novels, and then selling them to the second-hand bookshops on Charing Cross Road to raise the money for a bottle of brandy, which would barely last a day, and his meagre diet of cheese and biscuits. Occasionally a cheque arrived. It would be turned into lunch at the Scala restaurant on Charlotte Street – roast beef with as much fat as possible and lashings of horseradish sauce.

Court-martialled in 1943, Maclaren-Ross was not hard to spot in the streets of Fitzrovia during the war. Who could miss the aviator shades, camel-hair coat and carnation, cigarette-holder jutting out of a tightly clenched mouth and malacca cane, which offered useful protection against those bent on attacking him for being 'queer'? He got little work done, leaving a legacy excitingly brief, full of false bravura, one of a number of writers bedazzled by the cultivated cosmopolitan squalor, by the all-pervading glamour of Bohemia, by the enticing streets, secret little restaurants and dark pubs. A passage in his *Memoirs of the Forties*, taken from a Soho encounter between the author and the Indian poet Tambimuttu, explains the dilemma.

'"Only beware of Fitzrovia," Tambi said. "It's a dangerous place, you must be careful."

"Fights with knives?"

"No, a worse danger. You might get Sohoitis you know."

"No I don't. What is it?"

"If you get Sohoitis," Tambi said very seriously, "you will stay there always day and night and get no work done ever. You have been warned."

"Is this Fitzrovia?"

"No, Old Compton Street, Soho. You are safer here."'

Fortunately, Maclaren-Ross remains cast for ever in literary London. In Anthony Powell's *A Dance to the Music of Time* series he is the incorrigible X. Trapnell, and in Rayner Heppenstall's *The Lesser Infortune* he is the character clothed in a 'jacket of mustard-coloured velvet, chocolate-coloured trousers, with sueded shoes to match, writing lists of books yet to be written, complete with publisher and price.'

So who was to blame for the bohemians' dismally brief output? The bohemians' own unconquerable indolence or the attractive enticements? Those dark pubs were too enchanting. Each was a siren luring the procrastinating wordsman to his doom. A few hundred yards south of the Fitzroy Tavern at 25 Rathbone Place was the Wheatsheaf. Mock Tudor, with leaded stained-glass windows, dolled up to look like an old coaching inn, this was where the Fitzroy set went when their original inspiration – the Fitzroy Tavern – became infra dig some time during the 1940s. The Wheatsheaf served Younger's Scotch Tavern, which was stronger than and preferable to the insipid brews found at the Fitzroy. It too was soon filled with the louche and libertarian: Dylan Thomas; the hack writer James Graham-Murray ('James the Shit'); and the artist John Minton, a master at black-and-white illustration who committed suicide in 1957, a few days before his fortieth birthday.

It was at the Wheatsheaf that George Orwell picked up the idea of Winston Smith's rat phobia in *1984* after listening to a conversation from set designer Gilbert Wood, who was working on a film entitled *Death of a Rat*. Here Julian Maclaren-Ross celebrated Labour's landslide victory at the 1945 General Election (any excuse) with alternate glasses of scotch and beer. The celebrations lasted for about a week, and were enjoyed not just by Maclaren-Ross, but by the poet John Heath-Stubbs, who somewhat spoiled the occasion by revealing that he had voted Conservative, at which point JMR shook his head in disbelief, though whether this was directed at the poet's choice of party or the fact that he dared *claim* to have voted Tory was not recorded.

At 6 Rathbone Place was the Black Horse where, according to Maclaren-Ross, 'old dears in dusty black toasted departed husbands with port and lemon from black leather settees'. The folk singer and army dodger Ewan MacColl ran his Ballads and Blues Club here in the early 1950s before moving it to the Princess Louise in High Holborn. To the north of Rathbone Place was Rathbone Street, home of three unmissable hostelries: the Duke of York, the Beer House (now the Newman Arms) and the Marquess of Granby

The Duke of York at No. 47 was famed for its eccentric landlord, Alf Klein, who liked to cut off customers' ties, one per customer, the first time they drank there. He collected some 1,500 as trophies. Anthony Burgess, trainee bohemian polymath, and his wife Lynne were enjoying a quiet drink here in 1943, or as quiet as anywhere could be once Burgess had begun fulminating in his broad Mancunian boom, when a razor gang marched in and ordered several pints of beer, which they immediately poured onto the floor. They then threw their glasses at the wall and began brandishing the jagged edges. When Lynne Burgess proclaimed: 'What a waste of good beer,' the gang's leader went behind the bar and pulled pint after pint which he ordered her to drink. Lynne downed the lot.

The Beer House sold just that. No spirits or wine, much to the delight of George Orwell, for whom it was a home from home. The Marquess of Granby at the corner of Rathbone Street and Percy Street was the favourite of Dylan Thomas who came here to pick fights with guardsmen, who themselves had dropped by to pick on homosexuals. As the pub was in a different licensing area from most of its neighbours it stayed open half an hour later and attracted a sizeable crowd once the Fitzroy Tavern and Wheatsheaf had closed.

Obviously no one, not even Julian Maclaren-Ross, could keep up so intense a bohemian lifestyle for long. He was constantly on the run from irate landlords, debt collectors, bailiffs and solicitors. He became obsessed with Sonia Orwell, George's widow, and when she refused to reciprocate would make for her flat on Percy Street, shouting obscenities up at the window. By the late 1950s he was sleeping rough in Euston station or in the Turkish baths on Russell Square. This probably explains why his masterpiece, *Memoirs of the Forties*, for which he was paid chapter by chapter, was still unfinished when he died of a heart attack in 1964, just after finishing an entire bottle of brandy to celebrate a new commission.

A contemporary of Maclaren-Ross, but yet to enjoy the same cultish twenty-first-century revival, was Gerald Kersh. He worked as bodyguard, debt collector, chippie, French teacher, wrestler and cinema manager. Kersh spent night after night in the 1930s in West End coffee bars, 'writing on stolen toilet paper', as one biographer put it, summoning up the spirit of Galsworthy, whose *In Chancery* from *The Forsyte Saga* depicts an 'untidy' Soho, 'full of Greeks, Ishmaelites, cats, Italians, tomatoes, restaurants, organs, coloured stuffs, queer names, people looking out of upper windows, [that] dwells remote from the British body politic'.

Kersh hoped to produce the ultimate seedy Soho novel, following in the tradition of Robert Louis Stevenson's *Dr Jekyll and Mr Hyde* ('"Yes," returned Mr Hyde, "It is as well we have met; and a propos, you should have my address." And he gave a number of a street in Soho.'). He succeeded with the atmospheric Soho soliloquy *Night and the City* (1938). It is a novel that reeks of neon lights, dark alleys and streetwalkers; of blue smoke, cold cappuccinos and lipstick traces of kisses the protagonists pretend to feel.

The story revolves around Harry Fabian, a would-be wrestling promoter, desperately trying to look and sound like an American gangster, who eventually succumbs to trafficking in the white slave trade. Kersh sold the film rights for $40,000, but the buyers butchered it. When he received the script, he suggested that they 'perforate it and hang it on a nail'. A new script was devised for a 1950 production starring Richard Widmark, one of the great British *films noirs*.

Unlike his fellow mid twentieth-century West End bohemians, Kersh fought in the Second World War. He joined the Coldstream Guards, for whom he was a good marksman, once winning 100 cigarettes in a shooting contest. After the war he hit the big time, providing a column for the *Sunday People* as Piers English, and winning commissions from bestselling American magazines like *Esquire, Playboy* and *Collier's*. He even found time for another Soho novel, the gorgeously titled *Prelude To A Certain Midnight* (1947), about the hunt for a child murderer. There were more romances, crime stories, horror stories, even some SF. There were big advances, bigger sales, but not enduring fame. How boho.

# MINISTRY OF FEAR

During the Second World War a frisson of fear spread across Fitzrovia. The bohemian, reeling from drunken night to hungover morning, could no longer ignore the real world of the blackouts, of the danger of being blown up suddenly without warning. Yet war ironically meant more opportunities to practise the louche life. The Ministry of Information, based at Senate House, the University of London administrative headquarters, provided many West End bohemians, those unsuitable for frontline combat owing to a combination of physical incapability, dypsomania and chronic unreliability, with useful employment for a few years. Or as Dylan Thomas put it, the Ministry attracted 'all the shysters in London ... all the half-poets, the boiled newspapermen, submen from the island of crabs ... trying to find a safe niche'.

Writers who worked here included not only Thomas, but John Betjeman and Graham Greene. The latter claimed staff often had to wait up to twenty-four hours to receive replies to memos, and that the building was like a beacon 'guiding German planes towards King's Cross and St Pancras stations', although some believe the Luftwaffe spared the block as Hitler wanted it for his post-conquest London headquarters.

The first author to depict the Ministry in literature was Evelyn Waugh, who described it as 'that great mass of masonry . . . the vast bulk of London University insulting the autumnal sky' in his 1942 novel about the Phoney War, *Put Out More Flags*. In the novel Ambrose Silk uses the offices not to further the Allied cause but to publish a literary magazine, *Ivory Tower*, and in one memorable scene a lunatic carries a bomb throughout the building, sent from one department to another as the contents of his bag tick away.

Dylan Thomas was taken on during the war by Strand Films of 1 Golden Square, who won a contract with the Ministry of Information to produce morale-boosting documentaries such as *Our Country* and *These Are the Men*. His golden rule was that he would not drink on the job. Instead, as Jonathan Fryer pointed out in his biography, *The Nine Lives of Dylan Thomas*, he would sit there counting down the minutes until the pubs opened. One night in 1943 Strand strangely asked Thomas to take fire-watch duties. If an incendiary bomb landed on the building someone needed to raise the alarm. Thomas made sure he was comfortable. He and his new lover, nineteen-year-old Pamela Glendower, whom he had met at the Swiss Tavern in Old Compton Street, spent the night tucked up in the fire-watcher's camp-bed.

George Orwell's *1984*, like *Put Out More Flags* and the sprawling Anthony Powell epic *A Dance to the Music of Time*, was not just a political warning but a satire which targeted the boho Fitzrovia scene. One of its targets, mercilessly mocked in the novel, was a fellow London writer and local figure – T. S. Eliot.

The presiding influence on English literature while Orwell was writing, Eliot was sombre and strait-laced, as unbohemian as it was possible to be, but was nevertheless a regular in the pubs and restaurants of Fitzrovia. George Orwell was obsessed with T. S. Eliot. He loved Eliot's poetry, but Eliot, an editor at Faber, had rejected Orwell's first work, *Down and Out in Paris and London*, in 1932. Orwell spent the rest of his career trying to get his revenge. In *Keep the Aspidistra Flying*, Orwell's deft critique of hypocrisy in the advertising world, we read how 'there were fifteen or twenty shelves of poetry. The squibs of the passing minute. Eliot, Pound, Auden, Campbell, Day-Lewis, Spender. Very damp squibs, that lot. Dead stars above, damp squibs below.'

In the same book Orwell has his hero, Gordon Comstock, read a copy of *The Adventures of Sherlock Holmes* 'his favourite of all books, because he knew it by heart' – another dig at Eliot, who could also recite chunks of Holmes from memory. In *The Road to Wigan Pier*, when talking about fascism, Orwell notes: 'Some such attitude is already quite clearly discernible in writers like Pound, Wyndham Lewis and even if one looks below the surface in su-superior conservative highbrows like Eliot and his countless followers.'

So, having dismissed Eliot as a damp squib and a fascist, it must have been no surprise to Orwell that in 1944 Eliot rejected *Animal Farm*. His letter to the author of what was to become one of the best loved books of the twentieth century read: 'Your pigs are far more intelligent than the other animals and therefore best qualified to run the farm. What was needed (someone might argue) was not more communism but more public-spirited pigs.' Orwell's final revenge was *1984* which, like Eliot's 'The Waste Land' begins in April, the cruellest month, and in which the pompous, priggish O'Brien, Big Brother's vicar on Earth, is obviously modelled on the poet.

After the Second World War Fitzrovia lost its boho edge; unconventionality moved south of Oxford Street into Soho. The untimely deaths of protagonists like Orwell (1950) and Dylan Thomas (1953) sapped the spirit. For decades Fitzrovia, still unnamed as such, quieter and gentler than Soho, became a West End obscurity, its restaurants more expensive and exclusive than those of Soho (a position which swapped round in the 1980s), its simple sturdy houses around Charlotte Street free of Soho's prostitutes, chancers, spivs and spielers.

Shockingly, Fitzrovian gatherings became respectable. The Wednesday Club, which met above Bertorelli's restaurant on Charlotte Street, was the haunt not of literary rebels and ruffians but establishment stars: Christopher Isherwood, Stephen Spender and T. S. Eliot. When asked during one meeting to name his favourite piece of prose Eliot stunned his fellow, well-read guests by citing not a chunk of Conrad or a tract from Trollope, but the Birdy Edwards passage from the Sherlock Holmes novella *The Valley of Fear*, quoting so faithfully that he ruined the plot for those who had never, and now never would, read it. How George Orwell would have laughed.

# 9

# War

Thoughts of London in two world wars don't usually embrace the West End. The Great War rarely assumes a London face, while the Nazis' Blitz on London centred mostly on the East End, as it was designed to destroy the capital's industrial base. War time privations in the West End meant that the railings came down in Berkeley Square. 'I regard this ruthless tearing up of old iron railings as a barbaric piece of socialism,' thundered one MP. It meant that the telephones barely worked and that there was hardly any hot water at Claridge's, the most luxurious hotel in London.

Yet in both world wars the West End was in the front line: the front line for subversion and propaganda. The smart offices, grand hotels and grander houses – from Edgware Road to Tottenham Court Road, from Green Park to Regent's Park – were requisitioned for covert operations. They provided ideal cover for the government's incessant and ingenious intelligence departments.

The first West End address to be so used was Crewe House, an antebellum oddity on Curzon Street with an exquisite stone façade, Hacienda touches and sumptuous grounds, and now Mayfair's most impressive surviving mansion. In 1915 Crewe House became home to the Ministry of Propaganda. The ministry was run by Lord Northcliffe, Britain's most powerful newspaper magnate, who owned the *Daily Mirror*, *Daily Mail* and *The Times*. He appointed the novelist H. G. Wells as director (Wells resigned when Northcliffe refused to employ anyone with German parents) and put Wickham Steed, the *Times*'s foreign editor, in charge of campaigns. Steed targeted the Balkans, where many had been forced into fighting for the Austro-Hungarian Empire, and at Crewe House produced thousands of leaflets decorated with nostalgic nationalistic east European imagery which the Allies dropped by aeroplane over divisions of wavering enemy troops.

Northcliffe's and Steed's *coup de grâce* was to send Allied soldiers near to enemy lines armed with gramophones that played nationalist songs. Hundreds of Polish, Romanian and Czech troops fighting unenthusiastically for Austria-Hungary downed arms, later admitting that the turning point was when they heard a few stirring bars of native melodies.

## 'SET EUROPE ABLAZE'

When the Second World War began in 1939 Baker Street, that dynamic stretch of Marylebone known the world over as the fictional home of Sherlock Holmes, attained special importance among intelligence agents. How appropriate was it that the authorities chose to base their clandestine Special Operations Executive organization here where Holmes, fictionally, had unravelled so much intrigue?

The purpose of the Special Operations Executive was to attack the enemy using non-military means, such as sabotage and subterfuge. To Winston Churchill, the SOE was 'the Ministry of Ungentlemanly Warfare – an army of shadows' – and when he became prime minister he urged the organization to 'Set Europe Ablaze'. Consequently, SOE agents went undercover into France, the Low Countries – even Germany – to engage in low-level disruption. They destroyed enemy equipment, attacked buildings, blew up bridges and tampered with machinery. Terrorism was another word for it. Agents would break into a depot filled with lorries and fiddle with the wires so that the vehicles couldn't be moved. But rather than just apply wanton destruction, they would doctor the same part of each lorry, so that the driver wouldn't be able to find an undamaged component and use it to repair a broken one. *None* of them would work.

Before the SOE could begin its campaign it needed to find suitably daring agents. The army had few such innovative personnel at its disposal. Some agents had already reconnoitred parts of Europe soon to become inaccessible to the British, such as Geoffrey Household, author of the captivating thriller *Rogue Male*, but although other suitable names were suggested they weren't enough. Recruiting officers could hardly advertise, and running a trawl through the various military units and training camps might take too long. Instead the authorities came up with an ingenious idea. Whoever had sent in a correct solution to the *Daily Telegraph* crossword (from a British address) over the previous five years was deemed to have sufficient intellectual gravitas to be considered further.

After the elderly, juvenile, monoglot, infirm and insane had been wheedled out the remainder were invited for interview. These took place at the Metropole Hotel near Trafalgar Square where in Room 424, unfurnished save for a table, two chairs and a bare lightbulb, Major Selwyn Jepson of the newly formed MI9 wing of military intelligence held court. He never told potential recruits his name or why he was interviewing them. All they knew was that they had been invited to discuss 'unusual' war work. Jepson would begin talking in English and switch mid-sentence into French. If interviewees flinched they had failed. Indeed they not only needed to be proficient in the language of the country where they were to land, they also needed to understand its customs and history; they needed to be like agent Nicholas Bodington, who worked for Reuters and spoke French so well he was often mistaken for a Parisian.

Training courses for new recruits included parachute drops and first-aid work at Ringway airfield, Manchester, followed by four weeks with radio and ciphers. Physical fitness, commando training and map reading were conducted in the Scottish Highlands. At country houses emptied of owners and servants agents were taught how to storm a building and conduct an ambush, they were woken in the middle of the night by guards dressed in SS uniforms for 'interrogation' or sent to remote sections of railway track which they would blow up and examine – with the full knowledge of the authorities. Yet SOE agents had little training compared to other secret networks. The Soviets liked to have ten years to work with a new recruit. But these strictures weren't put in place for all SOE agents, for some were crooks – excrooks it was hoped – as the Allies needed forgers to produce fake French ration books, for instance. SOE was regularly contacting police forces for willing cons.

On Baker Street itself there were no clues that the intelligence nerve centre of the war effort was here, although the plaques on some doors did mysteriously announce that this was the address of the Inter Services Research Bureau. HQ was No. 64, previously home to the Prison Commissioners. Here was based Sir Charles Hambro, a merchant banker who had won a Military Cross with the Coldstream Guards before he was twenty-one and who went on to run the Great Western Railway successfully. He had even once taken seven Winchester wickets for Eton for the loss of only six runs.

Also at No. 64 officers sorted clothing for agents. Garments had to be exact replicas of what people were wearing in France; even the buttons on men's suits had to be sewn on in the French style.

No. 82, what had been Marks and Spencer's main offices, was taken over by agents investigating ciphers and signals. Here the SOE also started new codebreakers. One recruit was Leo Marks, a member of the family that ran the bookshop at 84 Charing Cross Road later made famous by Helene Hanff's book of the same name.

On his first day Marks was given a coded message to break, but to his chagrin failed to solve it within the allotted half an hour. His presiding officer was unimpressed and revealed dismissively that most of his secretaries would have completed the task in that time. Marks took the rest of the day to solve the problem and, distraught, handed in his work with the code broken. The officer thanked Marks and asked him to hand back the codebreaker he had used in solving the message. Marks explained that he hadn't been given a codebreaker. He had solved the original cryptogram with no help. The officer was astonished. No one had ever attempted anything so ambitious before. He immediately made Marks head of department.

Marks soon found flaws in the signals system given to agents. Their poem codes, which enabled messages to be encrypted using a well-known English poem as key, were too easy to break, for the Nazis were well acquainted with Coleridge and Keats. Instead Marks began composing poems that he taught agents to memorize. These the Germans couldn't unravel.

Chiltern Court, the luxury Art Deco block of flats above Baker Street station, was home to SOE's Scandinavia section. The section's greatest coup came early in the war when their team destroyed the factory near Oslo that was producing deuterium for a Nazi heavy water atom bomb. Nearby, at 1 Dorset Square, was the French Section, housed ironically on land where that most English of bodies – the MCC – had once played.

Once a new recruit had been taken on they would be sent to a flat in Orchard Court at the southern end of Baker Street, a flat so small that agents had to wait in the bathroom to meet the section head, Maurice Buckmaster. If they satisfied Buckmaster he would introduce them to Vera Atkins, the real power within the organization.

Atkins, who was fluent in English, French and German, would try to identify recruits' particular field of expertise. Could they ski, fly a plane or fire a gun? She ensured that agents being sent to France had been rid of English coins, theatre stubs and hotel matchbooks, and gave them a smattering of typical French ephemera: photos of relatives, letters from old friends post-marked from French cities and Metro tickets. She provided the BBC with coded messages concerning agents' safety that could be read out on the news as innocent non-war stories which would also mean something understood only by the agents' relatives. She also drew up a code of conduct agents needed to know. Page after page filled with fascinating minutiae. Suggestions on how to change one's appearance: 'Nose. Find two small nuts. Bore holes into the nuts and place them inside the nostrils. This will give you a very squashed tipped nose, but it will be possible to breathe quite easily.' She even ordered one agent to have his teeth refilled in the French manner, in case he was arrested and questioned by an orthodontic Gestapo officer.

Vera Atkins was really Vera Rosenberg. Atkins wasn't her married name – she was single – but an assumed Anglicized surname created to hide her Romanian origins, which officially made her an 'enemy alien'. She had been checked in case there was anything suspicious in her background, but noth-ing was found. Her official file in the War Office intriguingly notes under Politics: 'None'. After the war she spent a year in Germany tracking down missing agents, discovering that over a hundred had been killed in action, sent to the various Nazi concentration camps or simply executed by disgrun-tled Germans as the war drew to a close, and that the one she couldn't account for had absconded with three million francs of SOE money to the casinos of Monte Carlo.

SOE's activities are still so shrouded in secrecy that even when Atkins was in her nineties, just before she died in 2000, she would divulge little. Her biographer, Sarah Helm, surmised that Atkins must have been harbouring some desperate secret. Sure enough, in pursuing a trail across Europe Helm discovered that Atkins was party to an intelligence disaster that had cost hundreds of lives, those of a French Resistance section, following a lapse in security.

SOE agents had to work with an assortment of imaginative paraphernalia. Things like caborundum powder which when mixed with oil caused moving mechanical components to seize up, and thus was vital for wrecking railway stock. Or the Air Pen, a black metal cylinder, slightly larger than a fountain pen, which contained a powerful spring capable of firing a dart forty feet. The traditional schoolboy irritant of itching powder was put to great use, being smuggled into submarines or sent to brothels in Nazi-occupied countries staffed by Allied sympathizers who would use it when German officers visited.

Much of this bizarre stock of almost surreal weaponry went through Section D's technical department, initially based at 35 Portland Place, a few hundred yards north of Oxford Circus. There agents learned how to wire up dead rats with explosives, how to kill with their bare hands, how to remove a pair of handcuffs with a piece of thin wire and a pencil, how to derail trains (for which they were sent to practise on a stretch of track in the Midlands) and how to use a hand-held sticky bomb against a tank, which Churchill urged the French to take but which they stalled over until it was too late. At Portland Place they also produced an unusual body of literature: *The Art of Guerrilla Warfare*, *The Partisan Leaders' Handbook*, and *How To Use High Explosives*. These pamphlets were never officially published in Britain, but hundreds of thousands of copies made their way across the world and were translated into a variety of languages.

Before SOE agents left for the continent they assembled in a flat in Ivor Court, Gloucester Place, a few yards west of Baker Street. From there they were driven to the Kent coast and put on a plane making the short journey to a disused French airfield. SOE agents who took this journey included Hardy Amies, later dress designer to the Queen, who as head of the organization's Belgian Section was in charge of Operation Ratweek during which prominent Nazis and sympathizers were assassinated. Another was David Murray, who later ran Murray's Cabaret Club on Beak Street where Christine Keeler and Mandy Rice-Davies were showgirls. However, officers preferred to use women, as they believed the Germans were less likely to stop them and conduct a bodysearch, and it was the female SOE agents that had the most dramatic war. There was Violette Szabo who was half-French, had the best shot in the SOE, and whose life was celebrated in the film *Carve Her Name With Pride*. Another was Pearl Witherington, alias Madame Cornioley, who played a crucial role during the D-Day landings and was so skilled at blowing up bridges Hitler put a million franc bounty on her head. Then there was Noor Inayet Khan, who was descended from the last Mogul Emperor of southern India, and had been born in the Kremlin as her father was lecturing in Moscow at the time; Yvonne Rudelat who was sent to the Loire valley to blow up 300,000-volt electricity cables; Odette Sansom; and Christina Granville.

Odette Sansom took a small sailing boat from the Kent coast to the French

Riviera. She needed little luggage but made sure, as did all her colleagues, that she had her cyanide pills, vital if faced with torture that might force her to disclose the names of collaborators. Landing near Cannes, she made contact with her supervisor, Peter Churchill, but both were soon betrayed by a double agent and imprisoned. Despite being tortured, Sansom stuck to her cover story that Peter Churchill was the nephew of Winston Churchill and she his wife, hoping that the Nazis might thereby refrain from murdering them. Although they condemned her to death at Ravensbrück concentration camp, she somehow survived.

Christina Granville was in reality a Polish countess, Krystyna Skarbek. Hers was the most remarkable story of all. She was sent to Hungary to produce propaganda during the war, and from there left for Poland to aid escapes and collect intelligence, entering the country in the middle of winter after walking for six days through a blizzard in −30 degrees. Although Granville was arrested by police, she feigned tuberculosis to win release and resumed her covert missions, freeing the SOE leader in the south of France from a Gestapo-run prison. Alas she was arrested at gunpoint during the Battle of Vercours, but when ordered to raise her hands readily did so, proudly revealing to her captors two hand grenades which she threatened to drop unless they let her go.

After the war Granville took a number of mundane jobs, including that of second-class stewardess on a liner travelling to Australia. When the captain insisted staff wear their wartime decorations she was unwilling to do so at first but eventually came on duty in a uniform bedecked in a riot of colours, to the astonishment of the captain and a mass outbreak of jealousy among the male staff.

On the liner she also met her nemesis – Dennis Muldowney. He tried to inveigle his way into her affections and pursued her back to London. On the night of 15 June 1952 Granville climbed the stairs of her hotel, the Shellbourne on South Kensington's Lexham Gardens, only to hear a voice behind her. It was Muldowney. She cried 'get him off me' but when the night porter rushed to the scene he found Muldowney clutching a knife, crying 'I killed her.' Muldowney made no attempt to escape but sat still until the police arrived. He then blurted out, as if in a B-movie, 'I built all my dreams around her, but she was playing me for a fool.'

Following the murder the press, constrained by the very limited amount of information they were allowed to print about subjects still cloaked in secrecy, dubbed Granville 'the modern pimpernel no man could resist . . . the woman who ordered the Gestapo and set agents free'. Muldowney had one of the shortest Old Bailey trials on record – three minutes almost to the second – after which he was sentenced to death and hanged.

It was ironic that Granville survived such daring wartime escapades to die at the hands of a spurned admirer, for being an SOE agent was one of the most precarious wartime occupations. For instance, all fifty agents parachuted into the Netherlands in 1942–43 as part of the 'Englandspiel' programme were rounded up and killed by the Nazis. Indeed, of the 418 SOE agents sent to Europe, 118 failed to return.

Across the West End many smart houses adorned by Dutch gables and Baroque carvings harboured covert war activities. At 140 Park Lane was the SOE's N (Netherlands) Section run by David Boyle, an agent who had once unsuccessfully tried to kidnap Irish prime minister Eamon de Valera in New York. The section's war record was as poor as Boyle's bodysnatching, for almost every agent sent into Holland was captured and later murdered at Mauthausen concentration camp. Yet when one captured agent sent back coded warnings of the impending doom to 140 Park Lane he was ignored. This convinced him that HQ's disinterest was part of a grand plan, and it was only when twenty or so imprisoned agents began communicating at Mauthausen via the camp's central heating system that they realized they were the victims of major incompetence rather than pawns in a clever game.

At 10 Duke Street, near Selfridge's, General Charles de Gaulle, following his arrival at Croydon Airport in a Dragon Rapide on 17 June 1940, set up his Free French government-in-exile. From here agents engaged in espionage and sabotage activities against not just the Nazis but against the Vichy French government (which had collaborated with the Germans), against the French communists and even against their hosts, the British, whom, they suspected, were planning to install a puppet government in France at the end of the war. When a suspected German agent was found hanged in the basement at No. 10 in 1943 it took much persuasion by the various security services before the police agreed to drop the matter. That year de Gaulle moved his operations to Algeria.

An elegant flat on Mayfair's Hertford Street harboured one Elvira Chaudoir, daughter of a Peruvian diplomat, who was dissembling staunchly to the Nazis. A telegram she sent to her Spanish bank asking for £50 contained a coded message she knew the Nazis would read and translate as news that the Allied Invasion of 1944 was going to take place not in Normandy, but the Bay of Biscay. The *Abwehr*, the German intelligence service, thought Chaudoir was working for them. In reality she was a British double agent, employed by MI6 to spread false information as part of Operation Fortitude. But her British bosses evidently didn't think that much of her. In her security file they described her as a 'typical member of the cosmopolitan smart set and, though possibly lazy, not un-intelligent. There is some reason to believe she is living with a man who has a flat in the same house. It is not known whether she is continuing with her lesbian tendencies.'

Mayfair's Curzon Street, setting for the government's resourceful propaganda unit in the Great War, was home to a number of spies and spycatchers in the Second World War. At Nos. 1–4 was a new block, Curzon Street House, built in 1939 on land that had been occupied by some thirty houses. It had a fortified bunker, constructed as part of the mass tunnel-building programme devised by Minister of Production Lord Beaverbrook, which was so solid members of the royal family sheltered within during air raids. A few hundred yards west, at Curzon Street's junction with Chesterfield Gardens was the army's London District Command headquarters. A corner of the building was fortified with gun ports, just in case German paratroopers landed in the nearby parks and began street battles in Mayfair. Even after the war MI5 continued to man the ports, especially on Sundays when the mobs assembled at Speaker's Corner may have been thinking of storming the streets.

Not every West End espionage scheme went to plan. In 1940 Special Branch agents led by Dick White, who went on to head both MI5 and MI6, launched a frantic hunt around the West End's nightclubs and pubs for Wilhelm Mörz, a Nazi master-spy. Mörz, previously a Hamburg policeman, had come to Britain posing as a Dutch refugee, and was believed to be setting up a fifth column to create mayhem in London in readiness for a German invasion.

Agents discovered that his London contact was Hans Jaeger of 21 Anson Road, Tufnell Park. They swarmed there, but to no avail. Then information arrived that Mörz had been spotted in a Chinese restaurant on Piccadilly. Alas the suspect turned out to be a waiter who simply looked like Mörz. However, MI5's Jack Curry had recognized Mörz 'without a doubt' getting into a taxi in Regent Street. This new trail led to the El Morocco club on

Gerrard Street. Still no Mörz. Then a new lead appeared. MI5 identified the Nazi's signature in the register of a Kensington hotel. 'We are getting hot!' enthused the organization's G. Wethered. Yet they never did catch up with the slippery Mörz. In his summary Dick White wondered whether 'Mörz had in fact been in Britain at all'.

The bigger the building, the greater its strategic importance was likely to be. For instance, Shell-Mex House on the Strand became the Ministry of Supply; Senate House in Bloomsbury the Ministry of Information; and in the West End the Grand Central Hotel at 222 Marylebone Road the London headquarters of MI9, Britain's escape and evasion unit.

The hotel, a monumental building of the 1890s, designed in the Flemish Renaissance style and decorated in mahogany, marble and stained glass, was where Airey Neave reported for duty after escaping from Colditz, the now legendary German prisoner of war camp. 'It's MI9 you'll be wanting,' he was told by the officer at the desk without a flicker of emotion, 'They're upstairs.' After debriefing Neave was allowed to contact relatives. He phoned his father but the latter was shaving and couldn't think of anything to say to his escaped son. Neave later became a Tory MP and was assassinated by the INLA at the Houses of Parliament in 1979.

It wasn't just inside those buildings requisitioned by the government that unusual wartime espionage activities took place. Being the West End, it was always possible that the well-heeled folk popping in and out of a solid Georgian door with fancy fanlights were not putting in the required war effort, their connivance not quite as blatantly anti-social as those residing in the East End's 'Deserters' Corner', but probably just as damaging.

For instance at 5 Bentinck Street, near Wigmore Hall, a house owned by the millionaire peer, scientist and intelligence officer Victor Rothschild, lived Anthony Blunt, who later became the Queen's art adviser and an infamous spy, and Guy Burgess, one of the Cold War's most notorious double agents. MI5, unimpressed with the two men's sexuality, later described the property as a 'homosexual bordello serving as a viperous nest of Soviet spies'.

When Blunt applied to the War Office for intelligence work he received two separate letters in return, one of acceptance and one of rejection. Ignoring the rejection, he took up a training post with the War Office which soon summoned him to an interview to explain why a security check had unearthed a suspicious left-wing past. Blunt convinced his superiors that he presented no danger, and was enlisted. But he soon established contact with Soviet agents, his chief collaborator being . . . Burgess. At No. 5 Blunt used his artistic skills to copy technical data from government documents that Rothschild had brought home, documents that included details of how to construct the nuclear bomb Rothschild and other scientists were perfecting at Imperial College. He then handed the information to the Soviets.

Darker still were the deeds dealt at 47 Gloucester Place, one of a long stretch of formidably austere Georgian terraced houses on the road that runs parallel to Baker Street. This was the early 1940s home of Tyler Kent, a clerk in the codes department at the American Embassy who was sympathetic to the Nazi cause. Kent stole from the embassy some two thousand documents, including a number of secret communications which had sped back and forth between Winston Churchill, before he became prime minister, and American president Franklin D. Roosevelt. He was planning to use the stolen letters to prove, with the help of a compliant Nazi-supporting MP, Captain Archibald Ramsay, that the two politicians had been plotting to replace Neville Chamberlain as prime minister and bring America into the war. Joe Kennedy, the American ambassador in London, waived Kent's diplomatic immunity, and on 20 May the authorities raided the flat, seizing huge bundles of papers, including 1,929 classified documents. A trial took place in secret and Kent received seven years, a relatively lenient sentence as he was an American citizen. Ramsay was arrested at his Kensington home just before he was able to raise the matter in the House of Commons. Had he done so the public embarrassment may have spelled the end of Churchill's career and likely a swift Allies' defeat to Germany. This being the war, there was next to no mention of the Kent affair in the papers, merely a small paragraph in the *Evening Standard* of 1 June 1940 stating that a clerk had been 'detained'.

## 'COLLAR THE LOT!'

Fascist activity in the West End was once socially acceptable. In the 1920s the word 'fascist' and its various Italian versions had no semiological cachet, and no one baulked at the idea of spending a Saturday evening socializing at the various local fascist clubs.

As Benito Mussolini tightened his grip on Italian society, Soho's Italian community grew more beholden to the new movement. From the HQ of the Italian Fascist Party at 25 Noel Street and the Club Cooperativo at 15 Greek

Street, fascists took control of every aspect of Italian social life in London. Every summer hundreds of local youngsters of Italian extraction were sent to summer schools that were little more than fascist recruitment camps for the movement. Even those Italians opposed to the movement were obliged to sign up as fascists. Signor Grandi, the foreign minister, insisted that all British-based Italians send a telegram to the Secretary-General of the Fascist Party in Rome registering their name and details of which societies they belonged to. Refusal to do so would inevitably result in *la spalla frigido* at the Italian embassy, culminating in rejection when applying for new passports.

By the late 1930s fascists were the enemy, without and within. So when the war began in 1939 Soho's large Italian community feared for its existence. It would only be a matter of time before the home country was embroiled, they assumed, given Italy's fascist predilections. However, those at the upper end of the social scale felt themselves to be untouchable.

Such was the case with F. V. Cochis. He was general manager of Claridge's, the prestigious Mayfair hotel, or at least he was until 24 April 1940 when the owners told him to leave his employment, and his grace and favour flat in the hotel at once. Cochis sought help from Claridge's owner, the Savoy chairman, Rupert D'Oyly Carte, son of the Gilbert and Sullivan impresario, Richard. 'The company has nothing against you personally,' D'Oyly Carte told him, 'but it has decided to make a change owing to the serious anti-British attitude taken by the Italian press.' Cochis gained support from friends until the Savoy group unearthed the interesting snippet that he was near the top of a blacklist of London Italians discovered to be enthusiastic fascists.

Anti-Italian attitudes in the British press were typified by an article in the *Daily Mirror* that April which hysterically claimed that: 'every Italian colony in Great Britain is a seething cauldron of smoking Italian politics. Black fascism. Hot as hell. Even the peaceful, law-abiding proprietor of the back-street coffee shop bounces into a fine patriotic frenzy at the sound of Mussolini's name.' Two months later on 10 June Italy declared war on Britain. Prime Minister Winston Churchill ordered that all London's Italian males between the ages of sixteen and seventy be rounded up and interned. Ignoring the Cabinet's pleas to intern only 'dangerous' members of the Anglo-Italian community, he told police to 'collar the lot!' This neatly avoided the need to differentiate between those who felt allegiances to their ancestors' homeland and those who wanted to fight for their birthplace.

Police raided the Italian Club on Charing Cross Road at 8 p.m. Waiters were ejected from the Ritz Hotel and Carlton Club mid shift. Ferraro, the well-known maître d' at the Berkeley, suddenly disappeared. Even Peppino Leoni, owner of Leoni's restaurant on Dean Street, was taken in. He later recalled how while walking to his cell he felt a 'sudden hatred for the police, for the British government which had issued the instructions for my intern-ment, and for all forms of authority. I had starved for 33 years to establish my restaurant. I deeply resented the fact that after 33 years in England with no political or police blemish on my record I had been scooped up without proper consideration.'

Violence broke out immediately throughout Soho. A group of women marched along Broadwick Street, heading for the Italian shops of Old Comp-ton Street, ready to carry out the prime minister's injunction themselves, until they were thwarted by an Italian woman, Rose Blau, who pleaded with them to reconsider, explaining that Soho's Italians were mostly English born and did not support Mussolini. The march broke up.

George Orwell in his wartime diary for 12 June 1940 recorded his thoughts as he wandered through Soho noting the effect Italy's joining the war was having on Italian shops. With quick thinking many owners had renamed them as 'British' or cleverly erected placards claiming 'We are Swiss.' The Spaghetti House (now one of London's longest-running Italian restaurants) had overnight become the 'British Food Shop'. Orwell noted how the placards were so professional they must have been prepared some time before and kept in readiness.

Nevertheless, nearly all London's Italians were rounded up. The owners of the Camisa delicatessen on Old Compton Street were taken to the local police station for questioning. From there, like thousands of London Ital-ians, they were sent first to Lingfield racecourse in Surrey and then to Warth Mills in Bury while the Foreign Office decided on their future. When a list of those who were to travel on the luxury liner the *Arandora Star* for a new life in Canada was read out, the Camisas, to their disappointment, found that they were to be sent to the Isle of Man instead. A few days later the Germans torpedoed the *Arandora Star* in the Atlantic, even though it was flying the Swastika, and 730 lives were lost.

At least the Camisas were alive, but they were bored beyond repair. Used to spending twelve hours a day running their delicatessen, they had next to nothing to do on the Isle. When the war was over they returned to Soho, only to find that they had lost control of the shop to another branch of the family.

They opened their own deli on Berwick Street (it is no longer there), while the branch of the family that took over the Old Compton Street shop eventually moved across the street to No. 61 where they still prosper, selling London's finest ravioli and olives.

Also interned were a number of German Jews. The authorities didn't know what to do with them. One such refugee was Erwin Frenkel. A talented pianist, Frenkel had come to London from Vienna in May 1938 after his mother had told him to flee lest his temper got him in trouble. Frenkel wanted all the family to go, but his father chose to stay loyal to the local synagogue where he was cantor. Frenkel's mother bade him a tearful goodbye, crying that she would never see him again, and she was right. He went to London, rented a flat on New Cavendish Street, north of Oxford Circus, where he lived with a gentile Austrian girl, and made a living playing piano in a pub in Finsbury Park. Nevertheless, he was summoned to an 'aliens" tribunal where testimonials from rabbis were no match for a chairman who accused him of living off the immoral earnings of his girlfriend. Frenkel cracked up. He denied the allegations but was interned nonetheless. Later he claimed that he had been denounced by a rival pianist who wanted his job.

## AMERICAN BEAUTIES

Once the USA entered the war in December 1941 a new phenomenon hit London – Americans. Previously these exotic creatures had only been seen on celluloid, but they were even more electrifying in the flesh.

Two types of Americans arrived in the capital. There were the fresh-faced graduates hired by the US army's intelligence outfit, the Office of Strategic Services (OSS), and the rank and file GIs. The historian Malcolm Muggeridge described the OSS boys, whose number included William Casey, later the head of the CIA, as being like '*jeune filles en fleur* straight from a finishing school'. In October 1943 they moved into the heavily guarded 70 Grosvenor Street, Mayfair, and after a few weeks in London gained enough confidence to go on to the roof of the building rather than take shelter during air raids, as they could now tell from the sound whether the aircraft were coming from Hyde Park, St James's Park or Regent's Park.

The OSS took over a number of other West End addresses. They trained their agents at 40 Berkeley Square and ran a clothing department from 68 Brook Street. Their best agents lived on Hay's Mews, built as stables and coach houses for Berkeley Square properties in the 1740s, home of Ian Fleming shortly before he began writing the James Bond thrillers in the 1950s. Their signals' centre was deep under Tottenham Court Road by Goodge Street station, taking up space that had been outlined in 1939, at the outset of the war, for a planned new express tube system with stops at occasional Northern Line stations, which was eventually scrapped.

General 'Ike' Eisenhower, commander of the US armed forces during the Second World War, had his military headquarters at 20 Grosvenor Square. It was an excellent location: classy, central and accessible, but not exactly safe. When Eisenhower asked his British hosts for a base at least fifty miles outside London he was told that was impossible as he wouldn't be able to drive 'even twenty miles in the blackout'.

Eisenhower stayed mostly at the concrete-clad Dorchester Hotel on Park Lane, but at first lodged at Claridge's, the luxury hotel on Brook Street, where staff and guests were astonished to see his staff bringing him a crate of fresh fruit, goods unknown in London since war began. His room, he claimed, looked like a 'goddam fancy funeral parlour decorated in whorehouse pink' and he felt uneasy in Claridge's luxurious atmosphere, revealing to an aide: 'I feel like I'm living in sin.' Eisenhower didn't move out until it was pointed out to him that the hotel was 'a hunk of sugar; one bomb and the whole building will dissolve'.

Had Eisenhower learned of the fate endured by Lord Selbourne, minister for economic warfare and a member of Churchill's war cabinet, at Claridge's, he may have insisted more on avoiding London altogether. It was here that Selbourne dallied not with his wife but with a charming foreigner – Mathilde Lucie Carre – unaware that she was also 'Victoire', a double agent who was also working for the Nazis and eventually betrayed ninety members of the French Resistance to save herself. She knew that Selbourne was technically in charge of the Special Operations Executive, but not that he was too badly informed to divulge anything important. Victoire was eventually arrested, and interned for the rest of the war, narrowly escaping execution in 1949.

The London-based OSS officers weren't just planning for D-Day. In November 1943 they discovered that Hitler had only eight months' worth of industrial diamonds left and that a continuous supply was vital for his war machine. As Edward Jay Epstein explained in *The Diamond Invention*, only diamonds were hard enough to produce the precision parts of airplane engines, tanks, torpedoes and other weapons of war. Only diamonds were able to draw the fine wire needed for radar and its associated electronics. Only diamonds could provide the bearings necessary for the guidance systems of submarines and planes. And without diamonds work on the V1 and V2s would not be able to proceed.

Unfortunately for the Nazis the diamond mines were mostly closed, and De Beers, a Jewish firm, controlled the world's supply. Nevertheless, the Nazis succeeded in obtaining the jewels. The OSS spent considerable resources investigating how, and it wasn't until nearly the end of the war that they were able to establish the leak: the Forminiere mine in the Belgian Congo and a corrupt police chief in Leopoldville, the capital, through whom the gems were being smuggled out of Tangier and Cairo in Red Cross parcels.

Not every American soldier seconded to General Eisenhower's Grosvenor Square team worked solely for military intelligence. John Sweet, a clerk at No. 20, won a part in the era's most remarkable British film, Powell and Pressburger's *A Canterbury Tale*. The film follows the fortunes of a group of army innocents loose in the Kent town, its themes linked with Chaucer's medieval religious epic *The Canterbury Tales*. Sweet was lucky. The production teams had sought permission to use established Hollywood names, but the US army wouldn't sanction the release of Burgess Meredith or Tyrone Power. Sweet took the part of Sergeant Bob Johnson, what he described as a 'sort of Jimmy Stewart American from Oregon, a country boy', and was released from the army for six months to shoot the film in Kent and at Denham Studios, west London. Undissuaded by the Blitz and the bombs, Powell and Pressburger sped across the West End finding suitable locations for their other great war classic, *The Life and Death of Colonel Blimp*, which Churchill hated and tried to suppress. Their favourite location was the handsome block on the corner of Park Lane and North Row, which they used as the Home Guard HQ in the film.

The ordinary soldiers, or GIs, occupied a different part of the West End – the neon-lit centre. Their base was the Rainbow Club on the corner of Shaftesbury Avenue and Piccadilly Circus. When the Rainbow opened in November 1942 the key was symbolically thrown away to demonstrate how it would be open '24/7', as its users so eloquently put it in their impatient Ameringlish. In the lobby a distance post proclaimed: 'Leicester Square 100 yards, Berlin 600 miles, New York 3,271 miles.' American soldiers came to the Rainbow to socialize, read US papers and play pinball, but not to eat hot dogs, for they considered the English sausage inedible. After the war the building became a school for GI brides, where they could learn about American mores and how to drink eight glasses of water a day to make up for the lack of moisture in the American air.

The influx into London of thousands of GIs thrilled those who saw the war as one long party, albeit one with the lights mostly dimmed. An added delight for many came from the fact that one in ten of the US soldiers in London was black, even though foreign secretary Anthony Eden had urged the Americans not to send them to the UK. Some of the black GIs found the West End to be not completely welcoming. A sergeant complained that he was turned away from a Soho dance hall, and another was assaulted by two white US marines in Lyons' Corner House near Piccadilly Circus. There were also problems of racism within the American contingent, for many white American soldiers from the Deep South treated their black colleagues with a paternalism which both sides found natural but shocked the British. When a group of US officers refused to share a restaurant with an African trade delegation the matter was discussed at Cabinet level where Winston Churchill advocated giving the Africans a banjo so that they could pretend they were part of the band.

Initially the Americans were unpopular. They would demand of the barman 'Gimme a beer as quick as you got out of Dunkirk', or 'I hear the British flag has four colours – blue, red, white and yellow.' But eventually the GIs were warmly embraced by Londoners, particularly those whom Evelyn Waugh described as 'ill-favoured adolescent girls [who with] their aunts and mothers swarmed out of the slums into the squares of Mayfair and Belgravia. There they passionately and publicly embraced and were rewarded with chewing-gum, razor blades and other rare trade goods.'

For the Americans the law was occasionally different. Rape, for instance, was a capital offence in some US states. Consequently eight American servicemen were hanged on British soil. Not that the public would have been aware of such drama at a time of strict news rationing. Had they been, how great would have been their shock on discovering the even more extraordinary news that one absconding GI, a Ben Sutherland, was shot at on Park Lane, no less, by *American* police . . . in broad daylight . . . in London . . . !

War meant that people needed to take refuge. The poor went down the overcrowded tube stations, the rich to the Dorchester Hotel, reputedly one of the safest buildings in the capital. The Dorchester's air raid shelter was more comfortable than those on the Central Line tube stations or the Tilbury shelter house of horrors in the East End. Here the sleeping berths were two feet, rather than two inches, apart. There were even pillows, with slippers laid out neatly at the foot of the bed. Despite rationing the menu at the Dorchester remained barely affected, offering oysters, smoked salmon and lobster, but only until 1944 when the sandwiches started to be made of soya paste. At the Dorchester the well-heeled could mix with members of Churchill's War Cabinet, the novelist Somerset Maugham, who was wrongly thought to have gone missing when France fell to the Germans in 1940, and society hostesses such as Diana Cooper and Lady Cunard who knew their parties were more likely to attract the great and good here than in a decaying, servant-less Mayfair mansion.

Invitations from Emerald Cunard were the most coveted, and her dinners were free. When the air-raid sirens sounded she would crawl under the table and read Proust to her guests. An unimpressed visitor was Ernest Hemingway. When Lady Cunard asked him what he thought of Russia, he replied: 'There is the pro as well as the con about Russia. As with all these fucking countries.' Ronnie Greville, the society hostess who had flirted with Nazism before the war, was another who signed in at the Dorchester. Even as late as spring 1942 her Dorchester parties were attracting those who should have known better; those better known for embodying the moral righteousness of the Allied war effort, such as Lord Mountbatten. Four months later she was dead. Alas she had ordered her butlers to burn all her private correspondence.

A different set of establishment figures took root further along Park Lane at the Grosvenor House Hotel. It was here that the French resistance leader, Charles de Gaulle, rallied his followers with a speech on Bastille Day, 1941. And it was here too at a party on 1 December 1944, held to celebrate the twenty-fifth anniversary of the entry of women into Parliament, that Lady Astor, who had been the first woman MP to take her seat, announced she was not seeking re-election to the House of Commons, telling the gathering: 'I believe I have something to give to the House of Lords, but I'm not sure they want what I've got.'

Although the Nazi bombs largely ignored the West End – Hitler wanted it relatively intact for his own nefarious purposes after he had conquered the country – some bombs did fall. One significant casualty was the Café de Paris, the chic nightclub on Leicester Square where twin staircases curved down from a balcony based on the Palm Court of the *Lusitania* ocean liner to a dance-floor modelled on the ballroom of the *Titanic*. At the outset of the war the singer Inge Anders premiered a new novelty song at the Café which went: 'We're going to hang out our washing on the Siegfried Line', a jokey reference to the Germans' WWI western defensive line. It soon became one of the most popular numbers in the country. Harry Roy's Band, the club's regular act, contributed to the war effort with the song 'God Bless You, Mr Chamberlain', a nod to the prime minister, its chorus, 'We're all mighty proud of you. You look swell holding your umbrella, All the world loves a wonderful feller . . .'

But the most popular Café de Paris bandleader was Ken 'Snakehips' Johnson, a native of British Guiana. When war began Johnson announced: 'I'm determined to make them like swing at the Café or die in the attempt.' Alas he did both, for on 8 March 1941, as his band was playing to a packed crowd, two fifty ton landmines fell through the roof, killing the band leader and thirty-three others. The explosion was so intense the musicians and dancers were instantaneously killed, frozen in their dance poses.

There were survivors. One was a Dutch officer who had his injured leg washed by champagne, the only liquid at hand. Another was Betty Baldwin, daughter of the erstwhile prime minister, Stanley, who complained about looters arriving on the scene, tearing rings off the fingers of the dead and making off with handbags.

Although thousands of Londoners had been evacuated to the countryside, with those left in the capital living in fear of buzz bombs, death rays and imminent German invasion, at least the West End was bustling with illicit activity. There were illegal gambling schools – *spielers* – such as the heavily fortified Forty Four Club at 44 Gerrard Street and so-called 'bottle parties'. Guests at these had to sign a chit which enabled them to drink spirits previously ordered but not paid for. In the West End the best-known venue for wartime bottle parties was the Chez Nous. When the *Daily Telegraph* newspaper exposed the club's activities the owner sued, claiming the newspaper article had damaged his reputation, but lost the case when the judge told him 'You have no reputation to lose.' Eventually the authorities decided to ignore illicit West End drinking as it was too difficult to monitor the hundreds of such establishments that had sprouted across the area. That or they buckled under pressure from the American war machine which needed somewhere to relax.

Despite rationing it was possible to pick up all manner of illicit goods – most popularly silk stockings – during the war, particularly at Hymie Schnatz's stall on Berwick Street; never on the counter, but underneath or around the corner, from a man with a Ronald Colman moustache. Such figures soon acquired the name 'spiv', a corruption of the Romany word for sparrow, and they continued operating well into peacetime – as long as rationing lasted – much to the annoyance of prime minister Clement Attlee who told the House in 1947 that there was a 'section of the public which renders no useful purpose. Its members continue to make money in all kinds of dubious ways. We shall take all action open to us against these – I think they call themselves "spivs" and other drones.'

There were even spiv films. Typical was *The Noose*, a 1948 concoction by Edmond T. Greville featuring a gang of black marketeers headed by a Soho nightclub owner aided by the usual characters – boxers, market porters and cab drivers. Eventually there was a 'spiv' law – the Regulation of Employment Order (1947) which forced people to sign on for 'essential work' and allowed Ministry of Labour officials to search premises where they were likely to find shirkers, draft dodgers, deserters and other defaulters. So much bureaucracy; so little success.

# MINISTRY OF TRUTH

When Britain stood alone against the Nazis in spring 1940 the BBC made plans for dealing with the expected German invasion of London. 'Operation Stronghold' they called it. To reassure the public well-known voices such as the writer J. B. Priestley would conduct most of the broadcasts, giving instructions to the population on whether to resist and what to sabotage until the Nazis took over the airwaves, after which contrary messages, in suspiciously authentic and slightly-out-of-date English, would have been inserted by compliant fifth columnists, no doubt.

Propaganda was disseminated during the war from a number of select West End addresses. Some were requisitioned by the government for the BBC as soon as hostilities were declared. For instance, at 55 Portland Place George Orwell, then barely known outside the literary world (the lucid writing of his mostly autobiographical quasi-novels such as *Down and Out in Paris and London* jarring with the fashionable writing styles of the day), was one of a number of writers and intellectuals hired to take part in wartime broadcasts which were beamed to India, Burma and Malaya to maintain morale in the Far East in the face of the Japanese onslaught.

In June 1942 Orwell's office moved to the huge Peter Robinson store near Oxford Circus. There, as Malcolm Muggeridge explained, 'from a studio deep under Oxford Street, Orwell beamed at listeners in Cawnpore, Kaula Lumpar and Rangoon, assuming of course that there were any, poems such as "The Waste Land" [read by the author, T. S. Eliot, himself]. When I delicately suggested that this may well have failed to hit its target, the absurdity of the enterprise struck him anew and he began to chuckle, deep in his throat.'

Wandering around the local streets while taking a break from the BBC propaganda unit, Orwell's mood failed to brighten. In his wartime diary for 25 October 1940 he noted with the kind of anti-Semitism that had propelled Hitler: 'The other night examined the crowds sheltering in Chancery Lane, Oxford Circus and Baker Street stations. Not all Jews but I think a higher proportion of Jews than one would normally see in a crowd of this size. What is bad about Jews is that they are not only conspicuous, but go out of their way to make themselves so. A fearful Jewish woman, a regular comic-paper cartoon of a Jewess, fought her way off the train at Oxford Circus, landing blows on anyone who stood in her way.'

Orwell cut a figure sartorially and psychologically distinct from the typical broadcaster. At that time BBC announcers wore full evening dress, and could be fired if they got divorced. They were not allowed to mention certain topics, such as gambling, on air. But Orwell wore his normal, everyday clothes, those of a typical down-at-heel writer of the time – the bottoms of his trousers rolled, the elbows of his jacket leather-patched. He wasn't the most easygoing of souls. Paranoid that his mic wasn't wired up, he told a colleague that it was possible that someone pretending to be George Orwell was broadcasting more politically acceptable information from another room in the building. Orwell resigned from the BBC in September 1943 complaining that he had been 'wasting his own time and public money on doing work that produces no result'. But at least the BBC continued to maintain rigorous standards of political fairness throughout the war. For instance, they made sure Hitler was paid royalties whenever excerpts were read from *Mein Kampf*.

## BUNKER MENTALITY

The war that followed the Second World War – the Cold War – had an equally dynamic effect on the West End. It was played out in the exclusive apartment blocks and elegant town houses of Mayfair and Marylebone. Guy Burgess, one of the three most famous Cold War defectors to Soviet Russia (along with Donald Maclean and Kim Philby), had his last London address at Clifford Chambers, 10 New Bond Street. In 1950 he was sent as a diplomat to the USA. He failed to impress and gained notoriety for his unusual behaviour – chewing garlic as if it were gum and emptying a plate of prawns into his pocket which he left there for a week. On 25 May 1951 Burgess fled to the USSR.

Before fleeing to Moscow Maclean spent the same night (which was also his last in Britain) at Schmidt's restaurant, 33–37 Charlotte Street, with its legendarily rude waiters. On leaving he was followed to Charing Cross station by MI5 agents, who suspected him of passing atomic secrets to the Russians and wanted to make sure he was taking his usual train home. They left him at Charing Cross but he outsmarted them, slipping out of the station and being picked up by Guy Burgess, who was waiting for him outside the station in a car.

Expecting to return swiftly to Britain, Burgess left his Austin A70 at Southampton Dock. But neither man came back. Once MI5 realized they had defected, deputy director General Guy Liddell and Anthony Blunt, who was then Director of the Courtauld Institute, searched Burgess's flat for incriminating evidence. Liddell couldn't have made a worse choice. Blunt, art adviser to George VI and later Queen Elizabeth, was himself a Soviet agent, and during the search, according to the espionage historian Roy Berkeley, made sure he removed anything suspicious from the flat, particularly documents relating to himself. To the end of his life Burgess continued ordering his suits from Savile Row rather than from the heroic, proletarian Moscow stores.

It wasn't simply the presence of communist agents in the upper echelons of British society that made the Cold War years interesting, it was the way that so many smart West End addresses were at the mercy of the security services, just as they had been for the military during the Second World War. Rather than casting an innocent eye over the desirable streets of Marylebone and Mayfair, it is better to assume a cynical view. Those ornate West End

houses with their Baroque embellishments, gargoyles and stone dressings:
what arch clandestine machinations must they have witnessed!

Take Claridge's, one of London's most exclusive hotels, for instance.
When Winston Churchill was prime minister during the Second World War
he used the hotel to hold all-night meetings with US army intelligence personnel. These would end at 6 a.m. when the hotel barber would appear and
whisk the prime minister off for a haircut and shave. Churchill moved into
the hotel penthouse in 1945 after his shock defeat at the general election left
him homeless.

Some ten years later Nikita Khrushchev, the Soviet premier, stayed at
Claridge's during his April 1956 visit to Britain. His rooms were bugged by
MI5 who used a radio beam to activate his phone. Outside the hotel Khrushchev faced a different kind of attention. Wherever he went he was booed, a
noise he had never previously heard, coming from a regime where he was
permanently surrounded by toadying sycophants. What, he asked his Foreign
Office escort, was that 'boo,ooo' sound coming from the back of the crowd?
The diplomat explained that it was booing, that the people were expressing
disapproval. Rather than feeling hurt Khrushchev was bemused. In the back
of the car he began to say 'Boo' and 'Ooo', over and over again. When he got
back to Claridge's he continued the banter for the rest of the day, exclaiming
'Boo! Ooo!' to everyone he met.

Had Khrushchev slipped out of the hotel, headed down Davies Street,
along Berkeley Square, continued south along Fitzmaurice Place, turned
right onto Curzon Street and stopped by Leconfield House, at the junction
with Chesterfield Gardens, he would have found himself at MI5's headquarters. MI5, according to Stella Rimington, who later became its first female
chief, was then in the company of 'a small group of military officers, all male
of course, who all seemed to live in Guildford and spent their spare time
gardening. One had been a Dambuster, and had flown the most dramatic
and dangerous sorties when he was very young. He regularly withdrew into
his office and locked the door after lunch. I used to jump up and down in the
corner to look over the smoked glass in the partition, to see what he was
doing, and he was invariably sound asleep.'

MI5 was then run by a director-general whose name was unknown to
nearly every member of the organization – all part of the necessary mystique – but who was readily identifiable in the Curzon Street corridors, it
was joked, by being the only agent allowed to wear dark glasses. When

Rimington expressed an interest in promotion to officer class, causing apoplexy within the solely male, braces-wearing ranks, she was put on an intensive training course. This involved going into a given pub, striking up a conversation with a man at random and finding out all about his private life. She needed a plausible cover in advance and had to be prepared for her superior entering the pub at any moment, recognizing her and blowing her cover – just to see how she coped. MI5 moved to Gower Street near Euston in 1970 and returned to Curzon Street in 1976, this time taking premises at Nos. 1–4, Curzon Street House. The organization left for Thames House on Millbank in the 1990s, and the building has since been renovated into offices.

Should Khrushchev have contemplated a less high-profile trip, he could have surreptitiously headed for the No. 8 lamp post on Audley Square in Mayfair, where Soviet spies would make a blue chalk mark so that their contacts knew they had to go to Brompton Oratory church and pick up a package. Audley Square was a good choice. Nearby, at No. 3, Eon Productions film company later worked on the early James Bond features.

Towering over a West End held in the icy grip of the Cold War were four gleaming, reaching, secret service-run skyscrapers: Euston Tower; the MI5 headquarters at 140 Gower Street; the Post Office (now BT) Tower; and further south, Centrepoint. It was just as George Orwell had prophesied in 1984; each a monstrous new presence; vast, impersonal, futurist, sinister.

Euston Tower and the now demolished MI5 HQ had little to distinguish themselves architecturally, whereas the slender frame and massed aerials of the BT Tower, built as the Post Office Tower between 1963 and 1966, and then the tallest building in London, make it one of the most potent symbols of that era. In a near future all structures would look like this, so people thought at the time. Brick, stone, Classical embellishment, Renaissance décor, Baroque flourishes, Gothic adornments would disappear in a hi-tech world of glass, granite and vitrolite.

Centrepoint at St Giles's Circus, one of the West End's eastern gateways, was the most controversial of all these new Cold War creations. To deflect attention from Centrepoint's secret state status, the Government threw up a smokescreen around its construction, supposedly as part of a Ministry of Transport initiative, announced in July 1956, to 'clear-up' the intersection of roads at St Giles Circus. The scheme ran into delays, due to problems involving the paying of compensation to affected property owners and shopkeepers, until a developer, Harry Hyams, offered to buy the site in exchange for a 'Land for Planning Permission' deal.

Hyams, despite not owning the land, outlined plans for a thirty-seven-storey 380-foot honeycomb tower, and was soon granted an extremely lucrative deal, as well as a 150-year lease. The press and public were amazed at how planning permission had been rushed through, and complaints came from many quarters, including the Royal Fine Art Commission, who were told it could only adjudicate on buildings if development was referred to it in the first place, and that this one, unfortunately, hadn't been. Four days *after* Richard Seifert submitted his design for the tower, the Town and Country Planning Act 1959 came into force, outlawing the practice whereby developers sought (and often received) planning permission for land they did not own.

These skyscrapers were constructed in the 1960s at a time of intense government paranoia. They were equipped with all the latest hi-tech wizardry: air conditioning, super-fast lifts, swivel chairs, drinks machines. They were made ready for housing civil servants, who if war was imminent would move in, poised to run London from the bunkers below.

The government believed World War Three would be a prolonged struggle like its predecessors. The communists would drop an A-bomb, which would devastate the urban centres, but below these towers government officials would be preparing for the time when they could re-emerge and rebuild London. That was the initial thinking, but rapid developments in technology soon made their ideas obsolete. By the early 1960s government scientists knew that nuclear war meant gross annihilation. London would cease to exist. Nevertheless, some use had to be found for these leviathans. So MI5 housed its telephone network on the seventeenth floor of Euston Tower, where an 0800 number allowed its agents to phone HQ for free from any phone box in those pre-mobile days. The Ministry of Defence used the Post Office Tower for bouncing high-frequency microwave beams across the country as part of a national chain. The next building in line was in Stanmore, twelve miles north-west, and after that Dunstable, Bedfordshire, further north, and so on up the entire length of the country. Once the building's original Cold War purposes were no longer viable the Post Office allowed the public access to the observation tower. Around a million people took advantage until a bomb was found in the roof of the gents' toilets in 1971. It was a convenient excuse to shoo the public out so that the original strategic defence purposes could resume under more-advanced technology.

Centrepoint was finished in 1967, just as the Ministry of Transport, with great timing, announced that the road system outside had been shelved. As the government's original Cold War civil-defence policy was now redundant, Seifert's tower stood empty for six years while the authorities contemplated its future. The public was told that as office rents were rising sharply it was better to leave the tower empty than rent it out and tie its value down to a particular rent-review period. But the controversy over Centrepoint has never been solely based around its uselessness as an office block. What the 1950s and 1960s public found distasteful was the mass destruction of the locale – old St Giles and the stretch of shops at the northern end of Charing Cross Road which included London's first women's bookshop, opened in May 1910 to cater for growth in suffragist literature – to build a 380-foot, honeycomb-windowed white elephant.

Each of these towers was also deliberately placed above the tube network. For instance Euston Tower stands above Warren Street station, the now demolished MI5 headquarters at 140 Gower Street above Euston Square station, the BT Tower above the Victoria Line between Oxford Circus and Warren Street, and Centrepoint above Tottenham Court Road station. The reason behind building the towers above the network was primarily one of civil defence. During the Second World War the government decided to construct a number of bomb-proof tunnels that could take cables between strategically important buildings: Buckingham Palace, understandably; Curzon Street House, with its royal bunker; the Museum Telephone Exchange in Fitzrovia, home of the BBC's national distribution centre, on which the BT tower now stands; and the railway termini of Euston, St Pancras and King's Cross.

Once the war was over the authorities decided to build tunnels large enough for trains to run alongside the cables, hence the route of the Victoria Line, which connects all these sites. More recently other important, strategic buildings have been built above the line to make use of those connections, namely MI6 (by Vauxhall station) and the British Library, two of whose subterranean floors sandwich the line between Euston and King's Cross stations. Whether these lavish preparations will be of use in future wars is not yet known.

# 10

# Foul Play

The West End has long been the crime capital of London. Although gibbets for hanging criminals in public were dotted all around the capital, particularly in lonely spots such as the southern tip of the Isle of Dogs, the most famous London gallows of all was in the West End by the Tyburn stream, a few yards from where Marble Arch now stands. From 1196 to 1783 more than 50,000 people were hanged there.

Originally the Tyburn gallows was a basic site, but in 1511 it was expanded into the Tyburn Tree. This was an enormous triangular construction of three posts, eighteen feet high, known popularly as the 'Never-Green Tree', capable of hanging twenty-four prisoners at the same time, eight on each horizontal beam. Hangings took place seven or eight times a year, at events which were treated as public festivals. Spectators sat in grandstands, the wealthy on the best seats, by the tree, or in the rented rooms of the upper storeys of nearby houses and pubs. And for those who had to make do with a cheaper or free view among the masses there was always the added thrill of having one's pockets picked by someone who might end up at Tyburn a few months later.

In charge of the seating arrangements were the so-called Tyburn pew-openers. One such figure, Mammy Douglas, raised her prices from 2/- to 2/6 in 1758 for the demise of a Dr Florence Henesy (a man, despite his emasculated name – at that time there were only male doctors), who was hanged for treason. Mammy was publicly decried for profiteering, nevertheless the public paid up, grudgingly, until at the last minute when the doctor was reprieved, which understandably led to a riot as the mob tried to replace the fortunate doctor with Mammy Douglas.

The hangmen were all nicknamed Jack Ketch in mock honour of the executioner who botched the job when doing away with the Duke of Monmouth at the Tower of London in 1685. The hangman had the right to keep the clothes of the dead, and so as a snub many prisoners wore rags. But some of the condemned wore quality threads, hoping that a grateful executioner would ease their suffering by pulling on their legs and beating on their chests so that they died quicker. The hangman could also make a little cash on the side from members of the crowd who would pay for the right to stroke the dead or dying body, as they believed this had health benefits. Finally, at the end of the day's events, the hangman could sell the rope for sixpence. The more notorious the victim the more the rope would fetch.

The great writers and artists often came to Tyburn for inspiration. Samuel Pepys described in his diary for 21 January 1664 how he 'got for a shilling to stand upon the wheel of a cart, in great pain, about an hour before the execution was done'. Dr Johnson's biographer, James Boswell, seeing the highwayman Paul Lewis hanged in May 1763, exclaimed: 'I was most terribly shocked, and thrown into a very deep melancholy.' As for Tyburn art, in William Hogarth's *Industry and Idleness*, Plate 11: 'The Idle 'Prentice Executed at Tyburn', a huge crowd gathers to enjoy the executions, indulging in feasting, drinking and making merry while a group of boys overturn a fruit cart and pick the pocket of a cake salesman. Amongst the usual Hogarthian detail a Methodist minister urges the condemned man to repent as the officiating Anglican clergyman sits unconcerned in his carriage.

## GALLOWS HUMOUR

Hanging days had a well-defined macabre programme of activity. At daybreak well-wishers would start to line the route from the jail to the hanging tree. Victims would rise at seven o'clock at Newgate prison, where they were held prior to execution, and be led in fetters into Newgate Yard. There a blacksmith would take off their chains, and the Yeoman of the Halter would tie their hands in front of them, so that the hands would be in a praying position when they reached Tyburn. He would place a rope round their necks, the free end left to coil around their bodies, and lead them to the start of their journey.

The first stop was St Sepulchre's church on Newgate Street, where the condemned were given a nosegay of flowers. The Newgate church bell would sound, and the clerk would chant: 'You that are condemned to die, repent with lamentable tears; ask mercy of the Lord for the salvation of your souls.' The procession would then move down Snow Hill, across the Fleet Ditch and up the hill to High Holborn. Through the narrow streets of St Giles it would head for a tavern by St Giles's Hospital where prisoners took their last drink, known as the Cup of Charity, without having to pay, although some jokingly promised to buy a round on the way back. Then it was back on the wagon – never to drink again (hence the phrase 'on the wagon'). Lastly, at the start of Tyburn Road (Oxford Street), they were placed behind their coffin on a hurdle, to be dragged along the rest of the trip, a stretch that would last several hours.

As the condemned went to the gallows they would be approached by authors seeking their approval in publishing material already written as 'last confessions'. In return the condemned would advertise the forthcoming work to the crowds before they were executed, and the families would be duly rewarded. Finally there was the execution itself. The blindfolded victim, a hood over the head, the hands tied behind the back, would stand on a wagon with a rope around the neck and wait while the horse was whipped into running off. As the wagon moved away the prisoner would be left to dangle, dying a slow death from asphyxiation that might last nearly a painful hour, which was the whole point as far as the sentencers were concerned. Those singled out for really severe punishment were disembowelled while only half-hanged. The crowd knew that death had overcome life when they saw the dribble of urine down the leg.

The public wasn't horrified by these spectacles. On the contrary many took delight in the drama. Cheers would increase if the prisoner put up a fight, especially if he or she fought to the end as they dangled and swung; and life expectancy being so short in those days it was not as if many were dying prematurely.

Tyburn victims were mostly commonplace felons. There were a few murderers, more bread thieves, many who had simply tampered with haystacks, and many more who had fallen foul of the bewildering number of 'crimes' that precipitated hanging in those days. Among those executed here were Roger, Earl of Mortimer, who deposed Edward II in 1330; Perkin Warbeck, who rivalled Henry VII for the throne; and the Jesuit, Robert Southwell. He survived thirteen torture sessions and an imperfect hanging after the noose was placed improperly around his neck. The hangman then took mercy on him and pulled his feet to end his agony. At a time when the authorities didn't believe in half measures, Southwell was finally beheaded, quartered and disembowelled.

Then there were those deemed responsible for executing Charles I: Oliver Cromwell; his son-in-law, Henry Ireton; and John Bradshaw. In December 1660, after the country had reverted to a monarchy, Parliament voted that their bodies should be exhumed from their tombs at Westminster Abbey, drawn to the gallows, and hanged and buried under it. En route the three dead men were displayed overnight in the Red Lion pub on High Holborn. As Bradshaw's corpse had not been satisfactorily embalmed, and had badly decayed, the tavern was filled with a considerable stench during the exhibition. The next day the corpses were taken to Tyburn where though dead the three men were hanged and decapitated. The heads were then skewered onto poles outside Westminster Hall.

In the late eighteenth century the best-known Tyburn victim was Dr Dodd, a clergyman who had forged a £4,200 bond in the name of the Earl of Chesterfield. He was hanged in 1777, and after friends cut down the body they took it to a Goodge Street undertaker's where John Hunter, the eminent surgeon, tried unsuccessfully to bring Dodd back to life, even going as far as to give the unfortunate doctor a hot bath – all in vain. Three years later scores of West Enders went to the drop after being involved in the anti-Catholic Gordon Riots. Samuel Rogers, a witness, recollected seeing 'a whole cartload of young girls, in dresses of various colours, on the way to be executed at Tyburn'. Their crime? Watching as the mob burned down the homes of Catholics.

Some received a pardon just in time. In 1447 five men who had been placed on the gallows were lucky enough to win a reprieve while still alive. They were cut down and stripped by the hangman. Being allowed to keep the clothes of victims, he refused to part with the garments, despite the pleas of the men, who were obliged to walk home naked. Some who were hanged lived to tell the tale. One man pushed open the lid of his coffin and asked for a drink. A kindly spectator offered him a jug of wine, which he drank, only to drop down dead on the spot, this time for good. Sixteen-year-old William Duell, who was hanged after being convicted of rape and murder, recovered at the Surgeons' Hall on Newgate just as he was about to be dissected. He had his sentence commuted to transportation. A John Smith, who was hanged at Tyburn on Christmas Eve, 1705, was left to dangle for fifteen minutes until the crowd shouted 'reprieve'. He was cut down and taken to a nearby house where he soon recovered. Asked what it was like to be hanged Smith replied: 'When I was turned off I was, for some time, sensible of very great pain occasioned by the weight of my body and felt my spirits in strange commotion, violently pressing upwards. Having forced their way to my head I saw a great blaze or glaring light that seemed to go out of my eyes in a flash and then I lost all sense of pain. After I was cut down, I began to come to myself and the blood and spirits forcing themselves into their former channels put me by a prickling or shooting into such intolerable pain that I could have wished those hanged who had cut me down.' After that he was known for ever more as 'Half-hanged Smith'.

The practice of disembowelling and dismembering the victims ended through the efforts of the medical profession. Doctors wanted the bodies intact. So did relatives, but not to help the dissectors, for it was commonly believed that only an intact body led to life after death. By the late eighteenth century roughly half of those condemned to death were being spared the gallows for a worse punishment – banishment to Australia. Nevertheless, by then the residents of Mayfair and Marylebone wanted the Tyburn hangings stopped, not out of human compassion, revulsion at hangings and everything associated with it, but distaste at the rabble coming through their increasingly affluent area. After 1783 hangings took place within the prison walls at Newgate in the City.


## FLASH HARRYS

Frank Norman, the Barnardo's boy who became an unlikely celebrity in the 1960s after writing his prison memoirs, once explained the route into the West End underworld. 'You are fourteen years old. You walk down the Charing Cross Road. You are accosted by a man wearing a flashy tie. The rest follows on from there.'

This is the world the West End villain enters, one of dazzle, glitter, glitz, glamour. But where the lawbreaker and villain preying on the other side of London, in the East End, has tended to leave a name reverberating down history – the Ratcliff Highway murderer, the London Monster, Jack the Ripper – his West End counterpart has tended to operate incognito outside his chosen territory, obscured by the bright lights, able to reap the rewards without the public infamy.

And what rewards! They certainly were ample for Adam Worth, a Fagin-like master of a gang of thieves working Piccadilly in the late Victorian era. Born to poor German Jews in 1844, he and his parents emigrated to Cambridge, Massachusetts, in the United States. Worth fought in the American Civil War and gradually eased his way into established society, making his money initially from pickpocketing before moving on to cheque forging, swindling, safe cracking, burglary and diamond robbery.

In the London of the 1870s Worth took a flat at 198 Piccadilly, in the heart of the rich man's playground, under the alias Henry J. Raymond. Every morning Worth was out on the streets tending his flock of Artful Dodgers. By noon he could be found in the gentlemen's clubs of Pall Mall, discussing the finer points of cotton and silk with the industry's entrepreneurs. He was at the apex of a hierarchy of crime, aided by lieutenants with such wonderful names as 'Piano' Charley Bullard, Little Joe Elliott, Carlo Sesicovitch and his Number two, Jack Phillips, aka 'Junka', who was also his personal valet, a man with a face Worth's biographer Ben Macintyre described as looking 'like it had been carved out of Parmesan cheese'. The Pinkerton Detective Agency called Worth 'the most remarkable criminal of them all' and Scotland Yard dubbed him 'the Napoleon of Crime', a label picked up by Arthur Conan Doyle, who used it for Professor Moriarty in the Sherlock Holmes stories.

Worth rarely got his hands dirty. His villainy excluded knives and guns, and his motto was 'A man with brains has no right to carry firearms. Exercise your brain!' He joined a long list of men to have fallen in love with Lady Georgiana Spencer. Too late for a corporeal relationship – she had died in 1806 – he had to rely on Thomas Gainsborough's depiction on canvas which was being displayed in Agnew's art gallery at 43 Old Bond Street in spring 1876. The painting was drawing crowds of admirers, but not for long. Worth stole it at midnight, cutting the portrait from its frame and rolling it up with the paint facing outward to avoid cracking the surface.

Junka couldn't wait to see the Gainsborough turned into liquid gold. But that was not what Worth intended. He hadn't stolen the painting for profit, but because he wanted to look at it. A few weeks after the heist Junka invited Worth for a drink at the Criterion Bar on Piccadilly Circus. Worth, not one for mindless tippling and certainly not at the Cri, with its raffish male crowd, smelt a rat. His suspicions increased when he spotted a man in a bowler hat sat near them listening to every word. They were confirmed when Junka began to draw Worth into loud conversation about the stolen painting.

Worth attacked his ally, leaving him on the floor covered in a melange of tipped up alcohol, and fled.

Police searched 198 Piccadilly but found nothing as Worth was continually moving the masterpiece to different hidey-holes. Whenever he went on long-distance voyages he would carry it in a specially made Saratoga trunk with a false bottom. William Agnew, owner of the gallery from where Worth had stolen the painting, who had bought it at an auction for 11,000 guineas, offered a £1,000 reward for information relating to the theft. But when ransom letters arrived at the shop claiming that the painting was in New York he refused to negotiate. Agnew assumed the thief would run out of patience, but he didn't. There wasn't any further news of the whereabouts of the work until 1901 when Worth's crew contacted the Pinkerton Detective Agency and arranged a meeting in a Chicago hotel. Agnew's son, Morland, travelled to the American city, went to the hotel, and after some wait was handed a brown-paper parcel containing the rather mutilated portrait in exchange for an undisclosed amount of cash. The painting, since repaired, now hangs in New York's Metropolitan Museum.


## BROTHERS OUT-OF-LAW


By the start of the twentieth century the West End was a prominent location for both commerce and nightlife. The first offered the prospect of rich pickings, the second, ruled by late nights, soaked in alcohol and the enticing prospect of semi-legal drugs, was barely able to operate without the help of the shady underworld.

Within a half-mile radius of Piccadilly Circus there was entertainment of every kind, appealing to all classes: rough pubs, gentlemen's clubs, cheap tarts, gambling dens, high-class hookers, expensive restaurants, theatres, music halls, society nightclubs, drinking clubs and dance halls – all magnets for up-to-no-goodniks. Or as Scotland Yard's Ted Greeno put it, 'in the West End you could buy anything and see everything; and you could get your throat slit more promptly than in a pirate ship on the China Seas'.

By the 1920s Soho was dedicated to money laundering, illegal gambling in cellar *spielers*, pimping, violence and racketeering. The illicit profits from this business went mostly into the hands of the five Sabini brothers. Their leader was Darby, on whom Graham Greene based the gangster Colleoni in

*Brighton Rock*. His brothers were Fred, Joseph, Harry-Boy and George. They specialized in loan-sharking, and were happiest working the race tracks at Epsom and Brighton, but they also gallantly protected the West End from other hoods, especially those of European origin, looking to muscle in.

Darby Sabini executed his first West End job when a Clerkenwell girl was lured into prostitution by Juan Antonio Castanar, a gangster and tango-dancing Spaniard who owned a dancing school in Soho's Archer Street. Sabini visited Castanar and had a 'quiet word'. Castanar took no notice – obviously Sabini hadn't made himself loud enough – so a week later Sabini firebombed the premises. Yet it was not Sabini who took the blame for the blaze, but Castanar's Soho rival, Casimir Micheletti, a Frenchman. The Sabinis ensured this by spreading wicked rumours through the West End about Micheletti – that Micheletti had been responsible for the firebombing. Soon most of the London underworld was convinced that Micheletti was the culprit. Certainly Castanar thought so and tracked him to Montmartre in Paris, where he shot him dead.

When Italy joined the Second World War in 1940 the Sabinis were interned as undesirable aliens. But how Italian were they? At an Old Bailey trial, where Darby Sabini was accused of gang warfare in a Clerkenwell club, the judge, Mr Justice Darling, a proud linguist, addressed Sabini in Italian, to the latter's bemusement; he had only ever spoken English. Harry Sabini protested at being interned alongside his fellow second-generation compatriots. He was not Italian, he claimed with some justification, having been born in London, and never having been to Italy in his life. He appealed unsuccessfully, shocked to hear Mr Justice Humphreys denounce him as a 'violent and dangerous criminal of the gangster type'.

The few remaining Italian gangsters left in the West End during the Second World War soon found a new foe, not in the police or the army conscriptors but in the West End's Jewish gangsters, who were more than happy to introduce a touch of politics into their street battles. Wartime fights between Soho's Jewish and Italian gangsters culminated in the fatal stabbing in 1941 of Harry Distleman, doorman of the West End Bridge and Billiards club, at 37 Wardour Street. The knifeman was Antonio 'Babe' Mancini (he was the Italian). As the blade went in (five times) Distleman cried out: 'Babe's stabbed me in the heart. I'm dying.' In October 1941 Mancini became the first drop for the man destined to be Britain's best-known twentieth-century hangman: Albert Pierrepoint.

## KING OF THE HILL

The exeunt of the Sabinis left a power vacuum at the top in West End gang-land. In the 1940s Soho's leading villains joined battle to win the title of King of London's Underworld. In contention were the Whites, the Elephant Gang, Billy Hill, and Benny the Kid, aka Jack Spot, the legendary East End Jew who had wrestled Oswald Mosley's bodyguard to the ground at the 1936 Battle of Cable Street.

The Whites were briefly the main contenders, even though the under-world was still chuckling at the sight of one of their boys being pursued along the Ascot racecourse by a member of Jack Spot's gang in full view of the Royal Enclosure. But first they had to do something about Hill. On 9 July 1947 one of the Whites went to Hill's flat in Somers Town to agree on a truce: 'My boss says there's room for both of us,' explained the White aco-lyte. Hill thought not and slashed the man's cheek, carving on it a 'V' for Victory mark. He then bundled him up and took him to Soho, where he dumped him in the street with a note pinned to his coat stating that any other of White's 'ambassadors' could expect the same treatment. When Hill and his cronies raided the Whites' lair, Harry, the *paterfamilias*, gave in: 'Okay, Billy, you're the guv'nor,' he conceded.

Hill, one of twenty-one children from Seven Dials, was a master of safe-breaking, smash-and-grab raids, illegal gambling and chivving – sweeping a razor down the face, like he had done with White, never across, so as not to sever an artery. His gang became London's biggest. It was also the best named, given that it included Franny the Spaniel, Horrible Harry, Bear's Breath, Tony the Wop (somehow not interned), Soapy Harry and Square George, although these were probably not their real names. In the 1940s they launched a series of smash-and-grab raids in the West End. Ironically Hill was only able to lead them into battle because the authorities had freed him from Chelmsford jail so that he could be of some use to his country at time of war, which he promptly thanked them for by deserting.

One day in March 1940 Hill made for a jeweller's at 130 Regent Street in his maroon Phantom Corsair. Instead of parking outside he drove the vehicle on to the pavement and straight into the doorway, causing the com-missionaire to make a split-second decision whether to guard the shop or his life. Right behind Hill in a black sedan were Long Stan, Tosh and Big Jock.

Quickly the men loaded up with anything they could grab – as long as it glistened – and then drove away up Regent Street, again using the pavement, not the road, just for dramatic effect. Hill was later arrested and placed on an ID parade, but none of the victims managed to recognize him, well not in connection with the crime, at least.

His confidence pampered, Hill became more daring. His gang became untouchable. For their next job they drove the car along the pavement *before* the raid. The target was Philips, a jeweller's on New Bond Street. This time one of the gangsters stood upright in the car and leant out the sunroof to conduct the robbery. The gang then made off, again along the pavement. But as their car turned into Grosvenor Square, a police vehicle approached. For a while it looked as if the officers would catch up with the thieves. Alas another car then swerved into place between the two vehicles. With the officers cursing their bad luck, the second car stopped dead and the occupants ran off. The police could now go no further, and got out in exasperation. They were not amused by the number plate on the stationery car that had blocked their way: MUG 999. A call to Scotland Yard soon ascertained that this was not a valid registration.

The smash-and-grab raids came to a surprise end on 26 June 1940. Hill, Square Georgie and Harry Bryan (real name!) staked out Hemmings and Co., jewellers of Conduit Street, Mayfair. They devised a plan in which Hill would once again stand up through the sunroof, wield his sledgehammer and grab as much as he could. Unfortunately, that day Bryan was unable to drive properly. As he left New Bond Street he nearly hit a policeman, which was not a good start. When they reached the shop Hill got to work, but when the time came to go Bryan couldn't move the car, and worse still a crowd was heading their way. Although the gang had prepared well, with a second car nearby waiting for them, PC Higgs had copper's instinct on his side. As the second car passed he threw his truncheon at the windscreen, and smashed it. But copper's instinct wasn't enough. Hill sped up New Bond Street and left into Bruton Street. He then headed up, literally, making for the roof of an office block. Quickly he was on to another, and then down the stairs of a third, all the way down to the street, out the door ... into the arms of a policeman. Sharper than ever, Hill pleaded with the startled officer, 'He's in here,' pointing to the building he'd just left. Alas it was too late. The crowd had caught up by then, shouting, 'That's him!' Hill received two years.

After the war Hill became more daring. He moved on from smash-and-grab raids to kidnapping. The plan was not to lift the rich and powerful off the streets for a hefty ransom, but to frighten their staff. On 5 December 1945 the gang followed the manageress of a jeweller's on South Molton Street, Mayfair, home to Tottenham, where they bundled her into a car, and bound and gagged her. Hill explained to the woman that he meant her no harm. His gang just wanted the keys to her shop, which she happily handed over in exchange for her imminent freedom. The gang dumped the manageress on Hampstead Heath, and she called for help. By 8.30 one of the shop owners had arrived in South Molton Street, as had the police, but by then tens of thousands of pounds worth of jewels had been stolen.

The police knew Hill was behind it, and carried out a trawl of ruffians loitering around Piccadilly Circus, searching every lowdown caff, dive bar and clip joint. They hauled in two van loads of assorted uninvolved villains, just to shake up the town. They even sealed off all the main roads leading out of London, to no avail. When Hill, who was having a drink in his Camden Town local, found out about the hunt, he phoned the Yard himself, demanding the phone number of Robert Stevens, the Detective Inspector in charge of the case.

'I hear you want to see me,' Hill breathed softly to Stevens, who was relaxing at home.

'You?' replied the startled Stevens. 'Who are you? I don't know who you are.'

'I'm Billy Hill. You know, the villain.'

[Pregnant pause followed by the sound of ever-loudening breathing.]

'Who the hell do you think you are, Al Capone?'

Hill was arrested, but again was not identified by any of the protagonists.

While Hill's team was helping itself to the West End's jewels, his wife, Aggie, an expert at shoplifting, was helping herself to the area's finest goods. Aggie's nickname was the 'Queen of the Forty Elephants' on account of her size when laden down with stolen clothes. She and her fellow elephants would descend on the West End in chauffeur-driven cars, park outside (this being before parking restrictions were installed) and load up with everything they could carry before speeding off.

There was one infamous West End jewel robbery of the time with which Hill was *not* associated: the Jay's job at 73–75 Charlotte Street, Fitzrovia, in April 1947. As three robbers fled with their booty, a passing motorcyclist,

Alex de Antiquis, decided to indulge in a spot of heroics and prevent the getaway, only to be shot for his pains. As de Antiquis lay in the street wounded, who should walk past but Superintendent Robert Fabian (the inspiration for TV's *Fabian of the Yard*) and the hangman Albert Pierrepoint, on their way to their local, the Fitzroy Tavern. If only they had been accompanied by a doctor. De Antiquis died soon after in Middlesex Hospital. Police eventually caught up with the robbers and two of them were hanged ... by Pierrepoint.

In the early 1950s Billy Hill's team carefully planned the Big One – the Eastcastle Street job. This was Britain's first major post-war armed robbery, a crime so central to London history it even earned a mention in the script of the Ealing comedy *The Ladykillers*. Eastcastle Street is a short, quiet road to the north-east of Oxford Circus. Nothing much had ever happened there, and nothing much has happened since 21 May 1952 when Hill's gang, posing as a film crew making a gangster movie, stole £287,000 from a mail van at quarter past four in the morning.

Hill and co. planned the raid with military precision. They followed the van for months, so that they would be acquainted with all its movements. The night before the heist the gang was taken to a secret location where they were locked in and briefed. At two o'clock on the morning of the robbery one of the gang, dressed in a postman's uniform and carrying a post bag, calmly walked through the yard of the General Post Office HQ on St Martin's le Grand in the City, nodding to the man on duty at the lodge as if he had worked there all his life. The gang member approached the targeted van, opened the bonnet and disconnected the alarm. As he left the premises he made sure he again nodded to the duty officer. After all, the duty officer must have thought, if a man nods at you he must know you, and you him, even if you've never seen him before.

An hour and a half later the disalarmed van arrived at Paddington station, where another Hill acolyte watched it being loaded up with money bags. The van left Paddington en route, once again, for the big City post office. Thanks to road works it would likely leave Oxford Street and head along Eastcastle Street, as it had done previously. Sure enough it did! There, at 4 a.m., the main players in the drama lay in wait. As the vehicle turned into Eastcastle Street it found its path blocked at both ends by a car. Six men leapt out and attacked the van. The postmen pressed the button, which should have activated an alarm that would continue to scream until the vehicle's battery ran out, yet before they had a chance to contemplate the alarm's failure to sound they were attacked by masked men who had appeared out of the blocking cars. They were forced out and left in a heap on the pavement.

Hill's gang drove the van to Somers Town and offloaded the cash into boxes which they placed on a fruiterer's lorry. This they drove to Spitalfields Market where they carefully watched over it, just in case the usurpers were usurped by a gang even more daring than they, or in case the police came by. When neither happened the fruiterer's lorry was driven to Dagenham marshes and the cash finally retrieved. Later that day Billy Hill celebrated the coup at the Dorchester Hotel on Park Lane. As Jack Spot later recalled: 'There he was, dressed like Noël Coward ironing bank notes with his moll, Gypsy, standing alongside him. Across the room was a clothes line with more notes drying out attached with clothes pegs.'

The booty – £287,000 they counted, some £5 million in today's prices – was the largest single sum that had ever been stolen. The prime minister, Winston Churchill, was mortified and ordered daily updates on the police investigation. A thousand officers from Scotland Yard tore up London in trying to solve the crime, but never managed to apprehend anyone.

Naturally Hill was their main target. Although he had appropriate alibis for the time of the robbery, the police closed down his spielers, took an associate's car to pieces and tapped all the gang's telephones. The head of security at the robbed post office joined in the hunt for the cash, tailing Hill day and night, which did wonders for Hill's personal security. When Hill went on holiday to north Africa, his Post Office minders surreptitiously followed him everywhere at a respectful distance, even on the Tunisian camel trails. When Hill returned to his hotel he found his room had been thoroughly searched . . . as if he was going to leave used notes from the Eastcastle Street stash lying around. As Hill wrote three years later in his memoirs: 'I have reason to think that now Scotland Yard may know who actually carried out that job.' It didn't take Sherlock Holmes to work out who Hill meant. None of the money was ever recovered.

Nothing and no one could touch Hill. His power was even noticed by the non-criminal world. Henrietta Moraes, the artists' model and leading *bohémienne*, explained how 'Hill's men were everywhere, collecting protection money from the dutiful and carving up the faces of the obdurate.' But, she concluded, adding a vital unwritten rule, 'we were outside the circle of extortion, and were left alone.'

It was lucky for society that Hill wasn't more politically minded, or that Britain wasn't run along American lines, for what could have prevented him from becoming mayor? On 16 June 1955 Hill threw a party at Gennaro's on Dean Street, what is now the Groucho Club, to mark the publication of his autobiography, *Boss of Britain's Underworld*. It was a beautifully presented confessional, impeccably ghosted by Duncan Webb, doyen of Fleet Street's crime writers. The invitations for the party read: 'The above-named person is hereby appointed as a free and virtuous citizen of the inquitous and uninhibited province of Soho . . . known for its burglars, bandits, gangsters and con men.' In the book Hill explained how if the reader were to stand in any part of Soho 'at any hour of the day or night, you will be spotted by at least six of my men. This is the centre of my empire, the district from which I rule the underworld. Walk up Shaftesbury Avenue and ask who rules the underworld. Ask a copper. He'll tell you Billy Hill is the guv'nor.'

Nevertheless Hill had rivals. There was Tommy Smithson, a minder for the Mayfair vice bosses. When Smithson began getting too powerful Hill invited him to a showdown at a nearby factory. Gathered there were many of the post-war underworld's finest, including the two leading Jewish gangsters of the time, Jack Spot and Morris Goldstein, known as Moishe Blueball after the colour of one, just one, of his testicles. Hill told Smithson: 'Look, you know you're carrying a gun. Give us the gun.' Smithson obliged, but Hill hit him over the head with it. His men then attacked Smithson with a knife. In all Hill's gang administered no less than forty-seven V-shaped cuts on Smithson's face before leaving him for dead. At least they phoned the police, to let them know a man was in trouble, but by the time officers arrived Smithson had forgotten the names of his assailants. He was later rewarded with a £500 present for his silence.

In April 1955 Hill, sated with his ill-gotten riches, chose to retire to Australia. He took a ship. In his absence Jack Spot tried to muscle in. Spot certainly looked the part in his perfectly tailored suits, fedora and crombie. His real name was Jack Comer, and he had been known as Jack Spot ever since someone quipped 'wherever there is trouble Jack is on the spot'. He also acted the part as well. Every day Spot would make his way from his flat in Hyde Park Gardens to his barber's in Soho for a shave, wash, brush-up, and important chat about horses, women and hoods. He would then head off, sauntering along the road, waving and wishing passers-by good morning, en route for the Cumberland Hotel's Bear Garden on Oxford Street where he would hold court, dispensing advice and homilies to people seeking his advice on a wide range of topics.

To stake his claim as king of the West End, Spot turned for help to a pair of up-and-coming hoods from the East End – the Kray twins – who came west to protect his bookmakers. But a Jewish gang boss in Soho? The West End may have been irrevocably cosmopolitan but the *goyim* would never tolerate a *yiddishe* godfather. An Italian was more likely, so Albert Dimes felt. Strictly by trade Dimes, real name Albert Dimeo, was a bookmaker. He also organized bare-knuckled boxing contests at racecourses, and had earned his spurs by being charged with unlawful wounding after the 1941 murder of the Jewish bouncer Harry 'Scarface' Distleman. He was a sophisticated and cultured man, unlike Spot, he would explain to people. Once, when he visited a leading Mafia capo, he took with him as a present a collection of opera recordings made by the great tenor Enrico Caruso. But this was no ordinary collection, that an ignorant man may have presented. No. This collection was encased in a walnut wood box.

Then suddenly, to everyone's amazement, Hill was back. The Australian authorities, strangely, had refused to let him in. When Hill learned about the arrival of the Krays in Soho he was furious at the brazen cheek of these troublesome tyros and invited them to a showdown in an Islington pub, a location exactly halfway between the West End and East End. The Krays failed to show – they didn't do Islington – but not to turn up was an act brazen enough to cement their growing reputation.

With Hill back things began going wrong for Spot. Hill discovered that Spot had given evidence against his men in an assault case back in 1937, rooted out the relevant documents and had them pasted up in West End pubs. The best drama was yet to come. On 11 August 1955 Spot was drinking in the Galahad club in Soho when he heard that Dimes wanted to see him. Spot was already sore over lack of protection payments he claimed Dimes owed him. He rushed out of the Galahad, ran down Frith Street, and found the Italian at the eastern corner of Frith and Old Compton Street.

'Mambo music was blaring from the juke-boxes. Men in slouch hats and draped suits were taking the air on the corner,' as the *Daily Express* evocatively put it. The two men began trading blows. Soon they found their knives. Each stabbed the other before the badly injured Dimes stumbled into the Continental Fruit Stores. Instead of finding refuge from the mean streets Dimes found himself being hit on the head with a heavy scoop by the shopkeeper. Spot, meanwhile, staggered into an Italian barber's where he shouted: 'Fix me up' and fainted.

Both men were taken to hospital, arrested as they were discharged, and later tried at the Old Bailey. There Spot was supported from the witness stand by the eighty-eight-year-old Rev Basil Andrews, who testified that Dimes had started the fight. Also making a big impression for Spot was his wife Rita, whose wild Irish gypsy looks, green stilettos and diamond necklace even had the judge purring. Spot was acquitted, and so was Dimes. A fight had taken place but no one was guilty of starting it. Surely the first classified criminal case of spontaneous pugilistic combustion.

The underworld, not to mention Spot and Dimes, was in stitches. They knew the Rev Andrews was a far from reverend cleric, known in criminal circles as 'the knocking parson', thanks to his predilection for opening accounts with bookmakers and welching on the bets. He later admitted that the gangsters Bernard Schack ('Sonny the Yank') and Moishe Blueball (him again) had paid him £63 to act as a character witness for Spot.

Sonny, Moishe and the perjuring parson were arrested. The latter starred in court. When asked why he had lied previously he contritely explained how it was 'very wicked. I was hard up and I was tempted and I fell. I was desperately hungry. I had had continental breakfasts and nothing in between. I was very poor and hungry and I should not have yielded but I did. Thank God I have asked to be forgiven.' So why now had he decided to tell the truth? His response came straight out from the pages of a Gerald Kersh B-novel. 'In the silence of the night, when things come back to you, it was brought to my mind the sin I had committed and the wickedness I had done.'

Guilty sentences were handed out. Spot then announced that he was quitting the rackets. It was a convenient time to retire. His standing had been going downhill since a bullion raid at London Airport he had organized went awry. Hill didn't believe him. Six months later he arranged for Spot to be severely beaten up outside his Hyde Park Mansions residence. The culprits were two young thugs, 'Mad' Frankie Fraser and Alf Warren. Fraser went on to become London's most notorious twentieth-century henchman, and after many years inside began running coach tours of east London gangland sites in the 1990s.

Spot claimed he had no idea who the men that attacked him were, or so he told the police. 'I'm the toughest man in the world. I am staying in London. Nobody will drive me out.' His wife had no such scruples and readily named the assailants. A trial took place at the Old Bailey. The jury found Fraser guilty and he got seven years.

The trial marked the end of an era. Hill retired to Spain, the first resident on what became the Costa del Crime. The vanquished – Blueball, the Rev, Spot and Dimes – suffered a squalid demise. Moishe Blueball received two years for perjury. He later joined the Krays team but remained strictly small time. The Rev Andrews went to live in Oxford on a miserly church pension. Spot retired from the underworld around the same time as Billy Hill, stayed in London and bought a furniture store, but was later declared bankrupt. Dimes joined the Richardsons, the 1960s most brutal, but not most glamorous gang, scourge of the Krays. He oversaw slot-machine takings throughout the capital and was even allowed to meet the Mafia. But he didn't impress the MP Anthony Greenwood, who described him in the House of Commons as a 'squalid, cowardly small-time hoodlum'. When Dimes died the Krays sent flowers and a message, 'To a fine gentleman', but his relatives refused to accept them as it may have brought disgrace to the family.

## BOSS OF THE WEST END

By the late 1950s Billy Hill was in Spain, Jack Spot was in disgrace and Frankie Fraser was inside, doing seven years for stabbing Spot. A power vacuum had formed at the top of the West End underworld. Who would fill it? Perhaps the Krays? Before Hill left London he had sanctioned their promotion, hoping to unite East and West in crime. Reggie Kray was always thankful for Hill's patronage: 'Bill was the ultimate professional criminal,' he later wrote. 'I like to think that in some ways I have come close to emulating him, but in many other ways he stands alone. There will never be another Billy Hill.'

A new group of Italians, based in a social club in the Clerkenwell Road, fancied their chances of settling some old scores and becoming the new Sabinis. Ronnie Kray paid them a visit. After a brief conversation he drew out a Mauser pistol and fired three shots. No one was hit, and no one tried to stop him as he walked back to those waiting for him outside. Ronnie basked in the electric glow sparked by such bravado. This was what being a gangster was all about. No one could stop him and Reg now. Indeed the police were happy to leave the twins alone as long as they didn't kill anyone or harm members of the public.

The Krays turned their attention to Soho's clubs. On Greek Street a set of Cambridge-educated Hooray Henrys, including Peter Cook, had opened a cabaret venue. The Krays decided to extract protection money from the owners. It would be a cinch. Associates advised them not to. These graduates might be wet behind the ears, but they had famous friends. This was more dangerous for the Krays, with their social pretensions, than tapping the management at Dodgers' illegal kalooki club on Brick Lane. The journalists on Cook's new scurrilous magazine, *Private Eye*, were not bound by the same rules as the car dealers and three-card trick merchants of Aldgate, the twins were told. The magazine writers would fearlessly, or perhaps naively, go to print on the twins, using terms like 'raving homosexualist' and 'raving pooftah' in questioning the twins' sexuality, which was then illegal and more disconcerting to the establishment than a little bit of GBH. It just wasn't worth it.

The Krays complied and turned instead to a more typical West End nightclub – the Hideaway on Gerrard Street. One night in autumn 1964 a Kray associate, Teddy 'Mad' Smith, visited the place, smashed it up and threatened the owner. Later the twins arrived on the scene and pointed out that if their men were in charge of security such wanton destruction wouldn't take place. What they didn't reveal was that such wanton destruction had taken place solely because they had ordered it.

Surprisingly the owner, Hew McCowan, called the police. The underworld was astonished when McCowan insisted on pressing charges. Hadn't he heard of the Ten Underworld Commandments, in particular Commandment Number One: 'Thou shalt not grass'? Scotland Yard selected a recently promoted detective inspector, Leonard 'Nipper' Read, to handle the case. McCowan, courageously, told Read all about the twins. They were arrested, remanded and sent for trial at the Old Bailey. Read was certain that people would now come forward to testify against them. But what came next was all too predictable. In court the twins were represented by the finest silks money could buy: Paul Wrightson QC and Sir Peter Crowder QC. Out of court the twins leant on the members of the jury, having acquired all their names and addresses. Was that enough to bend the law? Just about. Only one juror voted in their favour, but that was enough in the days of unanimous verdicts to force a retrial.

The Krays had earned time for research and development. They researched Hew McCowan's background, and discovered he had been a police informer. Now counsel could convincingly argue that the prosecution's main witness was unreliable. The trial collapsed and Nipper Read was redeployed for a few years before relaunching what was eventually a successful coup against the twins. Meanwhile, the Krays rubbed McCowan's nose in it by buying the Hideaway, which they renamed El Morocco.

By expanding into the West End the twins came to the attention of the Mafia. The Mob was keen to launder hundreds of thousands of dollars of negotiable bonds stolen from the Royal Bank of Canada, and the Krays were ideal stooges. In 1964 Ronnie had a lengthy meeting at the London Hilton on Park Lane with Angelo Bruno, the head of the Philadelphia crime family. Could the twins 'take care' of $250,000 worth of such bonds? Sure. They took the money back to their East End HQ and burnt it in the dustbin at the back of the house. Of course the pyre was worthless; the incident had been contrived to see if the Krays could obey orders.

Despite their reputation as the most powerful criminals London has ever seen, the Krays were incapable of taking over the West End. Even though they had various outposts up west they lacked the administrative skills necessary to run an empire that at one time looked as if it would stretch from Esmerelda's Barn, a swanky nightclub off Knightsbridge, across Park Lane and Regent Street into the proto casinos and clip joints of Soho, all the way to the Grove Drinking Club in dismal Maryland, Stratford, beyond the East End. Petrol bombs through windows, cigarette punches, long firms, extortion, a knife in the guts – those were the easy things. Bureaucracy, strategies, profile building; that was beyond them.

Some of the Krays' less palatable West End activities stayed out of the spotlight for years. Little known is the story of how one night in 1965 they picked up a boy from the line of male prostitutes practising their polari around Piccadilly Circus, took him back to a house in Belgravia and after having their fill choked him to death before ridding themselves of the body in one of their favourite concrete motorway hidey-holes.

At the same time they were becoming involved in schemes so outlandish and absurd it is a wonder they lasted long enough to be sentenced to thirty years' imprisonment each at the Old Bailey. One of these was a plot to seize the former Congo president, Moise Tshombe, from his Algerian hideaway. Another was to build a new city in Nigeria. Ronnie flew out and was given what almost amounted to a state reception. The affair ended in disarray. The Krays were forced to nurse the wounds of frustration with pints of mild and bitter in the Grave Maurice pub on Whitechapel Road while their better-organized, better-looking and even more ruthless West End rivals – the Richardsons – sealed lucrative deals in South Africa.

Although the Richardsons were nominally south London scrap-metal dealers, by the mid 1960s they were running several lucrative London scams – 'long firm' frauds, extortion, money laundering, protection rackets like the Krays – and were earning a fortune from slot-machine takings. Charlie Richardson, the clan chief, even had a prestigious Mayfair HQ at 65 Grosvenor Street, mainly to impress his wealthy contacts in the South African diamond industry. Not so impressed was a Mafia hitman who turned up one day, asked the gangster if he was 'Mr Charlie Richardson', and when Richardson affirmed he was, pulled out a gun and began loading the chamber, resulting in the London gangster running off at full speed out the back door.

One of Richardson's most powerful clients was BOSS, the apartheid-propping South African security service, who asked him to do a few jobs for them in exchange for protection over his South Africa mines. Or to put it another way, a BOSS agent approached Richardson during a lucrative diamond deal and warned him: 'Charles, terrible things could happen to you, and we must really protect you against any possibility that one of our officers should unwittingly stumble on something that could hurt you ... so you WILL agree to help us out in London, although if you get caught : ..'

Richardson's first BOSS job in London was to break into the Anti-Apartheid offices at 89 Charlotte Street, Fitzrovia, and remove the membership lists. His non-political status in London gangland made him the ideal candidate. If caught he would be branded as a common burglar, rather than be linked with any political machinations. The job was not one of Richardson's most taxing. He went to the Charlotte Street offices late one afternoon, hid in the toilet, and when the staff left walked into the main room and removed the documents, which he then airmailed to his contact in Johannesburg. More exciting was the day Richardson and his boys went down to 10 Downing Street, and posing as workmen mending the phones planted a bug in the prime ministerial HQ, again for the benefit of the South African security services, bravely ignoring the knowledge that the penalty for treason was at that time execution.

At night various Krays, Richardsons and their posses would congregate at the Colony Casino Club on Berkeley Square, one of the few London institutions owned by the American Mafia, whose attempts to pay the Krays to stay away failed. Another favourite was the nearby Astor Club. It was here one night that Frankie Fraser, the veteran freelance gangster, and Eddie Richardson watched a fight take place that for once had nothing to do with them, only to be told by a Kray acolyte, Eric Mason, that he was off to tell the twins that Fraser, who was then an enemy, had started it. Fraser responded by kidnapping Mason, or as he later explained it, 'I slung him in me motor, took him to our headquarters and chopped him up with me chopper, me axe. I then took him to the London Hospital and dumped him out there with a blanket around him.'

It was also at the Astor in December 1965 that the Krays met the Richardsons formally for the first time. They tried to reach an agreement over territorial rights and future plans, but made little progress. The Richardsons also wanted information on the Krays' Mafia connections, and when these were not forthcoming insults flew. George Cornell, one of the Richardson gang, described Charlie Richardson who profited from as a 'fat poof', bringing the meeting to an abrupt end. For this insult, among other things, Kray murdered Cornell in the Blind Beggar pub, Whitechapel, a few weeks later.

It was not only the brilliantined Charlie Richardson who profited from association with the riches of the West End. One villain, known only as 'Denis', stumbled out of a Park Lane casino one Saturday night in the 1960s and watched as a van left the premises to be driven only a short distance to a bank where security guards posted what were surely the night's takings into the safe-deposit box. Denis returned the next week and observed the same procedure happen again, at exactly the same time.

Later that week he rented a ground-floor office near the bank, and with a bit of DIY installed his own safe-deposit box in the wall. On the following Saturday evening Denis sealed up the real bank's box, placed a few bricks and some scaffolding around it, and erected a notice explaining that as building work was in progress customers should use an alternative deposit box (his) where he had placed a sign bearing the bank's logo. He then went to a vantage point on Park Lane and sat with a flask of tea watching the local casinos drop off their night's takings, one by one, at his 'branch' of the bank.

Running a nightclub could be a dangerous business. Even the swishest, swankiest venues were not immune. For every George Shearing crooning over cuckoos, larks and doves, or a Tony Hatch scribbling a luscious string-driven melody on a napkin, there was someone like Ronnie Kray overdressed in a dinner jacket planning a punch-up or worse. On 25 July 1965 the former boxing champion Freddie Mills was found shot dead in his car in Goslett Yard, a tiny dog-leg backstreet behind the nightclub he owned at 143 Charing Cross Road. His wife found the gun, a .22 fairground rifle, by her husband's dead body.

Only a few days previously Mills, who had won the world light heavyweight championship in 1948, had been rowing with the Kray twins over who was really in charge of the club. So had the Krays added him to their killing list or was it suicide? Some crime experts believe that Mills took his own life, not because he was heading for the bankruptcy court but because he was the serial killer who in the early 1960s had killed a number of prostitutes in the London area by choking them to death on his penis in the so-called 'Jack the Stripper' murders.

Another nightclub owner who met a sticky end was Tony Zomparelli. He was playing the Wild Life pinball machine in the Golden Goose amusement arcade on Old Compton Street in September 1974 when two men in dark glasses and false moustaches approached him from behind and shot him dead. Zomparelli had recently served a four-year stretch for the manslaughter of David Knight, the twenty-one-year-old brother of well-known London villain, Ronnie Knight, one-time husband of Barbara Windsor. Ronnie Knight was hauled in for questioning, but no charges held. In 1980 one of the two hitmen involved, George Bradshaw, who had been a regular visitor to Ronnie Knight's club in Charing Cross Road, confessed to the killing. Knight was again arrested, this time at his home in Stanmore, while Barbara Windsor remonstrated with officers over their cavalier attitude to her recent house tidying.

Knight again denied involvement. 'No, I never had a hand in it,' he asserted. 'I was told that someone else had a grudge with this Zomparelli. Once I knew he got in there before me, I was sick, 'cos it was my brother and I wanted to do it myself. I admit that, I admitted that in court. I told the judge, I was looking for him myself, but someone beat me to it.' Knight was acquitted at the Old Bailey of killing Zomparelli, but in his book *Memoirs and Confessions*, published eighteen years later, he boasted of how he had ordered Zomparelli's killing in revenge for his brother's murder. It was a clever admission. Under Britain's 'double jeopardy' ruling he couldn't be tried again.

Yet neither the Richardsons nor the Krays, Fraser or Knight bossed the West End. Careful examination of criminal patterns show that someone else was operating and organizing behind the scenes. Who was the mystery godfather? Many thought it was Albert Dimes. Why else did he eat for free every night in the smartest Frith Street Italian restaurants? Why else were chickens and joints of meat brought to his table to be taken away for the luscious Mrs Dimes? Why had the Inland Revenue not received a penny in tax from him since 1951? Why did he never have to pay to have his hair cut, a serious business which took place practically daily in Soho and involved much shaving, shampooing and schmoozing amidst generous measures of tea tree, myrrh and ylang-ylang?

But it wasn't Dimes who was king of the Soho Underworld post Billy Hill. It was a different Italian: Pasqualino Papa, a Frith Street bookmaker who ran an off licence in Old Compton Street where he went by the severely Anglicized name of Bert Marsh. His ambition was to be kept out of the public eye at all costs, and it largely worked. Little mention of him has appeared in the press or in books. Few have had a bad word to say about him, concentrating instead on his charming manners and dapper clothes, compulsory qualities for the Mafia's top man in Britain.


# THE VICEROYS


Sabini and brothers, Billy Hill, Jack Spot, Albert Dimes, Kray and Kray, Richardson and Richardson were the gangland faces of West End crime. But there was a separate branch of West End villainy that enjoyed its own code of conduct, its own heroes and losers, and will for ever be aligned with Soho – vice.

The first Viceroys were a Maltese mob: the Messinas. Like the Sabinis they came as a fist of brothers: Carmelo, Salvatore, Attilio, Eugenio and Alfredo. Experienced in running brothels around the Mediterranean coastal cities, they arrived in London in two batches in 1932 and 1934, and set up their HQ on Curzon Street in the most fashionable corner of Mayfair. There, each brother remodelled himself with a suitably English title. Attilio became one 'Raymond Maynard', Salvatore masqueraded as 'Arthur Evans', Carmelo as 'Charles Maitland', Alfredo 'Alfred Martin' and Gino 'Edward Marshall'.

The Messinas began pimping prostitutes, ruling their women with fear.

They played on the fact that many of them were illegal immigrants, most of whom were quickly married off to English men (for a large take of their earnings) so that they couldn't be deported. The girls were then trapped into a life of prostitution, often on Gerrard Street, Soho (long before it was reborn as Chinatown). Any girls who didn't play ball, as it were, could expect the severest penalties. For instance in 1936 three prostitutes were found strangled in Soho *pour l'encourager les autres*. The perpetrators may or may not have been the Messinas. Nevertheless, in the aftermath the Messina girls became more compliant. And just to ensure they remembered to stay compliant the Messinas hired a Corsican cut-throat who would arrive in England on the overnight ferry from France, stab or wound a targeted victim, and immediately head back. But there was an upside to this web of vice. The Messina girls earned £50 a week at a time when the national average wage hadn't reached double figures.

The cosy world of Messina-run West End vice was spoilt in the 1940s by the arrival of another Maltese gang. This new troupe was led by Carmelo Vassallo, who began demanding protection money from the girls, driving around Piccadilly, winding down the window of his car and shouting at them: 'It's better for you to give us the money, otherwise I will cut your face.' When Eugenio Messina heard about this he was not pleased. Not pleased at all. He sought out Vassallo, and cut off two of his fingertips. For this he was convicted at the Old Bailey of GBH and sentenced to three years in prison. There was no room at Wandsworth gaol for his fifteen Savile Row suits, which was just as well in an age of strict clothing rationing.

The brothers kept things ticking over sweetly while Eugenio served his time, and when he was released he celebrated by investing in a yellow Rolls Royce. But Eugenio didn't have much time to cruise the West End in it, for by now questions were being raised in the House. MPs were aghast to discover that the Messinas were making half a million pounds a year from West End vice. But rather than launch an inquiry, home secretary Chuter Ede excused himself and the government with a tame cop-out, announcing that 'Any inquiries would not help the police because their difficulties arise from the fact that . . . they are sometimes unable to obtain evidence upon which criminal proceedings could be based.'

Instead it was a journalist, Duncan Webb of the *Sunday People*, who made the Messina empire crumble. On 3 September 1950 Webb splashed an exposé headed 'ARREST THESE FOUR MEN [Alfredo somehow missed out] . . . The Messina Gang Exposed.' Webb accused the brothers of 'ruling women . . . by persuasion, threat or blackmail and the use of the knife', of organizing marriages of convenience 'by bribery and corruption'. He breathlessly informed his public that he 'could not be bought or sold'; that despite the lure of temptations that would have trapped St Antony he had daringly extricated himself from scenes of depravation overseen by these viceroys of vice using a phrase he coined that is now one of the archetypal newspaper clichés – 'I made my excuses and left'.

Webb was nearly undone by his own sanctimoniousness. Walking along Old Compton Street he came close to being run over by a car. A prostitute told him: 'That was meant for you, dearie.' When he heard that one gang member had threatened to cut his throat, he sought out the villain and offered himself up. 'Here's my throat. Cut it.' The villain resisted. He was laughing too much.

Nevertheless, Webb's campaign succeeded. The Messinas didn't wait for British justice. Eugenio and Carmelo quickly headed for Dover in that yellow Rolls Royce, and then took a ferry to France, never returning to Britain (legally). Webb celebrated by placing an advert in *The Times* thanking St Jude, patron saint of the impossible. Yet how morally virtuous was this intrepid incorruptible investigator? When Webb ghosted Hill's memoirs, *Boss of Britain's Underworld*, he described his charge as 'a genius, and a kind and tolerant man'.

Alfredo Messina stayed in London, but in March 1951 was arrested by police, to whom he quickly offered a £200 bribe, an interesting piece of evidence the emergence of which in court didn't help his case. Perhaps his apparel did? 'He dresses in a semi-flashy style and oozes a lubricious self-satisfaction,' one journalist waxed, which may explain why the judge gave him only two years.

Although the Messinas were mostly on the continent or inside they continued to run their West End vice empire *in absentia*, with Marthe Watts, Eugenio's top girl, as Soho caretaker. The system went awry when Eugenio was kidnapped in November 1953 and the other brothers were arrested in Brussels for gun-running. Watts eventually rescinded her support and had the tattoo on her left breast, 'Gino le Maltais, homme de ma vie', surgically removed. How at that moment she must have wished she had originally plumped for a simple 'Gino'.

The Messinas were replaced by a joint Maltese-Jewish partnership: Bernie

Silver and Frank Mifsud. They had been vice kings in Brick Lane but now wanted bigger spoils. Soon they were more feared even than the Messinas. Mifsud was a former Maltese copper known as 'Big Frank'. According to local police vice chief Bert Wickstead: 'When you heard Big Frank wanted to see you it struck terror into the hearts of even the hardest men.'

Mifsud and Silver never attained the status of household names. Their villainy was too straight. It lacked finesse and *chutzpah*. But they did attain immense power. During the 1950s and 1960s they ran practically every strip club in Soho. They dealt severely with anyone considered to be a threat. In June 1956 Tommy Smithson, the champion racketeer who had been roughed up so severely by Billy Hill's boys, who could make as much as £500 a night 'protecting' Soho's clubs, was found dying from gunshot wounds outside the house of one of Mifsud's henchmen. He hadn't just been killed. According to the *Daily Mirror* he had been murdered 'Chicago style in broad daylight by crepe-soled killers who walked in Indian file to the upstairs room at Number 88 where there were two dull plops – the sound of a silenced pistol.'

It was not until 1973 that the police caught up with Mifsud and Silver. Alas the pair had fled abroad after a tip-off. Bert Wickstead, the detective put in charge of the operation to bring the two men to justice, wreaked his revenge with a flourish. He convinced a friendly newspaper editor to print a story entitled 'The Raid That Never Was', hoping that Mifsud and Silver would read the piece from their Costa del Crime hideaway and assume invincibility. Wickstead was right. Soon the two men were back in London. A party at their club, the Scheherazade in Soho, was raided, but although the pair were not there they were arrested soon after at the Park Tower Hotel. Scores of villains and revellers were carted off by Black Maria. Not to Savile Row police station – too many dodgy eavesdroppers at the West End nick – but to Limehouse.

Silver got six years for living off immoral earnings, a sentence he couldn't really understand: there *was* no immorality in the Soho vice world. Mifsud got only five, and that was quashed on appeal. The two men were soon able to enjoy the £50 million it was claimed they had stashed away in Swiss bank accounts.

It didn't help law-abiding London that some of the police were bent. One of the worst was Detective Sergeant Harry Challenor. He was based at Savile Row nick and once explained how 'fighting crime in London was like trying to swim against a tide of sewage; you made two strokes forward and were swept back three. For every villain you put behind bars there were always two more to take their place.' And Challenor certainly knew what he was talking about. His penchant was for planting knives, hatchets and iron bars on innocent citizens. He got away with it until 1963. During a state visit by Queen Frederika of Greece that year he arrested some demonstrators and claimed that pieces of brick had been found in their pockets. Alas no trace of brick dust could be found, and the accused were all cleared. Challenor went on trial for conspiring to pervert the course of justice. He was found unfit to plead and detained in a mental hospital at Her Majesty's pleasure.

Then there were the moral police to contend with. Bobbies began to take an interest in works of art. They raided a greetings-card shop on Regent Street in August 1966 and seized all the Aubrey Beardsley cards and posters they could find. How could these delicate black-and-white drawings, including *Lysistrata Haranguing the Athenian Women*, be porn given that they were all on display at the Victoria and Albert Museum, argued the shop manager? Bad move. Metropolitan police commissioner Sir Joseph Simpson went to the museum himself to see if a public art gallery was indeed displaying 'obscene prints'.

There was a public outcry led by members of the public who objected to living as if in a police state in which officers monitored the nation's morals. The Director of Public Prosecutions, Sir Norman Skelhorn, ordered the officers to take the cards back to the shop. A month later the police raided the Robert Fraser Gallery in Duke Street, Mayfair, a popular counterculture location. The Obscene Publications Squad seized twenty paintings and drawings by the American artist Jim Dine.

Now it was Jennie Lee, Labour's minister for the arts, who was outraged. She wrote to home secretary Roy Jenkins: 'Can I be sure that no policeman, plain-clothes or uniformed, will again set himself up as an expert on works of art?' Similarly, Lord Goodman, Harold Wilson's lawyer, raged 'can there be any argument at all for a police officer invading a national collection such as the Tate? Surely simple instructions could be given to the police with accredited national collections – they could be given a list of them – that they do not visit them to inspect alleged pornographic portraits. If the director of the gallery is exhibiting pornography and not art, his trustees can be expected to deal with him and not the police.' Jenkins confronted the Met's commissioner over the antics of Savile Row's 'dirty books squad' in July 1967. He told Sir Joseph that they were to stop seizing books by reputable publishers and that there should be no repeat of the embarrassing raids on the V&A or Tate Gallery. Interestingly the Inspector in charge, Bill Moody, was later indicted for corruption.

Some West End officers were keen to get out of town, even as far as Cyprus where they were guests of Soho club owner Jimmy Humphreys. In 1962 Humphreys opened a venue on Moor Street, off Old Compton Street. His dancers included Norma Levy, the prostitute who caused the downfall of Tory defence minister Lord Lambton, and June Packard, whom Humphreys married and reinvented as the stripper Rusty Gaynor. The couple bought holiday homes in Ibiza, when it was still a classy place, before the Manchester ecstasy fiends took it over; well, classy enough for Soho vice merchants. There they began organizing regular visits to the island's sun-kissed beaches for Soho's finest, particularly those usually seen in uniform such as Bill Moody, then head of the Obscene Publications Squad, Commander Ken Drury, head of the Flying Squad, and Commander Wally Virgo – all bent coppers who used to raid Soho porn shops and offer Humphreys the confiscated magazines in return for a £3,000 bung.

One summer Drury went over to Ibiza. At a champagne-quaffing contest he was drunk under the table by Rusty Gaynor. The holiday was meant to be a private affair, except it was soon splashed across the front page of the *Sunday People*, for Humphreys had recorded their sangria-soaked, siesta-free Balearic bacchanals. Drury had prepared his excuse well. He wasn't being entertained by a Soho vice king at all. Oh no. He was on the trail of the fugitive Great Train Robber Ronnie Biggs ... some 10,000 miles from Rio. What did for Drury was that his story was backed up by Humphreys. If you're a high-flying copper the last thing you want is an alibi from a slag. In March 1972 Drury was suspended. In May he resigned and sold his story to the *News of the World* for £10,000. The police launched an investigation. In all, seventy-four Scotland Yard officers, mostly from the Vice Squad, were caught up in the biggest police-corruption probe London had ever witnessed. Twelve resigned, twenty-eight retired, eight sacked and thirteen jailed including Drury, who received eight years, and Virgo and Moody twelve apiece. Moody was also convicted of conspiring to take money – more than £40,000 – from pornographers. Fellow officers were pleased to see him squirm. On his first day in the Vice Squad he had roared up in an Alfa Romeo, 'a real bird puller', as he put it, and sneered at a colleague with a modest family saloon, 'Is that the best you can do?'

Humphreys was rewarded for his help and given a royal pardon in 1978. He left Britain to run betting shops in Mexico, but couldn't resist the lure of raising illicit cash in the West End, colder and gloomier than Central America but more fun. In the 1990s he and Rusty were back in Soho pimping, and in 1994 they were jailed for eight months.

# HEAVEN, EARTH AND MAN

Occasionally a lone criminal makes life uncomfortable for West Enders. Such was the case on 30 April 1999 when David Copeland, a Nazi sympathizer waging a one-man war against minority groups, nervously asked the barman of the Admiral Duncan, a well-known gay pub on Old Compton Street, for directions to the nearest bank, and made off leaving a holdall containing a bomb packed with 500 nails in the bar. Fifteen minutes later the bomb exploded, killing three people and injuring scores of bystanders. Copeland had detonated similar bombs in Brixton and Brick Lane over the previous few weeks which by chance caused much less damage. It was later revealed that the police, suspecting that Old Compton Street could be a target, had alerted some gay businesses and organizations, but had sent the gay rights group, Stonewall, a warning letter with a second-class stamp. It failed to arrive until the day of the bombing.

Mostly West End crime is run by gangs. Two main gangs rule the early twenty-first-century West End, and both originate overseas. The Albanians run vice, the Chinese everything else. Some 70 per cent of Soho brothels are now in the hands of Albanian warlords. Thanks to the break-up of the old Iron Curtain countries, their empire has now broken free of Tirana, and has laid down feelers in Italy and New York as well as London.

It has been an efficient coup. The Adriatic viceroys have simply smuggled into London – often through kidnapping – women who continue to cut the locals' rates. And their pimps meanwhile cut their rivals' faces. There is a seemingly endless stream of girls pouring out of the Balkans, brought to London by white slave traders nastier than any previously known. They are organized into clans and are bound by an ancient code of honour – the *kanun* – which dates back to a fifteenth-century Albanian feudal prince.

The Chinese underworld is run by the Triads, a name that supposedly represents the harmony between heaven, earth and man. The Triads stem from the Hung League, a secret Chinese society with a long and proud ancestry. They are hierarchical and mathematically precise. At the top of each branch sits the 'chairman'. Under him is a 'treasurer', followed by an 'incense master' and three 'red poles'. Ranks are given numbers, all of which begin with a '4' to denote the four ancient alchemical elements, the four compass points and the four seas of Chinese lore.

The Triads specialize in day-to-day protection, guarding lucrative Chinatown restaurants on Lisle Street and Gerrard Street at the southern end of Soho, mostly from each other. They are heavily armed and uncontrollably violent. Their *modus operandi* is to torture victims and hold them prisoner in Britain until the family back home pays up. They are also keen on kidnapping, vice, drug trafficking, extortion, video piracy, loan sharking and credit card fraud. The Triads' main trade is smuggling illegal immigrants into Britain, and there are believed to be around 200,000 already in the UK. They are expert at wrapping their villainy in mysticism and mythology so that it is almost impossible to separate rumour from reality. Although there are said to be around fifty Triad gangs in Hong Kong, Britain is home to only four, including the renowned 14K, which is the biggest, and the Wo Shing Wo. Their main rivals are the Snakehead gangs from the Fujian province on the Chinese mainland.

Incidents of Triad behaviour in Soho are irregular and unpredictable. In June 2003 a Chinese man, Yu Yi He, an illegal immigrant, was shot dead in the crowded BRB bar on Gerrard Street. The killer calmly left, mingling with the crowds outside. What surprised crime watchers was that a gun was used. Usually the Triads use a machete or meat cleaver, rather more common in Chinatown than firearms, and always to hand. Indeed, five years previously a man was hacked to death by a gang armed with machetes only a few yards away from Gerrard Street. As soon as the crime was committed the papers blamed the Triads. Yu Yi He had been involved in money-lending, and only a week or so before being murdered had been ejected from Napoleon's Casino on Leicester Square for attacking customers. Still the murder remains unsolved ... well, unsolved by the Metropolitan police. His fellow hoods know whodunit.

# 11

# Day

The war over, Soho, with its potent mix of loose women, foreign foods, shabby narrow streets and exotic attitudes, came into its own. In a grey era of austerity, conformity, rationing and increasing state involvement, Soho meant louche, loose, licentious living. Here was everything that was being frowned out of everyday England, in particular sex, glamour, jazz, unusual drugs and weird people. Here one could behave outrageously, promiscuously, bibulously and guiltlessly. Here was an entire community geared not just to pleasure, but to pleasure with an intellectual, continental, bohemian edge.

In the 1950s just being in Soho became an existence in itself, a well-trod pattern experienced by many, coveted by more. Money was no problem. One could scrounge a drink or cigarette here, a cup of coffee there. One could blag into a club, befriend one of the well-heeled, who were now only too keen to venture east of Regent Street, and spend the day careering from coffee bar to pub, from boho drinking den to restaurant, back to pub, with maybe a half an hour in the second-hand bookshops of Charing Cross Road en route.

Breakfast of rich pastries and dense Hungarian coffee at Patisserie Valerie, where the walls were festooned with Toulouse-Lautrec cartoons, the décor chic and swish, and which has remained gloriously unchanged since. Then a stroll up Frith Street, past Moka at No. 29 with its gleaming espresso machine, Soho's first, dispensing real froth. Past No. 22, where in an upstairs room John Logie Baird transmitted the world's first recognizable television pictures in October 1925, stopping off for some more froth in the café below, Bar Italia.

Then off again, past No. 20, next door, where the eight-year-old Mozart lodged with his father, Leopold, and sister in September 1764 before playing to George II at Buckingham House. And then along to Soho Square, just to loaf and lounge in the grounds, laughing at the near-toppling mock Tudor hut built as an exotic folly to hide a transformer for the Charing Cross Electric Light Company. Now south again, this time along Greek Street. Here's the Gay Hussar at No. 2, which has just opened. A real continental restaurant in this most continental of London villages. There's the Pillars of Hercules pub at No. 7. It's been there two hundred years or so shrouded in romantic gloom. The Pillars of Hercules was where Francis Thompson, the dypso cricket poet ('For the field is full of shades as I near the shadowy coast, /And a ghostly batsman plays to the bowling of a ghost'), lying in a drunken stupor in the doorway, was rescued by Wilfrid Meynell, editor of *Merry England*, who cleaned him up and made him fit for society again.

Beyond, the pièce de résistance: Old Compton Street. Time for a mid-morning snack, probably at Camisa delicatessen. Give thanks. Only by a stroke of good fortune were the Camisas not deported during the war on the *Arandora Star*, torpedoed by the Germans, otherwise it would have been a longer walk to Lina's on Brewer Street, the only place in London selling Mediterranean squid. Next a rest in the churchyard of St Anne's on Wardour Street. Pity about the bomb that has destroyed most of the building. At least the graves are still there, including that of Theodore von Neuhoff, the so-called King of Corsica, whose treasure lies buried somewhere in Epping Forest.

How about a pre-lunch pint at the York Minster, where the landlord's father, Victor Berlemont, drank during the war with Charles de Gaulle himself? Lunch: must be the Café Torino at the corner of Dean and Old Compton, with its wrought-iron tables topped with marble; vol-au-vents at 1/6 each. Mr and Mrs Minella are such amenable hosts they even let that arch Sophophile, Daniel Farson bring his own pâté in to place on their toast. Then a post-lunch pint in Compton's. Here in 1957 Harry Webb would officially change his name to Cliff Richard.

After 3 p. m. closing it's time to start thinking about an afternoon tipple at a private drinking club. Perhaps the Colony. Up the narrow stairs, past the paintings and posters, into a paint-peeling room heavy with smoke and indefinable atmosphere, furnished with piano and cigarette-stained carpet. Here, where day is twisted through a timeless lens, there is no hiding place from the gimlet eye and rasping tongue of its *patronne*, Muriel Belcher, or an eyeballing from Francis Bacon, perhaps even Christopher Isherwood.

Excess drinking induces a desperate need for dining. Fish to soak up

Ballantine's Finest at Wheeler's, 'a temple devoted to shell-fish', according to *Bon Viveur in London* which tells how 'oysters in season are whipped open by Jack, once a wrestler, now a renowned oyster opener'. Or perhaps dinner of Dover sole and lobster cooked in any one of thirty-two different ways, but with no vegetables.

To end the day a lively, nasty pub: the Marquess of Granby, just north of Oxford Street, out of Soho, at the corner of Rathbone Street and Percy Street. It stays open half an hour later than the Fitzroy or Wheatsheaf. There is the chance of seeing Dylan Thomas pick a fight with a guardsman. The chance of solving the world's most pressing problems. Should Mr Atlee allow Britain to have its own Atom Bomb? Surely it will make us sitting ducks . . . can't trust the Russians. Jazz: be-bop or trad, dad? And what about trousers? Turn-ups or no turn-ups . . . ?

## ABSOLUTE BEGINNERS

It needed serious hard work to maintain an idyllic hedonism that could reduce the entire world to a series of rational arguments debated over a frothing coffee or a pint of Younger's Scotch Tartan. Few could keep pace. Aleister Crowley: dead in 1947 from various sexually induced diseases, not to mention large quantities of drugs. George Orwell: succumbing to TB, dead by January 1950. Dylan Thomas: dead from alcoholic poisoning at thirty-nine, three years later. Nina Hamnett, gifted artist, model for Modigliani and Gaudier-Brzeska: washed up and wrecked by the middle of the decade, usually on a Soho barstool, shaking an Oxo tin into drinkers' faces to raise the money for a drink, threatening to expose her breasts to those not paying up.

A new generation soon took their place. Henrietta Moraes, Colin Mac-Innes, Daniel Farson and Jeffrey Bernard. Henrietta Moraes became *the* muse of post-war Soho. Francis Bacon painted her eighteen times, they both claimed, though neither could count the amount exactly, many of which were based on pornographic photographs. She was the living embodiment of dangerous Soho: violent, often drunk, drug-ridden and foul-mouthed, but lovable, as many have recalled. Every day Henrietta could be found in the York Minster (aka The French House) where the same ritual would take place: 'Good morning, Gaston. Could I have a glass of Pernod? I mean, could you possibly lend me a fiver.' He would then supply her with a drink and the change from a fiver.

Of course no one could be born with so evocative a name as Henrietta Moraes. Originally she was plain Audrey Abbott, brought up by a strict grand-mother, who disciplined her in Jumping Jack Flash style – 'with a strap right 'cross her back'. After the war she became a model in London art schools, and married film-maker Michael Law, who renamed her Henrietta and set up home with her in a Dean Street attic.

Now she could begin the rounds: the Torino café, Nellie Dean's, the Gar-goyle and Gay Hussar. With the bodybuilder Norman Bowler, her next husband, she raised two children, as well as running a coffee bar in Soho's best bookshop: David Archer's on Greek Street. Here in 1956 she met the Indian poet Dom Moraes, who became her next beau. They married in 1961 and honeymooned in Jerusalem while the Adolf Eichmann trial, which Dom was covering, was taking place. Back in London they lived in a mansion off Cheyne Walk, Chelsea, until Dom left the property one day to buy cigarettes and never came back. Eventually Henrietta moved into a gypsy caravan in a New Age commune in the West Country. A trail-blazing hippy, she worked as an assistant to Marianne Faithfull, but spent her later years in Holloway for burglary. When she died in 1999 'Mick and Jerry and Family' sent a bouquet of lilies to the funeral.

Equally difficult but less loved was Colin MacInnes. Cousin of Rudyard Kipling and Stanley Baldwin, he was the author of what is now a cult peren-nial, *Absolute Beginners* (1958), written in a breathless, contrived, but engaging teen argot. Describing Soho in one scene, he finds the air 'sweet as a cool bath, the stars peeping noisily beyond the neons, and the citizens of the Queendom, in their jeans and separates, floating down the Shaftesbury Avenue canals, like gondolas'. George Melly said MacInnes was 'one of the great quarrellers of our time'. Some said his irascibility stemmed from self-disgust at his own homosexuality. According to onlookers he behaved with 'appalling arrogance' when he worked for Field Security Section in Germany in 1944, interviewing suspected collaborators, and impelled staff to bow to him. By day, after the war, he would trawl the newly opened clubs that catered for young black men looking for lovers. A favourite was the Myrtle Bank in Berwick Street, Soho, where the food came in combinations unprecedented in English culinary history – chicken and rice.

MacInnes was one of the few early post-war chroniclers who understood the changes that would soon be wrought on English culture by the increasing presence of black people. He was the first major white writer to portray blacks sympathetically. Yet he could be as patronizing as a colonial official in a Somerset Maugham short story. Unsurprisingly his stock increased only after his death from cancer in 1976.

Daniel Farson chronicled the West End at length in countless articles, broadcasts and memoirs, particularly *Soho in the Fifties*. In a radio broadcast in 1991 he described a Soho type of person: 'someone who enjoyed drink and food and conversation and laughter, who would never cash a cheque at a bank but always with a friend or pub or shop, who'd probably cry quite a lot and enjoy it, and would miss the train back home if a party was going on.' Of course Farson was describing himself, but he never went as far as describing how he would often mimic Soho's most famous schizoid character – Dr Jekyll / Mr Hyde – with a Colony Room monologue that descended into a rant along the lines of 'I loathe you, I can't stand you. You're so clever, so patronizing', before being thrown out and heading off to a secret gay pub, the Elephants' Graveyard.

Critics have condemned Farson's studies of Soho as being refracted through a glass always tinted a rose colour, that the real Soho was a darker and deeper place than his picaresque pen portraits acknowledged. Indeed, his version of Soho omitted much, as Norman Bowler once explained: 'Soho was a very painful place to be. People weren't getting drunk and abusing each other out of fun. It was pain.'

Jeffrey Bernard was best known for his role as a piece of human furniture in the Coach and Horses pub, 29 Greek Street, where he would cadge drinks from strangers before telling them to 'piss off', and for his witty if frustrating 'Low Life' column in the *Spectator*. In the 1980s he was asked to write his autobiography. This was going to be a bit difficult, given that he had experienced life through a near-impenetrable alcoholic haze, so he placed an advertisement in the papers asking if anyone could tell him what he had been doing between 1960 and 1974. The following decade Keith Waterhouse turned his life into a hit West End play, *Jeffrey Bernard is Unwell*, the phrase usually found in the spot which his *Spectator* column should have occupied had it not been abandoned after a particularly nasty bout of Sohoitis. Waterhouse once described Jeffrey Bernard as the 'Huckleberry Finn of Soho. The rest of us were going home and paying mortgages and educating children, but Jeff was paddling his raft up and down Old Compton Street.'

Alongside these there was a cast of thousands. Colin Wilson, the country's most dynamic new writer in the 1950s, fêted internationally for the intellectual muscle of *The Outsider*, a book mostly written in the Reading Room of the British Museum after nights sleeping rough on Hampstead Heath. Wilson should have been Britain's answer to Albert Camus but he spoiled the necessary mystique with too much party-going and too many naff books; over a hundred by the end of the century and none as powerful as the first. Then there was Brendan Behan, the Irish wit, who, when asked why his drinking input was so large his writing output but so small, quipped: 'I am a drinker with a writing problem'. The artist John Minton, a revered illustrator, committed suicide at thirty-nine. John Deakin, photographer, alcoholic, died precipitately in 1972. After his death his negatives and prints were found in a box under his bed. All great Soho-ites. All prematurely removed from its streets.

# FROTH ON FRITH

In Soho eating and drinking has long been a lifestyle in itself. No one went to Wheeler's on Old Compton Street for the quality of the fish. They went because either they were friends of Francis Bacon or because their lack of fear of being insulted by him was stronger than their revulsion at his lifestyle. Or perhaps they were friends of Prince Philip, and had been invited to his Thursday Club gatherings, where the actors Peter Ustinov, David Niven and James Robertson Justice told bawdy jokes and sang raucous songs, the Queen willing to let her consort have such a safety valve on the grounds that it was less taxing for her than having him try to escape the palace grounds by climbing over the walls.

They may have gone to the Gay Hussar on Greek Street, a rare (for London) Hungarian restaurant, for the food, even though the goulash was really *borju porkolt* – veal stew. But mostly they went for the chance of mixing with the most sparkling of socialists: Tony Benn, Barbara Castle and Michael Foot, as well as Soviet diplomats whom the management was obliged to discourage for fear of the restaurant becoming known as a centre for intelligence gathering.

The Gay Hussar was opened in 1953 by Victor Sassie, a Barrow-in-Furness native of Italian stock who had studied catering in Budapest, and was therefore the closest thing London then had to a continental restaurateur. He named it after the Magyar cavalrymen who in Hungary would gallop up to such places demanding buckets of wine for their horses. The restaurant remained popular in exalted left-wing circles throughout the 1960s. It was here that Mick Jagger, Marianne Faithfull, journalist Paul Foot and the incorrigible Labour MP Tom Driberg met to discuss forming a new socialist party, Logos (Greek for word), a venture that never came to fruition.

Leoni's Quo Vadis, a few streets along at 22–26 Dean Street, has always been a more conspicuous, extrovert restaurant than the Gay Hussar. Peppino Leoni, an Italian, opened it in 1926. Interned during the Second World War, he returned to the restaurant at the end of the 1940s and transformed it into one of the finest in the capital. When the authorities chose to erect a blue plaque to Karl Marx at the front in honour of the 1850s residency of the founder of communism Leoni was outraged: 'My clientele is the very best . . . rich people . . . nobility and royalty, and Marx was the person who wanted to get rid of them all,' he thundered.

In the 1990s, after the founder had passed away, the restaurant was bought by superchef Marco Pierre White and the artist Damien Hirst. Now Marx's sojourn upstairs is not only deemed more socially acceptable, but his name has been added to the signboard, which reads 'Leoni Quo Vadis Marx', as if the scourge of bourgeois society was co-owner of this most bourgeois of establishments. But then the owners can parade his sojourn in the knowledge that a Marxist revolution is unlikely to sweep them away.

For those who couldn't, or preferred not to afford Wheeler's, the Gay Hussar or Leoni's, there was and still is – just – the New Piccadilly Café on Denman Street. Here, Formica tops and swivelling chairs, décor unchanged since the days of the beat poets and CND Aldermaston marchers, frame simple, cheap, enjoyable unfussed food: sausage, egg and chips; steak, chips and peas (not tinned) fused with a hint of mint; mixed grill; dishes with a continental twist, such as Risotto Bolognese. In 1956 the café was a meeting point for Hungarians fleeing the Soviet invasion. Many years later the owner recalled one Magyar migrant coming up to the till to pay his bill and proudly showing his father, who was then the proprietor, a political rival's severed finger wrapped in a handkerchief.

Eating at Jimmy's, another Soho institution, found down a basement in Frith Street, has also long been an experience in itself, a brief entry to a now mostly vanished world of all-night card sessions, wrestling bouts and mohair suits. In the 1950s Jimmy's was popular with GIs relaxing in London at the weekends, and the menu was suitably Americanized. Today Jimmy's reeks of an authenticity that comes from serving Balkan food long before London was saturated in kebab houses.

The other side of Oxford Street – what was still masquerading as North Soho after the war, not yet officially converted into Fitzrovia – offered more options for interesting eating. There was Schmidt's on Charlotte Street, all of whose staff – Germans – had been interned between 1939 and 1945. Like Bloom's, the celebrated Jewish salt beef bar in Whitechapel, it used the old European custom whereby staff bought the meals from the kitchen and then sold them to customers. Schmidt's notoriously employed the rudest waiters in the world and never advertised. 'Our advertisement is on the plate,' Herr Schmidt himself used to boast.

A few doors along Charlotte Street is Bertorelli's, founded in 1913 by the Italian Bertorelli brothers, one of whom died in 1995 aged 101. It was home in the 1950s of the Wednesday Club, a literary group founded by the reviewer Philip Toynbee, named in honour of Richard Hannay's Thursday Club from John Buchan's *The Three Hostages*, whose members included Christopher Isherwood and T. S. Eliot. The restaurants existed side by side in harmony until the Spanish Civil War, when the two sets of waiters emphatically took political sides and set about each other in a political streetfight.

Much of the fuss surrounding places like the New Piccadilly and Jimmy's lies in their 'authenticity': period menus; mid twentieth-century furnishings; a world without crass dieting. At one time not just Soho, but London, was full of such places. Now, because so many family-run eateries have been replaced by boutiques and American coffee chains they look odd; lost in a time-warp.

To many West Enders, to drink was more important than to eat. During the day the responsible, and those without a private income, stuck to the only Soho-ly acceptable non-alcoholic liquor – coffee. Soho, fittingly, was home to Britain's first espresso coffee bar: Moka, at 29 Frith Street. Behind the venture was a Scotsman, Maurice Ross, who bought Britain's first Gaggia machine from Pino Riservato, a travelling salesman specializing in dental equipment who was so concerned at the poor quality of coffee on offer in Britain he acquired the UK concession for the machine. The Gaggia offered a whole new way of dispensing coffee. A hand-operated spring-lever piston forced hot water on to the ground beans at a pressure of nine atmospheres, producing a head or *crema* on the top. It was a technique which couldn't be replicated at home with a kettle and a cup.

Ross began Moka in 1952, the opening ceremony presided over by the esteemed Italian actress Gina Lollabrigida. From that moment coffee quickly went from being a minority drink, which had virtually disappeared during Second World War rationing, to being exotic, a luxury. The coffee bar attained hip status, and Soho had more coffee bars than the rest of Britain put together. There was Les Enfants Terribles on Dean Street, which boasted of 'music, songs and laughter *à la française*', and Act One Scene One on Old Compton Street, which had been the Au Chat Noir, 1930s hang-out of the flamboyant and infamous cross-dresser Quentin Crisp. It boasted of 'Real French coffee, where the film and theatrical celebrities gather'. The Torino, a few doors nearer Dean Street, was fitted with rose-coloured marble-tiled tables often filled with plates of vol-au-vents made of chicken and rabbit. This was the favourite gathering place for the beats in the 1950s.

Round the corner from the Torino on Frith Street, by now popularly renamed Froth Street, was another authentically Italian rendezvous. Not considered anything special in the early 1950s, when there were so many similar establishments, Bar Italia, like Moka and the Torino, acquired the necessary Gaggia but aimed its services at workers in the local catering industry rather than beats and beatniks. It now has legendary status, an essential part of the tourist trail for any self-respecting up-and-coming London aesthete, not just because of its longevity, but for retaining the correct period detail: neon signs, chrome pedestal bar stools, mirrors, two-tone Formica striped with steel, Rocky Marciano shrine, scooter club, whose members preen and parade outside in good weather, revving their machines as if auditioning for *Quadrophenia*, and for always being busy and buzzing with bonhomie.

The post-war Soho coffee-bar scene was satirized memorably by Tony Hancock in his 1960 film *The Rebel*. Hancock, playing a troubled clerk who dreams of becoming a fêted artist, enters a Moka lookalike establishment furnished with rubber plants and sends the staff apoplectic by ordering a 'cappuccino, no froth. I don't want any froth, I want a cup of coffee! I don't want to wash my clothes in it!' The outraged proprietor grudgingly accords, pouring milk from a bottle into the coffee as comfortably as a maître d' of a swanky Parisian hotel tipping a glass of 1923 Clos-de-Bèze into a paper cup.

Twenty years later a more anarchic cultural icon, the cult US writer William S. Burroughs, subjected the Moka to what he called 'para-psychic bombardment' – sessions of recordings and pictures. 'Now to close in on The Moka Bar. Record. Take pictures. Stand around outside. Let them see me. They are seething around in there. The horrible old proprietor, his frizzy haired wife and slack jawed son, the snarling counter man. I have them and they know it.' Evidently Wild Bill wasn't enamoured with the espresso.

A deeper, longer, filmic look at the Soho coffee-bar scene can be found in the 1959 film *Beat Girl*, filmed on the real streets of the square mile of froth. *Beat Girl* was the first British film with a long-playing soundtrack, courtesy of composer John Barry and singer Adam Faith, and was furnished with an unforgettably corny dialogue: 'Love – that's the gimmick that makes sex respectable, isn't it?' and 'If you wanna fight, go join the Army – that's for squares.' Alas, by the end of the decade the explosion of coffee bars in Soho had been tempered by a decline in the quality of the coffee which had vanished in a sea of desperate, milk-heavy cappuccinos, never to return.

# DYPSOMANIA ON DEAN

By the afternoon coffee was no longer the most important concern. At a time of strict licensing, the pubs shut at 3 p. m., and so the semi-illicit afternoon drinking club became a vital refuge. By the mid 1950s there were some 500 of them in the West End. Almost any upstairs flat with room for two chairs and a counter made do. Some were that basic. Others were more sophisticated, in that the lights were dimmed and the staff rude beyond endurance. At the Galahad, frequent haunt of the gangster Jack Spot, entrance was possible only by uttering a secret password to the sour-faced attendant behind the flap at the door, although most patrons never realized that any word they uttered would have got them in.

The most renowned drinking club was the Colony at 41 Dean Street, home from home to Francis Bacon, Colin MacInnes and more recently Damien Hirst and Tracey Emin. In charge was the fierce-tongued Muriel Belcher, who would greet friends with the charming homily: 'Hello, Cunty' and gave all male frequenters semi-funny women's names, such as 'Miss Hitler'. When John Braine, author of *Room at the Top* made an appearance, she remarked to no one in particular: 'There's plenty of room in her top.' He was so upset he sought advice from his lawyers who told him not to be so silly. Such was the Colony's reputation the crème de la crème society would pay homage. Perhaps Princess Margaret wanted to be insulted, but she was not (conspicuously) when she paid a visit. Nor was David Bowie when he asked for a cup of tea. Less hospitably greeted were two rats which peeked their heads through the floorboards one day. 'You two can fuck off,' Belcher stormed, when she saw them, turning to one nonplussed drinker, to whom she explained: 'They're not members.'

Francis Bacon was Belcher's hero, and she paid him ten pounds a week to bring gamblers from Charlie Chester's casino on Archer Street to the club. Eventually he was rich enough not to need the money. In fact, after selling his paintings for seven-figure sums he was rich enough to stand everybody champagne, often with the quip: 'Here is champagne for my real friends, and real pain for my sham friends.' In the 1970s Belcher's mental health took a turn for the worse. Bacon took her on holiday to Jamaica, but regretted it. 'She thought she was at the club the whole time,' he wailed to George Melly.

When Belcher died in 1979 the even more bad-tempered Ian Board, who had been head barman, took over. Board wasn't around or alive long enough to secure as esteemed a place in Soho history as his predecessor, for he himself passed away in 1994, replaced by the more reasonable Michael Wojas. The Colony was lucky to survive a major scare in 1996. Jeffrey Bernard, Soho's best-known twentieth-century drinker, announced publicly that 'hardly anyone worthwhile goes to the Club any more', probably because by that time he was wheelchair-bound and could no longer climb the rickety stairs. Despite the new almost-liberal licensing laws it survives.

Not everyone was welcome at a private drinking club. Most had to make do with pubs, of which Soho has long boasted London's most interesting, most cosmopolitan, most learned and most colourful clientele. No one ever drank in Soho for the quality of the beer; rather it was to sup in the presence of glamorous ghosts hovering over the bar stool – Dylan Thomas, Nina Hamnett, George Orwell, Charles de Gaulle, Arthur Rimbaud, Karl Marx … the thought that some of the mystique that made those names so celebrated might rub off.

The inspired imbiber had and still has a boundless choice. Within a few streets of Soho Square there is the mouth-watering prospect of the Crown and Two Chairmen at 32 Dean Street; the John Snow, 39 Broadwick Street; De Hems on Macclesfield Street; the Dog and Duck at 18 Bateman Street;

the French House, 49 Dean Street; the Golden Lion, two doors along at No. 51; the King of Corsica at 90 Berwick Street; the Sun and 13 Cantons on Great Pulteney Street; and the Coach and Horses of 29 Greek Street.

Of these some have so enticing a reputation it is barely possible to walk past without being sucked in. A pub has stood on the site of De Hems, to the south of Shaftesbury Avenue, since 1688 when it opened as the Horse and Dolphin. A retired Dutch seaman, De Hem, took over the premises early in the twentieth century. He had a passion for molluscs, and decorated the walls with some 300,000 oyster shells, the last of which were removed in the 1950s. Fittingly it was here during the Second World War that Dutch Resistance fighters gathered. In the 1960s De Hems became popular with music business people, for it was said that the bottom three places in the charts could be bought in the pub's Oyster Bar. The rumour attracted Pete Meaden, the Who's first manager, who described himself as 'neat, sharp and cool, an all-white Soho Negro of the night' and would come here every lunchtime to buy rounds of scotch and coke.

The French House has long been the haunt of Soho's literary crowd, and was so especially in the 1950s and 1960s. It was here that Brendan Behan ate his *boeuf bourguignon* with both hands. It was here that Dylan Thomas left the only copy of the handwritten manuscript for *Under Milk Wood* a few weeks before he went to America – for good – in 1953. Thomas told a BBC producer, Douglas Cleverdon, that if he found the original he could sell it. All Thomas knew was that he had dropped it somewhere in Soho, probably in a pub, but had no idea where. Eventually Cleverdon realized that the French House was a likely choice. He found the script and sold it for £2,000 (£35,000 in today's prices).

The French opened as the Wine House in 1910. It was run by a German, Schmidt, who was then Britain's only foreign landlord. Unsurprisingly, Schmidt was deported when the Great War began. He was replaced by a Frenchman, Victor Berlemont, who would eject troublesome customers by announcing: 'I'm afraid one of us will have to leave, and it's not going to be me.' Berlemont changed the pub's name to the York Minster, and during the Second World War it became a meeting place for the French Resistance. Charles de Gaulle, their leader, drew up his Free French call-to-arms after lunch upstairs one day in the early '40s, according to local legend.

After the war painters such as Lucian Freud and Francis Bacon became regulars, this at a time when rationing meant that scotch could only be obtained under the counter by one in the know, who would ask for *un vin blanc ecossaise*. In 1951 Berlemont was succeeded by his son, Gaston. Despite being born in Soho and serving in the RAF during the war, Gaston played up his Gallic background to the full by sporting a flamboyant moustache and engaging in much hand-kissing. It was he who changed the name from the York Minster to the French House.

## THE CARNABYTIAN ARMY

The West End's most impressive characters of the 1950s were mostly artists and writers; Francis Bacon and Colin MacInnes for instance. By the 1960s tailors, hairdressers, photographers and actors were more typical.

By a combination of luck, hard work and ingenuity the West End briefly came to be at the centre of the fashion world. The area had set the tone for how Britain should dress in Regency days when Beau Brummel revolution-ized men's apparel by wearing a starched cravat. According to one contemporary commentator, Beau's dress struck dandies dumb with envy and caused washerwomen to miscarry. Brummel also encouraged men to wear trousers rather than knee breeches, discouraged fancy trims and stressed the cut of the garment, leading Lord Byron to remark how there was 'nothing really exceptional about Brummel's dress save "a certain exquisite propriety"'.

Less fêted but equally successful a hundred years later was the Hanover Square-based dressmaker Lucy Sutherland (Lucile). The first Londoner in her field to succeed in France, Lucile took advantage of the Parisians' embarrassment at having their models move on the catwalk, and so in her fashion shows they did not stand still. She specialized in 'cascades of chif-fons, of draperies as lovely as those of ancient Greece', as one customer described them, and her gowns for Lily Elsie in *The Merry Widow* in 1907 brought the high waistline, narrow clinging skirts and giant, plumed hats into fashion.

In 1912 Lucile made plans for opening a branch in New York, and booked herself a passage on White Star Liners' new flagship, the *Titanic*. Discon-certed by the size of the vessel, she went to bed each night fully dressed, which was just as well, for on 14 April an iceberg fatally struck the ship at around midnight. Lucile and her husband, Sir Cosmo Duff Gordon, secured a berth on the almost deserted No. 1 boat. After it escaped the wreckage one of the crew explained that with the ship sunk their pay would be stopped. Duff Gordon promised to meet the men's costs, and presented them with a cheque on board the rescue vessel, a scene photographed by the ship's doctor. When the party reached New York one of the crew went to the papers and denounced Duff Gordon for trying to bribe the men into keeping quiet about how he had paid them to row away from the *Titanic* so that they would not be swamped by drowning passengers. Although Duff Gordon was exonerated at the inquiry, his and Lucile's reputations were besmirched, and she never regained her standing.

A few hundred yards south of Hanover Square runs Savile Row, built in 1695 over the kitchen garden of Burlington House (now home of the Royal Academy). By the mid nineteenth century Savile Row had acquired tailors' shops, and its reputation soon grew. In the 1930s the firm of Kilgour, French and Stanbury at No. 8 made Fred Astaire's morning coat for the film *Top Hat*, and this set the pattern for the biggest Hollywood names – Cary Grant, Bing Crosby and Frank Sinatra – to come to Savile Row for their suits.

Hardy Amies, who had worked in the Intelligence Corps during the Second World War, opened an outfitters in 1946 at 14 Savile Row. He started to specialize in the quintessentially English gentlewoman's look of tweeds by day and jewel-framing silks by night, as well as more continental-style dresses which took up the influence of Christian Dior's New Look of 1947, that of rounded shoulders and full skirts. In the 1950s Amies began providing dresses for the Queen, and was awarded a Royal Warrant in 1955. Long the model of discretion, he broke with diplomatic protocol in 1999, not to reveal his secret agent past but to brand the creations of the new young British designers, John Galliano and Alexander McQueen, as being 'more appropriate to the Folies Bergère'.

Next to Hardy Amies's at No. 15 is Henry Poole, named after the founder, who dressed local huntsmen and bankers such as the Rothschilds in the early nineteenth century. Poole inadvertently created the tuxedo in 1860 when a visitor from Tuxedo Park in America asked Poole if he could make him a new type of short smoking jacket which he had seen on Edward, Prince of Wales, at Sandringham. After Poole died in 1876, the store was enlarged and began concentrating on civil rather than military tailoring. By the twentieth century Poole's had become the largest tailors in the world, with more than 300 staff. It has since absorbed several other firms.

At No. 1 Savile Row, a 1732 town house with touches by William Kent, is Gieves and Hawkes, founded as two separate firms by a Mr Gieves (in 1785) and a Mr Hawkes (in 1771). The two firms later merged, and in the nineteenth century Gieves and Hawkes developed the Kitchener and Wolseley sun helmet, an essential item for those travelling in hot climates, such as Livingstone and Stanley. Coincidentally, it was here that Livingstone's corpse laid in state after his death in 1874 before being interred at Westminster Abbey.

Savile Row accidentally pioneered Britain's first post-war youth cult look in 1948. Local tailors began to promote an Edwardian revival style of long single-breasted jackets, overcoats with velvet collars, and narrow trousers as being symptomatic of English 'class'. But after delinquent working-class teenagers adopted the style, calling themselves 'Teddy Boys', such clothes became socially unacceptable among the middle classes overnight. As one Savile Row customer put it, 'the whole of one's wardrobe immediately became unwearable.' Savile Row tailors usually showed restraint, so when Tommy Nutter set up his House of Nutter outlet at No. 35 in 1968 thanks to a cash injection from Cilla Black, laid a chocolate-coloured carpet and installed a nameplate that read simply: 'Nutters', his staid neighbours were shocked.

By that time, however, it was not Savile Row that was attracting the public's attention, but a different street also situated a couple of hundred yards from Regent Street – on the east side – Carnaby Street. Built in the 1680s, Carnaby Street was named after a demolished local mansion, Karnaby House, and in the early nineteenth century was known for the Nag's Head pub, a hotbed of revolutionary political activity where the toast was 'May the last of the kings be strangled with the guts of the last of the priests'. The rag trade was long established around here. There were some seventy tailors on and around Golden Square by the First World War, although Carnaby Street itself had no connection with the industry until the 1950s when it was lined with small, blackened terraced houses, tobacconists and attic workshops that were cheap to rent.

In the mid 1950s photographer Bill Green opened a select clothes shop, Vince, at 15 Newburgh Street, one street along from Carnaby, selling imported Levi's (few people in Britain then owned jeans) and dandified clothes. Ready-to-wear stuff as opposed to Savile Row's tailored suits. Green's target customers were mostly homosexuals, as noted by George

Melly who once explained how it was the only shop where 'they measured your inside leg each time you bought a tie'.

Vince's soon gained a reputation. Wolf Mankowitz celebrated the shop in his Soho beat novel *Expresso Bongo* in which 'sweating teenagers [wear] Vince Man's Shop jeans with heavy rollnecks, close-fitting Charing Cross Road teddy trousers and velvet-collared coats bought on hire purchase'. One of Vince's assistants, John Stephen, soon branched out and opened his own menswear shop, His Clothes, on nearby Beak Street. His Clothes specialized in scarves loosely knotted around the neck, velvet suits and cheap throwaway garments. When a fire damaged the premises in 1960 Stephen opened a new branch at 41 Carnaby Street. There he introduced new concepts into marketing clothes such as experimental window displays and racks on the pavement displaying goods. The clothes were Italian-styled – round-collared shirts, inch-wide ties, short jackets with side vents, five inches long – aimed at a young narcissistic crowd known as Mods.

The Mods were one of the first British youth tribes to succeed the Teds, their style antithesis. They began as devotees of the modern movement: modern jazz, existentialist literature, modern architecture, who also wore the latest fashions. By 1960 that look, if not the intellectual tastes, had been appropriated by bands of suburban working-class and lower-middle-class youth more concerned with the correct image, the right press on their trousers and a precise haircut than with the latest books and sounds.

It was a vapid but stylish attitude, personified in public by the naff Australian singer Frank Ifield, who told the press: 'You can knock my talent but never ever knock my tailor.' And Mod was a paternalistic movement. Females – girl Mods – were considered expendable, there to do little other than contribute to the image with the 'correct' mufti of seamless stockings, stilettos, elfin hair and corpse-coloured face with a dash of mascara.

On Saturday afternoons the Mods would gather on their scooters at roadside junctions where they could parade and preen, occasionally gazing in the shop windows of the trendiest West End clothes stores. Apart from His Clothes, these included Anello and Davide's by Cambridge Circus, Cecil Gee on Charing Cross Road, Thea Porter's boutique on Greek Street and Gear at 35 Carnaby Street. Anello and Davide's sold Cuban-heeled boots with elastic edges that became a Beatles trademark. Cecil Gee on Charing Cross Road was excellent for mohair suits, stove-pipe trousers and full-draped jackets. It was Eric Clapton's favourite clothes shop in the days before he sold his soul to MOR. Thea Porter's boutique on Greek Street was where Pink Floyd bought the flamboyant togs they wore on the covers of their early records. And at Gear on Carnaby Street Michael English designed one of the most important 'Swinging London' fashion accessories – sunglasses with a Union Jack underlay printed across the lenses.

Mods could be found in the new clothes-conscious pop / R&B London groups such as the Small Faces, the Yardbirds and the Who, who regularly used these shops. It was at His Clothes that the Who's drummer, Keith Moon, and the eccentric performer Viv Stanshall tried out their trouser-testing gag. This involved Moon and Stanshall demanding the 'strongest pair of trousers in the shop', tearing them apart, to the horror of the store manager, and then being joined by a one-legged man who had been waiting outside. With the store manager fuming, the one-legged man would grab the trousers, announcing that they were 'just the thing he was looking for' and order the confounded shopkeeper to 'wrap them separately!'

By the mid 1960s John Stephen owned around a third of Carnaby shops, each sporting a variation of his name, such as Stephen John's Man's Shop. Carnaby Street, along with its Chelsea equivalent, King's Road, was now the shop window for youth fashion in England, and crowds flocked there at weekends. For most Britons the first indication that something interesting was happening in Soho came in the *Daily Telegraph Weekend* magazine of 26 April 1965. An article written by an American, John Crosby, headlined: 'London, the Most Exciting City in the World', focused in soon-to-be-dated purple prose on the activities of rich, upper-class dandies such as 'Rupert Lycett-Green, Mary Quant and a bunch of other pretty Chelsea birds'. It brought the Carnaby scene to national attention. The Kinks simultaneously lionized and sent up the scene with their February 1966 single 'Dedicated Follower of Fashion', about a dandyish fop who 'does his little rounds / 'Round the boutiques of London Town / Eagerly pursuing all the latest fads and trends'.

Soon the rest of the world caught up with the idea of London, rather than Paris, as a fashion centre. On 15 April 1966 an article in the American magazine *Time* entitled 'You Can Walk Across It On The Grass [*sic*]' drooled over how 'on any twilight evening when the day's work is done, Carnaby Street pulses with slender young men in tight, black pants that fit on the hips like ski-pants, their tulip-like girlfriends on their arms, peering into the garishly-lit windows at the burgundy coloured suede jackets with the slanted, pleated pockets'. The article also coined the term 'Swinging London', a phrase dreamt up by one of the editors.

Inevitably the publicity killed Carnaby Street, which soon began to attract chain stores. By the end of the decade it was filled with cash-in shops stuffed with inferior hipster jeans and second-rate Cuban heeled boots, patronized by what detractors denounced as 'weekend hippies'. The street enjoyed a brief revival at the end of the 1970s, when its stores latched on to punk, stocking tartan bum-flaps, knee-length lace-up boots and zip-festooned leather jackets, but by the 1980s it had succumbed to nostalgia and over-priced tat.

One criticism of the new boutique-ridden London was that the innova-tors had been replaced by those looking for a quick cash-in, by merchants who knew nothing of the culture and just fancied making a quick buck. So where did the Beatles fit in to that? They not only understood the new cul-ture, they had pioneered it. They also wanted to spend money and make money, in ever-increasing amounts. The Beatles opened a boutique as part of their Apple Corps business empire at 94 Baker Street in December 1967. The shop was easily identified by the swirly psychedelic mural on the south wall, the subject of many complaints from 'straight' neighbouring shop-keepers, which the council eventually ordered to be painted over. The shop would be a 'beautiful place to buy beautiful things', the group claimed, and they were set to open more stores in Manchester, Birmingham and Liver-pool. Nothing came of their grandiose plans, which was hardly surprising given that Paul McCartney announced that the Baker Street boutique would be run according to 'Western communism principles'. Communist or not, the store was a financial disaster, and when it closed on 30 July 1968 all £15,000 worth of stock was given away to members of the public.

Clothes weren't the only items on the menu at Apple Corps. Aside from the record label, which *was* a success, showcasing the Beatles' later works and most of their solo output, there was Apple Electronics. This branch was run by Yanni Mardas – 'Magic Alex' – and was geared towards creating weird and wonderful gadgets. Mardas impressed Lennon with his 'nothing box', a small plastic device which emitted randomly blinking lights, and Apple fitted him out with his own laboratory in the basement of 3 Savile Row, Apple's HQ. There he designed new recording equipment, and boasted of plans to create the world's first 72-track tape machine. The lab was a disaster. Rather than being state-of-the-art, it was poorly planned, unusable and cramped.

There was no soundproofing, no intercom (visitors had to knock on the door . . . in a studio!), and no 72-track tape deck. Mardas was fired from Apple in 1969. Every British patent he applied for on Apple's behalf was turned down. It later transpired that his main electronic experience was as a TV repairman. So much for 'Western communism principles'.

The Beatles, undisputed rock trailblazers, rarely played gigs in the West End, but ironically their last gig took place here, not in a sweaty Soho club at night, but on the roof of their Apple HQ in Mayfair's Savile Row, amongst the bespoke tailors, by day. The unannounced live show took place on 30 January 1969 to the astonishment of local office workers who could hear a group that sounded like the Beatles but could not see exactly where the noise was coming from until they realized that as it could only be coming from the roof of 3 Savile Row it probably *was* the Beatles. Everything was going fine with the gig – well, the Beatles were at each other's throats by then, but they were playing the same song at the same time – until the police, based further up the road, came along and pulled the plug. Perhaps the Beatles should have waited until nightfall when gigs seem more appropriate and the corruption-ridden Savile Row police would have been out clubbing themselves.

## THE TEASY-WEASIES

It was not enough to wear the correct clothes. There was an important attachment to the body that needed to be right – hair. The West End could never have been taken seriously as a fashion centre without an equally talented body of hairdressers, and of these there was no shortage. At 171 New Bond Street in 1963 an East End Jew who had fought the new post-war fascists on the streets of Aldgate in the late 1940s rearranged Mary Quant's hair with geometric Bauhausian precision. 'I'm going to cut your hair like you cut material,' Vidal Sassoon told Quant, founder of the first London boutique on Chelsea's King's Road, and in doing so invented the Bob.

The new style sent reviewers at the fashion show at which it was revealed into ecstasy. It was photographed by Terence Donovan, and propelled across the world in the pages of *Vogue*. Sassoon had learned his skills at the Grafton Street salon of Paul 'Teasy-Weasy' Raymond ('We'll do a teasy-weasy here, and a teasy-weasy there'), who could boast of London's most star-studded celebrity client list. When Sassoon left Raymond's for New Bond Street in

1954 he hired a succession of immaculately dressed sharp young blades as assistants. These included Leonard Lewis, also Jewish, but from distinctly non-*heimishe* Shepherd's Bush, who later went on to become the revered Leonard of Mayfair, and Nigel Davies, whose embarrassment at his pedestrian name eventually resulted in a reappearance as Justin de Villeneuve, mentor to Twiggy.

At 171 New Bond Street, Sassoon, with his hand-held blow-dryer (no fixed, space-helmet-style dryers here) and fancy conditioners, became the best-known hairdresser in London. One new West End luminary who was not a fan of the Vidal Sassoon look was the era's most celebrated photographer, David Bailey. After being demobbed in August 1958 Bailey obtained a job as a gofer to photographer David Olins in his Charlotte Mews studio. He soon found a more appealing post in the studio of John French, the suave, gay and married photographer. French admired Bailey's jazzed-up Boho look – long hair, Cuban boots, jeans and leather jacket at a time when no one in Britain, not even the Beatles, looked like that – and his new charge soon became part of a new group of meritocratic, iconoclastic anti-establishment trend-setters.

That group also included the actors Terence Stamp and Michael Caine, working-class boys made good, who took a flat in the heart of old-money London at 64 Harley Street, the house where the painter J. M. W. Turner had lived in the early nineteenth century. One day Caine, who had married young and divorced soon after, was visited by bailiffs acting for his former wife, who wanted alimony. Caine was obliged to attend debtors' court, where the magistrate refused to believe that the actor had no money yet lived in Harley Street.

A few yards away at 57 Wimpole Street was the most fêted, most chased, most eligible, most fawned over of the new 'classless' pop culture celebrities – Paul McCartney. He was living in the Georgian town house belonging to the parents of his girlfriend, Jane Asher. It was here on Wimpole Street that McCartney wrote a number of early Beatles songs, including 'I Want To Hold Your Hand' (together with John Lennon in the basement) and 'Yesterday'. McCartney claimed the latter song came to him in a dream, on waking from which he went over to the piano beside the bed and played the melody complete. He named the new piece 'Scrambled Eggs' in honour of Booker T & the MGs' instrumental 'Green Onions', and quickly contacted the group's producer, George Martin, worried that he may have subconsciously lifted the tune from an existing song. His fears turned out to be unfounded; 'Yesterday' has since become the most commercially successful song in the history of recorded music. At the height of Beatlemania in the mid 1960s McCartney used to escape from the house by clambering on to the flat roof of the adjacent property, No. 56, where he had an arrangement with the owner. He would then make his way out of the front door of the neighbour's property when no one was looking. Such was the temporary price for being a marketable cultural innovator.

Some, but not all, of the old class barriers alongside which the monied, leisured, upper classes ruled Britain were being broken down so that in the near future the monied, leisured, middle classes could rule Britain. Although the West End, London and the country were changing culturally at a phenomenal rate, during the period from autumn 1963 to autumn 1964, which saw the rise of Swinging London, the prime minister was the Scottish laird Alec Douglas-Home, the fourteenth Earl of Home. He had been obliged to resign his seat in the Lords to contest a seat for the Commons to stay in office, having been chosen for the premiership not by the country, or even by the Conservative Party, but by the Queen.

## ROOM SERVICE

The 1970s were always likely to be an anti-climax. Soho descended into a sea of sleaze and sordid sex around its strip clubs, massage parlours, clip joints and hostess bars. It became a byword for seediness. The number of local sex shops grew to such levels that by the end of the decade there were some 200 of them, their presence dissuading many people from visiting. A saviour came in the shape of the Soho Society, formed in the 1960s to campaign for the preservation of the area's character. The society pressed the council to act, not out of concerns for morality, but to combat the shabbiness. MP Tim Sainsbury pushed a private member's bill through Parliament to ban overtly sexual window displays, and in 1982 a law was passed forcing sex establishments to be licensed, which effectively led to scores of properties closing down. Soho was down to thirty-five sex shops by the end of the decade, and the number has since dropped again.

By the 1980s, with the '60s a distant memory, there was a new generation of daytime West End gadabouts looking for somewhere safe to play, a place where they could suffer their Sohoitis untroubled by the rest of society. Having deemed pubs passé, as they were stuffed with dirty old men and students, having considered the private drinking dens relics from another age, and noting that the gentlemen's clubs suffered from an obvious sexist malaise, the alternative was obvious. Why not set up a club; a new, better, different, more dramatic kind of club; a club for the kind of people who don't belong to clubs? Using Groucho Marx's adage about not wanting to join anything that would have him as a member, the publishers Carmen Callil and Liz Calder set up the aptly named Groucho Club. It opened in May 1985 in the former Gennaro restaurant on Soho's Dean Street, the place where the 1950s gangster Billy Hill had launched his autobiography, and soon became the favourite hang-out for the new A-List arts celebrities – Julie Burchill, Salman Rushdie, Ben Elton, Anna Ford, Damien Hirst et al – keen for somewhere of their own in the centre of London now that Fleet Street had left the City for windswept and empty Wapping and Millwall.

Even if many of its patrons passed their time in a haze of mind-mashing white powder, the Groucho was the setting for a thousand unforgettable incidents that have enticed successive generations of media wannabes. There was the time that style journalist Robert Elms and a pal racked up a bar bill for seventy-eight bottles of Beck's, one bottle of champagne and a sandwich – a bill that was framed on the wall for ages. There was the time the *Modern Review* journalist Tony Young had sex in the toilets with a Princess Di look-alike, obviously and unarguably more exciting than the real thing. There was the time the cartoonist Tony Husband, chewing on a bowl of teeth-grinding nuts, noticed one of his party take something out of his mouth and place it back in the dish, only to be told when he remonstrated with the fellow that they were not eating nuts but olives, and that he was finding a home for the stone.

But there was also the dark side to the Groucho day. Liam Gallagher of Oasis went on the rampage with a snooker cue and caused £5,000 damage to the table and a TV, for which he was banned – for life – although why they let him in in the first place was a more pressing question. There was too much priapism from Damien Hirst and Chris Evans. There was too much coke taking – on the stairs, in the lift, in the rooms, in the corridors. There was the ultimately unsuccessful attempt to buy the club in 2000 launched by Sloane Ranger Benjamin Fry.

That battle captured the media's imagination in a manner unseen since the abdication of Edward VIII. On one side were those desperate to display their hip credentials by siding with the new bohemians against the sad, straight, conservatively attired Fry; on the other were the Hooray Henrys who didn't care a dried fig for the Groucho's reputation but just wanted to make some money from the deal. That almost all the participants shared the same advantageous background and education, and earned the same kind of telephone-number salaries, was all part of the fun for independent onlookers.

When Fry was asked why he wanted to buy the Groucho he gave a reply that won prizes for its mangling of the English language: 'The Groucho has a strong brand, which has obvious synergy with the rest of the leisure industry', to which the interviewer might have added the obvious: 'Yes, Mr Fry, but is it any good?' Of course the real questions that should have been asked were why would anyone want to belong to a club not simply that would have them as a member but that would regularly entertain the likes of Patsy Kensit, Damien Hirst, Kylie Minogue and Alex James? Were these really appropriate successors to the great Soho tradition of exclusive clubbers that once included Dr Johnson, James Boswell, Francis Bacon and Colin MacInnes? Was it worth paying some £500 a year for the privilege of buying second-rate beer and third-rate food in the company of a man who pickled sheep for a living or, even worse, a man who played bass for Blur? Was this the best way to spend that most priceless of commodities – a day in the West End?

# 12

# Night

After dark the West End comes to life. Revellers new to the area soon learn what Londoners take for granted: that a night out is a night remembered in the West End.

At first it was music hall that pulled the night-time crowds. The most popular West End halls were the Trocadero and London Pavilion, both by Piccadilly Circus, and the Oxford Music Hall near St Giles's Circus. Acts at the Trocadero, which opened in 1882, would quickly whip up the crowd with jokes such as: 'Are your relatives in business?' 'Yes – in the iron and steel business.' 'Oh, indeed?', 'Yes – me mother irons and me father steals' and 'How long has your father been in his present position?' 'Three months,' 'And what is he doing?' 'Six months.' A longer duologue ran:

> Where were you born?
> Liverpool.
> What part?
> All of me.
> Have you lived there all your life?
> Not yet.
> Any great men born there?
> No, only babies.

The London Pavilion was more ambitious. It contained bowling alleys and restaurants as well as a music hall. Here some of the genre's best-known songs were premiered, including Charles Coburn's 'Two Lovely Black Eyes' and Albert Chevalier's 'Wot Cher! (Knocked 'Em in the Old Kent Road)'. It was also here in 1877, during the Russo-Turkish War, that G. H. Macdermott unveiled a new political number, 'War Song'. Macdermott was concerned at the reception he might meet, given the sensitivity over the conflict. 'All eyes were on me,' he later recalled, 'as I sang the first verse: "The Dogs of War are loose and the rugged Russian Bear /All bent on blood and robbery has crawled out of his lair."' But as Macdermott launched into the next verse: 'It seems a thrashing now and then, will never help to tame / That brute, and so he's out upon the same old game / The Lion did his best, to find him some excuse / To crawl back to his den again', the crowd leapt to their feet. Eventually they were standing on the tables cheering, whipped into euphoria by the chorus: 'We don't want to fight / But, by Jingo, if we do / We've got the ships / We've got the men and got the money, too / We've fought the Bear before . . . and while we're Britons true / The Russians shall not have Constantinople.' From this a new set of words soon entered modern parlance – jingo, jingoism, jingoistic – the art and act of supporting one's country in a militaristic fashion.

The Oxford Music Hall at the eastern end of Oxford Street, by The Tottenham pub, had been an old coaching inn. It was claustrophobic and always crowded, and a huge mirror at the back of the stage reflected the entire hall. Upstairs, prostitutes patrolled the galleries. The audience would noisily and heartily join in the choruses. When Marie Lloyd, dressed as a schoolgirl, sang 'What's That For, Eh?' amidst a number of suggestive phallic symbols, the venue nearly lost its licence. In 1917 it was converted into a theatre.

Music hall in London, especially in the West End with its greater crowds, reached its peak during the Great War as singers stoked patriotic fervour in numbers like 'Keep the Home Fires Burning', 'Pack up Your Troubles' and 'It's A Long Way to Tipperary'. Once again Marie Lloyd's take was more risqué: 'I didn't like you much before you joined the army, John, but I do like yer cockie now you've got your khaki on.' Somehow she got away with it.

As London grew at an unparalleled rate during the late Victorian era so people began heading in ever greater numbers to the West End at night. Leicester Square, a fashionable residential address in the eighteenth century, perfectly positioned near the royal courts, became *the* major night time destination in the nineteenth century.

On the east side of the square was the Alhambra Theatre, which opened in 1858 in a building that only four years previously had been unveiled as the Royal Panopticon of Science and Art, showcasing scientific exhibits. Whereas the Panopticon had been a disaster, resulting in its founder Edward Clarke going bankrupt, the Alhambra fared better. The grand Moorish design enticed revellers to what were mostly circus shows, and even though within two years it was a music hall, the shows were a success until the building was demolished to make way for an Odeon cinema in the 1930s.

Similar quick-fire changes occurred on the north side of the square where the site once occupied by the aristocratic Savile House was covered with the Royal London Panorama in 1881. The venue opened with exhibitions of scenes from the Charge of the Light Brigade but made little money. Within a year it was converted into the Empire Theatre, putting on operettas and ballets. Still no joy. There was only one solution – a music hall. Now customers began to flock there, even, ironically, to see ballet. Everyone had a wild time until 1894 when the London County Council decided the promenade where patrons paraded and preened was too raucous, and revoked the Empire's licence. The venue was only able to reopen on condition that a canvas screen separated the auditorium from the ungainly prom area. Punters, who included the young Winston Churchill, were unimpressed and tore it down in protest. The Empire was demolished in 1927 and replaced with a picture palace. Now, nearly a hundred years later Leicester Square is still best known for its cinemas.

Until the Theatres Act of 1843, only two London venues, including Covent Garden Opera House, were allowed to present drama. The change in the law saw theatres open across London, some concentrating on serious works, although given the limitations there had been on the genre it was some time before there was any British drama of note, some plumping for musical works, many veering between the two.

By a quirk of popular misnaming the phrase 'London theatre' gradually metamorphosed into 'West End theatre', even though the catch-all title includes venues in Covent Garden and even as far away from the West End as Sloane Square, home of the formidable Royal Court. As far as West End theatres are concerned they have all nearly always been solely in Soho, where the stage has mostly been the setting for light-hearted farces and romps, rather than serious drama.

For instance, at 73 Dean Street, right amongst the blackened brick-terraced properties of Victorian Soho, Frances Maria Kelly opened the Royalty Theatre in 1840. The first night was a disaster, as the scene-changing machine made such a damnable noise it drowned out the sound of the actors, while the vibrations induced fits of shaking in the audience. It was at the Royalty on 25 March 1875 that the earliest surviving Gilbert and Sullivan production, *Trial By Jury*, was premiered. The manager of the theatre was Richard D'Oyly Carte, who went on to become the duo's mentor.

While looking for a two-act opera to precede the staging of Offenbach's comic opera *La Périchole* D'Oyly Carte bumped into Gilbert and persuaded him to produce a piece which would be suitable for the slot. Gilbert had featured a primitive version of the work in *Fun* magazine. All he needed now was to expand it and find a suitable composer. When Arthur Sullivan's name came up Gilbert trudged through the snow with the complete text to Sullivan's Battersea flat. By the time he arrived he was in a foul mood. As the composer later recalled: 'He read it through, as it seemed to me, in a perturbed sort of way, with a gradual crescendo of indignation, in the manner of a man considerably disappointed with what he had written. As soon as he had come to the last word he closed the manuscript violently, apparently unconscious of the fact that he had achieved his purpose so far as I was concerned, inasmuch as I was screaming with laughter the whole time.'

A decade later, flushed with the success of the partnership's works, which were run mostly in the Savoy Theatre off the Strand, D'Oyly Carte built the flamboyant Palace Theatre by Cambridge Circus, a riot of terracotta and Moorish embellishments. He hoped the venue would become the home for English opera but had to settle for a music hall, the Palace Theatre of Varieties, when he realized his original ideas were too ambitious. In 1911 the theatre was the setting for the first Royal Command Performance, the music-hall star Marie Lloyd excluded from the bill for being too vulgar. Since the 1960s it has been the setting for long-running performances of musicals, such as *The Sound of Music* (1961–67), *Jesus Christ Superstar* (1972–80) and *Les Misérables* (1985–2004).

Similar stories chart the life of a large West End theatre, such as the Prince Edward on Old Compton Street. Too large and too close to the bright lights for 'straight' plays, it has always put music before dialogue. The Prince Edward opened in 1930 with the musical *Rio Rita*, which ran for only fifty-nine performances. When its follow-up, *Nippy*, fared only slightly better, the owners decided that the best way to stem the losses would be to convert the premises into a cabaret restaurant. The new venture – the London Casino – which opened in 1936, was a success, but during the Second World War the building was seconded by the authorities who used it for the Queensbury All Services Club. After the war, musicals, including *Pick Up Girl* and Ivor Novello's *The Dancing Years*, were staged until 1954 when the Prince Edward became a cinema, pioneering wide-screen Cinerama. It reverted to a theatre in the 1970s, putting on Andrew Lloyd Webber's *Evita* in 1978 and later *Chess*. In the 1990s Lord Delfont and Cameron Mackintosh oversaw a £3.5 million refurbishment that saw a successful three-year run for *Mamma Mia!*, the Abba musical, ideally placed in the heart of camp London.

Four prominent theatres can be found on Shaftesbury Avenue near Piccadilly Circus, in the heart of the West End: the Apollo, Lyric, Gielgud and Queen's. It was at the Queen's in 1937 that John Gielgud took the title role in *Richard II*, Peggy Ashcroft playing the Queen. How unusual to see Shakespeare in the West End, where producers could rarely be convinced that the plays would attract enough people and were reluctant to take financial risks. More typical of the Queen's bill is the musical *Les Misérables* which opened there in 2004.

# NIGHTCLUBBING

The nightclub was a British invention arising directly, as strange as it may seem, from the drinking laws passed with the Defence of the Realm Act in 1914 at the outset of the Great War. Until then Londoners could drink more or less when they liked. Pubs would open at 5.30 in the morning and stay open till after midnight. But with the new laws their hours were 12–2.40 p.m. and 6.30–10 p.m. As the magazine *Tatler* mourned: 'No khakied lad or cherub in gold and blue may now sup after 10 p.m.'

The new law threw up a number of absurdities. For instance, a 'No Treating Order' meant that people could not buy alcoholic drinks for others. There could be no rounds. Opposition was silenced on the grounds that this was only a temporary measure that would barely last the war, perhaps no later than the following Christmas, and then Britain would revert once more to the civilized concept of those who wanted to tipple being able to do so anywhere, anytime. Instead, once the war ended, the licensing laws were altered instead of scrapped, and drinking hours were only grudgingly extended.

Unsurprisingly, there was no shortage of entrepreneurs willing to cater for the huge market in the West End for those who wanted to drink outside the legit hours. These public-spirited, if outlaw, figures were also quick to spot that it was not enough just to supply booze. The voracious late-night reveller would also want a bit of music and some dancing girls. The result was a new kind of venue – the nightclub – which sprang up in the West End, particularly around Leicester Square, the area the poet Arthur Symons so eloquently described as: 'Never really normal London ... an escape, a sort of shame-faced and sordid and yet irresistible reminder of Paris and Italy.'

In 1921 the passing of the Licensing Act allowed drink to be served until 12.30 a. m., as long as it was accompanied by food, and there were soon more than 150 nightclubs in Soho to take advantage. Clubs opened and closed with bewildering speed. The Grafton Galleries, a large basement in a Mayfair art gallery, were converted into a nightclub after dark, the nude drawings covered up with tissue paper to save the embarrassment of the revellers (or was it the other way round?). The Grafton had sandwiches, but no alcohol, and a jazz band with real black people in it. Then there was Rector's cellar on Tottenham Court Road. Here the band dressed in firemen's helmets and ran around the room playing cornets to an audience consisting entirely of women in full evening dress and men in white ties and tails. Alter-natively, clubbers could go to Gerrard Street, to the Big Apple, a black club – rare for the 1930s – run by the boxer John Margot who had champion potential until he began drinking too much Red Biddy (red wine and meths) which addled his brain. One night he went berserk and attacked six police-men. That was the end of the Big Apple.

At Ciro's, according to a breathless reporter in the *Tatler*, there were 'hostesses rushing in quick with little dances (and daughters), and lots of nice things to drink, to try and make up for that gorgeous dancing floor, and noisy niggers and top-hole ched, and free-and-easy ladies'. At the Nest Club in Kingly Street dope was available off the menu. At the Trocadero by Piccadilly Circus the Bright Young Things could enjoy the incentive of a 25-guinea clothes voucher awarded to the best-dressed lady. Or they could go to Uncles in the basement of Mayfair's Albemarle Club, scene of Oscar Wilde's down-fall. Patrons must have thought they were in an authentic American speakeasy, for the décor spoke of prohibition and suggested moral subversion, while the *liquor*, as opposed to mundane alcohol, was served in tea cups.

After a quick snort of cocaine behind a rococo screen at the Café Royal (activities featured in Aleister Crowley's 1922 novel *Diary of a Drug Fiend*), young men in tight suits and nail varnish would head to *the* club: the Embassy at 6–8 Old Bond Street. Entry was a matter of negotiating a route past the bouncers who, according to Mayfair chronicler Michael Arlen, would 'sift out the low and vulgar from the fashionable crowds', and past a one-legged man sat at the entrance selling buttonhole carnations. Once inside they could mix with the Prince of Wales, the greatest clubber of his age, who described the Embassy as 'the Buckingham Palace of nightclubs' and had a table permanently reserved for him and his oddly named friends, such as 'Fruity' Metcalfe, of whom King George V, his father, so vigorously disapproved.

It was at the Embassy that dress standards began to decline to the point of anarchy. When Edward appeared in a dinner jacket, rather than white tie and tails, members were outraged. Barbara Cartland later recalled people exclaiming: 'the cad, the swine; how disgraceful when ladies are here.' And it was also at the Embassy, during the economic crisis of 1932, that George V phoned the prince and ordered him to hand over £10,000 from his personal Duchy of Cornwall funds to the Treasury.

But only the most devout bohemian would dare enter the sybaritic portals of the Cave of the Golden Calf. The Cave opened in 1912 in a former draper's basement on Heddon Street, halfway between Oxford and Piccadilly circuses. Visitors included the novelist Rebecca West, and the poets W. B. Yeats and Ezra Pound. The MC was Madame Strindberg, former wife of the Swedish playwright, whom the painter Augustus John once described as the 'Walking Hell-Bitch of the Western world'. The Cave was sumptuous and spectacular, the atmosphere a heady mix memorably described by Osbert Sitwell as a 'super-heated Vorticist garden of gesticulating figures, dancing and talking while the rhythm of the primitive forms of ragtime throbbed through the wide room'. Here the men were attenuated, white-faced and kohl-eyed, the women bare-backed, stockinged, lithe and lissom, a cigarette holder in one hand, a cocktail glass in the other; stark black-and-white in geometric form.

Mme Strindberg's aim was for the Cave to be 'a place given up to gaiety ... brazenly expressive of the libertarian pleasure principle'. To this end she hired some of the finest artists of the time to brighten it up. Spencer Gore decorated the walls with murals inspired by the Russian ballet; the sculptor Jacob Epstein added contributions which held up what Wyndham Lewis, who painted abstract hieroglyphics around the walls, called the 'threateningly low ceiling'; and Eric Gill, the sculptor notorious for having sex with his sisters, daughters and dog, designed its main motif: a phallic Golden Calf. And how apt was that auric animal, for it was a golden calf that the Children of Israel created in the Sinai desert to help them engage in their unbridled hedonism when Moses ascended to the mount to receive the two tiny sapphires on which was written all knowledge, symbolized by the Ten Commandments.

As exquisite as the Cave of the Golden Calf was the Gargoyle on Meard Street, off Dean Street. The Hon. David Tennant bought the building in 1925. Before opening the club he engaged the finest interior decorators. There was no trawling through the 1920s version of the Yellow Pages. Instead Tennant hired Henri Matisse, who covered the walls and pillars with glass squares to provide infinite vistas and give the venue its nickname – 'the Club of Twenty Thousand Reflections'. Just for good measure he also commissioned no less an architect than Edwin Lutyens, doyen of imperialist constructions in Delhi, and the financial districts of London and Manchester, to knock the building into shape and added touches for the inside such as leather curtains with an African motif. Tennant also spent £56,000 on the top-floor ballroom where a musical combo, unoriginally named Alexander's Ragtime Band, played the latest dances, particularly the Black Bottom. The clientele was as refined as it was possible to find this side of the Île-de-France: princes and princesses, King Carol of Romania, Fred Astaire.

At all these places the soundtrack was a sort of jazz. Not quite the syncopated, blasted Dixieland swirl of Harlem, but a stripling version alien enough to scare the wits out of those who felt the country was receding into imminent anarchy, self-destruction, or worse. 'Jazz was crude and vulgar,' the *Observer* alleged. 'It is performed by niggers whose chief business is to make noises. In fact the dance has been defined as a "number of niggers surrounded by noise".'

Less refined was the décor of the Café de Paris on Coventry Street, a few yards from Piccadilly Circus. Its restaurant was a replica of the Palm Court on board the *Lusitania* but it failed to attract many customers until the owner, Martin Poulsen, had the bright idea of phoning the Prince of Wales himself at York House. 'Your Royal Highness. You promised me that when I opened my own club you would visit.' From the prince came back the question 'Where are you?' 'At the Café de Paris, Coventry Street,' replied Poulsen. 'When do you want me to come?' 'As soon as possible, Your Royal Highness, things are desperate with me'. The Prince arrived with his usual posse: Mrs Dudley Ward, Fruity Metcalfe and Trotter, the one-armed Brigadier-General. The Café de Paris was saved. The only problem was that the band was obliged to dance as long as the prince was dancing. Edward remained on the floor for an hour and fifty-five minutes, the band playing continuously without a break for that time.

It was fun to break the law, to ignore the half-past midnight drinking up entreaty. And no one took more pride in those days in teasing the authorities than Kate Meyrick. She was the undisputed queen of the London clubs, immortalized as Ma Mayfield in Evelyn Waugh's *Brideshead Revisited*. Her first venture was Dalton's, located next to the Alhambra on the east side of Leicester Square. In January 1919 it was raided by Sgt. Goddard, who was so well disguised his own men failed to recognize him as they stormed the premises at the appointed time. The police found 292 'low-class' women on the premises and Meyrick was taken to court where she heard the prosecuting counsel describe Dalton's as a 'sink of iniquity and a noxious fungus growth upon our social system'.

This didn't stop the redoubtable Kate. She was soon running clubs all over the West End: the Folies-Bergere, Newman Street; the Little Club in Golden Square; the Manhattan of Denman Street; and best of all the 43 Club at 43 Gerrard Street, set in the cellar of what had been the poet John Dryden's house. Regulars at the 43 included dilettantes, aristocrats, royals, Britain's best artists (Augustus John and Jacob Epstein) and even the world's greatest writer (Joseph Conrad). On one occasion the Northern millionaire Jimmy White turned up with six Daimlers filled with 'showgirls' who spent £400 on champagne. The actress Tallulah Bankhead was drinking at the 43 one night when an old flame approached, delighted and gushing, 'Dahlink, I haven't seen you for 15 years, mwah mwah', to which Bankhead replied: 'Dahlink, I thought I told you to wait in the car.'

The 43 Club had a secret exit round the back which led through a courtyard and an unlocked door of an adjoining shop's backyard into Newport Market. When the club was raided on 20 October 1924 a number of celebs took advantage of this route. 'Fun is fun,' the proprietress would say, 'but vulgarity is vulgarity. Out you go, my boy!' Meyrick was charged at Bow Street magistrates with selling intoxicating liquor without a licence. London society was shocked. No one had ever seen her in broad daylight before. She was given six months in jail.

Not to be dissuaded, she opened a new establishment, the Silver Slipper, on Regent Street. No sooner had it opened than the police dropped by once more, again uninvited. They charged on to the dance floor while a Cossack dance was being performed and made scores of arrests. In 1928 Meyrick was back in court, accused of selling alcohol without a licence at the 43. The prosecuting counsel was unrelenting. 'She is the most inveterate lawbreaker with regard to licensing matters that the police have ever dealt with in the metropolis,' Mr Muskett told the court. Six months. But 1929 was the most dramatic year for Rex v Meyrick. At the Old Bailey on 21 January, Detective Sergeant Goddard handed the jury wads of £10 notes, notes Kate Meyrick had used in trying to bribe him. She received fifteen months' hard labour.

With the owner inside, the 43 Club patrons went out of control. One minute on the evening of 4 April 1929 Lord Loughborough was in a cheerful mood. A couple of hours later, back in Shepherd's Bush, he had fallen through a fourth-floor window on to some crazy paving. Later that summer the youthful Lord Howard of Effingham was one of seventy revellers who took part in a fight outside the club. Luckily for him, he was only bound over to keep the peace.

That same year the vice squad officer in charge of the raids on nightclubs like Meyrick's was jailed for corruption. He had been receiving so many backhanders from worried entrepreneurs he had a luxury car, a fine house in Streatham and £18,000 in savings. Kate Meyrick, unsurprisingly, was one of the nightclub impresarios who had a financial 'arrangement' with the cops. Evelyn Waugh depicted this accurately in *Brideshead*: 'Now look here my good man, there's no need for you to notice anything; we've all been to Ma Mayfield's. I reckon Ma Mayfield pays you a pretty good retainer to keep your eyes shut – well you keep them shut on us as well, and you won't be the loser by it.'

# BIRTH OF THE COOL

On 7 April 1919 an unusual noise was heard in the Hippodrome Theatre by Leicester Square – jazz. Responsible for this extraordinary amalgam of blaring horns and discordant rhythms, never before heard in London, was the Original Dixieland Jazz Band, mostly white musicians from New Orleans playing piano, cornet, clarinet and trombone. The magazine *Performer* was not impressed and wrote how 'the best qualification for a jazzist is to have no knowledge of music and no musical ability beyond that of making noises.'

London had to wait a few years for its next instalment of this strange, exotic, foreign music, and when Louis Armstrong was brought over from the Cotton Club, Los Angeles, at great expense in July 1932 he was greeted with similar bafflement. The organizers, displaying the kind of blasé incompetence that would get London a bad name in live music circles until the late 1960s, gave Armstrong a scratch band to play with and put him on a bill of variety acts. The audience didn't know how to react to a jazz instrumentalist, and one journalist remarked to the *Daily Herald*'s Hannen Swaffer: 'That man, why he did everything with the trumpet but play it.' A theatre manager at the back of the auditorium later explained that although he almost left immediately he stayed because he wanted to know what Armstrong was going to do next. 'I have never seen such a thing. I thought he might even play the trumpet before he was through.'

London's first jazz club, which opened in the 1930s, was the Bag O' Nails on Kingly Street, a few hundred yards south-east of Oxford Circus. *Melody Maker* once explained that 'the Bag O' Nails was to the history of British swing music what Hampton Court Palace is to the history of England'. The venue later hosted meetings of the Rhythm Club, Britain's first jazz society.

Jazz in Britain has always been a mostly desperate affair, promoted and patronized by white intellectuals ignorant of the culture from which it sprang and ignored by a public that rarely gets to meet it on equal terms, and almost never on the radio (something that had barely changed by the twenty-first century). Remarkably, during the music's 1950s hey-day, UK audiences weren't able to hear Miles, Monk, Mingus, Dizzy, Dexter or Duke, or almost anyone remotely resembling them, thanks to a Musicians' Union ban on American jazzmen playing in the UK unless a British equivalent was invited to the US in return. As there *was* next to no worthwhile British jazz to send to the States – only Ronnie Scott and Tubby Hayes could be guaranteed an invite – the nation missed out immeasurably.

One of the last acts to tour before the ban were Teddy Hill and his Orchestra, who were allowed to play the Palladium near Oxford Circus with the stipulation, written in Hill's permit, that neither he nor his band were allowed to 'move'. And if anyone broke the ban, as Sidney Bechet did in 1950, there was hell to pay – a conviction and big fines from the courts. One British act which did take part in such an exchange was Ronnie Scott's in 1957. Dave Brubeck's group toured the UK while the Ronnie Scott Sextet left for the USA. The ship taking them to New York docked at 52nd Street – *the* jazz street. Yet Ronnie Scott and co. ended up playing on an all black rock 'n' roll / R&B package, playing stadiums alongside Fats Domino and Chuck Berry. As the veteran bop pianist Stan Tracey later wondered: 'Why the fuck they needed a British bebop band I've no idea!'

There were ways around the ban. Benny Goodman and his pianist, Buddy Greco, were allowed to play the London Palladium after the union informed the Ministry of Labour that the men were 'variety artists'. Greco responded by playing local jazz clubs after hours. There were also occasional visits from authentic musicians stationed in London with the US army who had been booked to play airforce bases, technically US territory and free from trades union interference, and who naturally gravitated to Soho clubs in the early hours. In this way the alto sax player Art Pepper's cool sophistication intoxicated the Soho audiences, who were frustrated all the more to hear him say: 'If you dug that, you should hear Charlie Parker.'

Not only was jazz under attack from outside in the 1950s – the MU ban – but in the West End there was civil war. On one side were musicians aligned with traditional ('trad') Dixieland jazz – endless versions of the Negro spiritual 'When the Saints Go Marching In' murdered by twenty-five smiling guys wielding clarinets and cornets dressed in matching waistcoats and bowler hats. On the other side was bop: genuine sensual innovation, sounds no one had ever previously thought possible stretched out of a smooching saxophone or dug deep from the lesser-used keys on a tinkling piano as the drums burst behind the trumpet in a burst of unparalleled excitement.

During the jazz wars (which still take place intermittently) everyone was obliged to take one side or the other; there was no middle ground. When traditionalists heard bop there was an outcry. Having grudgingly accepted Duke Ellington's elliptic departures, they were not prepared to move on any further from the sound that New Orleans had dispensed with several decades earlier. They savaged the new music and refused to accept it, remaining unaware that like the earliest jazz this was authentic black street culture, as opposed to Hollywood-affected showbiz. They also failed to appreciate the politics of the new music – that the black man was obliged to invent bop as a means of preventing the white man stealing his music again, like he had with the first jazz sounds before removing the passion, the technique, the sex and the originality, and replacing it with a big band mush.

With trad were musicians like Ken Colyer, a trumpeter who had once jumped a merchant navy ship to reach New Orleans, where he had jammed with local musicians before being arrested and deported. Amongst the boppers was Ronnie Scott, who went on to open Britain's best-known jazz club in Soho. An early battle site was the Leicester Square Jazz Club, situated above the Café de l'Europe. Here in 1948 the BBC, in a rare outside broadcast, cast Humphrey Lyttelton's Band, hardcore traditionalists led by an Old Etonian, versus a bop group. When the boppers played Humph's supporters booed loudly, claiming that theirs was the real music – 'the right notes and chords,' as trombonist Chris Barber later explained, failing to realize that there were no right notes and chords, that the music only worked if it freely embraced heart and brain rather than following a copybook. (Later Lyttelton embraced the new sounds. But when he added the saxophonist Bruce Turner into his band for a concert in Birmingham, Turner was greeted by students armed with placards that read: 'Go home, dirty bopper.')

The boppers may have won the intellectual and moral battles, but they also needed to eat. They wouldn't be able to survive solely on playing the new music. Yet if they could master its complex harmonies they would have no trouble with old-fashioned dance band material. To get work at one of London's many dance halls, in an era before audiences danced solely to pre-recorded sounds, jazz musicians would line up on shabby Archer Street by Shaftesbury Avenue most mornings awaiting the opportunity to audition *al fresco* before venue managers and impresarios looking to make bookings for the evening gigs. The musicians took up every inch of the pavement, berating, bickering and bawling, haggling and hassling, a saxophone on a strap slung over a shoulder; a hand clasping *Melody Maker* and a drum stick, just to show versatility. Cries of 'You must remember me, I played in that all-nighter with Mick Mulligan' . . . 'of course I know the bass part to "Think Deep" . . .' would fill the air.

The Archer Street auditions were like a bohemian version of the East End 'Call-on' by which jobs were secured at the docks, the Harmony Inn café taking the place of the Steamship pub recruiting ground on East India Dock Road. Unlike the dockers' Call-on, most of the contenders secured jobs, even if only briefly. Beggars couldn't afford to be too choosy. Ronnie Scott took up a stint with a dance band at the Cricklewood Palais while dreaming of a call from Dexter Gordon at Birdland. 'Don't try to lead the saxophone section,' he was warned. One night old-school trumpeter Jack Jackson hired Scott for a stint at Churchill's, a swanky dining and dancing venue on New Bond Street. Socializing at a table, Jackson noticed that Scott had led the band into a bop-inspired flight of fancy. Fuming, he approached the band, who by now were grooving high, and thundered: 'What the hell is going on?' at one of the less involved members of the ensemble. 'It's okay, Ronnie's got the message,' came the reply, above the clash of cymbals. 'Right, here's another one,' retorted Jackson. 'Tell him he's fired.'

Around this time the only London club solely putting on jazz, run by jazzers rather than by entrepreneurs, was Club 11 at 41 Great Windmill Street, opposite the Windmill Theatre. Club 11, which opened on 11 December 1948, was a claustrophobic dive, enlivened by a couple of threadbare old sofas where the house band was Ronnie Scott's Sextet, and the patrons pursued a lifestyle of alcohol-fuelled, amphetamine-rush excitement propelled by the newest, brashest, wildest sounds imported from America. To emphasize their originality they dressed in a bizarre uniform of drape-back jackets with outlandish shoulders, loud ties with louder knots or a polka-dot bow tie like Thelonious Monk (it was easier to dress like him than play like him), silk shirts and corduroy trousers, mostly bought from Cecil Gee on Charing Cross Road.

Followers adopted such fundamentalism to show the outside world that they were more than merely hedonists, that they were cultural innovators armed with a political credo. After all, the jazz they were championing was not the music of Uncle Toms such as Louis Armstrong, with their plastic smiles and gleaming teeth, it was serious Art, whose practitioners had avoided the patronization of an American establishment that wanted to dilute the music of its sex and rebellion, and had withdrawn into a boho world, distinguished by its own language, drugs, clothes and attitudes.

In April 1950 Club 11 moved to 50 Carnaby Street, just over a decade before the street attained worldwide hip status for its clothes stores. The new address was an even shabbier venue. It was guarded outside by a black boxer who also acted as rent collector for the soon-to-be-infamous Notting Hill murder site of 10 Rillington Place. Those who ran Club 11 were ambitious with their booking policy. They invited Billie Holliday to play, offering her $250 but overlooking the small matter of air fares. As neither they nor anyone else knew where Holliday was they sent the request to the US jazz magazine *Downbeat*, naively suggesting that all her drugs requirements could be met. Club 11 received no reply, but it did receive a visit from the drugs squad. On the night of 15 April 1950 police descended in large numbers. They arrested the actor Mario Fabrizi for possessing cannabis, and Fabrizi spent a night inside crawling across the cell floor, banging on the door croaking: 'Water, water!' Another taken in was an RAF servicewoman whom the police accused of possessing a 'low moral standard and fraternising with buck niggers'. As a bonus officers netted an army absconder, Denis Rose, who had been helping run the club.

In court the magistrate, in the time-honoured tradition of m'lud posing memorably naive questions ('Who is Bruce Springsteen?', 'Who is Gazza?'), asked those gathered: 'What is bop?' He was given an original definition by a police inspector from Savile Row station: 'It's a queer form of modern dancing. A Negro jive.' There were fines, rather than prison sentences, and a closed-down club. Billie Holliday did eventually play Soho – at the Downbeat Club, 20 Old Compton Street, in 1958. The show was nearly ruined when a member of the audience began using the payphone during one of her numbers, much to the annoyance of the saxophonist Kenny Graham who became so irate he had to be restrained from physically assaulting the offender.

Meanwhile Cy Laurie, a trad man, took over the old Great Windmill Street premises. Here he began hosting London's first all-night raves in a club that lasted the decade. He later gave up jazz to take up with the Maharishi Mahesh Yogi in India, long before the Beatles had even left Liverpool.

Jazz was also on the menu at 100 Oxford Street, a wonderfully intimate basement dive that had been Mack's restaurant. It had first put on jazz in 1942 when a jazz fan named Feldman hired the venue on Sunday nights to showcase the talents of his child-prodigy son Victor, a drummer dubbed 'Kid Krupa' in honour of the legendary big band jazz drummer, Gene Krupa.

American GIs stationed in London would often turn up at 100 Oxford Street; even Glenn Miller himself came along before his mysterious plane crash. In the 1950s Humphrey Lyttelton took over bookings, renamed it Humph's, and attracted a fashionable crowd that included fashion pioneer Mary Quant, who would wear clothes – black tights – that caused an outrage, though not as much of an outrage as her companion, Alexander Plunkett-Green, who was wearing his mother's cast-offs. By 1964 the venue had become the 100 Club (the name unkindly claimed to derive from the number of people it could hold in comfort, rather than from its address), putting on beat groups. It later emerged as a key venue in the development of punk.

## HOMETOWN SKIFFLE

Not every budding musician could master the complexities of jazz – trad or bop. For the enthusiastic amateur who just wanted to be able to belt out a memorable song with a few mates, the music played by live bands in clubs or heard on what few shows existed on the wireless was too sophisticated and needed too much study. As for traditional forms of popular London music-making – an upright piano and a melodramatic singer in a pub – these were considered too antiquated. However, thanks to a couple of enterprising West End musicians, an alternative soon arose.

In 1954 Lonnie Donegan, a banjo player in Chris Barber's trad-jazz group, and Wally Whyton, a guitarist, went on a fact-finding mission to the American Embassy's Information Service Library at 1 Grosvenor Square, Mayfair. The library was a treasure trove of US blues and folk records made by artists then barely known in England, such as Big Bill Broonzy, Leadbelly and Muddy Waters, 'records you could learn in ten minutes that would last you a lifetime,' as Whyton later explained.

The two men and some friends began trying to replicate such sounds on ad hoc instruments: guitar, stand-up bass and home-made drums. They dubbed the style 'skiffle', borrowing a word coined in the Deep South American black ghettos to describe the spontaneous house parties thrown to raise money for the rent. The name had been used for a 1928 album *Hometown Skiffle*, a compilation of American jug-band styles and western swing played on what George Melly described as 'kazoos, tea-chest and broom-handle basses, seven-gallon jugs and empty suitcases, presumably because its practitioners either had no money for real instruments or the real instruments had been seized by the bailiffs'.

Donegan began taking the spotlight at Barber's West End gigs, which took place in the basement of a church on Bryanston Street near Marble Arch, playing blues songs he had learnt from those embassy library records in the skiffle style. Before long punters were turning up primarily to hear Donegan's skiffle rather than Barber's traditional jazz. In 1955 he recorded a skiffle version of Leadbelly's 'Rock Island Line', a story about a US train driver who deceives the inspector at a toll gate outside New Orleans. It was released as a single in late 1955, despite the scepticism of executives from Decca Records, the label that went on to turn down the Beatles and Jimi Hendrix.

The recording had a vitality and rhythmic intensity that at the time was unknown in British popular music. It became a major hit – the first debut record to go gold in Britain, although Donegan earned no extra money beyond his original session fee. It even reached the top ten in the US. To British ears the skiffle sound was a revelation. Few – young or old – had heard the blues. They didn't realize that Donegan's rendering was revivalist, and were intoxicated by the romance of living just outside the law in the American wilds. It was just the right time for this sound to hit the UK en masse for the first time. Memory of the war and its attendant Blimpish attitudes was fading fast. Meat rationing had ceased. At last people had money to spend on the new goods appearing in shops; comfort goods never before available on a mass scale – TVs, fridges, cars, washing machines.

This spirit of optimism was quickly captured by young musicians armed with cheap guitars, basic drum kits and bucket-loads of youthful exuberance. Thousands formed skiffle groups across the country, an early version of the Beatles amongst them. In London the skiffle bands headed to Soho with its coffee bars, atmospheric pubs dominated by barstool philosophers, and glamorous women in tight clothes. One of the new skiffle venues was a steakhouse on Old Compton Street. Owned by the Irani brothers and named the 2I's, it had a frontage that consisted of a large pane of plate glass, a glass door with a chromium handle, and a 7-Up sign which, according to Ian Samwell, Cliff Richard's first guitarist, was 'either an inducement to purchase or placed there to prevent the inattentive from walking headlong into it'.

There was little to separate the 2I's from scores of similar Soho establishments, and it began to lose money, especially after the more exotic Heaven and Hell opened next door, until Wally Whyton stopped by on 14 July 1956 during the annual Soho Fair and asked Lincoln Irani if he and his group could busk inside. Soon large crowds began turning up to see skiffle groups playing the 2I's. But skiffle was too limited to sustain interest for long. Its songs seemed able to draw on no experiences beyond those endured on dusty American trains, picking cotton and hanging around New Orleans, or a mixture of all three. However, by 1956 other unusual sounds were being heard on British radios. Bill Haley, a white Texan singer, had taken rhythm 'n' blues songs such as Big Joe Turner's 'Shake, Rattle & Roll', songs of everyday working-class experiences in the black community, voiced in slang and complete with sexual references, and with an eye on the white teenage market cut them anew, removing the sex and excitement to produce 'respectable' cover versions.

Haley achieved instant success in the US and UK charts. White American and British youth, at whom the songs were aimed, had never heard such sounds before – in any form – and embraced Haley with excitement bordering on frenzy. When another American singer emerged who looked more sexually threatening than the bland Haley – Elvis Presley – accompanied by songs of erotic depth, what had looked like a short-lived craze attained gravitas.

The most popular of the new acts playing a mix of skiffle and rock 'n' roll at the new Soho venues were the Vipers. They were fronted by a number of different singers, in particular Tommy Hicks, a merchant seaman. One night some A&R men from London's record companies, including EMI's George Martin, who later produced the Beatles, dropped into the 2I's as Hicks took the mic. Martin was unimpressed, but Hugh Mendl from Decca Records was won over and signed Hicks. Under the tutelage of the Svengali-like Larry Parnes, Hicks had his name changed to Tommy Steele and became one of the era's most successful all-round entertainers.

Through Hick's success, the 2I's began to attract agents, managers and impresarios looking for the next star. An advert of the time proclaimed:

'When in London visit the 2I's coffee bar 59 Old Compton Street, W1, Home of the Stars – Tommy Steele, The Vipers, Terry Dene. Presenting every night skiffle at its best with Les Hobaux, The Cotton Pickers, The Eastsiders etc etc'.

The advert caught the eye of a north London singer obviously modelled on Presley called Harry Webb. In April 1958 Webb and his backing band, the Drifters, secured a two-week residency at the 2I's: 'I kind of expected that Lionel Bart would come in and say "This lad's gonna be great" and make us stars overnight,' Webb later recalled. 'After all, it happened that way for Tommy Steele. Not a bit of it. The audience was blasé and the wage just about covered a late-night taxi home.'

The Drifters had no bass player. Electric bass guitars were then almost unknown in England (when Jet Harris later joined he was one of only three people in the country to own one), but the Drifters were good enough to be signed by EMI, Britain's main record label. Webb, in a move that would be later echoed by Richard Starkey (Ringo Starr), John Miller (Joe Strummer) and numerous others, decided his name wasn't rock 'n' roll enough. He and the group went to the Compton pub near the 2I's to find inspiration for a new title. They went through scores of combinations before whittling them down to two – Russ Clifford and Cliff Russard. The party remained unconvinced about both choices until someone proposed Cliff Richards. Guitarist Ian Samwell then suggested dropping the final 's' so that when people got the name wrong and called him 'Cliff Richards' Webb could correct them and say that it was Cliff Richard, thereby ensuring that the name was mentioned twice.

That August, 1958, at Abbey Road Cliff Richard and the Drifters cut their first single, 'Move It', Britain's first authentic rock 'n' roll record. It still sounds haunting and atmospheric, full of a sexual menace that Richard quickly dropped. Equally promising was another 2I's act, the Worried Men, featuring Terry Nelhams. After playing the venue for three months Nelhams was disconcerted at not having made it as a star, and when he won a spot on TV decided the time was right for a name change. Looking through a list of baby's names, he picked out 'Adam' in the boys' list and 'Faith' from a random list of girls' names, segueing the two.

To prepare correctly for his first TV appearance the newly renamed Adam Faith then lay in the bath in his jeans to make them skin-tight. He was soon given the chance of cutting a record. The label was EMI (Electrical and Mechanical Industries), Britain's foremost record company. On the fourth floor of EMI's Great Castle Street HQ, off Oxford Street, the talent spotters and A&R (Artists and Repertoire) men, such as George Martin, held court. They would invite in songwriting hopefuls who would play their latest number on the office upright piano. They would then make an instant judgement on whether the new piece really was 'just the thing' for Marty Wilde or Tommy Steele.

When in 1959 Johnny Worth devised a catchy, banal song he called 'What Do You Want?' which he thought ideal for Adam Faith, he made the usual journey to Great Castle Street. There he saw EMI's Norman Newell, who had just returned from a trip to the USA. Newell realized that when it came to rock 'n' roll he and his colleagues had no idea what they were doing. It was best just to copy whatever was hip in America. So at the recording session at Abbey Road, EMI's studios in St John's Wood, the producer added pizzicato strings as heard on Buddy Holly's recent hit 'It Doesn't Matter Any More' to Worth's song. Once cut, the record's makers took the acetates back to Newell and awaited his response. 'It's horrendous,' he wailed. 'Adam Faith can't enunciate his words! He says "biyabee" instead of "baby".' Faith's producer had not only copied Holly's arrangements but Holly's idiosyncratic diction, adding a touch of music hall, with just a hint of Petticoat Lane Yiddish to arrive at a final, yearning, 'Vish you vonted my luv, biyabee'. Nevertheless, the record sold in large quantities, and reached No. 1 at the end of 1959.

The complaints of rock 'n' roll detractors such as Newell that the singers spoke in their own bizarre language that only initiates understood were superbly sent up by Wolf Mankowitz in his Soho beat novel *Expresso Bongo*. An exposé of the ruthless superficial world of Tin Pan Alley, it was turned into a 1959 film starring Cliff Richard as Bongo Herbert, the young hopeful who is turned into a star; 'from rags to riches in five yelping stages – from dirty sweaty shirt to gold lamé sweat shirt' – in which Herbert's trademark chorus runs in glorious meaninglessness:

> 'Ex-presso – bongo
> Fla-menko – bongo
> Tooo-baygo – bongo
> Caa-lypso-bongo
> Bongo – bongo – calypso – bongo
> Olé!'

Cliff Richard used rock 'n' roll merely to propel himself into the public eye. He soon transformed himself from a gyrating, sub-Presley sexual predator to wholesome family entertainer, with only the occasional foray into anything more demanding. His backing group was more inspired. A month after the recording of 'Move It' they were joined by the guitarists Bruce Cripps and Brian Rankin who had come down to London from the North East, and had spent much time playing in the 2I's basement. Cripps decided to change his name to Bruce Welch, while Rankin, who could copy Buddy Holly solos note for note, went for the more rock 'n' roll sounding Hank Marvin. The Drifters became the Shadows.

In 1960 an associate of the group, Jerry Lordan, influenced by the reverb-heavy guitar sound of the Red Indian rock 'n' roller Link Wray, wrote an instrumental for the Shadows called 'Apache'. They recorded it for EMI. For a British group 'Apache' was a remarkable achievement. Marvin used every trick in his repertoire to strengthen the sound: tremolo arm, echo unit, and a Vox amplifier he bought from Charing Cross Road. 'Apache' begins with an ominous drum figure which quickly makes way for Hank Marvin's eerie Fender Stratocaster as it moves through textures that effortlessly summon up visions of the immeasurable New World. The Shadows even managed to improve on 'Apache' in 1962 with 'Wonderful Land', although by that time they were no longer confined to the West End.

'Apache' went to No. 1 in Britain, but remained largely unknown to several generations of Americans, presumably because record executives there were loathe to import a British take on their own culture. Surprisingly, it reappeared in the late 1970s as a major influence on New York's burgeoning hip-hop producers, who used it as a backing track on which they built new sounds.

## THE NEW ESTABLISHMENT

By the end of the jazz and skiffle decade West Enders were participating in a new type of nightlife. Soho basement dives were taking advantage of new technology to host nights at which the music came from discs spun by a compere, rather than by a live band. A new terminology was needed for this new set up. The venue came to be known as a discotheque, the fancy French name stemming from London's first such establishment – La Poubelle, which opened on Great Marlborough Street near Oxford Circus in 1959. The compere would now be known as a disc jockey, a term coined by one of the first such figures: Jimmy Savile.

La Poubelle was run by the twenty-four-year-old Louis Brown. It was suffocatingly small, there were no windows, air-conditioning or fire exit, but it attracted a steady stream of curious socialites including the Duke of Kent and the West Indian calypso singer Harry Belafonte. Brown later went on to launch London's most exclusive rock star night-time haunt – Scotch of St James, in Westminster.

But not all night-time entertainment in the West End of the 1950s took place in clubs or discotheques. Many heading down to the West End after a hard day's graft wanted to be amused, and there were no shortage of comedians willing to help them. Thousands enthused to the antics of the Crazy Gang, based around three double acts: Jimmy Nervo and Teddy Knox, Bud Flanagan and Chesney Allen, and Eddie Gray and Charlie Naughton.

Gray was the most manic. He was known as 'Monsewer' Eddie Gray, for he spoke Cockney laced with mangled French, and wore a ridiculous, glued-on curled moustache. 'Madame and masseurs,' he would begin, 'How are you, all right? Enjoyin' yourself? I'll soon put a stop to that.' Gray was a master of japes and practical jokes. On Charing Cross Road he and the older Charlie Naughton would often perform a skit which involved Gray helping a very frail looking Naughton across the road, regardless of the traffic. Drivers would wait impatiently, but feel guilty about tooting. When they were half way over the pair would suddenly burst into a manic song-and-dance routine, deftly skipping past the onrushing cars as the drivers shook their fists.

One time in a café on Old Compton Street Gray sat next to Naughton, who was bald, and despite promising those assembled that he would behave himself, started buttering Naughton's head. On another occasion Gray and the comic Tommy Trinder stopped by a pillar box on Broadwick Street. Gray peered into the hole and shouted: 'Well, how did you get in there? Don't panic. I'm sure we can get you out.' As a crowd gathered, he turned to Trinder and explained 'It's a postman. He's fallen in. I'm going to get help. Can you lot wait here?' He and Trinder then made their way off, never to return. The crowd would slink off embarrassed once they realized they had been duped.

For new acts the main venue was the Windmill Theatre near Piccadilly Circus. By day they would audition before the theatre's formidable owner, Vivian Van Damm, and assistants who had heard it all before. And who it was not easy to impress. When Benny Hill auditioned at the Windmill in the early 1950s he choked on his first gag and got the dismissive 'Next please!' At that time he was still billed as Alf Hill, but decided he wanted something more upmarket. His brother, Leonard, suggested Benny, as Jack Benny was one of his idols.

First, new acts had to get an agent, and the West End was full of them: on Charing Cross Road, Denmark Street, Beak Street and Golden Square. The sharpest was Harry Wright, who operated from an office near Cambridge Circus. One day the phone rang and a honeyed voice asked: 'Is that Harry Wright?' Harry took out his usual cigar, and replied 'Sure.' 'This is Richard Burton,' came the voice from the other end. 'Sure,' Harry responded. 'I'm doing a British tour. Could you handle my business?' asked the great Welsh thespian. Putting the cigar back in, Harry added 'Sure.' 'And oh,' continued Burton, 'my wife, Elizabeth Taylor, will be over here.' 'Sure,' added Harry. 'Can you handle her, too?' 'Sure.' 'Oh, and one other thing,' Burton added. 'You're not Jewish are you?' Quick as a flash Harry came back: 'Not necessarily.'

On Golden Square was Archie Parnell's agency, where in 1946 an unknown South African comic turned up looking for work. He had been raised as Solly Cohen but decided on a name change. With his battered features, wicked leer and dirty laugh, Sid James, as he now called himself, came over as the archetypal cockney wide boy, but the only east London he had been to was the town of that name in South Africa. Thanks to Parnell's agency, he was offered the part of the gangster Eddie Clinton in the film *Black Memory* just nine days after arriving in England. *Black Memory* bombed but Sid gradually got offered better parts, culminating in a role in the Ealing comedy *The Lavender Hill Mob*.

By 1953 Sid James was attracting interest from America. MGM cast him in *Crest Of A Wave* alongside Gene Kelly. That year the BBC commissioned a new series in which a pompous character holds court in a bedsit somewhere in London. The producers needed a straight man for the new show, and its writers, Ray Galton and Alan Simpson, knew exactly who they wanted – the new face in *The Lavender Hill Mob*. Alas they didn't know his name, and to discover his identity in those pre-internet days they had to find a cinema showing the film. Galton and Simpson did so in Putney, and sat through the entire run until the credits came up with James's name.

The new show, recorded in the West End at Broadcasting House, pitted Sid James against an even more formidable talent. He was described by one biographer as 'Anthony Aloysius St John Hancock II of 23 Railway Cuttings, East Cheam, dressed in a Homburg hat and heavy overcoat with an astrakhan collar of uncertain age; a failed Shakespearean actor with pretension of a knighthood. Age: 30s but claims to be younger; success with women nil; financial success nil; a pretentious, gullible, bombastic, occasionally kindly, superstitious, avaricious, petulant, over-imaginative, semi-educated, gourmandising, incompetent, cunning, obstinate, self-opinionated, impolite, pompous, lecherous, lonely and likeable fall guy.'

However, the king of the new West End comics playing the large theatres was neither of them but a hulking bear of a man who had begun entertaining troops in the desert. During one show in Egypt he whipped the fez off the head of a passing waiter, stuck it on and brought the house down. He had no need to change his name; for wherever it would be heard from now on grown men and women would collapse into a hysterical heap: Tommy Cooper.

Even the Queen wasn't safe from his wit. After one West End Royal Command Performance, Cooper was introduced to Her Majesty.

'Do you think I was funny?' he asked her.

'Yes, Tommy,' replied the Queen.

'You really thought I was funny?'

'Yes, of course I thought you were funny.'

'Did your mother think I was funny?'

'Yes, Tommy. We both thought you were funny.'

'Do you mind if I ask you a personal question?'

'No, but I might not be able to give you a full answer.'

'Do you like football?'

'Well, not really.'

'Can I have your Cup Final tickets, then?'

The arrival of the 1960s saw a new form of comedy hit the West End. In 1961 two Cambridge graduates, Peter Cook and Nicholas Luard, opened the Establishment Club at 18 Greek Street in the heart of Soho. They were keen to avoid censorship, so by setting it up as a private, members-only club they pitched themselves beyond the reach of the censorious Lord Chamberlain. Cook and Luard even convinced a number of celebrities, including the prolific writer J. B. Priestley and the violinist Yehudi Menuhin, to become members.

The Establishment had an unusual aim, largely unknown since John Wilkes's *Briton* publication of the late eighteenth century – to satirize and denigrate public figures of authority. People flocked to the club to hear acts launch into surreal dialogue along the lines of: 'How do you do? My name is God, and I'm here tonight because I'm omnipotent', which detractors considered blasphemous rather than an affirmation of His ubiquity. Subjects satirized on the opening night included Harold Macmillan, the prime minister; Alec Douglas Home, foreign secretary; and Jomo Kenyatta, the African nationalist who, asked during a chat show skit for a prediction on the outcome of an imminent Tottenham–Burnley match, replies: 'Yes, Ah shall be perhaps de first Negro man to be Queen of England.'

The Establishment audience was mostly middle class, which was hardly surprising given that working-class audiences have never understood satire and would have been upset at mocking Macmillan, the so-called Supermac. But to those drunk on the club's anarchic spirit Cook warned that the heyday of satire had been in Germany's Weimar Republic 'and see how it prevented the rise of Adolf Hitler'.

In April 1962 the Establishment gave the idiosyncratic American beat comic Lenny Bruce (who had evaded wartime service by persuading the medical team examining him that he was a compulsive transvestite) a residency to perform what theatre critic Kenneth Tynan described as 'outspoken harangues in an idiom I can only describe as jazz-Jewish'. When Bruce tried to return a year later the home secretary, Henry Brooke, banned him from entering the country. The Establishment didn't last long, but Cook's other venture did, for he also financed a magazine formed with the same irreverence and satirical edge – *Private Eye* – based in the West End ever since.

For those uninterested in loud rhythmic music or satire; for the establishment as opposed to The Establishment, there were cabaret spots, casinos and old-fashioned upmarket nightclubs untainted by the rise of 'Swinging London'. At Danny La Rue's club situated in the basement of 17 Hanover Square, below where Lucile had fashioned the finest *fin-de-siècle* lingerie, the host, Britain's first drag artist, appeared in the 1960s alongside Ronnie Corbett, half his size, as straight man.

The new legal casinos were quick to take advantage of a change in the gaming laws. One such legit gambling joint was the Pigalle, by Piccadilly Circus, where the greeter was none other than Joe Louis, former boxing world heavyweight champion. A life-size photo of the 'Brown Bomber' was pasted on the doorpost, and the man himself would greet gamblers softly with the chilling words: 'Hello, my name is Joe Louis.' There were also the high-class joints patronized by the sharp-suited neophytes: Michael Caine, Terence Stamp, David Bailey, places such as the Pickwick Club on Great Newport Street, opened by *Expresso Bongo* author Wolf Mankowitz who invited the 'thousand smartest people of the time to join' and was rewarded when Noël Coward and Brigitte Bardot turned up on the opening night.

Then there were ritzy nightclubs where men wore tuxedos and women mink stoles. Such was the Eve Club, 189 Regent Street, run by Helen O'Brien. Her real name was the more nocturnally impressive Elena Constantinescu, and she was never seen without a Balkan Sobranie cigarette or glass of champagne to her lips. Elena circumvented the licensing laws by charging punters a guinea a year membership. She also tempted them with extra charges. When club hostesses went to the toilet, which was often, they would leave their handbags open, and on returning would expect to find a tenner tucked in.

The Eve attracted AA List celebrities (Frank Sinatra, Errol Flynn), spies

(MI5 sent Elena a letter from Room 055 of the War Office when they saw her consorting with a dodgy Romanian) and sleazy politicians (John Profumo, soon to become the disgraced War Secretary, held his stag night at the Eve). Christine Keeler, who brought about Profumo's downfall, was rejected as unsuitable for hostessing; 'too easily led . . . I was proved right,' Helena later claimed. Norma Levy, the high-class hooker who was to become the nemesis of Lord Lambton in 1973, worked there for a few days without being taken on. 'Hard and mercenary, she really didn't have the requisite breeding,' explained Helena.

By the mid 1960s the high-class nightclubs had been joined by a loud newcomer: the Playboy Club at 45 Park Lane. A colourful mélange of slick sophistication, James Bond-era glamour and animalian eroticism, the Playboy Club enabled punters to be entertained by eager hostesses – Bunny Girls – partly dressed as rabbits. Before the Bunny Girls went on the floor the Bunny Mother would inspect their nails, tights and tails, and diligently ensure not a whiff of pubic hair could be seen. The Bunny Girls also wore two pairs of tights to ensure their legs looked as nylonly attractive as possible and would stuff toilet paper down a D-cup to heighten the effect of a breast about to overflow into the customer's Martini.

# SPONTANEOUS UNDERGROUND

Pre 1963 the notion that London would soon lead the world in developing new forms of music would have struck any knowledgeable person contemplating the idea as absurd. Britain, let alone London, had made little contribution to the world's music thus far. As far as the Western Classical tradition, pioneered by Italy, Germany and Austria was concerned, Britain was a minor player. Homegrown symphonies and orchestral works heralded as vital to the music's development by British critics, such as Elgar's *First* (1908) or Holst's *Planets Suite* (1918), had barely made a dent on the continent's cultural consciousness. Victorian Britain had produced no Beethoven, Brahms or Bruckner, twentieth-century Britain no Stravinsky, Sibelius or Shostakovich. Only Vaughan Williams's Third and Fifth symphonies could be ranked alongside the European masterpieces.

As for popular music, British versions barely travelled well outside their own locale, let alone beyond the coast. The music hall audience of London was nonplussed by Will Fyfe and the 'I Belong to Glasgow' school of Caledonian comics, and the sentiments were similar when it came to Scottish audiences' appreciating Charles Coborn, creator of such enduring cockney romps as 'Two Lovely Black Eyes'. And in any case, technology was too primitive to relay these localized working-class standards across the country in a way that might influence a change in taste.

Then came jazz, which swept across the dancefloors of the world, not least of all those of London's West End. As far as most West Enders were concerned the first jazz sounds they heard were examples of the correct way to play the music. It was only when musicians did manage to catch up with the new progressive bebop sounds coming out of America after the Second World War, that many realized they had to rip up their manuals and start again.

Yet as much as London musicians and audiences loved jazz, blues and rhythm 'n' blues, it wasn't *their* culture. They were simply borrowing sounds, lyrical ideas, styles of instrumentation from America . . . copying rather than innovating. Perhaps they had to learn how to copy properly before they could gain the confidence to innovate.

Of the copyers and homage-payers the most inspired were the set of young musicians centred around Cyril Davies and Alexis Korner. In various West End clubs in the early 1960s they played not jazz but the harsh, guitar-heavy rhythm 'n' blues of Muddy Waters and John Lee Hooker. At the Roundhouse, 83 Wardour Street, Davies and Korner started the Thursday-night London Blues and Barrelhouse Club. Occasionally they pulled off a coup, hiring real American blues artists such as Sonny Terry, Brownie McGhee and Big Bill Broonzy to play there, but most of the time they performed in front of an audience so small there were occasionally more people on stage than in the crowd, which led Davies to quip one night: 'You three are very privileged to hear us four play.'

In 1962 Davies and Korner formed a group, Blues Incorporated. They began a Thursday-night residency at the Marquee, then based below a cinema at 165 Oxford Street, with a constantly fluctuating line-up that included at various times Jack Bruce, Ginger Baker, Brian Jones and Mick Jagger – all soon to become cornerstones of the new rock sound. When Blues Incorporated were booked for a BBC radio session on 12 July 1962 Korner decided not to take along Jones or Jagger. Instead, the discarded pair teamed up with some friends, including Keith Richards, and took to the Marquee stage under the name 'Brian Jones, Mick Jagger and the Rollin' Stones'. The night ended in violence when the audience was attacked by a group of Mods.

When Korner found out what Jagger and Jones had done behind his back he sacked them from Blues Incorporated; not for moonlighting but for playing non-purist R&B songs by Chuck Berry and other rock 'n' rollers. Unperturbed, the gang carried on playing as the Rolling Stones, filling in during the twenty-minute break at the Marquee in the early weeks of January 1963 until the promoter decided they weren't good enough for the rise in fees they wanted. Only a clairvoyant could have watched the nascent group and predicted that within three years they would be world leaders in a new, international style of music.

Soho in the early 1960s was filled with beat clubs, located mostly in what had until recently been jazz venues. Some were so obscure and short-lived that to this day no one can be sure where they were situated. One of these was the Blue Gardenia, an illegal drinking club which may have been on St Anne's Court, the short alleyway connecting Dean and Wardour Streets. It was at the Blue Gardenia on 9 December 1961 that the Beatles played their first London gig in front of a handful of insomniacs and twenty-four-hour Sohoites. Yet the Beatles had been booked to play not in Soho that night but in Aldershot, Hampshire, about fifty miles from London. When only a handful of people turned up due to lack of advertising the group rushed through a short set and headed off for London, arriving in Soho about 2 a.m. Ironically, only John, Paul and Pete Best played – George spent the time at the bar chatting to someone he knew.

It was also in the West End, at HMV's Oxford Street store on 8 January 1962, that the Beatles made their first, primitive recordings out of the tapes from their unsuccessful audition with Decca Records. The engineer cutting the disc, Jim Foy, liked what he heard and was amazed when manager Brian Epstein revealed that the group had written some of the songs themselves. At that time there were few groups at all – it was mostly an era of solo singers – and songs were sought from established songwriters, rather than originated in-house. Foy recommended that Epstein met EMI's song publishers, and they signed up the rights to the two songs that comprised the Beatles' first single, 'PS I Love You' and 'Love Me Do'.

Better known than the Blue Gardenia was the Flamingo at 33–37 Wardour Street. There the club sound was mostly organ/sax-based R&B and the house band Georgie Fame and the Blue Flames, starring the virtuoso guitarist John McLaughlin, later a Miles Davis sideman. The Flamingo was the first London club to play West Indian music, and less typically was the location for Simon and Garfunkel's first UK appearance in the summer of 1964. No alcohol was sold, although a lot of the coke was laced with scotch. In 1963 the club gained public notoriety when a member collapsed outside and was later found to have 76 purple hearts (Drinamyl) in his stomach. This led to Henry Brooke, the Conservative home secretary, making an incognito visit to Soho's night clubs and announcing that anyone found with purple hearts would be fined £200 or face six months in jail. His warning had little effect on those US soldiers who, as pop manager Simon Napier-Bell explained in his autobiography, came to the Flamingo 'every weekend and paid for their night out by selling Benzedrine tablets taken from their cockpit emergency kits'.

The Scene was the West End's leading 1960s Mod club. Based on Ham Yard near the Windmill Theatre, a site that is now one of the West End's few empty lots, it was run by Ronan O'Rahilly (later proprietor of Radio Caroline), who employed a dancer to showcase new moves: the Swim, Jerk, Mashed Potato, Pony, Watusi, Fly *et al*. Here the soundtrack, courtesy of DJ Guy Stevens (who later produced the Clash's *London Calling*), was the slickest and most sophisticated: Major Lance's 'Monkey Time', Benny Spellman's 'Fortune Teller' – top-drawer American R&B that was never played on UK radio. The Scene's clientele dropped inordinate amounts of pills, and after closing time would head to a café in Fleet Street, before driving to the south coast on their scooters, or catching the milk train from Waterloo. The Scene earned its place in rock history by gaining a mention in 'I'm The Face', the first single by the Who (as The High Numbers): 'So many tickets down the Scene, honey, they'll likely blow a fuse.' Many musicians visited the club, including the Small Faces, Rod Stewart and the Animals' Chas Chandler (later manager of Jimi Hendrix and Slade), who came down from Newcastle and later recalled how 'there were no lights and no alcohol. When we saw it we couldn't believe it. On Tyneside people went to clubs to fight.'

For the new class of plutocratic rock stars there were exclusive nightspots decked out in modernist fittings: the Ad-Lib on Leicester Square; the Bag O' Nails on Kingly Street; and the Speakeasy near Oxford Circus. The Speakeasy was decorated as an American Prohibition-era joint, and was once described by 'Spanish Tony' Sanchez, the Rolling Stones' drugs consultant, as 'dark and crowded with the young and beautiful men and women who had turned London, momentarily, into the hip capital of the western World'. Here the rock aristocrats would stumble in after a gig knowing that the ordinary screaming fans who had made them rich but who they were spending so much time running away from were safely tucked up. Others came here to play. Jimi Hendrix visited the club on 16 September 1970, the night before he died, expecting to jam with Sly Stone who had just arrived in London but who failed to show.

For a few years the Marquee remained *the* venue for hearing the new hybrid music: rock, as opposed to rock 'n' roll; loud, crashy, guitar heavy, still reliant on R&B for the chord changes, still reliant on 'moon-and-June' lyrical simplicity for a few years. The Yardbirds shared the bill on the opening night at Wardour Street, 13 March 1964, with the Arkansan blues singer Sonny Boy Williamson II, their collaboration later released as the album *Five Live Yardbirds*. Others who played during the first few weeks included John Mayall's Bluesbreakers, the Alex Harvey Soul Band, the South African pianist Michael Lubowitz, a fine jazz and blues pianist who soon began trading as Manfred Mann, and the Who, who secured a Tuesday residency at the end of the year advertised as 'Maximum R&B'.

A pattern was set where a group, whose musical interests amounted to little more than being able to belt out passable versions of American R&B standards, would hone their craft live at venues like the Marquee, garner a following, hit the charts, move on to bigger venues and arrive in the studio for their early albums having smoothed out the mistakes and attained the confidence to experiment and innovate, to create a worthwhile body of music out of their own culture.

London's main studios catering for the new sound were Olympic in Barnes and Abbey Road in St John's Wood, but there were several important sites in the West End. For instance, at ATV House, 17 Great Cumberland Place, near Marble Arch, the Kinks recorded much of their 1960s output. Also recorded at Pye was the Who's 'My Generation', which antagonized critics with its aggressive stance and muted swearing. The group's guitarist, Pete Townshend, author of the song, had made a home demonstration version of the song with a 'Bo Diddley' shuffle rhythm, but a single recorded in that style had to be scrapped when drummer Keith Moon refused to play the beat. Manager Kit Lambert diffused the tension by suggesting Roger Daltrey sung the words with an exaggerated stutter – 'Why don't you all f-f-f fade away?' It was an inspired move.

The Rolling Stones were regular customers at IBC, 35 Portland Place, a few hundred yards north of Oxford Circus, in the mid 1960s. There they recorded the driving and tortuously named single 'Have You Seen Your Mother, Baby, Standing In The Shadow?' in 1966. So were the Yardbirds, honed from the same raucous R&B template as the Stones, who went to IBC in December 1964 to record their first non-blues song, 'For Your Love', written by a young Manchester songwriter, Graham Gouldman (later of 10cc), around an unusual pairing of harpsichord and bongos. The song's catchiness disappointed Eric Clapton, the group's guitarist, a blues purist, who quit in disgust. Ironically, Clapton soon moved towards blatantly commercial records with Cream while the Yardbirds continued to experiment and break new boundaries.

In January 1966 New Yorker Steve Stollman began organizing a new type of mixed-media event at the Marquee on Sunday evenings. Under the name 'Spontaneous Underground' it featured beat poets, film-makers, magic artists and props such as a huge mound of pink jelly which would inevitably induce patrons to strip off and roll in it. The flyer produced to advertise the 13 March event read: 'TRIP, bring furniture toy prop paper rug paint balloon jumble costume mask robot candle incense ladder wheel light self all others. March 13th 5pm, Marquee Club, Wardour Street W1 5/-.' It also asked: 'Who will be there? Pop singers, hoods, Americans, homosexuals (because they make up 10 per cent of the population), 20 clowns, jazz musicians, one murderer, sculptors, politicians and some girls who defy description.'

People turned up to Spontaneous Underground events in a variety of period clothes, mixing Edwardian jackets, velvet trousers, leather boots and cravats. At first the soundtrack was free jazz, rather than anything connected with rock, and was provided by the free-form outfit AMM, whose Cornelius Cardew played in a white lab coat. Cardew was England's leading exponent of arch experimentalist John Cage, and had spent two years with the German electronics innovator Karl Heinz Stockhausen. He then turned against his mentor with the vituperative book *Stockhausen Serves Imperialism*, and began to perform catchy Chinese revolutionary songs such as 'We All Love the Three Old Articles of Chairman Mao'. Cardew once explained that an AMM performance had 'no beginning or ending. Sounds outside the performance are distinguished from it only by individual sensibility.' This meant that for some AMM concerts Cardew would play the piano by tapping a leg with a small piece of wood.

Soon Spontaneous Underground had a house band: a group of architecture students bent on twisting R&B and rock 'n' roll into new shapes. They played to a backdrop of films, multicoloured lights and stage props, deliberately contrived to make the performers look anonymous, but which were then innovative. Led by singer, guitarist and songwriter Syd Barrett, they called themselves the Pink Floyd Sound, an amalgam of the names of two obscure Carolina blues musicians: Pink Anderson and Floyd Council.

Thus far the group had been playing mostly free-form jazz at the Goings-On Club, 3–4 Archer Street, as the Abdabs, ending shows by discussing their work with the audience. Now at the Marquee they began to play absurdly loud versions of the R&B standards 'Louie Louie' and 'Roadrunner', with what Julian Palacios described as 'freak out explorations in the middle' and which culture journalist Mick Farren claimed sounded 'like a guitar solo by the Who, only it was a solo with out any song to go round it – like a sandwich without bread. They were very loud with no musical form save that every forty minutes or so they stopped, paused a while, and started again.'

To help him gain the right sort of mindset to play live, Syd Barrett would lay out stacks of sugar cubes, drop a globule of LSD on each one and lick the cube. He would then sit and look at three objects: an orange, a plum and a matchbox, which in his mind became the moons of Uranus – Oberon, Titania and Miranda – as he later recalled in the song 'Astronomy Domine'. The Pink Floyd Sound took chances and made mistakes. At the Marquee Syd would take a basic rock 'n' roll riff and distort it through his guitar by rolling steel ball-bearings up and down the frets to create strange noises. From these experiments came the ten-minute, mind-expanding, stoned space trip 'Interstellar Overdrive', the defining sound of the era. Again, as with the Stones' raucous R&B at the Marquee in 1962, it would not have been possible to experience these performances and foresee that it was the harbinger of a new music, a new form of rock – cleverer, wittier, more eloquent, more elegant, more literate than what had gone before; to see at that stage that it *was* possible to combine the visceral thrust of the Stones' 'Satisfaction' with the ethereal bliss of Miles Davis's *Miles Ahead*.

And it was not just with avant-garde, experimental free-form rock that there were surprises and exciting new developments in the West End. The arrival in September 1966 of an unknown American jobbing guitarist, who had played in the backing band of Little Richard and the Isley Brothers, showed that there was a lot more work to be done with the electric guitar.

Indeed, Jimi Hendrix proved in a few West End gigs and several more studio appearances at Olympic in Barnes that until he arrived in London work on maximizing the instrument's sound hadn't really begun.

Straight from London Airport Hendrix's manager, Chas Chandler, took him to a house in West Kensington to jam with Soho gigging regulars Andy Summers (later of the Police) and Zoot Money. Those lazing round the house were stunned into speechlessness at Hendrix's virtuoso technique and his exuberant style. Ronni Money, Zoot's wife, rushed upstairs to urge the tenant, Kathy Etchingham, to come down because 'Chas has just brought this guy back from America and he looks like the Wild Man of Borneo'.

Over the next few days the unknown guitarist was paraded around the West End as a prize exhibit. Nothing had been seen like it in Soho since the appearance of Giovanni Giacomo Casanova in 1764. First Hendrix was taken to the exclusive Scotch of St James club, off Pall Mall, where he was introduced to his idol, Eric Clapton. When Clapton heard Hendrix play he turned to Chandler and whispered 'He's *that* good?' But Hendrix himself, however, was strikingly modest. He genuinely thought his vocals to be substandard. He had no wish to be a solo artist but wanted to form a band.

Auditions took place at the Gaslight Club off Piccadilly, and a press conference was thrown at the Bag O'Nails on Kingly Street on 25 November 1966. According to the singer Terry Reid, when Hendrix broke into his first number, 'Wild Thing', the other guitar players 'began weeping. They had to mop the floor up. He was piling it on, solo after solo. I could see everyone's fillings falling out. When he finished it was silence. Nobody knew what to do. Everybody was in complete shock.'

Hendrix moved into 34 Montagu Square, Marylebone, a Georgian town house nominally leased by Ringo Starr. Walking the streets of the West End, he would often dress in quasi-military outfits. One day he was stopped by the police near the flat and berated by five or six officers for being dressed so. 'You shouldn't be wearing that,' one of the officers exclaimed, 'men fought and died in that uniform', to which Hendrix replied 'What, in the Veterinary Corps, 1898?' It was at No. 34 in January 1967 that the guitarist wrote the haunting 'The Wind Cries Mary', with its shimmering, restrained harmonics, after a row with Kathy Etchingham which involved much smashing of plates. Hendrix locked her in the bathroom while he completed the number and when he opened the door she ran off. After cooling down, Etchingham returned to the flat and Hendrix played her the song. Unsurprisingly she relented.

There were also plenty of West End venues willing to showcase the new rock sounds. In the Blarney Club, an Irish venue located in the basement of 31 Tottenham Court Road, producer Joe Boyd began hosting 'UFO Presents Night Tripper', soon contracted to plain UFO, from 23 December 1966. Amidst the orgiastic atmosphere there were screenings of underground films, poetry readings, impromptu stage shows, acid deals and a clothes stall run by Michael Rainey of the Chelsea boutique, Hung On You. Arthur Brown swung from a trapeze wearing a flaming helmet of burning meths while singing 'Fire'. Soft Machine from Canterbury, full of jazzy improvisations and bohemian attitudes, played passable psychedelic pop. The house band was Pink Floyd.

No alcohol was sold at UFO, which was just as well given the claustrophobic heat and lack of air. To save their energy the audience sat on the floor watching the group, except for a few 'leapers' at the front who would soar through the air in kaftans and bells, and odd individuals gyrating their bodies to a rhythm indiscernible to anyone else. At the top of the stairs an old man wearing a paper crown would wait for the inevitable police raids and tape conversations for purposes indefinable, especially given that the tape recorder was fake.

## A VERY CELLULAR SONG

Alongside the new R&B/beat scene of the mid 1960s, folk – restrained, vernacular, both radical and traditional, a guitar and affixed mouth harp the only overheads for most of its purveyors – underwent a revival as musicians sought simple emotional honesty in the face of the bombast of rock.

In some cases folk was merely a style to be explored until it was time for a change. This was the case with the most important performer in the genre, Bob Dylan; not that anyone realized this when he played the King and Queen pub, 1 Foley Street, Fitzrovia, in December 1962. At that time Dylan's first album was captivating those in the know but the artist was largely unknown to music fans. Dylan wasn't even scheduled to perform, but just happened to be part of the throng gathered in the pub that night.

Also there was Martin Carthy, who went on to become England's most influential folk guitarist. Carthy went up to Dylan and asked: 'Excuse me, your name is Bob Dylan, isn't it?' When Dylan affirmed that it was Carthy asked him if he would like to sing, to which Dylan replied: 'No. Well, maybe I will later on; ask me later.' Carthy did and the two sang 'Talkin' John Birch Paranoid Blues', a dig at McCarthyite America. After the gig Carthy gave Dylan a grounding in English folk which took him in new directions on his third album, *The Times They Are A-Changing*. Dylan also found time to visit Dobell's record shop at 77 Charing Cross Road, turning up with a bottle of Guinness but no bottle opener, where he joined a crowd bellowing into a primitive recording machine, later assuming the name Blind Boy Grunt on the release for contractual reasons.

To some, folk was a political rite of passage, an affirmation of not just socialist credentials but of a passion for full-bloodied Stalinism: the ability to tow the party line, to take orders and not veer from the dogma, lest one became an unperson. Such was the case with Ewan MacColl, whose Ballads and Blues Club was held at the Black Horse pub, 6 Rathbone Place, Fitzrovia. MacColl had been James Miller, a Salford-born songwriter, composer of 'Dirty Old Town', until the outbreak of the Second World War encouraged him to change his name to dodge conscription. At his Ballads and Blues Club he would sing miners' laments, sea shanties – anything as long it took the side of the downtrodden common man against the boss class – with one hand cupped over an ear. It was primitive, but to many a welcome respite from the mass outbreak of beat groups.

In the mid 1960s folk split apart. Some (Martin Carthy, Dick Gaughan, Christy Moore) stayed true to the purist line, but remained marginalized by the public. Some (Fairport Convention, Pentangle) ignored tradition, creating a new blend, folk in the rock format: timeless songs with traditional themes underpinned by strong rhythms and ensemble playing.

The schisms led to much in-fighting, particularly in the West End. According to the purists, folk was being ruined by exposure to capitalist rock 'n' roll. There was muttered dissatisfaction at the way folk singers were toying with electric instruments, were diluting the pure message with commercialization, rock 'n' roll and noise. By 1966 the West End was full of solo artists busy developing a body of work based around their songs in which they were accompanied mostly by just a guitar. But each soon aligned themselves with rock; each had their own unique romantic vision, and they gravitated to Soho in a wave of talent the strength of which London music had never previously seen, the choice staggering: Paul Simon, Bert Jansch, John Renbourn, Donovan, Cat Stevens, Al Stewart, John Martyn, Nick Drake, Roy Harper . . .

Some were American (Simon), some Londoners (Stevens was raised above a restaurant on New Oxford Street). Others, like Jansch, Martyn and Stewart, had come from Scotland, the latter honouring his new locale in two songs, 'Soho Needless To Say' and 'Old Compton Street Blues'. Their West End home was Les Cousins at 49 Greek Street, a tiny auditorium with room for only three rows of seats run by Andy Matthews, whose parents owned a Greek restaurant, Dionysus, located in the premises above.

But the most exciting folk act to play Soho was not one of the singer-song-writers, as the new breed began to be called, but a group – a loose collective might be a better description – from Scotland: the Incredible String Band. Adepts at a vast trove of unusual instruments – gimbri, harp, harpsichord, sitar, whistle, pan pipe, oud, chahanai, water harp and hammer dulcimer – they fused western folk with eastern instrumentation alongside fabulist, psychedelic lyrics. They wrote mystical chants, nursery rhymes, heart-wrenching love songs and nonsense rhymes drenched in dreamlike imagery, their sets beginning with the fantastical 'Koeeoaddi There', which noted, alchemically and cryptically, 'Earth, water, fire and air met together in a garden fair, put in a basket bound with skin, if you answer this riddle, if you answer this riddle, you'll never begin . . .'

The West End had not heard such a mind-melting marriage of myth and music since William Blake had sung his own poems at the Reverend Matthews' house on Rathbone Place.


# DR MARTEN'S APOCALYPSE

Music usually develops amidst two warring tribes: the traditionalists and the modernists. The first argue that *this* is the way it sounded at its peak, there-fore *this* is the way it should always sound. The latter claim a new sound has arrived, better than the old sound. That *this* is the new way. One generation's modernists often become a later generation's traditionalists.

By the mid 1970s rock had created within itself the kind of divisions that had previously beset jazz and folk. Those groups intent on creating a body of art to rival the great symphonists could no longer be found at the West End's Marquee club in front of a few hundred devotees on a wet Tuesday night. They had become rock gods; untouchable, distant, their pictures not even appearing on their albums.

Consequently, the groups that *were* playing the Marquee and other Soho clubs in front of a few hundred devotees on a wet Tuesday night stacked themselves in opposition to the intellectual rockers. They harked back to the early days of Soho R&B pop, to the three-minute, guitar-heavy chimes of the Kinks, Who and Pretty Things. The most popular of these mid 1970s revivalists were Eddie & the Hot Rods, nominally from Southend but sufficiently cockney in style to attract a capital following. Yet barely had these groups begun playing the West End than a breakaway movement appeared. Some of the new groups realized that there was little point reviving nostalgically; social change meant it was impossible to view things with the same eyes. When Eddie and the Hot Rods played the Marquee on 12 February 1976 the support group, the Sex Pistols, trashed their equipment and terrorized members of the audience.

Whereas the Hot Rods were part of a scene that wanted to preserve the status quo, so that they could eventually join its upper reaches, the Pistols' motive was revolutionary: the old order had to be destroyed and replaced. As guitarist Steve Jones explained in an interview with the *New Musical Express*: 'We're not into music. We're into chaos.' It was not the first time the Sex Pistols had brought anarchy to the West End. It began at their first ever gig, which took place in Soho at St Martin's School of Art on 6 November 1975. After rehearsing in a room on Denmark Street, London's Tin Pan Alley, the Pistols wheeled their equipment across Charing Cross Road through the rush hour crowd to play a short set that consisted of mangled versions of Small Faces and Who songs. After twenty minutes the unimpressed promoter pulled the plug. It was not that the Pistols were playing aesthetically unsound music, as a trad jazzer might have accused a bopper twenty years before, it was that the Pistols were not, as far as most of the audience were concerned, playing anything remotely connected to music at all. They were amateurish. They could barely play. They were rude and anti-social. They were terrifying. As singer John Lydon later related, 'There was not one single hand clap. The college audience had never seen anything like it. They couldn't connect because our stance was so anti-pop, so anti-everything that had gone before.'

By summer 1976 the Marquee had banned punk. Looking for a West End berth, the Pistols gained a foothold – a Tuesday-night residency – at the 100 Club on Oxford Street. The violence that surrounded their music and their manifesto now materialized at this club. On 29 June a member of the Pistols' entourage taunted the well-known rock critic Nick Kent, kicking and jostling him at regular intervals. When Kent asked him to stop he was attacked by another Pistol hanger-on, John Beverly, soon to be renamed 'Sid Vicious'. Vivienne Westwood, then part of the Pistols' management team and now one of Britain's leading fashion designers, apologized to Kent, promising that 'that psychopath' (Vicious) would never be allowed to attend one of their gigs again, a promise not only ignored (Beverly was soon invited to join the band) but deliberately scorned, for when Beverly replaced Glen Matlock on bass Malcolm McLaren, the main Pistols manager, issued a press release which ran: 'His best credential is that he gave Nick Kent what he deserved many months ago at the 100 Club.'

Throughout the summer of 1976 the storm the Pistols were creating around the country through their nihilism and lack of compromise was exciting the public and terrifying the establishment. On 20 September 1976 there was a punk 'festival' at the 100 Club. It was the wasted generation's Woodstock. By now the Pistols had quite a collection of fellow iconoclasts. On the bill were the Sex Pistols, the Clash, the Damned, Buzzcocks and Subway Sect. The night was stolen, however, by another new group, a band of David Bowie devotees mostly from Bromley: Suzie [sic] and the Banshees. Their line-up, agreed only minutes before they went on stage, included Sid Vicious on drums. Most of them had only just met their instruments for the first time.

Rock fans in the crowd were horrified. This was even less authentically musical than the Sex Pistols. The Banshees played half an hour of guitar-based white noise – allegedly a version of the Velvet Underground's 'Sister Ray' – over which Suzie (later Siouxsie), wearing Nazi armbands and a see-through plastic mac, recited 'The Lord's Prayer', telling the audience: 'We may not be able to have anarchy on the streets but at least we can have it in our little club.' When Sid Vicious tired of drumming the 'song' ground to a halt.

Yet out of this muck came gold. The Banshees had gone further than the Pistols in defining the precepts of the new era: that anyone could make music, if they had the right spirit, ideas, vitality and a fresh approach; that music was more about people's instinctive reactions to their own culture than a formula prescribed by a producer; that technical competence could be acquired at a later date. Even more revolutionary, the Banshees showed that night that a rock group could be led by a woman unwilling to occupy traditional 'rock chic' poses; that from now on women – the Slits, Kate Bush, Bjork, Siouxsie herself over the years – would produce rock that rivalled the best men had to offer.

This night, more than any other, paved the way for the sudden growth of a vast new body of music that quickly left the confines of the West End to dominate the next few decades. Gradually the West End lost its status as the night home for the avant-garde. Instead, the large number of venues meant that the area could capitalize on the vast number of choices night-time revellers now had. Those who wanted jazz one night, a new romantic club the next, and comedy at the weekend knew that they could find everything they wished for in the West End.

By the 1980s the West End was known more for its nightclubs than its live venues. A major destination was the Wag on Wardour Street, situated above the 1960s Flamingo. The Wag reached its peak one night that decade when David Bowie was drinking with Mick Jagger at the bar, Boy George was gyrating on the dance floor and Jack Nicholson was schmoozing upstairs. But sadly even the Wag could not resist the onslaught of the fake Irish pub craze of the late twentieth century, and it was converted into an O'Neill's, run by a Birmingham firm.

Louise's on nearby Poland Street was more of an acquired taste, home in the early 1980s to punks in bondage gear bought from Vivienne Westwood's Seditionaries shop on King's Road, a lesbian DJ with Swastikas painted on her clothes, and an MC in a suit and tie complemented by a T-shirt emblazoned: 'Fuck Your Mother'. At one time the Gargoyle on Meard Street, decorated many decades earlier by Matisse and Lutyens, was Gossip's, origin of the 1980s new romantic scene which grew around the nights when the DJ played records only by David Bowie and Roxy Music. By 1982 Wednesdays had been handed over to those running the Batcave who concentrated on gothic punk as pioneered by Siouxsie and the Banshees, of which there were by now numerous followers.

Few venues have ever been put to so much use as the old Gargoyle. For it was here in 1979 that Don Ward imported into London the idea of the American Comedy Store format. Comic hopefuls would take the floor before a cynical audience and a compere with a gong who would strike off unimpressive performers. It didn't help that the gong was often kept by the bear-like Scouse wit Alexei Sayle. Some never even got as far as trying to tell any jokes. Arnold Brown was gonged off before he had even opened his mouth.

Soon the new scene and its main performers were being labelled under the banner 'alternative comedy'. Older comics were horrified by these tyros with their left-wing attitudes and punkish manners. Many were heard to say: 'Alternative comedy? Alternative to what, being funny?' Alternative comedy tried too hard. It was clever rather than funny; too knowing. Like the satire scene of twenty years previously it had built-in limited appeal. Punters had to be well versed in offbeat culture, football, up-to-the-minute trends in music and Trotskyite politics, otherwise they would not be able to respond accordingly. Sayle himself told the story of how he grew up in a hard-core Communist household. One day in primary school the teacher handed them all little glasses of milk and told the kids: 'Let us give praise for the milk. Milk comes from God . . .', only to be interrupted by the young comic hopeful, who piped up: 'No, miss, milk comes from the Milk Marketing Board, which is a semi-autonomous, government-owned management co-operative which regulates milk production according to the Total Production Quota (TPQ) to ensure sufficient milk production to meet consumer needs', and so on ad nauseam. The Comedy Store later moved to Oxenden Street, nearer Leicester Square, where it still draws crowds.

One venue continues to entrance those looking for a memorable night out in the West End, and has outlived all its one-time rivals. Ronnie Scott opened his jazz club in the basement of 39 Gerrard Street, where illegal Second World War bottle parties had taken place, in October 1959. It moved in December 1965 to its current site, and remains Britain's best-known jazz club, even though Scott died in December 1996.

Scott was an engaging and witty compere who buried his own insecurity in his playing to showcase the best the music had to offer to West End audiences. Born into the Jewish ghetto of Aldgate, his musical epiphany came touring the US in 1947 when a few days grace in New York meant that he could visit the clubs of 52nd Street and hear Charlie Parker, Dizzy Gillespie and Thelonious Monk in the flesh, at a time when even their records were unavailable in Britain. Consequently the club's longevity can be traced to Scott's determination to immerse himself in a culture that was alien but which sought converts. He may not have been black, born in St Louis or the son of cotton pickers, but he could play a mean saxophone. He understood intuitively that jazz ran not according to a rigid rule book but through a mix of sensitivity and sensuality; that as a musical form it was fluid and adaptable.

Few places anywhere in the world can still offer so vast and exciting a range of night-time experiences as the West End. Imagine staying in Hazlitt's, the refined, immaculately mannered eighteenth-century hotel based in the former home of the essayist William Hazlitt, on Frith Street in the heart of Soho. You have arrived in the West End knowing nothing of London but are well versed in staying in skyscraping executive hotels across the world. In the time it would normally take you to get from your air-conditioned double-bedded room with its computerized card key on the fifty-seventh floor to the nearest bar or restaurant in any other city you could make it from your room in Hazlitt's to Bar Italia, Ronnie Scott's, L'Escargot, the Coach and Horses, the Gay Hussar, Leoni's Quo Vadis, the French House and the whole of Chinatown. That's not to mention the length of Old Compton Street. You may need more than one night.

# 13

# Style

A battle for the West End's soul is raging. For now the West End remains the capital of style, but for how long? Lined up on one side are the franchises – restaurants, coffee bars and clothes stores – and the venal politicians. On the other side are the people, the great mass who use the West End. A few are residents, most are visitors, many are unconcerned or unaware of the changes, and will remain so until it is too late and the West End has been cleaned of its character and history, sanitized into a gigantic Nandoed, Starbucked, pedestrianized American-style shopping mall of vapid café bars, retail 'units', and granite and glass office blocks.

Once, the average Londoner – indeed the average Briton residing anywhere in the UK – could safely assume that any culinary deficiencies they found in Stoke-on-Trent or Ashton-under-Lyne could be redeemed by stylish eating and drinking in Soho or Fitzrovia. The West End was practically *the* only place in Britain where the knowledgeable epicurean could indulge in good food, washed down with drinkable coffee. What the citizen abroad – from Aarhus to Ankara, from Cottbus to Caesarea – took for granted, that their average local high-street eaterie would provide quality food and strong coffee at a reasonable price, without too much fuss or fake obsequiousness from the waiters, the typical tasteful Briton has long realized was available mostly only in London, rarely outside the West End, and even then rarely at a cheap price.

For generations the world reeled in embarrassment at the British with their inability to eat properly, their laughable native diet of saveloys, pease pudding, shepherd's pie, liver-and-bacon, fish fried in beef dripping, and prawns and cockles rendered inedible by being saturated in vinegar. Now the newspapers wax over the supposed ever-improving British diet and restaurant variation, a supposedly staggering choice of fresh, continental-style options and a bewildering range of national cuisines that can satisfy every palate. But then eating in Britain, like sex, has long been a continental affair. In the early twentieth century it was French restaurants. After the war it was Italian joints. In the 1970s Chinese was the novelty. A decade later Indian. More recently the fad has been for Thai or tapas. Never British.

Now there is more choice but it is Hobson's Choice. What profit a West Ender Nobu, overpriced sushi in the company of Boris Becker on Old Park Lane, when the original Pollo on Old Compton Street with its authentic Italian food (as Italians might eat it) served up in liberal portions, with its ox-blood booths, beanpole railings and hungry queues lining the street outside, with its lack of red-checked tablecloths and seedy waiters, where Syd Barrett once hallucinated his ravioli into the moons of Uranus, has closed? How can it avail those looking for lunchtime sustenance near Frith Street when the choice is no longer between Wheeler's and the Court Café but between Soho Thai and Nando's?

The new West End restaurants are designed towards inducing feelings of nausea and inadequacy the moment the customer enters the premises. Instead of being run by a knowledgeable, friendly maitre d', intent on learning the name of every customer and dispensing sagacious bonhomie from table to table, they are identical, personality free, geared towards feeding Mammon rather than discerning Londoners, run by marketing men and design consultants, intent on zealously shooing off eaters who have strayed over the hour mark, concerned mostly with extracting maximum revenue from minimal effort.

For the British have long confused the notions of eating and pricing. Edible food in Britain has traditionally come at a price – an excessive price. So has value and service. Whereas in France the scuzziest, seediest, most Gitane-ridden street bar, stuffed with paid-up Jean-Marie Le Pen supporters and knife-wielding desperadoes' will serve up the finest Salad Niçoise at minimal cost, the bread, fresh, luscious, divine, the water elegantly presented in a carafe with a twist of lemon, their British equivalent can only be cajoled into treating the customer accordingly by threatening to take the staff hostage. An unhealthy price tag is attached to each link in the chain: bread? at a cost; fresh bread? extra cost; water? tap at a price, bottled pricier. And that's before the main meal and drinks arrive.

# SLEEPLESS OUT OF SEATTLE

Nothing threatens the survival of style in the West End more than the rise of the American coffee bar. Just like in the first decade after the war the West End is being overrun with places geared towards turning into a lifestyle what should be something that is simply an unobtrusive end to a meal. Except that the new coffee bars are not the preserve of local entrepreneurs providing their particular product with an independent eye. They are not new versions of Bar Italia on Frith Street, swish, sleek and stylish, unique and individual, but a triumph of the bland over the bold, the mass-produced over the personally moulded, run from corporate skyscrapers closer in spirit and location to Seattle than Soho, or even Sorrento.

Each coffee bar, homogenized and indistinguishable from each other, the décor controlled and uninspired, has the same inescapable, insipid, ersatz jazz soundtrack, the same mania for fad-ridden diet and decaf versions; the same rude and ignorant staff attempting to offer the customer the same flat, featureless, tasteless, nauseous concoctions: 'expresso [sic]' – with sugar! – or milk-laden mush served in unnecessary gallon-size quantities, presented in – horror of horrors – a paper cup.

Of course other cities have fallen under the same spell, but Birmingham, Basingstoke and Barnstaple were never able to rival the West End as a cultural and social pinnacle in the first place.

# STYLE COUNSEL

It is not just the new nonsense coffee bar that is threatening the West End's unique identity. The change in shopping patterns in the early twenty-first century is having a debilitating effect on what was once Britain's greatest shopping centre. Bond Street may still have the highest number of royal warrants of any street in Britain, but it is Oxford Street, which touches all four West End enclaves – Mayfair, Marylebone, Soho and Fitzrovia – that symbolizes the West End.

Oxford Street has long been short of style. Despite the great department stores, there has long been what Virginia Woolf decried as far back as 1932 as 'too many bargains, too many sales, too many goods marked down . . . the buying and selling too blatant and raucous'.

This long, slow decline was exacerbated at the end of the twentieth century with the arrival of discount stores on Oxford Street run by boorish MCs with *Eastenders* accents advertising alarmingly cheap goods at ear-splitting volumes. Commentators and chroniclers lined up to announce the death of the street. By 2006 the same discount stores had largely disappeared, but they had been replaced by an even more alarming mix of cardboard-pizza takeaways, mobile phone shops and *bureaux de change*.

The grand shops that once attracted customers from across the world are closing down one by one. Dickins and Jones shut at the beginning of 2006, leaving a prime site by Oxford Circus vacant. It joined a too-long list of departed department stores that includes C&A and Peter Robinson. Shoppers may well be only experimenting by heading away from the West End to the new undercover, sanitized out-of-town malls like Bluewater, but when the novelty wears off they will be crawling back to the West End. They may, if they are lucky, find some of the great names – John Lewis, Selfridge's, Fenwick's, Hamley's – remaining amidst the dross. More likely they will find an Oxford Street reduced to the prosaic state of Manchester's Market Street or Liverpool's Bold Street.

The West End at least still has its mainstream theatres and musical venues. Indeed, Soho has more places devoted to middle-of-the-road entertainment in the *Guys and Dolls*/Andrew Lloyd Webber/*Rocky Horror Show* mould than the rest of the country put together. Yet where the West End was once packed with groundbreaking venues such as the Marquee, Vortex, Bunjies, Roundhouse and Les Cousins, where the music lover might experience the first stirrings of a major new movement soon to rule the world, there are now next to none left.

Similarly with nightclubbing. Where West End nightclubs once showcased the latest sounds and dances, the cutting edge is now found in Hoxton or Hackney, Brixton or Brighton. The West End is now better known as the place for those in search of tasteless, footballers'-wives dives – China White, Ruby Blue, the Embassy – than for the next Haçienda or Ministry of Sound.

Perhaps the concerned West Ender can find salvation from the lead shown by the politicians? Sadly not. It is the West End politicians who have promoted a succession of ill-considered anti-social schemes which, if enacted fully, would have wiped out what is so special about the area. In the 1950s it was the mania for sky-scraping glass towers, scores of which were planned for Soho, to be connected by walkways in the sky, topped with heligarages for a pan-West End helicopter service, only one of which (Kemp House on Berwick Street, with no heligarage) was built. In the 1980s it was the West End politicians who actively sought to sanitise Soho with cluttery street furniture and pedestrianization, fortunately and blissfully abandoned in the face of commonsense opposition.

More recently, those looking for a lead in the fight to save the West End's soul from an elected leader would have been disappointed. The West End was ruled for ten years towards the end of the twentieth century by Dame Shirley Porter, leader of Westminster city council, in which the West End resides. In the 1990s Porter was involved in the sale of council homes to prospective Tory voters in politically vulnerable wards that saw the district auditor accuse her of 'wilful misconduct' and 'disgraceful and improper gerrymandering'. On the other side of the line, incorruptible and unshakeable, stands Ken Livingstone, mayor of London, whose solution to the traffic problems of Oxford Street in August 2006 was to suggest the introduction of a Manchester-style tram system to clog the streets more.

So if the West End is at the mercy of corporate empire builders and uninspiring politicians, who can protect its status and reputation? As with the East End the solution lies in the hands of the people who use it, the people who will benefit most from its resurrection. In the East End years of rogue political manipulation, economic deprivation and urban decay are being addressed, not by grand municipal schemes but by random groups of like-minded locals acting from their own volition.

It was a group of architectural historians squatting in crumbling Spitalfields silk workers' houses in the 1970s that saved the glorious Georgian streets of Fournier, Princelet, Wilkes and Folgate, now some of the most desirable addresses in east London. It was the ingenuity of Bengali immigrants taking over run-down Spitalfields shops and converting them into gleaming neon-lit curry palaces that helped transform Brick Lane from a violent unloved no-go zone into one of Britain's most remarkable locations.

The same self-help solutions will save the West End from Starbucks, Nando's, Soccer Scene, Phones4U, Eat and Subway, from all the gross, solecistic purveyors of 'pizzas' (sic) and, worse still, 'paninis' (sic). A noise of guitar against drum or computer bleep against rhythm-generator pulse will be heard from a Beak Street basement; a brush will sweep across a canvas on Charlotte Street; a fervent debate will rage above a pub on Great Windmill Street; a restaurant will open for those whose desire for food comes from a rumbling in the stomach and a memory in the mind rather than a recipe page in a celebrity-chef cookbook. The remaining outposts of distinction – Andrew Edmunds on Lexington Street, the New Piccadilly Café, Lina's and Camissa's delicatessens, Pollock's Toy Museum, the Wigmore Hall, the Theatre Bookshop by Fitzroy Square, The I Am The Only Running Footman pub in Mayfair – will be joined by delights yet unknown.

It is already happening. The great success stories of the modern West End owe their status to no government quango directive or council initiative. Marylebone High Street and its environs had no particular cachet a generation ago. It offered little more than, say, Kingsland High Street in Dalston in terms of quality of goods. But with the mass homogenization of shopping across the country and the decline of so many London high streets Marylebone has taken the opposite route and now attracts people from across the capital, each with a different agenda; some who want to spend two hours in Daunt's bookshop and others who intend to buy nothing but simply breathe in the air of stylish sophistication that wraps itself around those dull-named streets filled with delights (St Christopher's Place, Thayer Street) and those whose romantic titles lead nowhere (Bentinck Mews, Spanish Place).

And when visitors have finished on Marylebone High Street they can wander along the tiny lanes to the south, their narrowness contrived by the now buried presence of the Tyburn stream, where they will find spicy sausage-laden delicatessens and a restaurant selling fish and chips made out of cold-eyed monsters and real potatoes, unlike the deep-frost pap available in most 'chippies'. Or they might find themselves wandering around the northern reaches of Wardour Street during the working day desperate for a lunch whose contents has not been planned from a brutalist concrete office block in East Finchley or does not contain the misnomers 'skinny', 'tall' and 'grande'. They may chance upon the Malletti pizzeria on Noel Street and recall that pizza is an Italian way of dishing up everyday foodstuffs on baked rather than boiled bread, need not be a mulch of tomato and processed cheese and need not come with an eat-as-much-as-you-can-carry salad bar.

Come the end of work, they will muse on the qualities of bitter made with care and distinction by a company geared towards brewing beer, rather than being part of a 'leisure' chain, and head for the John Snow on Broadwick

Street, where amidst the delicately engraved glass and broody wood they will delight on handing over a £2 coin and receiving change for their pint. Their next stop could well be the cinema, and how they will marvel at being able to choose between a Hollywood blockbuster, an art-house treasure or a rep classic at a small friendly venue such as the Curzon Soho or the cheaper than cheap Prince Charles near Leicester Square, rather than having to drive to a mind-numbing megaplex at the end of a sixteen-mile queue of traffic in Swiss Cottage.

Then there are the success stories that sweep through an entire section of the West End. There is the style makeover that has seen Old Compton Street, long Soho's high street, go from a vibrant street of famous bars, restaurants and shops into the country's most famous gay street. Why Old Compton and not Wardour, Frith or Beak? Through word of mouth, maybe? Like-minded individuals slowly began to turn the Admiral Duncan and Compton's pubs into havens for those taking advantage of the liberalization of laws on homosexuality in the late 1960s. Perhaps it was a nod to the cavortings of Quentin Crisp on the street in the 1930s or an ironic tribute to Cliff Richard's local sojourn in the 1950s. No 'official' reason has been found. It was history on the hoof, unrecorded, inexplicable. But it brings tens of thousands to the place, particularly at weekends, particularly around midnight, in a so un-English way.

Another is the transformation of a handful of streets between Leicester Square and Shaftesbury Avenue from seedy backwaters of shabby shops and hard-to-let flats into a dynamic territory thronged with visitors and buzzing with life. Chinatown's arrival in the West End was also an accident – the World War Two bombing of Limehouse, London's original Chinatown. Its growth has been organic and market-led, its product desired and revered, its future bright, buoyed by the power of personal choice and value for money. It works. It draws in people from all over to marvel at its scope and ingenuity. It is brash but stylish. Typical West End really.

# Acknowledgements

Once again I must declare an immense debt to my agent Faith Evans and editor Margaret Bluman, without whom this book would have been impossible and who were always at hand with advice and encouragement. John Nicholson, as ever, provided me with the most remarkable sources and suggestions. Without Katy Walsh Glinert journeys from Montagu Square to Cambridge Circus, and from Old Park Lane to Fitzroy Square (via Spanish Place and Goslett Yard), wouldn't have been so enjoyable. Many thanks also to Marian Walsh and Martin Rose.

I would like to thank a number of people for all their ideas and guidance: Richard Aron, Clive Bettington, John Breslin, Celia Boggis, Rosie Glaisher, Peter Golds, Mark Gorman, David Grant, Fiona Hayes, Gill King, Cormach Moore, Martin Morris, Anne Orsi, Tim Richard, Sarah Shannon, David Stone, Lucie Sutherland, and the staff of the London Library and Westminster Archives.

# Bibliography

Allfrey, Anthony, *Edward VII and his Jewish Circle*, Weidenfeld & Nicolson, London, 1991.

Bacon, Tony, *London Live*, Balafon, London, 1999.

Barrow, Andrew, *Gossip: A History of High Society from 1920–1970*, Hamish Hamilton, London, 1978.

Bearse, Ray and Read, Anthony, *Conspirator: The Untold Story of Churchill, Roosevelt & Tyler Kent*, Macmillan, London, 1991.

Beckson, Karl, *London in the 1990s: A Cultural History*, W. W. Norton & co, NY, London, 1992.

Berkeley, Roy, *A Spy's London*, Leo Cooper, London, 1994.

Binney, Marcus, *The Women Who Lived for Danger: The Women Agents of the SOE in the Second World War*, Hodder & Stoughton, London, 2002.

Bloom, Clive, *Violent London: 2,000 Years of Riots, Rebels and Revolts*, Sidgwick & Jackson, 2003.

Borer, Mary Cathcart, *Mayfair: The Years of Grandeur*, W. H. Allen, London, 1975.

Brooker, Peter, *Bohemia in London: The Social Scene of Early Modernism*, Macmillan, 2004.

Bryan, Cyril, *Roundabout Harley Street: The Story of Some Famous Streets*, John Bale, London, 1932.

Cartland, Barbara, *We Danced All Night*, Hutchinson, London, 1970.

Clarkson, Wensley, *Hit 'Em Hard: Jack Spot, King of the Underworld*, HarperCollins, London, 2002.

Cook, Andrew, *M: MI5's First Spymaster*, Tempus, Stroud, Gloucestershire, 2004.

Ellman, Richard, *Oscar Wilde*, Hamish Hamilton, London, 1987.

Farson, Daniel, *Soho In The Fifties*, Pimlico, London, 1987.

Fiegel, Eddi, *John Barry: A sixties Theme*, Constable, London, 1998.

Foot, M. R. D. *SOE: An outline History of the Special Operations Executive 1940–46*, BBC, London, 1984.

Fordham, John, *Let's Join Hands and Contact the Living*, Elm Tree, London, 1986.

Gillman, Peter and Leni, *Collar the Lot!: How Britain Interned and Expelled Its Wartime Refugees*, Quartet, London, 1980.

Godbolt, Jim, *A History of Jazz in Britain 1919–50*, Quartet, London, 1984.

Green, Jonathan, *All Dressed Up*, Pimlico, London, 1999.

Gilbert, R. A. *The Golden Dawn: Twilight of the Magicians,* The Aquarius Press, Wellingborough, 1983.

Hay, Douglas and others, *Albion's Fatal Tree: Crime and Society in Eighteenth-Century England*, Allen Lane, London, 1975.

Helm, Sarah, *A Life in Secrets: The Story of Vera Atkins and the Lost Agents of the SOE*, Little, Brown, London, 2005.

Hill, Billy, *Boss of Britain's Underworld*, Naldrett, London, 1955.

Hobhouse, Hermione, *A History of Regent Street*, Macdonald and Jane, London, 1975.

Houlbrook, Matt, *Queer London*, University of Chicago Press, Chicago, 2005.

Jones, Steve, *London Through the Keyhole*, Wicked Publications, Nottingham, 1991.

Kennedy, Carol, *Mayfair: A Social History*, Hutchinson, London, 1986.

Kohn, Marek, *Dope Girls: the birth of the British drug underground*, Granta, London, 1992.

Linnane, Fergus, *London The Wicked City: A Thousand Years of Vice in the Capital*, Robson, London, 2003.

Linnane, Fergus, *London's Underworld: Three Centuries of Vice and Crime*, Robson Books, London, 2003.

Mackenzie, Gordon, *Marylebone: Great City North of Oxford Street*, Macmillan, London, 1972.

Marriott, Oliver, *The Property Boom*, Hamish Hamilton, London, 1967.

Masters, Brian, *Great Hostesses*, Constable, London, 1982.

McDevitt, Chas, *Skiffle: The Definitive Inside Story*, Robson, London, 1997.

Mellor, David, *The Sixties Art Scene in London*, Phaidon, London, 1993.

Melly, George, *Owning Up*, Weidenfeld and Nicholson, London, 1965.

Miles, Barry, *In the Sixties*, Jonathan Cape, London, 2002.

Moraes, Henrietta, *Henrietta*, Hamish Hamilton, London, 1994.

Morgan, Ted, *Somerset Maugham*, Jonathan Cape, London, 1980.

Norman, Frank, *Norman's London*, Secker & Warburg, London, 1969.

Pearce, David, *London's Mansions: The Palatial Houses of the Nobility*, Batsford, London, 1986.

Pearson, John, *The Profession of Violence*, Weidenfeld and Nicholson, London, 1972.

Pentelow, Mike and Rowe, Marsha, *Characters of Fitzrovia*, Chatto and Windus, London, 2001.

Platt, John, *London's Rock Routes*, Fourth Estate, London, 1985.

Remy, Michel, *Surrealism in Britain*, Ashgate, Aldershot, 1999.

Richardson, Nigel, *Dog Days in Soho: One Man's Adventures in Fifties Bohemia*, Victor Gollancz, London, 2000.

Spalding, Frances, *British Art Since 1900*, Thames & Hudson, London, 1986.

Summers, Judith, *Soho: A History of London's Most Colourful Neighbourhood*, Bloomsbury, London, 1989.

Summerson, John, *Georgian London*, Pleiades Books, London, 1945.

Symonds, John, *The Great Beast: The Life and Magick of Aleister Crowley*, Macdonald, London, 1971.

Tames, Richard, *Soho Past*, Historical Publications, London, 1994.

Thomas, Donald, *An Underworld At War*, John Murray, London, 2003.

Thomas, Donald, *Villains' Paradise*, John Murray, London, 2005.

Vansittart, Peter, *In the Fifties*, John Murray, London, 1995.

Walker, John A., *Provocation, Controversy and the Visual Arts*, Pluto Press, London, Sterling Virginia, 1999.

Wedd, Kitty, with Peltz, Lucy and Ross, Cathy, *Artists' London: Holbein to Hirst*, Merrell, London, 2001.

Wheatcroft, Geoffrey, *The Randlords*, Weidenfeld and Nicolson, London, 1985.

Wheen, Francis, *Karl Marx*, Fourth Estate, London, 1999.

Willetts, Paul, *Fear and Loathing in Fitzrovia: the Bizarre Life of Writer, Actor, Soho Dandy, Julian Maclaren-Ross*, Dewi Lewis Publishing, 2003.

Ziegler, Philip, *London At War 1939–45*, Sinclair Stevenson, London, 1995.

# Index

*A Hard Day's Night* (film) 14
Abberline, Inspector Frederick 105
Abbey Road recording studio 271
Abel-Smith, Tim 55
Accum, Friedrich 50–51
Ackroyd, Peter 89, 126, 127
Ad-Lib, the 270
Adam, Robert 8, 35, 37, 41
Adam Brothers 35
Adler, Alfred 98
Adulteration of Food Acts (1860) 51
Aesthetes, the 148–50
Aesthetic Movement 131, 132
African-Americans 179
Agnew, Morland 195
Agnew, William 195
Agnew's gallery 194
Ailesbury House 6
Albanian warlords 217
Albany 44–5, 107
Albemarle Club 107, 247
Albemarle Street 49
Albert Victor Christian Edward, Duke
        of Clarence 106
Albion Hotel 120
Aldford House 16
Alex Harvey Soul Band, the 271
Alexander II, Tsar 75
Alexandra, Queen 106
Alhambra Music Hall 115

Alhambra theatre 243–4
Ali, Tariq 86
All Saints church 96
All Souls church 47
Almack's club 11
alternative comedy 280–281
Alvanley, Lord 8
American Embassy 40, 55, 87
Amies, Hardy 168, 232
AMM 272
anarchists 73–7, 77–8, 82
Anders, Inge 181
Anderson, Robert 72–3
Andrews, Rev Basil 204, 205
Anello and Davide's 234
Anglers' Club 80
Angry Brigade, the 40
Animals, the 270
Anne, Queen 7
Anson Road, Tufnell Park 171
anti-Semitism 16, 183
Antients, the 127
Apollo public house 71
Apollo theatre 246
Apple Corps 236–7
Apple Electronics 236–7
Applebe, Ambrose 29
Apsley House 8, 9
*Arandora Star* (ship) 140, 175
Archer, Jeffrey 120–122

Archer, Thomas 36
Archer Street 254, 273
architecture, Regency 45
Argyll, Ethel Margaret Whigham,
    Duchess of 118
Argyll, Margaret Sweeny, Duchess of
    30
Ark, the 28
Arlen, Michael 41, 248
Arlington, Lord 11
Armstrong, Eliza 103–104
Armstrong-Jones, Anthony, Lord
    Snowdon 45
Armstrong, Louis 252, 255
Asher, Jane 238
Asprey's jewellers 22, 43
Asquith, Cynthia 24
Asscher, Abraham 15
Asscher Brothers 15
Astaire, Fred 232, 249
Astor, Lady 180
Astor Club, the 209
Atkins, Fred 108
Atkins, Vera 166–7
Atlee, Clement 182
atomic structure 51
ATV House 271
Au Chat Noir 115–16, 227
Audley Square 186
Autonomie anarchist club 76

Bach, Johann Christian 42
Bacon, Francis (artist) xii, 141–3,
    221, 224, 228, 229, 230–231
    *Three studies for Figures at the Base
    of a Crucifixion* 141–2
Bacon, Francis (philosopher) 91, 94
Bag O'Nails club 252, 270, 274
Bailey, David 238, 266
Baird, John Logie 51–3
Baker, Ginger 268

Baker, Robert 43
Baker, Terence 121
Baker Street 164–7, 236
Bakerloo Line, the 22
Baldwin, Betty 181
Ballads and Blues Club 276
Bankhead, Tallulah 23, 250
Bar Italia coffee bar 219, 227
Barber, Chris 254, 257
Barber's West End Gigs 257
Bardot, Brigitte 266
Barnato, Barney 14, 17, 58
Barnato Joel, Jack 20
Barrett, Syd xii, 153, 273
Barry, John 228
Barthelemy, Emanuel 72
Bastard Arms public house 153
Bateman Street 229
Bath, Dowager Marchioness of 130
Bathurst, Earl of 19
Battola, Jean 75
Bauer, Edgar 71
Bauhaus, the 58
Bavarian Chapel, the 61
Bayswater x, xi
BBC 82–3, 167, 182–3, 254, 264
Beach Boys 98
Beach, Thomas Miller 73
Beak Street 33, 114, 234
Beardsley, Aubrey 149, 150, 215
beat clubs 269–70
*beat Girl* (film) 228
Beatles, the 14, 86, 153, 236–7,
    238–9, 269
Beaverbrook, Lord 171
Bechet, Sidney 252
Becker, Boris 29
Bedford Park 132
Beecham, Lady 26
Beer House, the (now the Newman
    Arms) 83, 158, 159

Beerbohm, Max 150
Behan, Brendan 224, 230
Beit, Alfred 14, 15–17
Belafonte, Harry 262
Belcher, Muriel 228–9
Belgravia 4
Bell, Graham 140
Benn, Tony 224
Bennett, Arnold 45
Bentinck Street 172–3
Berkeley, Roy 184
Berkeley House/Devonshire House
    6–7, 22, 25–26, 41
Berkeley of Stratton, Lord 6, 40–41
Berkeley Square 11, 39, 40–42, 163,
    177
Berlemont, Gaston 231
Berlemont, Victor 220, 230
Bernard, Jeffrey 221, 223, 229
Berners Street 146
Bernsdorff, Count 34
Bertorelli's restaurant 162, 226
Berwick Street 109, 176, 222, 230
Bethell, Richard 97
Betjeman, John 160
Big Apple night club 247
Bingley, Lord 36
Birkenhead, Lord 28
Black, Cilla 233
*Black Dwarf* 86
Black Horse public house 71
Black Horse public house, Rathbone
    Place 158, 276
blackmail 111
Blake, James 89
Blake, William xi, 63, 89–90, 101,
    123, 125–8
    *The Marriage of Heaven and Hell*
    89–90
    'Songs of Innocence' 127
    'Tyger' 126, 127

Bland, Florence 37
Blandford, Lord 30
Blarney Club, the 274
*Blast* (magazine) 136
Blau, Rose 175
Blind Beggar public house,
    Whitechapel 209
Bloomsbury x, ix
Bloomsbury group, the 138
Bloomsbury Way 84
blue film racket 113
Blue Gardenia beat club 269
Blue Posts public house 71
Blue Stocking Society 37
Blues Club 153
Blues Incorporated 268–9
Blunt, Anthony 172–3, 184
Blunt, Wilfred 134
Board, Ian 229
Bodington, Nicholas 165
Boer War 16
Bohemian Soho 144
Bolingbroke, Henry St John, Viscount
    33
Bomberg, David 137
Bond Thomas 43
Bond Street 39, 43, 285
Bond Street Stroll, the 43
BOSS, South African security service
    208
Boswell, James 109, 123, 190
    *Life of Johnson* 10
bouncers 248, 255
Bourdin, Martial 76–7
Bourdon House 29
Bow 39
Bowie, David 229, 280
Bowler, Norman 222, 223
Boy George 280
Boyd, Joe 274
Boyle, David 170

Bracken, Brendan 84
Bradshaw, George 210
Bradshawe, John 192
Braine, John 228–9
Braun, Sigismund von 118
Brewer Street 33, 101
Britannia Hotel 55
British Library 140, 147, 188
Broad(wick) Street 33, 89, 125, 127, 175, 229, 288–9
Brompton Oratory church 186
Brook House 15, 27
Brook Street 177
Brooke, Henry 58, 266, 270
Brothers, Richard 90–91, 93
Brown, Arnold 280
Brown, Arthur 274
Brown, Ford Madox 35
Brown, Louis 262
Brown, Peter 86
Brownell, Sonia 84
Bruce, Jack 268
Bruce, Lenny 266
Brummel, Beau 8, 231
Brüning, Heinrich 29
Bruno, Angelo 207
Brunt, John 65
Bruton Street 23, 141
Bryan, Harry 198
Bryanston Street 257
BT Tower 147, 186, 187–8, 188
Buckmaster, Maurice 166
Building Act (1774) 37
Burchill, Julie 240
Burgess, Anthony 158–9
Burgess, Guy 172–3, 184
Burgess, Lynne 158–9
Burke, Thomas 115
Burlington, first Duke of 44, 124
Burlington, third Earl of 44
Burlington Gardens 23, 139

Burlington House 44, 124, 232
Burne-Jones, Edward 132
Burney, Fanny 37, 123
Burns, John 76
Burroughs, William S. 146, 228
Burrows, Anne 127
Burt, the Reverend Robert 8
Burton, Decimus 46
Burton, James 46
Burton, Richard 263
Butterfield, William 96
Butts, Thomas 126–7
Byng, Admiral John 41
Byron, Lord George Gordon 45, 231
    Don Juan 12, 92

Cadogan Hotel 108
Café de l'Europe 254
Café de Paris 181, 249–50
Café Royal 107, 115, 150, 247
Cage, John 272
Caine, Michael 238, 266
Calais 124–5
Calder, Liz 240
Callil, Carmen 240
Cambridge Circus 234
Camden Town Group, the 134
Camisa delicatessen 175–6, 220
Campbell, Colen 44
Canaletto (Giovanni Antonio Canal) 33
cannabis 152
Canonbury Tower 56, 91, 94
Canons 36
Cantlie, James 79, 80
Cape Colony 16
Cardew, Cornelius 272
Cartland, Barbara 25
Carleton, Billie 151
Carlisle, second Earl of 32
Carlisle House 32, 100

Carlisle Street 86
Carlton Club 175
Carlton House 46
Carlyle, Thomas 127
Carnaby Street 1, 233–6, 255
Carnarvon, Lord 97
Carol, King of Romania 249
Caroline of Brunswick, Princess 102
Carow, Edith 43
Carpenter House 3
Carre, Mathilde Lucie 177
Carter, Howard 97
Carthy, Martin 275–6, 276
Carvalho, Don Sebastian Joseph de 34
Casanova, Giovanni Giacomo 32, 100
Casement, Roger 115
Casey, William 176
Cassel, Ernest 15–16, 27
Castanar, Juan Antonio 196
Castle, Barbara 224
Castlereagh, Lord 64–5
Catherine of Braganza 43
Cato Street Conspirators 40, 54, 55, 64–5
Cave of the Golden Calf, the 136, 248–9
Cavendish, Lady Dorothy 23
Cavendish Square 36, 48
Cecil Gee 234, 234–5, 255
Central Line, the 15, 49
Centrepoint 186, 186–7, 188
Challenor, Detective Sergeant Harry 214–15
Challoner, Bishop Richard 61
Chamberlain, Austen 24
Chambers, William 44
Chandler, Chas 270, 274
Chandos, Duke of 36
Chang, Brilliant 151–2

Channon, Chips 23
Chaplin, Charlie 26
Charing Cross, xi, 123
Charing Cross Road x, xi, 117, 166, 174, 188, 234, 276
Charles I, King 192
Charles II, King 5, 32
Charles Street 3, 24
Charlotte Street x
    anarchist activity 75, 77–8
    Anti-Apartheid offices 208
    artists based on 129, 155
    brothels 101
    the Jay's job 199–200
    Russian Social Democrats meeting 80–81
    Schmidt's restaurant 184, 226
    the Wednesday Club 162, 226
Chartists, the 65–6, 68–9
Chatsworth House 22
Chaudoir, Elvira 170–171
Chesterfield House 3, 21
Chesterfield Street 3, 21, 22
Cheyne Walk 222
Chez Nous 181
child prostitution 103–4, 110
Chiltern Court 166
Chinatown xi, 218, 289
Chinese Legation 78–80
Chippendale, Thomas 7
Chiswick 125
Churchill, Peter 169
Churchill, Lord Randolph 19
Churchill, Winston 27, 28, 164, 168, 173, 174, 179, 185, 201, 244
Cibber, Caius Gabriel 32
cinemas 1, 113, 244, 246, 289
Ciro's nightclub 247
City Centre Properties 57
civil defence 188
Clapton, Eric 234–5, 272, 274

Clarence, Duke of. *see* Albert Victor Christian Edward, Duke of Clarence
Clarendon, Edward Hyde, Earl of 6
Clarendon House 6
Claridge's Hotel 3, 81, 174, 177, 185
Clark, Alan 45
Clark, Thomas 48
Clarke, Edward 243
Clerkenwell House of Detention 72
Clerkenwell Road 205
Cleveland Street 105–6, 129
Cleverdon, Douglas 230
Clifford Chambers, 10 New Bond Street 184
clip joints 112–13
Clipstone Street 95, 153
Clive, Robert (of India) 41
Clore, Charles 55–6
The Club 10
Club 11 255–6
Club Cooperativo 173
Coach and Horse public house 223, 230
Coates, Wells 138
cocaine 151–2, 240, 247
Cochis, F. V. 174
Cock Tavern 63
Cockerell, Charles 46
coffee bars 219, 226–8, 285
Cold War, the 184–8
Coldstream, William 140
Cole, Superintendent 110
Coleridge, Samuel Taylor 144, 146
Collins, Michael 27–8
Collins, Norman, *London Belongs To Me* 29
Colman Hedge Lane 32
Colony Club 142, 209, 228–9, 229
Colyer, Ken 253
comedy store, the 280–281

Comer, Jack. *see* Spot, Jack, aka Benny the Kid
Communism 66–72, 74, 80–81, 85
Communist Club, the 81
Communist League, the 66–7, 69, 71
Connaught, the 3
Connolly, Cyril 156
Conrad, Joseph 137, 144, 250
    *Heart of Darkness* 16
    *The Secret Agent* 76–7, 101
Conservative Party 122
Continental Café 81
Cook, Peter 206, 265
Cooper, Diana 180
Cooper, Tommy 264–5
Copeland, David 217
Corbett, Ronnie 266
Cork Street 3, 138, 141
Cornell, George 209
Cornelys, Teresa 32, 100
Corrigan, Laura 20, 30
Corrigan-McKinney Steel Company 20
Cotton, Jack 56, 57–8
Coughlin, Monica 120–121
Coulon, Auguste 75
Covent Garden xi, 31, 108–9, 123
Covent Garden Opera House 244
Coventry Street 115
Coward, Noël 266
    *Private Lives* 29
Cranley Gardens 117–18
Crazy Gang, the 262–3
Cream 153, 272
Cream, Dr Neill 109
Crewe House 23, 39, 163–4
crime 189–218
Crimean War (1853–56) 38, 43
Criminal Law Amendment Act (1885) 104, 105, 107
Crisp, Quentin 115–16, 227, 289
Criterion Bar 194–5

Crompton Cinema Club 113
Cromwell, Oliver 60, 192
Crook, Annie Elizabeth 106
Crosby, Bing 232
Crosby, John 235
Cross, John 42
Cross Picture Company 52
Crowder, Sir Peter, QC 206
Crowley, Aleister xi, 95–6, 98, 155, 156, 221, 247
Crown and Two Chairmen public house 229
Crown Jewels, the 15
Cullinan, Thomas 14
Cullinan I, Star of Africa 14–15
Cumberland Hotel 202–3
Cunard, Lady Emerald 180
Cunard, Lady Maud 23, 30
Curry, Jack 171
Curzon, Sir Nathaniel 39
Curzon Cinema, Shaftesbury Avenue 1
Curzon Soho cinema 289
Curzon Street 13, 39, 42, 171, 185–6, 211
Curzon Street House 171, 186
Cyprus 216

D. H. Evans 48
Dadd, Richard 129
Daily Herald 22
Daily Mirror 58, 174, 214
Daily Star 121, 122
Daily Telegraph 82, 164–5, 181
Daily Telegraph Magazine 235
Dali, Salvador 139
Dalton's night club 250
Daltrey, Roger 271
Daly's 115
Daunt's book shop 288
David Archer's bookshop 86, 222
Davidson, William 64–5

Davies, Cyril 268
Davies, Nigel 238
Davy, Humphrey 49–50, 51
Dawson, Peter 53
de Antiquis, Alex 200
De Beers 16, 178
de Gaulle, Charles 170, 180, 229, 230
De Hems public house 229, 230
de Quincey, Thomas 144–6
Confessions of An English Opium-Eater 145–6
de Valera, Eamon 170
de Walden, Howard 2, 48
Deakin, Joe 75
Deakin, John 224
Dean Street 32, 70
  coffee bars 227
  the Colony Club see Colony Club
  the French House see French House, the
  the Groucho Club 70, 202, 240–241
  Quo Vadis restaurant 175, 225, 282
  public houses 229, 230
  the Royalty Theatre 244–5
Debenham, William 48
Debenhams's 48
Defence of the Realm Act 150, 246
Defoe, Daniel 35–6, 39–40
Delfont, Lord 246
Denham, Sir John 44
Denis (criminal) 209
Denman Street 225, 250
Denning, Lord 118
D'Eon, Charles 100–101
Derrick, Samuel 109
Deschamps, Marie Claire 33
Devonshire, William Cavendish, second Duke of 7

Devonshire, William Cavendish, fifth
     Duke of 7
Devonshire, Edward William Spencer
     Cavendish, tenth Duke of 22,
     25
Devonshire House 6–7, 22, 25, 41
Devonshire Street 79
diamond market, the 14–19, 177–8
Diana, Princess of Wales 7
Dickens, Charles 37, 131
     *Nicholas Nickleby* 34
Dickins and Jones 286
Dietrich, Marlene 26
Dimes, Albert 203, 203–4, 205, 211
Dine, Jim 215
discotheques 262
discount stores 286
disembowelment 191, 193
Disraeli, Benjamin 2, 13, 38
dissectors 192, 193
Distleman, Harry 'Scarface' 196
Dobell's record shop 276
Dodd, Dr 192
Dog and Duck public house 229
Domesday Book 35
Donegan, Lonnie 257–8
Donovan 276
Donovan, Terence 237
Donworth, Ellen 109
Dorchester Hotel, the 3, 26–7, 177,
     180, 201
Dorchester House 26
Doré Galleries 136
Dorset Square 166
Dostoevsky, Fydor 109
Douglas, Lord Alfred 107
Douglas, Mammy 189
Douglas, William, fourth Duke of
     Queensbury 10
Douglas-Home, Alec 239
Dover Street 100, 140

Downbeat Club 256
Doyle, Arthur Conan 147–148, 194
D'Oyly Carte, Richard 245
D'Oyly Carte, Rupert 174
Driberg, Tom 153, 225
Drifters, the 259–60
Drinkwater, John 24
Druce, Mrs 36
Druce, Thomas 36
drugs 41, 145–6, 150–53, 240, 247,
     255, 270, 273
Drumlanrig, Viscount 107
Drummond, Malcolm 133
Drury, Commander Ken 216
Dudley, Earl of 14
Dudley House 14, 18
Duell, William 192
Duff Gordon, Sir Cosmo 231–2
Duke of York public house 158–9
Duke Street 170, 215
Dylan, Bob 275

East End, the 31, 287
Eastcastle Street Job, the 200–201
Eddie & the Hot Rods 278
Eddy, Prince. *see* Albert Victor
     Christian Edward, Duke of
     Clarence
Ede, Chuter 212
Eden, Anthony 178–9
Edgecombe, Johnny 119
Edward VII, King 15, 20
Edward VIII, King 9, 24, 25, 248,
     249–50
Edwards, George 64–5
Edwards, John 143
Edward's Hotel 109
Egg, Augustus 129
Eisenhower, General Dwight D. 177
El Morocco club 171–2, 207
Elephant Gang, the 197

Elgin Marbles, the 44, 45
Eliot, George 42
Eliot, T. S. 161–2, 226
Elizabeth I, Queen 32
Elizabeth II, Queen 49
Elizabeth, Queen of Bohemia 6
Elizabeth, the Queen Mother 8–9, 24
Elizabeth, Tsarina 100
Elmes, James 47
Elms, Robert 240
Elton, Ben 240
Embassy night club 247–8
Emin, Tracy 228
*Empire* (magazine) 150, 151
*Empire News* 151
Empire Theatre 244
Engels, Friedrich 66–7, 70
  *Condition of the Working Class in*
    *England in 1844* 66
  *The Manifesto of the Communist*
    *Party* 67–8
English, Michael 235
English, Piers 160
English Revolutionary Society, the 74
Eon Productions 186
Epicerie Francaise, the 77–8
Epstein, Brian 269
Epstein, Jacob 248, 250
Erdman, Edward 56–7
Ermakova, Angela 29
Establishment Club, the 265–7
Establishment for Gentlewomen
    During Illness 38
Etchells, Frederick 135
Etchingham, Kathy 274
Euston, Earl of 35, 106
Euston Arch 56
Euston Road x, 35, 140
Euston Road School, the 139–40
Euston Square station 188
Euston station 56

Euston Tower 186, 187, 188
Evans, Chris 240
Evans, Dan Harries 48
Eve Club, the 266–7
Evelyn, John 6, 6–7
*Evening News* 74
Express Dairy Company 84
*Expresso Bongo* (film) 26, 261

Fabian, Superintendent Robert 200
Fabrizi, Mario 255–6
Fair Trade League 76
Fairbanks, Douglas, Jnr. 118
Fairport Convention 276
Faith, Adam 228, 260–261
Faithfull, Marianne 222, 225
Fame, Georgie 269–70
Faraday, Michael 51
Farm Street 23
Farren, Mick 87, 273
Farringdon Road 93
Farson, Daniel 221, 223
Fascism 173–6
fashion industry 231–7
Fenians 72–3, 76
Ferguson, Lady Sarah, Duchess of York
    7
Fetter Lane 101
Firm, The 132
First International, the 72
First World War
    drug abuse 150
    music halls 243
    propaganda operations 163–4
    prostitution during 110
    Somerset Maugham's service 22
    Vorticists and 137–8
Fitzgibbon, Constantine 156
Fitzherbert, Maria 8
Fitzrovia ix, 1
    anarchist club 76

artists in 133
George Orwell's 82–4, 96–7
obscurity 162
origin of name x, 153–4
*Peeping Tom* (film) 114
Scientologists 98
Stalin visits 81
style 2
Fitzroy, Henry 35
Fitzroy Coffee House 153
Fitzroy Square 1, 35, 75, 136
Fitzroy Street 94, 98, 133, 140, 154
Fitzroy Street Group, the 133–4
Fitzroy Tavern x, 116, 153–8
Five Fields, the 4
Flamingo beat club 269–70
Fleming, Ian 177
Florence Restaurant 135
Foley House 47
Foley Street 275
Folies-Bergere night club 250
folk music 275–7
food 50–51, 283–4
Foot, Michael 224
Foot, Paul 225
Ford, Anna 240
Ford, Ford Madox 137
43 Club 97, 250, 251
Forty Four Club 181
Foster, Lady Elizabeth 7
Fountain Court 127
Fox, Charles James 7, 11
Fox and Hounds public house 71
Foy, Jim 269
Foyle, William 26
Foyle's 26, 74
France 124–5, 168–9
Francis, Ted 121–2
Francophilia 147
Fraser, Frankie 204–5, 209

Frederick, Duke of York and Albany 45
Frederick, Emperor of Germany 38
Frederick, Prince 6
Free Exhibition of Modern Art 130
*Freiheit* 75–6
French House, the 110, 220, 221, 230, 230–231
French, John 238
French Revolution 62
Frenkel, Erwin 176
Freud, Lucian 230–231
Frith, W. P. 129
Frith Street 32, 51, 53, 112, 219, 225–6, 226–7, 227
Fry, Benjamin 240–241
Fry, Roger 134–5, 136
Fryer, Jonathan 161
Futurists, the 135

Gainsborough, Thomas 16, 194–5
*Blue Boy* 18, 29
Galahad Club, the 203, 228
Gallagher, Liam 240
Galliano, John 232
Galsworthy, John, *In Chancery* 159
Galton, Ray 264
gambling 11, 181, 266
Graham-Murray, James 158
Garfield, John, *The Wand'ring Whore* 108
Gargoyle night club 249, 280–281
Garland, Judy 26
Garrick, David 10
gas lights 40, 50
Gaslight Club 274
Gaudier-Brzeska, Henri 155
Gaughan, Dick 276
Gay Hussar, the 220, 224–5, 282
Gaynor, Rusty 216–17
Gear 234, 235

Geneva International Convention on Narcotics Control 152
George I, King 6, 33, 42
George II, King 6
George III, King 7–8
George IV, King xi, 7–8, 8, 11, 43, 45
George V, King 248
George VI, King 8–9
Georgian Group, the 35
Gerald, Queenie 110
Gerald Street 10
German Crown Jewels 19
German Hotel, the 70
Gerrard Street 62, 172, 181, 212, 218, 247, 281
ghosts 41
Gibbon, Edward 38
Gielgud theatre 246
Gieves and Hawkes 233
Gilbert, W. S. 131, 133, 148–9, 244–5
Gilby, Sir John 26
Gilchrist, Alexander 127
Giles, John 127
Gill, Eric 134–5, 248
Gillingham Street 120
Gilman, Harold 133
Ginner, Charles 133–4
Gladstone, William 37, 150
Glendower, Pamela 161
Glorious Revolution, the 60
Gloucester Place 168, 173
Godwin, E. W. 131
Goering, Herman 20, 27
Goings-On Club 273
Golden Ball, sign of the 123
Golden Head, sign of the 124
Golden Lion public house, Dean Street 117, 230
Golden Square 33–4, 46, 161, 250

Goldsmith, Oliver 123
Goldstein, Morris, aka Moishe Blueball 202, 204, 205
Goodge Street 192
Goodge Street station 177
Goodman, Lord 215
Goodman, Benny 253
Gordon, Lord George 60–62
Gordon Hotels 26
Gordon Riots, the 9, 34, 40, 60–62, 192
Gordon Thomas estate agents 56
Gore, Spencer 133, 133–4, 248
Goslett Yard 210
Gosling, John, *The Shame of A City* 112
Gossip's night club 280
Gouldman, Graham 272
Gower Street 186, 188
Grafton, first Duke of 35
Grafton, Charles Fitzroy, second Duke of 35
Grafton, Augustus Fitzroy, third Duke of 40
Grafton Galleries nightclub 247
Grafton Gallery, the 134–5
Grafton Way 63
Graham, Kenny 256
Grand Central Hotel 172
Grand Jury of Westminster 39
Grandi, Signor 174
Grant, Cary 232
Granville, Christina 168, 169–70
Gray, Eddie 262–3
Great Fire of London (1666) 31, 32
Great Marlborough Street 262
Great Ormond Street 136
Great Pulteney Street 230
Great Windmill Street 67, 69–70, 74, 112, 255

Greco, Buddy 253
Greek Street
    boutiques 234, 235
    The Club 10
    De Quincy lives on 145
    and drugs 153
    the Establishment Club 265–7
    fascist activity 173–4
    origin 32
    restaurants and public houses 220,
        222, 223, 230, 277
Greeks 33
Green, Bill 233–4
Green Pamela 113
Green, William Curtis 26
Green Park xi, 25
Green Street (now Orange Street) 29,
    126
Greene, Graham 45, 160
    Brighton Rock 195–6
    Our Man in Havana 156
Greeno, Ted 195
Greenwood, Anthony 205
Greenwood, James 109–10
Greville, Edmond T. 182
Greville, the Hon Ronald 24
Greville, Ronnie 24–25, 180
Gropius, Walter 58
Grosvenor, Sir Richard 39–40
Grosvenor Estate 39–40
Grosvenor Gallery, the 132–3, 148
Grosvenor House 18–19, 22, 29
Grosvenor House Hotel 19, 29, 180
Grosvenor Square 19, 20, 23, 30, 39,
    40, 54–5, 87, 177
Grosvenor Street 20–21, 176, 208
Groucho Club, the 70, 202, 240–241
Gunter's tea rooms 41

Hague, William 122
Haile Selassie 26

hairdressers 237–8
Haley, Bill 258–9
Halifax, Lord 27
Hambro, Sir Charles 165
Hamelford, J. E. 53
Hamilton Place 14
Hammerson 18
Hamnett, Nina xi, 155–6, 221, 229
Hampden House 30
Hanway Street 71
Hancock, Tony xii, 264
    The Rebel 227
Handel, George Frederick 44
hangings, spectacle of 189–93
Hanover Gallery 142
Hanover Square 31, 39, 42, 231–2
Hanover Square Concert Rooms 42
Hanover Street 56
Harcourt House 36
Hardie, Keir 74
Harewood, Lord 49
Harley Street ix, 2, 37–8, 73, 128,
    238
Harmony Inn Café 254
Harris, Bob 54
Harris, Harry 54
Harris, Jack 109
Harris, Louisa 109
Harris Brothers, the 53, 54
Harrison, Laurence 25
Harris's List of Covent Garden Ladies
    108–9
Harry Roy's Band 181
Hart, John 53
Hartnell, Norman 23
Haydn, Joseph 42
Hayes, Tubby 252
Haymarket 39, 109, 110
Hay's Mews 177
Heaven and Hell 258
Heddon Street 248

Helm, Sarah 167
Hemingway, Ernest 180
Hemmings and Co 198
Henderson, Laura 114
Henderson, Nigel 140
Hendrix, Jimi 153, 271, 274–5
Henesy, Dr Florence 189
Heppenstall, Rayner, *The Lesser
    Infortune* 157
Hermitic Order of the Golden Dawn
    xi, 94–6, 98
Hertford, Marquess of 20
Hertford Street 39, 170–71
Hibernia Stores 147
Hicks, Tommy 259
Hide Park Road 43
Hideaway, the 206–7
High Holborn 192
Hill, Aggie 199
Hill, Benny 263
Hill, Billy 111, 197–205
    *Boss of Britain's Underworld* 202,
    213
Hilton Hotel 28, 56
Hippodrome Theatre 251
Hirohito, Emperor 154
Hirst, Damien 225, 228, 240
His Clothes 234, 235
Hitler, Adolf 24, 28, 138, 183
Hitler, Alois 81, 138
Hoare, Phillip 150
Hogarth, William 123, 123–5
    *Gin Lane* 32
    *Industry and Idleness*, Plate II
        190
    *Masquerades and Operas: The
        Taste of the Town* 44, 124
    *O The Roast beef of Old England
        (The Gate of Calais)* 125
    *The Rake's Progress* 124
Hogg, Thomas 146

Hohenlohe, Princess Stephanie
    Julianne von 27
Holborn xi
Holles Street 48
Holliday, Billie 255, 256
Holmes, Sherlock 148
Home House 37
homosexuality 115–18, 159, 233–4,
    289
*Horizon* (magazine) 156
Horseshoe public house 71
Hotel Provence 150
House of Fraser 48
House of Nutter 233
Household, Geoffrey 164
Howard of Effingham, Lord 251
Howland Street 147
Huguenots 33
Hulme, T. E. 137, 138
Humphrey Lyttelton's Band 254
Humphreys, Jimmy 216–17
Humph's jazz club 256
Hundred Marks public house 153
Hung On You boutique 274
Hungary 169
Hunt, Leigh 45
Hunt, William Homan 129–31
Hunter, John 192
Huntington, Clara, Princess 20
Husband, Tony 240
Hussein, Hasib 76
Huxley, Aldous 45
    *Chrome Yellow* 154
    *The Doors of Perception* 152
Hyams, Harry 187
Hyde Park x
Hyde Park Corner 12–14, 110
Hyde Park Mansions 204

IBC recording studios 272
Ifield, Frank 234

illegal immigrants 1–2, 218
*Illustrated Book of Sexual Records, The* 113
immigrants 1–2, 33, 74, 218
Incredible String Band, the 277
Independent Group, the 140
Ings, James 64–5
INLA (Irish National Liberation Army) 172
Institute of Contemporary Art (ICA) 140–141, 142
Inter Service Research Bureau 165
International Club, the 74
International Surrealist Exhibition 139
International Workingmen's Association 72
internment 173–6
Intrepid Fox public house 230
IRA (Irish Republican Army) 73
Ireton, Henry 192
Isherwood, Christopher 162, 226
Italian Club 174
Italian community 173–6, 196
Italian Fascist Party 173–4
Italian public house 71
Ivanov, Yevgeny 118, 119, 120
Ivor Court 168

'Jack the Ripper' 94, 106, 134
Jack the Stripper 210
Jackson, Holbrook, *The Eighteen Nineties* 149
Jackson, Jack 254–5
Jacobites, the 33
Jaeger, Hans 171–2
Jagger, Mick 225, 268–9, 280
James, Henry, *The Princess Casamassima* 73
James II, King 5
James, John 42
James, Sid 264

Jameson Raid, the 16
Jansch, Bert 276–7
Japanese Embassy 20
Jay's job, the 199–200
jazz 249, 251–6, 268, 272, 281
Jefferies, Anne 36
Jekyll and Hyde Alley 114
Jepson, Major Selwyn 165
Jews 33, 176, 183, 196
Jimmy's 225–6
John, Augustus 136, 144, 154, 248, 250
John, Gwen 154
John Lewis 48–9, 286
John Mayhill's Bluesbreakers 271
John Snow public house 229, 288–9
John Soane Museum 124
Johnson, James 62
Johnson, Ken 'Snakehips' 181
Johnson, Dr Samuel 10, 34, 40
Jones, Brian 268–9
Jones, Peter 48
Jones, Steve 278
July 7 2005 bombings 76
Justice, James Robertson 224
*Justice* (journal) 16

Karnaby Mansion 233
Kauffmann, Angelica 34, 37
Keeler, Christine 114, 118–20, 267
Keith, Alexander 42
Kemp House 55, 287
Kempton, Freda 151
Kendall, Duchess of 33
Kennedy, Joe 173
Kennedy, John F. 55
Kennington Common 69
Kensington xi
Kent, Duke of 262
Kent, Nick 279
Kent, Tyler 173

Kent, William 7, 44, 125, 233
Kentish Town 71
Kenwood House, Highgate 37
Keppel, Alice 20
Kersh, Gerald 159–60
    Night and the City 159–60
    Prelude To A Certain Midnight
        160
Ketch, Jack 5, 189–90
Khan, Noor Inayat 168
Khrushchev, Nikita 185
Kilburn High Road 54
Kilgour, French and Stanbury 232
Kimberley, Cape Colony 16
King, Gregory 31
King and Queen public house 65,
    275–6
King of Corsica public house 230
Kingly Street 247, 252, 270
King's Highway, The 34
King's Road 235
King's Square 31–2
King's Theatre, Haymarket 11
Kinks, the 235, 271
Kinsey, Alfred 112
Klein, Alf 158
Kleinfeld, Judah 153
Klinger, Michael 113
Knave's Acre 33
Knight, Paul 26
Knight, Ronnie 210
Korner, Alexis 268–9
Kravchinski, Sergius Michaelovitch
    (Stepniak) 77–8
Kray twins, the 203, 205, 205–8,
    209, 210
Kurtha, Aziz 121

La Poubelle 262
La Rue, Danny 266
La Tour Eiffel 137, 154

Laing Art Gallery, Newcastle 133
Lamb, Lady Caroline 45
Lambert, Kit 271
Lambton, Lord 216, 267
Langtry, Lillie 14
Lansdowne Club, the 41
Lansdowne House 41
Laurie, Cy 256
Law, Michael 222
Lawrence, D. H. 26
    Women in Love 154
Le Bureau Centrale de
        Renseignements et d'Action 170
Le Caprice 121
Le Caron, Henri 73
Le Gallienne, Richard 18
League of the Just 66
Leconfied House 185–6
Lee, Jennie 215
Lee, General Raymond E. 28
Lefevre Gallery 141
Legge, Sheila 139
Leicester House 6
Leicester Lounge, the 150
Leicester Square xi, 111, 115, 123,
        123–5, 150, 243–4, 250, 270
Leicester Square Jazz Club 254
Lenin, V. I. 60
Lennon, John 236
Leoni, Peppino 175, 225
Les Ambassadeurs Club 14
Les Cousins 277
Les Enfants Terribles coffee bar 227
Lessner, Friedrich 67
L'Etoile restaurant 155
Leverhulme, Lord 29, 154
Levy, Norma 216, 267
Lewis, John 48
Lewis, John Spedan 48–9
Lewis, Leonard 238
Lewis, Paul 190

Lewis, Wyndham 135–8, 248
Lexham Gardens 169
Liberty, William Lazenby 131
Liberty's 131
licensing laws 246–7
Liddell, General Guy 184
Liebknecht, Wilhelm 71
Limehouse 150
Lincoln's Inn Fields 61
Lindsay, Sir Coutts 132
Lisle Street 150, 151, 218
*Listener* (magazine) 137
Little Club, the 250
Little Newport Street 152
Littman, Joe 53, 54
Liverpool 26
Livingstone, David 233
Livingstone, Ken 287
Lloyd, Marie 243, 245
Lloyd George, David 18, 22
Lollabrigida, Gina 227
London, City of 31
London Casino, the 245
London Clinic, the 38
*London Magazine* 145–6
London Palladium 245, 252, 253
London Pavilion music hall 242, 242–3
London Street Commune 58
Londonderry, Charles Vane-Tempest-Stewart, Marquis of 27–8
Londonderry, Lady Edith 28
Londonderry House 22, 27–8
Long, John St John 37–8
Lord Chamberlain, the 114, 265
Lordan, Jerry 261–2
Loughborough, Lord 251
Louis, Joe 266
Louise's night club 280
LSD 152–3, 273
Luard, Nicholas 265–6

Lubowitz, Michael 271
Lucile (Lucy Sutherland) 231–2
Lutyens, Edwin 29, 249
Lyceum Club 135
Lydon, John 278
Lyons' Corner House, Coventry Street 115
Lyric theatre 246
Lyttelton, Humphrey 254, 256

Macartney, Sir Halliday 79–80
McCartney, Paul 236, 238–9
McClean, Mary Ann 98
Macclesfield Street 229
MacColl, Ewan 158, 276
McCowan, Hew 206–7
Macdermott, G. H. 242–3
MacDonald, Ramsay 28
MacInnes, Colin 221, 222–3, 228, 231
    *Absolute Beginners* 100, 222
Macintyre, Ben 194–5
Mackenzie, Morrell 38
Mackintosh, Cameron 246
McLaren, Malcolm 279
Maclaren-Ross, Julien 114, 156–7, 158, 159
    *Memoirs of the Forties* 157, 159
McLaughlin, John 270
Maclean, Donald 184
MacMillan, Harold 23
Macmillan, Harold 118, 119
Macnamara, Caitlin 154
McNeill, Dorelia 154
Macniece, Louis 155
McQueen, Alexander 232
Maddox Street 56, 110
Mafia, the 207, 208, 209
Mahler, Gustav 15
Malatesta, Errico 78
Malawian Embassy 20

Malcolm Sir John 41
Mall, the 74, 141
Manchester Street 91
Mancini, Antonio 'Babe' 196
Manette Street 73–4
Manhattan night club 250
Mankowitz, Wolf 266
    Expresso Bongo 234, 261
Mann, Manfred 271
Manning, Eddie 152
Manson, Charles 98
Manson, James 133–4
Marble Arch 39
Mardas, Yanni 236–7
Margaret, Princess 114, 229
Margaret Street 152
Margot, John 247
Marinetti, Filippo 135, 136
Marks, George Harrison 113
Marks, Leo 166
Marlborough International Fine Art
    143
Marlborough Street 126
Marquee Club 140, 268–9, 271,
    272–3, 277–8
Marquess of Granby public house 158,
    159, 221
Marriott, Oliver 56
Martin, George 259, 260
Martyn, John 276–7
Marvin, Hank 261–2
Marx, Jenny 69, 70, 71
Marx, Karl 66–72, 74, 225, 229
    Das Kapital 71
    The Manifesto of the Communist
        Party 67–8
Mary, Queen 27
Marylebone ix, 1, 2, 35–9, 90, 128
Marylebone High Street 2, 288
Marylebone Lane 31
Marylebone Road ix, x, viii, 35

Maschwitz, Eric, 'A Nightingale Sang in
    Berkley Square' 40
Mason, Eric 209
Mathers, MacGregor L. 95
Matisse, Henri 249
Matlock, Glen 279
Matthews, Andy 277
Matthews, the Reverend Henry 127
Maugham, W. Somerset 3, 21, 22, 180
    Of Human Bondage 21
    The Moon and Sixpence 22
Mayfair ix, x, xi, 1, 2–3, 4, 21–2, 23,
    39, 39–43, 54–5
Mayfair Chapel 42
Mayfair One 48
Mayor Gallery 138, 141
Meaden, Pete 230
Melbourne, Lord 44
Melbourne, Elizabeth 44–5
Melly, George 222, 229, 233–4, 257
Mendl, Hugh 259
Menuhin, Yehudi 265
Merlin, Joseph 32
Mescalin 152
Messina, Alfredo 212, 213
Messina, Eugenio 212, 213
Messina brothers, the 111, 211–13
Metropole Hotel 165
Metropolitan Hotel 28
Metzger, Gustav 140
Meynell, Francis 22, 220
Meyrick, Kate 97, 250–251
MI5 172, 184, 185, 185–6, 187, 267
MI6 188
MI9 172
Micheletti, Casimir 196
Middlesex, Forest of 31
Mifsud, Frank 214
Mikado, The (Gilbert and Sullivan)
    131
Mill Street 54

Millais, John 130, 131, 141
Millennium Hotel 40
Miller, Glenn 256
Miller, Tom 147
Mills, Freddie 210
Ministry of Information 84, 160–161
Ministry of Propaganda 23, 39, 163–4
Minton, John 158, 224
Modigliani, Amedeo 155
Mods, the 234–5, 270
Moka coffee bar 219, 226–7, 228
Money, Ronni 274
Money, Zoot 274
Monico site, the 57–8
Monmouth, James Scott, Duke of xi,
    5–6, 31, 189–90
Monmouth House 5, 31–2
Montague, Elizabeth 37
Montague House 37
Montague Square 37, 274
Montefiore, Sir Moses 12, 17
Moody, Bill 216
Moon, Keith 235, 271
Moor Street 216
Moore, Christy 276
Moore, DeGrimston 98
Moore, Henry 138
Moraes, Dom 222
Moraes, Henrietta xii, 201, 221,
    221–2
Moravian Chapel 101
Morning Chronicle 65
Morrell, Lady Ottoline 21, 154
Morris, William 129, 131, 132
Morrissey 116
Mortimer, Roger, Earl of 191
Mortimer public house 71
Mörz, Wilhelm 171–2
Most, Johann 75–6
Mountbatten, Lord Louis 27, 180
Mozart, Wolfgang Amadeus 219

Muggeridge, Malcolm 176, 183
Muldowney, Dennis 169–70
Murger, Henry 144
Murray, David 168
Murray's Club 114, 118, 168
music 267–8, 286
    folk 275–7
    jazz 249, 251–5, 268, 272, 281
    punk 236, 256, 277–80
    rhythm 'n' blues 268–70
    rock 270–5
    rock 'n' roll 258–62
    skiffle 257–8
music halls 113, 242–3
Mussolini, Benito 60, 78, 80, 81–2,
    173
My Fair Lady (musical) 43
Myrtle Bank club 222

N. M. Rothschild & Sons 13
Nag's Head public house 233
Napier-Bell, Simon 270
Naples, King of 32
Napoleon III 72
Nash, John 45–7
Nash, Paul 138
National Government, the 28
National Portrait Gallery 6
Naughton, Charlie 263
Nazarenes, the 130
Neave, Airey 172
Negri, Dominic 41
Negri's tea rooms 41
Nest Club 247
Netherlands 170
Nettleship, Ida 154
Neuhoff, Theodore von 220
Never Green Tree, the 189
Nevinson, C. R. 137–8
New Bond Street 20, 43, 132, 142,
    184, 198, 237

New Burlington Galleries 139
New Cavendish Street 176
New Inn public house 71
New Piccadilly Café 225
New Road from Paddington to
    Islington, The 35
New Street Act, 1813 46
*New York Times* 111
Newell, Norman 260–261
Newgate 189–90, 192, 193
Newlove, Henry 105–6
Newman Arms public house (the Beer
    House) 83, 158, 159
Newman Passage 83, 114
Newman Street night club 250
Newport Market 250
Newport Street 266
*News of the World* 112, 121, 152,
    216
Nicholas II, Czar 131
Nicholson, Ben 138
Nicholson, Harold 24
Nicholson, Jack 280
Nigeria 207–8
nightclubs 246–51, 266–7, 280,
    286
Nightingale, Florence 38
Nilsen, Denis 116–18
Nitsch, Herman 140
Niven, David 224
No. 1 London 8
Nobu restaurant 28–9
Noel Street 81, 173, 288
Noho x, 2
Norman, Frank 193
*North London Press* 106
North, Lord Frederick 32, 40
North Soho x, 226
Northcliffe, Lord 163
Northumberland Arms public house
    71

nuclear war 187
Nutter, Tommy 233

O'Brien, Helen 266–7
Obscene Publications Squad 215, 216
*Observer*, the 139, 249
O'Connor, Fergus 69
Office of Strategic Services (OSS)
    176–8
O'Kane, Margaret 102
Old Bond Street 43, 194
Old Compton Street ix, 50
    anarchist activity 82
    coffee bars 227
    homosexuality in 115–16
    Italian community 175
    jazz clubs 256
    origins 32
    prostitution 108, 112
    restaurants and public houses 142,
        147, 220
    style makeover 289
Old Soho 32
Olins, David 238
Olivier, Laurence 26
Olympic recording studio 271
Omega Workshops 123, 136–7, 155
100 Club 256, 278–9
100 Oxford Street jazz club 256
One Scene One coffee bar 227
opium 145–6, 150
O'Rahilly, Ronan 270
Orange Street 126, 127
Order of Chaeronea 107
O'Reilly, John 14
Orford, Earl of 11
Original Dixieland Jazz Band 251
Orwell, George 96–7, 144, 159, 175,
    182, 183, 221, 229
    *1984* 82–5, 158, 161, 162
    *Animal Farm* 85, 162

*A Clergyman's Daughter* 97
*Complete Works of George Orwell* 85
  *Keep the Aspidistra Flying* 161
  *Road to Wigan Pier* 161–2
Orwell, Sonia 159
Osnaburgh Street 108
Oxenden Street 281
Oxford, Lady 30
Oxford, Edward Harley, second Earl of 37
Oxford Circus 46, 47, 183
Oxford Movement 96
Oxford Music Hall 242, 243
Oxford Street ix, 1, 46, 63, 98, 145, 191
  development of 34–5
  the ICA 140–1, 142
  the Pantheon 10–11
  property developers 54
  shops 48, 49, 132, 285–6
  Tyburn Road renamed 39

Packard, June 216
Paddington Street 90
Paine, Thomas 63
Palace Theatre 245
Palacios, Julian 273
*Pall Mall Gazette* 103
Palladianism 44, 124
Palmer, Samuel 126, 127
Palmerston, Lord 74, 102
Pantheon, the 10–11
Paolozzi, Eduardo 140
Papa, Pasqualino 211
Paris 69
Park Lane 1, 4–5, 14–19, 26–7, 39, 55–6, 58, 170, 267
Park Street 8
Parke, Ernest 106
Parker-Bowles, Camilla 20

Parnell, Archie 263–4
parties, the inter-war years 23–5
Pasmore, Victor 139–40
Pasolini, Pier Paolo 113
*Patience* (Gilbert and Sullivan) 133, 148–9
Patisserie Valerie 219
Patmore, Coventry 148
Peace of Paris 35
Peckham Rye 89
*Peeping Tom* (film) 114
Penrose, Roland 141
Pentangle 276
Pepper, Art 253
Pepys, Samuel 6, 190
Percy, Henry 19
Percy Street 81, 84, 114, 137, 138, 159
Pesthouse Close 125
Philby, Kim 184
Philip, Prince 224
Philips, John 3
Philips, Lion 70
Philips jewellers 198
Phillips, Jack, aka Junka 194–5
Phillips, Lionel 19–20
Piccadilly x, 8–9, 12–14, 25, 30, 39, 43–5, 58, 110
Piccadilly Circus ix, 1, 46, 57–8, 110, 111, 111–12, 115
Pickadell Hall 43
Pickwick Club 266
Pierrepoint, Albert 196, 200
Pigalle, the 266
Pillars of Hercules public house 220
pillorying 105
Pink Floyd 235, 273, 274
Pinochet, General Ugarte 38
Plasters' Arms public house 71
Playboy Club, the 58, 267

Plunkett-Green, Alexander 256
Poet's Club, the 137
Poland Street 126, 127, 146, 280
Polari 116
police corruption 214–16, 251
political turmoil, 1848 68
Pollock, Jackson 140
Poole, Henry 232
pop art 140
Pope, Alexander 44
'Popish Plot', the 5
Porter, David 37
Porter, Dame Shirley 287
Portland, Duke of 36
Portland House 36
Portland Place 47, 79, 83, 168,
    182
Portland Street 103
Portman Estate, the 36–7
Portman, Henry William 37
Portman Square 37
Post-Impressionists, the 134–5
Post Office (now BT) Tower 147,
    186, 187–8, 188
Poulsen, Martin 249
Pound, Ezra 136, 137, 144, 248
Powell, Anthony, A Dance to the
    Music of Time 157, 161
Powell, Michael
    A Canterbury Tale 178
    The Life and Death of Colonel
        Blimp 178
    Peeping Tom 114
Pre-Raphaelites, the 127, 129–31
Presley, Elvis 259
Price, Sir Henry 53, 54
Priestley, J. B. 182, 265
Prince, John 35–6
Prince Charles cinema 289
Prince Edward theatre 245–6
Private Eye 87, 206, 266

Process Church of the Final Judgement
    98–9
Profumo, John 118–20, 267
property development, post-Second
    World War 53–9
prostitution 1, 47, 56–7, 101–2,
    102–4, 108–12, 120–122,
    196, 211–12, 217
Protestant Association, the 60
protesters 58, 87–8
Prussian Embassy 74
Public Morality Council 111
punk 236, 256, 277–80

Quadrant, the 46, 47
Quant, Mary 237, 256
Queen Anne Street 128
Queen's theatre 246
Queensbury, Marquess of 107–8
Queensbury, William Douglas, fourth
    Duke of 10
Queensbury All Services Club 245
Quo Vadis restaurant 175, 225, 282

Rainbow Club 178–9
Rainey, Michael 274
Ramsay, Captain Archibald 173
Ransome, Arthur, Bohemia in London
    144
Ratcliff Highway Murders 146
Rathbone Place 72, 127, 158
Rathbone Street 114, 158–9
Raymond, Paul 113–14
Raymond, Paul 'Teasy-Weasy' 237
Raymond's Revue Bar 113–14
Read, Herbert 138
Read, Leonard 'Nipper' 206, 207
Rebel Arts Centre 136
Recchioni, Emidio 82
recording studios 271–2
Rector's Cellar nightclub 247

Red Lion public house, High Holborn 192

Red Lion public house, Soho 67, 68, 69–70, 74

Regent Street ix, 1, 45–7, 131, 150, 151, 197–8

Regent's Park 46, 47

Regulation of Employment Order (1947) 182

Reid, Terry 274

Renbourn, John 276

Reynolds, Joshua 10, 34, 123, 128

Rhodes, Cecil 17

Rhythm Club, the 252

rhythm 'n' blues music 268–70

Ribbentrop, Joachim von 24, 28

Rice-Davies, Mandy 29, 114, 119–20

Richard, Cliff 259–60, 261, 289

Richard Green art gallery 43

Richards, Keith 268–9

Richardson, Charlie 208–9

Richardson, Eddie 209

Richardsons, the 208–9

Richmond, George 127

Rimbaud, Arthur 144, 147, 229

Rimington, Stella 185, 186

Rising Sun public house 71

Ritz Hotel 22, 175

Road, The 34

Robert Fraser Gallery 215

Robert McAlpine & Sons 26

Roberts, William 135, 137

Robinson, Crabbe 46

Robinson, J. B. 17–18

Roche, Sophie, von la 11

rock music 270–275

rock 'n' roll 258–62

Rockinham, Lord 11, 40

Rogers, Claude 139

Rogers, Samuel 192

rollerskates, invention of 32

Rolling Stones 88, 98, 153, 269, 272

Roman Catholics 34, 60–61, 62

Ronnie Scott's Jazz Club 281

Roosevelt, Theodore 43

Rose, Denis 256

Rose and Crown public house 71

Rose Street (now Manette Street) 73–4

Rosebery, Lord 107

Rosenkruez, Christian 93

Rosicrucian's 93–4

Ross, Maurice 226–7

Ross, Robert 134

Rossetti, Dante Gabriel 129–30
  *The Girlhood of Mary Virgin* 129–30

Roth, Andrew 119

Rothermere, Harold Sydney Harmsworth, Lord 27

Rothschild, Alfred de 12, 13

Rothschild, Evy 13–14

Rothschild, Ferdinand 13–14

Rothschild, Leopold 14

Rothschild, Baron Lionel Nathan de 12–13

Rothschild, Nathan Meyer 12

Rothschild, Victor 30, 172–3

*Round the Horne* (radio programme) 116

Roundhouse, the 268

Rowbotham, Sheila 86

Royal Academy 34, 44, 123, 124, 128, 130, 131, 132, 232

Royal Command Performances 245

Royal Court Theatre 244

Royal Fine Arts commission 58, 187

Royal George public house 117

Royal Institution, the 49, 51, 53

Royal London Panorama 244

Royal Observatory, Greenwich 76

Royal Panopticon of Science and Art 243
Royalty Theatre 244–5
Rubens, Peter Paul, *Adoration of the Magi* 18
Rudelat, Yvonne 168
Rudolph of Austria, Crown Prince 13
Rupert Street 135
Rushdie, Salmon 240
Ruskin, John 96, 130, 131, 132, 135
Russian Revolution 23
Russian Social Democrats 80–81
Russo-Turkish War 242–3
Ruthven, PC George 65

Sabini, Darby 195–6
Sabini brothers 195–6
Sainsbury, Tim 239
St Anne's church 220
St Anne's Court 269
St George's Baths 25
St George's church 42–3
St James's xi
St John's Wood Cemetery 92
St Martin's Hall, Long Acre, Covent Garden 72
St Mary-by-the Bourne ix
St Marylebone ix
St Nicholas's church 125
St Patrick's Catholic Church 32
St Paul's canons of 34–5
St Paul's Cathedral 56
*Salò, 120 Days of Sodom* (film) 113
Salvation Army 103
Samuel, Dudley 53–4
Samwell, Ian 258, 260
Sanchez, 'Spanish Tony' 270–271
Sandys, Lord Duncan 118
Sansom, Odette 168–9
Sanzio, Raphael 130
Sardinian Chapel, the 61

Sassie, Victor 224–5
Sassoon, Vidal 237–8
satire 265–6, 281
Saudi Arabian Embassy 39
Savile, Jimmy 262
Savile House 244
Savile Row 1, 3, 232–3, 236–7
Savory and Moore 43
Savoy Theatre 245
Sayle, Alexei 280, 281
Sbardellotto, Angelo 82
Scene, the 270
Schack, Bernard 204
Scheherazade club, the 214
Schmidt's restaurant 184, 226
Schnatz, Harry 182
science and scientists 49–53
Scientology 98
Scotch of St James 262, 274
Scott, Ronnie 252, 252–3, 254, 254–5, 281
season, the 23
Second World War
    air raid shelters 179–80
    American GIs 178–9
    BBC broadcasts 182–3
    the black market 181
    bombing 28, 35, 180–181
    bottle parties 181–2
    censorship 83, 84–5
    diamond supplies 177–8
    Dutch Resistance 230
    Free French government-in-exile 170
    gambling 181
    internment 173–6
    lack of effect on West End 53
    looting 181
    Ministry of Information 84, 160–161
    Operation Fortitude 170–171

Operation Ratweek 168
Operation Stronghold 182
the OSS 176–8
propaganda operations 163
prostitution during 111
rape 179
requisitioned buildings 172
SOE 164–71
spies 171–2, 173, 177
theatre closures 114
Sedgemoor, battle of (1685) 5
Seifert, Richard 187
Selbourne, Lord 177
Self, Will 146
Selfridge, Gordon H. 49, 51
Selfridge's 49, 51–2, 53, 286
Senate House 56, 84, 160–161, 172
Seven Years War (1756–63) 35
Sex Pistols 278–9
Seymour Place 13
Shadows, the 261–2
Shaftesbury Avenue 1, 78, 246
Shakespeare's Head public house 109
Shaw, Frederick Charles, *the Ladies
    Directory* 112
Shaw, George Bernard 20, 35, 74, 85
    *Pygmalion* 43
Shell-Mex House 172
Shellbourne Hotel 169
Shelly, Percy Bysshe 42, 144, 146
    'Mask of Anarchy' 64–5
Shepherd, Edward 39
Shepherd Market 3, 39, 110, 120–
    121
shoplifting 199
shopping 48–9, 285–6
Shrimpton, Jean 86
Sibthorp, Shurmer 25
Sickert, Walter 106, 133, 134, 149
Silver, Bernie 213–14
Silver Slipper night club 250–251

Simon, Paul 276–7
Simon and Garfunkel 270
Simpson, Alan 264
Simpson, Sir Joseph 215
Sinatra, Frank 232
Sinclair, Stephen 117
Sitwell, Osbert 24, 248
Skelhorn, Sir Norman 215
skiffle 257–8
Sloane Square 48
Small Faces, the 235, 270
smash and grab raids 197–8
Smell Society, the 29
Smith, Lady Eleanor 23
Smith, John 92
Smith, John (Half-Hanged Smith)
    192–3
Smith, Patti 147
Smith, Terry 'Mad' 206
Smithfield Market x
Smithson, Tommy 202, 214
Smollett, Peter 85
Smythers, Richard 65
Snowdon, Anthony Armstrong-Jones,
    Lord 45
Soane, John 46
Social Democratic Club, Rose Street
    73–4
Social Democratic Foundation 76
Social Deviants, the 87
Society of Friends of Russian Freedom
    77
Society of Spencean Philanthropists 64
Soft Machine 274
Soho ix, 1–2, 125
    coffee bars 226–8
    early development 31–4
    eating places 224–6
    the Gordon Riots 62
    Italian community 174–6, 196
    nightclubs 247–9

Soho (*cont.*)
  origin of name x, 31
  post-war 219–24
  private clubs 228–9
  public houses 229–31
  roofing plan 55
  sanitised 287
  seediness 239
  sex industry 100, 101–2, 109–10,
    111, 113–14, 212, 217, 239
  theatres 244–5
Soho Society, the 239
Soho Square xi, 5, 31, 100, 101, 145,
  219–20
Somerset, Lord 106
Sotheby's 43
South Audley Street 87–8
South Molton Street 127, 199
South Sea Bubble financial crash
  (1720) 36, 42
Southampton Arms public house 71
Southcott, Joanna xi, 90, 91–3
Southwell, Robert 191–2
Speakeasy, the 270–271
Speakers' Corner 98
Special Operations Executive (SOE)
  codes 166
  equipment 167–8
  N (Netherlands) Section 170
  offices 165–7
  operations 168–70
  recruitment 164–5
  training 165
*Spectator*, the 70, 223
Spence, Thomas 63–4
Spenceans, the 63–4
Spencer, Lady Georgiana 7, 194
Spender, Stephen 162
Speyer, Sir Edgar 20–21
spies, Soviet 172–3, 184, 186
spivs 182

Spohr, Louis 12
Spontaneous Underground 272–3
Spot, Jack, aka Benny the Kid 197,
  201, 202, 202–5, 228
Stacpoole, Michael 121
Stafford Street 95
Stalin, Josef 60, 80, 81, 82
Stamp, Terence 238, 266
Stanhope Gate 17
Stanshall, Viv 235
Star of Africa, Cullinan 1, the 14–15
Star of South Africa, the 14
Starr, Ringo 274
Stead, W. T. 103–4
Steed, Wickham 163–4
Steele, Tommy 259
Stieber, Wilhelm 74
Stephen, John 234, 235
Stephen John's Man Shop 235
Stephen Mews 74
Stepniak (Sergius Michaelovitch
  Kravchinski) 77–8
Stevens, Cat 276–7
Stevens, Guy 270
Stevens, Robert 199
Stevenson, Robert Louis, *Dr Jekyll and
  Mr Hyde* 159
Stewart, Al 276–7
Stewart, Douglas 117
Stewart, Rod 270
Stillingfleet, Benjamin 37
Stockhausen, Karl Heinz 272
Stollman, Steve 272
Strachey, Lytton 22
Strand 44
Strand Films 161
Stratford Place 34
Street Offences Act (1959) 112, 113
Strindberg, Madame 248
strip clubs 113–14
Strype, John 33

Stuart, James 'Athenian' 37
Stuart, James Edward (the Old
    Pretender) 33
Stubbs, John Heath 158
Stulik, Rudolph 137
Sublime Society of Beefsteaks 125
Suez Canal Company 13
Sullivan, Arthur 131, 133, 148–9, 245
Summers, Andy 274
Summerson, John 35
Sun public house 230
Sun Yet Sen 78–80
*Sunday People* 160, 216
*Sunday Times* 98
Sutherland, Ben 179
Sutherland, Billy 116–17
Sutherland, Duchess of 21
Sutherland, Duke of 25, 30
Sutherland, Lucy (Lucile) 231–2
Suzie and the Banshees 279–80
Swaffer, Hannen 252
Swallow Street 61
Swan Close 6
Swedenborg, Emmanuel 89
Swedenborgians 126
Sweeny, Margaret, Duchess of Argyll 30
Sweet, John 178
Swift, Jonathan 44
Swinburne, Algernon 148
Swinscow, Thomas 105
Symons, Arthur 149, 247
Szabo, Violette 168

Taine, Hyppolite 109
Talbot public house 71
Taplin, Thomas 62
Tate Gallery 143, 215
Taylor, Alfred 107
Taylor, Margaret 154–5
Taynton, William 52
Teddy Boys 233

Teddy Hill and his Orchestra 252
telegraph, the 51
Tennant, David 23, 249
Tenser, Tony 113
terrorists and terrorism
    7 July 2005 76
    anarchists 73–7
    Fenian 72–3, 76
Thackeray, William 37
    *Vanity Fair* 9, 41, 144
Thames House 186
Thames, River 4
Thatcher, Margaret 142
Thea Porter's boutique 234, 235
theatres 114, 243–6, 251, 286
Theatres Act (1843) 244
theatrical agents 263–4
Thévenon, Daniel 150
13 Cantons public house 230
Thistlewood, Arthur 64–5
Thomas, Dylan xi, 139, 144, 154–5,
    158, 159, 160, 161, 162, 221,
    229, 230
Thompson, Francis 220
Thursday Club, the 224
Thursday-Night London Blues and
    Barrelhouse Club 268
Tidd, Richard 64–5
*Time* magazine 235–6
*The Times* 80, 81, 91, 138, 151
*Titanic*, the 104, 231–2
*Top Hat* (film) 232
Torino coffee bar 227
Tottenhall Manor 34–5
Tottenham Court Road x, 35, 71, 75,
    140, 177, 247, 274
Tottenham Court Road station 188
Tottenham Street 74
Tower of London 56, 65
Town and Country Planning Act
    (1959) 187

Townsend, Pete 271
Toynbee, Philip 226
Toynbee Hall mission, Whitechapel 120
Tracey, Stan 253
Tractarians, the 96
Trafalgar Square xi, 76
Transvaal, the 14, 16, 19
Trebeck, Dr 42
Triads, the 217–18
Trinder, Tommy 263
Trocadero, the 242, 247
Trollope, Anthony 37
    Phineas Finn 37
    The Small House at Allington 37
    The Way We Live Now 9–10, 18
Trotsky, Leon 80, 81, 82
Truefitt's wigmakers 43
Tshombe, Moishe 207
Turk's Head tavern 61–2
Turner, Bruce 254
Turner, J. M. W. 128
Tutankhamun, curse of 97–8
Twiggy 86, 238
Tybourn, River ix
Tyburn ix, 39
Tyburn gallows 4, 34, 189–90
Tyburn Road 39, 191
Tyburn stream 31, 34, 39, 288
Tyburn Tree, the 34
Tyburn Way, The 34
Tynan, Kenneth 266

UFO 274
Ulrichs, Karl Heinrich 104
Uncles night club 247
Unit One Group 138
United Irishmen of America 73
University of London 84
Upper Brook Street 15
Upper Grosvenor Street 30, 118
Ustinov, Peter 224

Valentine, Lady Freda 29–30
Van Damm, Vivian 263
Van Gogh, Vincent 134, 135
Vassallo, Carmelo 212
Vauxhall station 188
venereal disease 110
Vere Street 105
Verlaine, Paul 144, 147
Vermeer, Jan, The Lady Writing a
    Letter 16
Vice Squad 216, 251
Vicious, Sid 279
Victoria, Queen 13, 74, 150
Victoria and Albert Museum 26,
    216
Victoria Line 188
Vietnam Solidarity Campaign 87–8
Vietnam Solidarity Front 88
Vietnam War 40, 87–8
Vince's Man's Shop 233–4
Vipers, the 259
Virgo, Commander Wally 216
Vogue 237
Voltaire 41
Voluntary Aid Detachment 22
Vorticists, the 123, 136–8
Voynich, Wilfred Michael 77–8
Voynich Manuscript, the 78

WI xi
Wag, the 280
Waitrose 2
Walker Art Gallery, Liverpool 26
Walpole, Horace 6, 10, 11, 42
Warbeck, Perkin 191
Ward, Don 280
Ward, Stephen 119, 119–20
Wardour Street 32, 220, 230, 280,
    288
Warner, Douglas, The Shame of A City
    112

Warren, Alf 204–5
Warren Street station 188
Warwick Street 61
Waterhouse, Keith 223
Waterloo, Battle of (1815) 12, 19, 54
Watts, Marthe 111, 213
Waugh, Evelyn 161
    *Brideshead Revisited* 250, 251
    *Vile Bodies* 23
Waverton Street 3
Waye, the 34
Webb, Duncan 202, 212–13
Webb, Sidney and Beatrice, *Soviet Russia: A New Civilization* 85
Wednesday Club, the 162, 226
*Weekly Despatch* 110
Welbeck Street 62
Welch, Bruce 261–2
Wellclose Square 31
Wellington, Arthur Wellesley, Duke of 8, 37
Wells, H. G. 163
Wembley Stadium 26
Wernher, Beit and Co. 16
West, Rebecca 248
West End
    battle for soul 283–9
    boundaries x–xi
    colonization by social elites 4
    extent ix–x
    origins 31
    social role xi–xii
    style 1–3
West End Riots 76
Westbrook, Harriet 42
Westbury, Lord 97–8
Westcott, Dr William Wynne 93, 94, 95
Westminster xi, 31
Westminster, Duchy of 40
Westminster, Hugh Lupus Grosvenor, first Duke of 16, 17, 18–19

Westminster, Hugh Grosvenor, second Duke of 29
Westminster, William Grosvenor, third Duke of 55
Westminster, Shelagh, Duchess of 18–19
Westminster City Council 287
Westphalen, Ferdinand von 74
Westwood, Vivienne 279
Wethered, G. 172
Wheatsheaf public house 158
Wheeler's fish restaurant 142, 221, 224
Wheen, Francis 67
Whig Party 44
Whistler, James McNeill 131, 132–3, 148, 150
White, Dick 171, 172
White Hart public house 71
White Horse Street 3
White House 101
White, Jimmy 250
White, Marco Pierre 225
White Swan tavern 105
Whitehall xi
Whites, the 197
Whitfield Street 98
Who, the 153, 235, 270, 271
Whyton, Wally 257, 258
Wickstead, Bert 214
Wiedemann, Fritz 27
Wigmore Street 98
Wilde, Oscar xi, 18, 106–8, 131, 132, 144, 148–50
    *The Importance of Being Earnest* 87
    *Lady Windermere's Fan* 19
    *The Picture of Dorian Gray* 106
Wilhelm II, Kaiser 18–19
Willetts, Paul 156
Williams, Kenneth 116

Williams, Owen 26
Wilson, Colin, *The Outsider* 224
Wimpole Mews 119
Wimpole Street 238–9
Windmill Street 76
Windmill Theatre 114, 263
Windsor, Barbara 210
Winnett Street 1–2
Witherington, Pearl 168
Wojas, Michael 229
Wollstonecraft, Mary 63
Women Police Volunteers 110
Women's Legion 22
Women's Patrols 110
Wood, Alfred 108
Wood, Gilbert 158
Woods Mews 15
Wooldridge's chemists 150
Woolf, Virginia 35, 286
Wordsworth, William 10–11
Workers' Educational Association 68

*World's Pictorial News* 151, 152
Worth, Adam 194–5
Worth, Johnny 260–261
Wren, Christopher 33, 42
Wright, Harry 263
Wright, Whitaker 21
Wrightson, Paul, QC 206
Wyatt, James 11

Yardbirds, the 235, 271, 272
Yeats, W. B. 94, 96, 248
*Yellow Book, The* 149
*Yokel's Preceptor* 105
Yoko Ono 140
York Minster, the
    *see* French House, the
Young, Tony 240
Ypres, Battle of 22
Yu Yi He 218

Zandfontein, South Africa 14
Zomparelli, Tony 210

# PENGUIN HISTORY

**EAST END CHRONICLES**
ED GLINERT

Medieval burial ground, Victorian hell hole, Blitz bombing target, modern artists' playground: the East End has always been London's strange alter ego, with an identity unlike anywhere else.

Here Ed Glinert tells the dark, unusual and arcane stories of its streets and people – from the mystics of Wellclose Square to the gory Radcliffe Highway Murders, from Huguenot silk weavers to the horrors of the Black Death, from the heyday of the great docks to the gentrification of Spitalfields – revealing the underbelly of the city as never before.

'Glinert clearly has a magpie-like mind, a boundless energy for wandering the streets of the city and a fascination with curiosities … a wealth of detail'
*Guardian*

'Lively … exciting … genuine illumination' *Sunday Telegraph*

'A nuanced, layered picture … fascinating details and links emerge … It is at moments when chronology is exploded and past events reappear in new guises that this book is most interesting' *The Times Literary Supplement*

'Rarely has a few square miles of Earth generated such notoriety … Glinert unearths the often horrifying, bizarre, cruel and occasionally just plain odd events that have taken place … there are fascists and terrorists, anarchists and revolutionaries, suffragettes and preachers' *Daily Express*